Thank you
Your friend

José Antonio

WORLD OF
GOLF
1980

**Edited by
George Simms**

Queen Anne Press

Macdonald and Jane's · London and Sydney

ABBREVIATIONS

A	Austria	H	Holland	SA	South Africa
ARG	Argentina	HK	Hong Kong	SC	Scotland
AUS	Australia	I	Italy	SING	Singapore
B	Belgium	IN	India	SK	South Korea
BUR	Burma	IND	Indonesia	SW	Sweden
BZ	Brazil	IRE	Ireland	SZ	Switzerland
C	Canada	J	Japan	TAI	Taiwan
COL	Columbia	M	Morocco	THAI	Thailand
DEN	Denmark	MAL	Malaysia	TRI	Trinidad
E	Egypt	MEX	Mexico	USA	United States of
ENG	England	NZ	New Zealand		America
F	France	P	Portugal	VEN	Venezuela
G	Germany	PI	Philippines	W	Wales
GB	Great Britain	PR	Puerto Rico	ZIM	Zimbabwe-
GR	Greece	S	Spain		Rhodesia

© **Macdonald and Jane's Publishing Group Limited 1980**

Photographs supplied by **H W Neale** unless otherwise credited

ISBN 0 362 02007 8

Published by Queen Anne Press, Macdonald and Jane's Publishing Group Limited, Paulton House, 8 Shepherdess Walk, London N1 7LW

Photoset in 10/11pt Times and printed and bound in Great Britain by Redwood Burn Limited, Trowbridge & Esher

Front cover: Severiano Ballesteros (*Brian Morgan*)
Back cover: Tom Watson (*Brian Morgan*)

CONTENTS

Foreword   4

FOCUS
World Tour Target is 1981   6
Golfers of the Year   10

THE MAJOR CHAMPIONSHIPS 1979
The Open Championship 1979   21
The US Open Championship 1979   29
The US Masters 1979   37
The US PGA Championship 1979   43

THE WORLD'S CIRCUITS – THE UNITED STATES
The US Tournament Circuit 1979   50
Results   57

THE WORLD'S CIRCUITS – EUROPE
The European Tournament Circuit 1979   83
Results   86

THE WORLD'S CIRCUITS – JAPAN, ASIA,
SOUTH AFRICA, AUSTRALASIA
The Japanese Circuit 1979   132
The Asian Circuit 1979   142
The South African Circuit 1979   147
The Australasian Circuit 1979   151

THE INTERNATIONAL SCENE
The Sun Alliance Ryder Cup 1979   161
The Walker Cup 1979   164
The PGA Cup 1979   167
The World Cup 1979   169
The Transatlantic Trophy   171
The Women's Professional Circuit 1979   173
The Pro-Amateur Year   177

THE AMATEUR YEAR   182
Results   185

THE YEAR IN SCOTLAND, WALES AND IRELAND   198
Results   203

THE TOP SIXTY   205

CHAMPIONSHIPS ROLLS   232

FOREWORD

World of Golf was first published as a yearbook in 1973, and the 1980 edition is as comprehensive as ever, with results, reports, and statistical data from the major theatres of Europe, the United States, Japan, Asia, Australasia and South Africa.

The Editor and the Publishers are especially grateful to the six companies associated with the game of golf who readily agreed to combine as part-sponsors of the Yearbook. They are:

Associated Tyre Specialists who for a number of years have sponsored a major Pro-Amateur Tournament which has established itself as one of the principal events of its kind in Britain. Stars from the world of show business, sports and entertainment regularly team with the professionals for the ATS Pro-Am event in aid of charity.

British Caledonian Airways have in recent years supported many of the younger professionals, as well as some of the more experienced ones, on the European circuit, and one of their number, Sandy Lyle, topped the Order of Merit in 1979. In addition, British Caledonian have for two years sponsored a match between their Young Lions and Texas.

Carlsberg Brewery Ltd have been the main reason why the new Women's Professional Golf circuit had such a successful baptism in 1979. Their sponsorship of 12 events within the Carlsberg European Ladies Championship, with over £20,000 in prize money, guaranteed the success of the first big step into women's professional golf in Europe. They will be increasing their involvement considerably in 1980.

Lynx Precision Golf Equipment have established themselves, in Europe as well as in the United States, as among the most sought-after of golf clubs. Their Prowler, Predator, and Tigress Elégance clubs are distributed on a 'professional shops only' basis in the UK by Trendan Sports, who are also the sole UK distributors of Munsingwear clothing.

Martini & Rossi Ltd linked the Martini name with the professional golf circuit with a £6000 tournament in 1961 and have been there ever since. They doubled their prize money to £30,000 in 1978, increased it to over £40,000 in 1979, and are going still higher in 1980 in what will be the 20th successive Martini International Tournament.

Sun Alliance Insurance Group are now synonymous with golf. They have sponsored the Ryder Cup matches against the United States, when played in Britain, since 1973, put their resources behind the PGA Match-Play Championship from 1975 to 1979, and in 1980 will be switching to the PGA Championship (stroke-play) for the first time.

In compiling a reference book of this nature, it is necessary to rely on the co-operation of many people in supplying statistics and data. My sincere thanks are accordingly due to:

The European Tournament Players' Division and the General Division of the Professional Golfers' Association; the Information Officers of the PGA Tour of America; the Royal and Ancient Golf Club of St Andrews; the English Golf Union; the Australian Professional Golfers' Association; the Asia Golf Circuit; the South African Professional Golfers' Association; Mike Mikami in Japan; Golf Photography International for permission to use their many photographs; Action Photos, for supplying the bulk of the photographs; and the many other contributors indispensable to the Yearbook.

George Simms, Editor, 1 January 1980

FOCUS

WORLD TOUR TARGET IS 1981 GOLFERS OF THE YEAR

Nobody in the world matched Tom Watson's achievements in 1979.

FOCUS

George Simms

WORLD TOUR TARGET IS 1981

On the eve of the Open Championship at Royal Lytham and St Annes in Lancashire, England, there took place a meeting that could well change the pattern of professional tournament golf in the 1980s. Represented at the meeting, which was held at The Belfry, in the Midlands, the National Headquarters of the British Professional Golfers' Association, were Australia, Canada, Hong Kong, Japan, New Zealand, South Africa, the United States, and Britain.

A further, less intensive, meeting was also held later at Lytham. A statement was issued after the first gathering to the effect that delegates concerned had exchanged views at this first international get-together of the world's PGAs, but the communique on their deliberations was largely lost in the clamour of the Open Championship itself.

The ideology behind the calling of the conference was that for many years each PGA had adopted a conservative and independent attitude, but that professional golf was now a growing commercial business, and that the getting together of those concerned in it would provide an opportunity to review mutual experiences and views. The outcome of this initial meeting, which will be followed at the end of 1980 with a further conference to be held in Australia, could be to bring about the oft-discussed dream of a World Golf Tour.

Such a dream has long been nurtured by Peter Thomson. The Australian's illustrious career with his five Open Championship titles, and a host of victories around the world, finally came to an end – in so far as major title-seeking is concerned – with the Open at Royal Lytham. He was one of Australia's delegates at The Belfry along with Graham Marsh, and it is logical to assume that he will devote himself to making reality of a dream.

Tournament golf, the shop window of the profession, shows nothing but growth around the world. In Australia, between mid-September 1979 and March 1980, their circuit will have offered well over a million Australian dollars in prize money. Around a quarter of a million more was available in pro-amateur events. Some dozen events were televised, either nationally or regionally. In 1970, the total prize fund in Australia was A$69,000! Thomson, who is the Australian PGA's President, made it quite clear at The Belfry that a World Body of PGAs was a first prio-

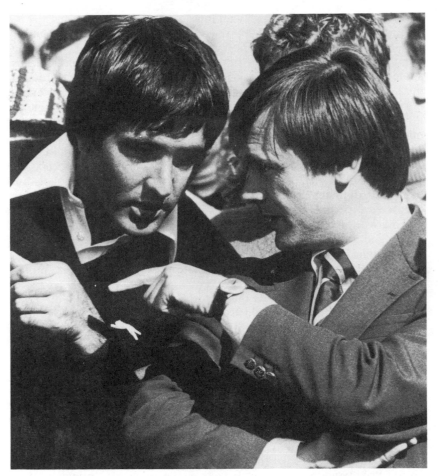

Europe's most marketable property Severiano Ballesteros with Tournament Players' Division Secretary Ken Schofield. Within two years, says Schofield, Ballesteros could be playing for £3,500,000 outside America. (Phil Sheldon)

rity. Asia will expect to achieve the US$1,000,000 mark in 1980 with its 10 national championships, plus the Philippine Masters.

Major events have been played in the Far East now for over 20 years. Nine of the 10 events on the Asia Circuit are promoted by the respective Amateur Federations, which means that the professionals have little say in regard to the Asia tour itself. None the less the story is one of continuous growth in prize money and the establishment of a Tournament Players' Division along similar lines to America and Europe is probably not far away.

South Africa and New Zealand do not match such prize funds. Nevertheless South Africa's major events totalled over R400,000, a figure swollen to over R600,000 by other events. New Zealand's four principal tournaments normally come to well in excess of NZ$200,000. Europe passed the £1,000,000 mark a few years back and is heading towards the second million. Their tour, run by the European Tournament Players' Division, now with a Qualifying School, Sunday finishes, standardised prize money breakdowns, and pro-ams built into tournaments, is second only to the United States in well-organised efficiency.

A World Golf Tour, should it come about, would be a misnomer, for it could never embrace the United States and Japan, although the latter might find it possible to schedule a couple of events in their calendar. The professional circuit in Japan extends over 10 months and spans around 50 tournaments. Their tour is currently offering over $5,000,000 in prize money, the vast majority of tournaments are televised, and nearly 20 of them are compulsory for the leading 30 players unless excused on medical grounds.

America, of course, is a law unto itself. The tour extends to some 44 weeks and attracted $13,000,000 of prize money in 1979, around half of which came from television contracts. Of interest is the fact that there are 300 members of the US tour and that despite the huge prize money only 70–80 make a profit or break even.

A co-ordinated calendar is the success point of a World Golf Tour. To this end South Africa hold the key in switching their season from November and December to January and February to avoid a clash with Australasia. A South Africa-Asia-Europe-Australasia World Tour is then a possibility.

What would be demanded would be a Grand Prix series of some 20–24 events, each with a minimum prize fund of £70,000 to £75,000. Foreseen are two or three at this level in South Africa and in Asia, 10 to 12 in Europe, and six or seven in Australia. New Zealand and Canada feel they could each produce one event at this with £70,000 in prize money.

An additional incentive for top players to support the 'International Grand Prix' would be a Circuit Prize based on a four-Continents Order of Merit. The meeting felt that £100,000–£125,000 minimum should be sought in such sponsorship for distribution to the leading players.

A Co-ordinating Committee, based on one representative per zone, will meet again in 1980 to further the proposals. The target for the World Golf Tour – 1981. Meanwhile Peter Thomson's formal proposal at The Belfry that a 'World PGA Federation' should be set up was seconded by the European TPD. The proposal will be put to the respective Executives and Tournament Committees prior to another meeting – in Australia in November 1980. The objects: 'The mutual benefit and furtherance of the game of golf'.

Ken Schofield, secretary of Europe's Tournament Players' Division, has no doubts that 10 or 12 tournaments with £70,000-plus in prize money will be on his 1981 Tournament Schedule, despite inflation running high in the difficult British economic climate. He says: 'The indications are that the upward trend in sponsorship of recent years will be continued. There is still no shortage of outlets for golf promotion and

*Delegates from Professional Golfers' Associations around the world at their meeting
prior to the Open Championship.*

sponsorship with so much more leisure time to be filled.'

Certainly the prize for the successful in professional tournament golf is becoming rich indeed. Tom Watson, in heading the US Money Winners' List for the third successive year, banked $462,636 as a result of his five tournament victories and 15 top-10 finishes. When he was number one in 1977 he won $310,653, while in 1978 his total was $362,429.

Severiano Ballesteros and Sandy Lyle, the two top attractions in Europe in 1979, found their exploits well rewarding. Lyle, who dethroned the happy Spaniard from the number one position he had held for three years, banked just under £50,000 in European tournament earnings. Ballesteros earned only slightly less, and has won nearly as much in four years as Neil Coles has won in 25!

They and other young players in Europe must view with relish the future prospect of playing for £2,000,000 in Britain and on the Continent, then moving on to what could be a further £1,500,000 Grand Prix tour of three more Continents, with an overall £100,000 Circuit Prize thrown in for good measure. It is a long cry from the prize fund of £200 for the first PGA Match-Play Championship in 1903!

GOLFERS OF THE YEAR

George Simms

In 1977 Tom Watson won the Open Championship at Turnberry, the US Masters, three home tournaments, and topped the Money-winners' List in the United States which is the yardstick of success on the American professional circuit. Few people opposed him as the Golfer of the Year.

Domestically he emerged as America's supreme golfer again in 1978. He set a new record in winning $362,429, beating the previous best by Johnny Miller in 1974, and added five more US tournaments to his tally.

Not everyone this time, however, voted him number one. In America a leading golf journal, for one, handed the accolade to Nancy Lopez for her nine victories on the US women's tour. And this particular Yearbook gave the edge in 1978 to Jack Nicklaus, who had not won a major title since 1975 but who triumphed at St Andrews in the Open Championship for the third time, at the age of 38, won three times at home, and journeyed to Australia to take their Open for the sixth time.

But major titles or no major titles nothing can prevent the naming of Watson again as the golfer of 1979. He won five home tournaments to take his career record to 16 US victories in eight years, amassed over $460,000, and was number one again in the United States for the third year in succession. He did not have Jack Nicklaus to contend with. Nobody did. Nicklaus cut his schedule to a dozen events, was second in the Open, fourth in the Masters, and ninth in the US Open, but finished down the Money List in 71st place. Since turning professional in 1961 he had never been lower than fourth, and the time is surely very near when golf's greatest player of the modern era, eight times number one in America, will cut away from the tournament circuits.

Tom Watson has long been the heir apparent, with already two Open Championships and a World Series to set alongside those 16 career victories. He did not entirely monopolise the 1979 spotlight.

Larry Nelson, who in 1969 wandered down to a driving range to see what the game was all about and was hooked from that moment on, not only won the first tournaments of his career – the Inverrary Classic and the Western Open – but lost a play-off in Memphis and finished number two to Watson with over $280,000. He also won all five of his Ryder Cup matches.

Internationally, probably no one matched Australia's David Graham. He won a nerve-tingling US PGA Championship in a play-off with Ben Crenshaw, then went home to win in Australia as well as in New Zealand.

Fuzzy Zoeller, like Nelson, began 1979 viewing a tournament career that had been steadily improving since it began in 1975. The sun shone for him throughout. He won by five shots in San Diego, and then confounded all the forecasters at Augusta by winning the US Masters in a play-off, courtesy of Ed Sneed. He emerged as a new star in the Trevino mould.

Hale Irwin had another fine year, despite finishing 19th in the Money List. At Inverness he held on to win the US Open Championship for the second time in five years, led in the Open at Royal Lytham & St Annes until the Ballesteros blitz in the final round, and in pairing with John Mahaffey to retain the World Cup for America in Greece, won the World Individual title that goes with it as well.

Male chauvinism, unintentional though it might be, tends to ignore the exploits of the Women's Professional Tour. To do so is to ignore Nancy Lopez who is dominating the game as few, if any, have done in the past. In 1978 she won nine times and set new record money-winning levels. In 1979 she won eight more, plus the 'unofficial' team event, and exceeded her previous prize money total with nearly $200,000 in tournament winnings.

Outside of the United States every circuit had its star. In Asia, with less than six months of professional experience behind him, Lu Hsi-Chuen from Taiwan, nephew of 'Mr Lu', took the 10-championship Asian Circuit by storm, winning three of them and finishing way ahead as the Circuit's number one.

Japan was again dominated by Isao Aoki whose reputation is now completely international, while in South Africa Gary Player sensationally walked away with the South African PGA Championship, the South African Masters, the South African Open and the Sun City Classic in successive weeks! At 44 he remains still a force in world golf.

Europe belonged to Sandy Lyle and Severiano Ballesteros. If the Spaniard did not quite have the protracted glory he enjoyed in 1978 he had a purple three weeks patch that culminated in a now historic victory in the Open Championship, the youngest champion of the century and the first Continental player to win it since the Frenchman Arnaud Massy triumphed in 1907.

It was Lyle who stopped him in his tracks in his quest for a fourth successive Harry Vardon trophy to match the Oosterhuis reign of 1971–74. In only his second full year as a professional, the 21-year-old former amateur international won four times, including the prestige European Open Championship, shared second place in the World Cup Individual competition, and was prominent wherever he played – and that embraced Britain, the Continent, Africa, and Japan.

Who then to follow Tom Watson as Golfer of the Year 1979? On consideration of achievement within a golfer's own particular sphere, and for the first time since the Yearbook began making such nominations in 1973, Severiano Ballesteros and Hale Irwin are named joint-second. For her continuing supremacy of women's professional golf Nancy Lopez is awarded the number four spot, with Sandy Lyle at number five.

Tom Watson. (Golf Photography International)

1 TOM WATSON

Watson lost no time in getting his game into shape for the $13,000.000 US Tour beginning in the second week in January and going through to the end of October. As early as the third tournament, the Andy Williams-San Diego, he finished tied for second place behind Fuzzy Zoeller, and three weeks later he was again joint runner-up in Tucson behind Bruce Lietzke, who had virtually sewn up the tournament with an opening 63.

Towards the end of March he placed second once more, this time five behind Lanny Wadkins, who scored a memorable victory in the Tournament Players' Championship in final-day winds that gusted to 45mph.

Then came the first of Tom's five tournament titles. He ran away with the Sea Pines Heritage Classic at Hilton Head Island, leading from start to finish and setting a tournament record with a 54-hole total of 199. His eight strokes lead of the field at that point remained a record for the year as well. He won by five from Ed Sneed, and he and Lietzke at Tucson were to prove the only start-to-finish winners during the season, a feat that Watson achieved twice!

Sneed's dramatic collapse in the Masters saw Tom in a losing three-way play-off with Zoeller for the title, but the following week at

LaCosta he again led all the way to win the Tournament of Champions by six strokes.

Byron Nelson has been something of a guide and mentor to Tom in his professional life, and Watson had repaid the interest by twice winning the Byron Nelson Classic. He was always in contention for the hat-trick when he opened with 64 at Preston Trail, in Dallas, and clinched his third victory of the year after a play-off with Bill Rogers, who had finished fast and caught him with a 66. A birdie on the first play-off hole settled it for Watson.

Two weeks later and Tom won again – this time on the home ground of the man everyone accepts he will succeed, Jack Nicklaus.

He had three strokes in hand in winning the Memorial Tournament at Nicklaus's Muirfield Village course in Dublin, Ohio, after building a four-stroke lead at halfway.

Watson started a warm favourite for the United States Open, but inexplicably missed the cut, shooting 75–77, mostly the result of wayward driving, and although he finished third in the Canadian Open he fell away again when he journeyed to Royal Lytham to bid for a third Open Championship title. Four shots behind the leader Hale Irwin after 36 holes, Watson dropped quietly out to a tie for 26th with 76–81. But he was not done, and in August came his fifth and final victory when he beat Johnny Miller at the second extra hole of a play-off to win the Colgate Hall of Fame for the second successive year.

His finest year saw him contest 21 US tournaments. He won five times, was second four times, third once, and had 15 top 10 finishes, only once being 'out of the money'. His stroke average for 82 rounds of golf was 70.27.

JOINT 1–2 SEVERIANO BALLESTEROS

Set alongside his exploits of the previous two years, the 22-year-old Ballesteros perhaps did not enjoy multiple success in 1979. But nothing could detract from his spectacular victory in the Open Championship at Royal Lytham & St Annes, nor the manner in which he accomplished it.

And at the end of the season, in which Sandy Lyle had finished less than £2,000 ahead of him in topping the Order of Merit, there were those who were prepared to argue that Seve's £15,000 for winning the Open, with its prize fund of £155,000, suffered by comparison with Sandy's £17,500 for winning the European Open with a prize fund of only £105,000! A reversal of those two achievements would have put Ballesteros at the top for the fourth successive year.

Seve had only modest success at the opening of the European season. He missed the cut in his own Spanish Open after dashing home from a joint-12th place in the US Masters, and then tied for ninth in the Madrid Open. There were signs of his real form in finishing fifth in Italy, and his tie for third in the French Open, two shots behind Bernard Gallacher, was achieved under the great strain of the death of his fellow-Spaniard Salvador Balbuena on the eve of the tournament.

It all built up to a glorious three weeks in June and July which compensated for missing the cut in the United States Open. In the new Lada English Classic at The Belfry, in the Midlands, he cruised to a six-shot victory, to register his first win since the Japanese Open of the previous November. The following week in Helsingborg he was locked in battle with Lyle in the Scandinavian Open, finishing second three shots in arrears . . . and so to Royal Lytham.

His progress to the Open title is fully chronicled herein. It was a remarkable accomplishment by one who was unknown until the same Open Championship three years previously. Seve did not win another title. But he ended the European year in second place in the Order of Merit with £47,411 in official money-winnings, and a total of £195,608 won since he began tournament play in 1974. That done, he went out to Japan where he finished seventh in the defence of the Japanese Open title he won in 1977 and 1978, and placed eighth in the Australian Open.

JOINT 1–2 HALE IRWIN

In 1978 Irwin set the sort of record that most golfers who want to win tournaments could well do without. He played in 22 events, made the cut in each, had 13 top 10 finishes, a stroke average of 70.65, banked $191,666 – and did not win a single US event! He did, however, get compensation by going out to Australia and South Africa to win the PGA title of each country.

Nevertheless Hale's last victory in America remained as the San Antonio-Texas Open of 1977 – until Inverness, Toledo, in June 1979. It was there that he won the United States Open Championship for the second time in five years, winning by two shots despite finishing double-bogey, bogey, when he had five strokes in hand with two holes to play!

Like Ballesteros at Royal Lytham & St Annes, winning an Open Championship title was the supreme moment in an otherwise unspectacular year for Irwin, in so far as play on the US circuit was concerned. He had three third-place finishes, but at the end of the year went out to Athens with John Mahaffey to retain the World Cup for America, and in doing so won the World Individual title as well. He also won three out of four points in helping America retain the Ryder Cup trophy in the match with Europe at White Sulphur Springs.

For a while it seemed that he might emulate Gene Sarazen, Bobby Jones, Ben Hogan, and Lee Trevino, by winning the US and British Opens in the same year. At Royal Lytham he led Ballesteros by two shots at the halfway mark, and was still two ahead going into the last round. But he lost that lead when taking six at the second hole in the final round, and was never again in contention. He finished sixth.

Two of Hale's third-place finishes came early in the season: at Orlando, Florida, he finished tied with Bill Rogers and Andy Bean,

Above: Severiano Ballesteros.

Below: Hale Irwin.

only one stroke behind the play-off pair Bob Byman and John Schroeder; the following week he finished a disappointing six strokes down to Larry Nelson in the Inverrary Classic, after setting a new course record with a 10-under-par 62 in the second round.

He was again in low-scoring mood in the Houston Open, shooting a seven-under 64 in the second round, but finished in a tie for third four shots behind Wayne Levi.

Hale Irwin is 34. In the 12 years he has been on the US Tour he has won 11 titles and over $1,500,000 in prize money.

4 NANCY LOPEZ

A golfing phenomenon, a superstar – just two of the many journalistic accolades that have been hung around the neck of Nancy Lopez since she took the Ladies Professional Golf Association tournament circuit by storm in 1978.

In that 'rookie' year she won nine tournaments – including a now legendary five in a row – took $189,813 in prize money, and was crowned Rookie of the Year, Player of the Year, and subsequently named female Athlete of the Year by the Associated Press.

It was no fluke. In 1979 she won another nine tournaments, including the unofficial team championship in partnership with JoAnn Washam, and ended the year at the top again, this time with $197,488. It is estima-

Nancy Lopez.

ted that in her brief two years of professional golf she has grossed £250,000 in earnings. Wiseacres declared they should rename it the Lopez Professional Golf Association!

For the record, Nancy won the Sunstar, Sahara National, Women's International, Coca-Cola Classic, Golden Lights, Lady Keystone, Colgate-European Open, Mary Kay Classic, and the Ping Classic (team) tournaments.

She played probably her finest golf of the year in the Mary Kay at Bent Tree, Dallas, when in the second round she became the first ever to record 10 birdies in a single round, going out in 30 and back in 36. She had needed an eighth birdie at the ninth to be out in 28!

Nancy is 23 and married to TV commentator Tim Melton. She was only 12 when she stunned everyone by winning the New Mexico Women's title. She won the US Girls' Open in 1972 and 1974, and in 1976 was on the Curtis Cup side that beat Britain at Royal Lytham. In 1975 she was second in the US Women's Open, and she was second again in 1977, her first tournament as a professional.

She was just eight years old when her father Domingo put a club in her hand and told her to 'knock the ball in the hole'. She has been knocking it in ever since. With her ruthless concentration and aggression she drives to around 230–240 yards, and is one of the game's deadliest putters. She has never had a golf lesson as such, although at the Mary Kay tournament in 1979 she was sufficiently concerned about her game to telephone a golf professional friend who flew down to put her right. She then shot 66 en route to her 17th tour title in two years.

5 SANDY LYLE

Three victories, eight top 10 placings, £49,232 in tournament winnings in Europe, and the Harry Vardon Trophy to go with it marked a wonderful year for Sandy Lyle at the young age of 21 and in only his second year as a professional. And he added the Scottish Professional title to it all for good measure.

Great things had indeed been expected of Sandy when he turned professional after an amateur career in which he had represented England at all levels, and Britain in the Walker Cup as well. But few expected him to 'come good' so soon.

Winner of the Nigerian Open in his 'rookie' year of 1978, he again played with success in Africa in 1979, and opened the European season with good placings in the Portuguese and Spanish Opens. But it was in the sunshine of Jersey that he had his first big success, winning the British Airways/Avis Open by three shots from Howard Clark with a 13-under-par 271.

He failed by a shot to join the four-way play-off for another £5,000 winner's cheque in the Welsh Classic, despite a heroic five-under-par 66 in the last round, and finished in a tie for fourth behind Severiano Bal-

Sandy Lyle.

lesteros in the Lada English Classic.

The following week, however, he fought one of the season's finest 36-hole battles with the Spaniard before wresting his Scandinavian Open title from him, outgunning him with an immaculate 65 when they were paired for the third round.

Sam Torrance took him to three extra holes before Sandy won the Scottish Professional title, and he moved on from there for his finest victory of the year in the European Open Championship at Turnberry. Lyle shared the 36-hole lead with Ballesteros and Ken Brown, but the advantage was with Neil Coles and Mark James as the field lined up for the final round and the first prize of £17,500.

Lyle chose the occasion to produce his greatest golf of the year. He birdied six of the first seven holes, wavered for a while, then finished off a round of 65 with two more birdies for a spreadeagling seven-shots victory. It took him to the top of the Order of Merit, from which Ballesteros was unable to dislodge him.

There was one more distinction to come. The former England amateur international, now representing Scotland, paired with Ken Brown to finish second, five strokes behind the United States in the World Cup in Athens, his own total of 287 giving him joint second place behind Hale Irwin in the World Cup Individual Standings.

THE MAJOR CHAMPIONSHIPS 1979

THE OPEN CHAMPIONSHIP 1979
THE US OPEN CHAMPIONSHIP 1979
THE US MASTERS 1979
THE US PGA CHAMPIONSHIP 1979

Severiano Ballesteros raises his arms in triumph after winning the Open Championship at Royal Lytham & St Annes.
(Golf Photography International)

Lynx Predators.
Lean. Light. Lion-Hearted.

Lynx Predators are America's most wanted golf clubs because they're years ahead in design and construction. They embody the exclusive Lynx head-shaft-grip concept that reduces overall weight significantly. This lets you generate more clubhead speed with less effort.

Predator Woods. Offset or conventional hosel. Investment casting technology imparts iron-like control to your wood game. Offset hosel helps keep hands ahead of ball at address and at impact for added control.

Predator Irons. These low-profile, hefty-hitting irons feature a low center of gravity which puts more mass behind the hitting area of the club face. This gets the ball up quickly with more power behind your shots for greater distance and control.

Shafts for all Predators availa in Lynx-Lite by True Tem Right or left-handed available.

See your golf pro today ab Lynx Predators. They'll help rule the most beastly course.

Carl Ross

Carl Ross, President

LYNX

THE OPEN CHAMPIONSHIP 1979

Norman Mair

BALLESTEROS ZIG-ZAGS TO TRIUMPH

With three strokes in hand on the last tee of the Open Championship, Severiano Ballesteros hooked a three-wood into the left rough, intent only on keeping the ball out of the assorted shrubbery down the right.

'What's it like there?' he enquired of his caddie Dave Musgrave.

'I don't know', said Musgrave with a grin, 'that's about the one place this week we've never been!'

Down the years, Royal Lytham & St Annes has always been known as a great driving course and yet Spain's King of the Jungle won the Open hitting only one fairway with his driver on each of the last two days. In fact, in the bullying wind of the final round, the strongest of the Championship in the opinion of many players, he nailed only five fairways even though he resorted frequently to an iron or three-wood off the tee.

It used to be said of Lytham that it had a bunker for every day of the year. But with many of them rendered obsolete by changes in the game, not least in terms of equipment and balls, that number has been cut by more than half. Even so, when Musgrave showed the young Spaniard a map of the course three weeks before the Open, he pointed out shrewdly the part that sand play was still going to have in the forthcoming Championship, and advised him to go to Lytham with that department of his game 'sharp as hell'.

In retrospect Ballesteros calculated that he had been in 15 greenside bunkers and 14 times had 'got it up and down'. It was a sandy statistic reminiscent of Gary Player's feat at Muirfield in 1959 in his maiden victory in the Open when he was 12 times bunkered and 11 times got down in two. Albeit I think it is fair to say that Seve's putting played a larger part, since Player so often came out close to the flag.

Player was 23 when he won at Muirfield, and so the 22-year-old Ballesteros became the youngest champion this century, and only the second Continental to take the title. The other was Arnaud Massy back in 1907.

Seve may make his audience laugh when he speaks approvingly of Lytham's narrow fairways, 'because then everyone misses them, not just me', but he is not just joking. He believes he has the strength, eye, and such a long zig-zag trail of much inadvertent practice, to have the beating of anybody in the world when it comes to recovering from what lies off the beaten path. There is, however, undeniably something to the American view that though he might still often win, he would not be

Salute to a champion. Ballesteros emerges through the crowds that swarmed across the 18th fairway in the closing stages to see the happy Spaniard apply the final touches to his victory. (Steve Powell, All-Sport Photographic)

able to play quite the same way in the United States because of their water and trees, and rough which may be shorter but is apt to be much more consistent and cloying.

At the close of the first day Ballesteros lay joint 16th, eight strokes off the pace, Bill Longmuir having come out of the unruly wind with a six-under-par 65 which drew from Jack Nicklaus: 'I don't believe the man or the score!'

Never having broken 30 before in any tournament, outward or homeward bound, the 26-year-old Longmuir, who cheerfully confessed to being almost flat broke, turned in 29 to recall the feats of Tom Haliburton and Peter Thomson in the 1963 Open on the same links. It also prompted memories of Tony Jacklin's front nine of 29 at St Andrews in 1970. Suitably inspired, Longmuir punched a six-iron to under three yards at the par-four 10th and holed it to dip seven under. The clouds were sombre, the day grey, but when Longmuir shaped a three-iron round on the wind at the 12th to steal to within four feet of the furtively hidden flag, and sank the putt for his eighth birdie, one would not have been surprised to see the former furniture-van driver bathed in a heavenly light.

Almost entirely self-taught, Longmuir read no books on golf but practised swinging hour after hour in the garden, studying his reflection in the French windows. On the very eve of the Championship, troubled by his form, he was to be seen swinging and hitting on the practice ground, with Australia's Noel Ratcliffe steadying his head with the grip end of a club held at arm's length.

Only three times in the previous 10 years had the player who led after the first round gone on to win – Lee Trevino in 1971, Tom Weiskopf in 1973, and Gary Player in 1974. All of which was a sobering reflection for the man who had originally got his tournament career off the ground with the proceeds from winning two personality contests – Mr Basildon (an Essex town) and Mr Tots (the Talk of the South club). The curriculum for the latter had included giving an on-stage golf lesson to Fiona Richmond whose swing he caught in one marvellously expressive word: 'Lumpy!'

Tucked in second was Hale Irwin who had gone to Lytham in 1974 also as the reigning US Open Champion. In coming home in a three-under-par 33 for the best back nine of the day he unfurled 'a handful of excellent strokes' with, among them, a prime specimen of the shot he had worked on specifically for the Championship – 'a little British six-iron to within six feet of the flag at the 10th, a shot struck with no follow-through, like Doug Sanders himself'.

The next day, having torn a second successive 68 from the wind to lead by two strokes from Ballesteros, Irwin put neatly in perspective the double of winning the premier Opens of the Old World and the New. 'It squelches the argument, no matter which side of the pond you are on, as to who won the Open!' Out in 32 with twos at each of the three short holes, the erstwhile All-American footballer never dropped a stroke to par all day, though he had need of that freshly honed 'British pitch and run' to rescue a four beating upwind at the 15th.

At first Irwin genuinely thought he was being kidded when told of the four blistering birdies of Ballesteros in the course of the last five holes. 'Practically the equivalent', he protested, 'of cutting across.'

Ballesteros had got out in two-under the par of 35 but it had been the stuff of guerilla warfare with Seve seldom on the straight and narrow. On the 10th tee he tugged a one-iron grotesquely, and it was then that Lee Trevino suggested that the cause of his problems was a failure to clear the left side. After which Ballesteros proceeded to play the remaining eight holes in five under, coming back in 32 with that famous finish plundered by this dashing blade of Spain to the tune of 3–3–4–3–3 against the card of 4–4–4–4–4.

His three at the notoriously costly 468-yard 15th was one of only five recorded over the first two days when the average for the field was, respectively and revealingly, 4.95 and 4.81. Moreover, it came after he had hit the wrong club, or what he had called the wrong club until he chipped in with it and decided, with a grin, that it had been a flash of intuitive tactical genius. As to that seeming contravention of Rule 9(1) involved in Seve's apparent acceptance of Trevino's conversational mid-round advice, authority turned a Nelsonic eye, no doubt telling themselves that you can never believe all you read in the papers anyway.

Mark James, with unfamiliar joy, celebrates a putt across the final green which earned him fourth place in the Championship.

On that second evening, Ballesteros touched warmly and gratefully on the value of the four practice rounds he had had with Roberto de Vicenzo 'a great player with long experience of golf and Lytham'. Above all, asserted Ballesteros, Roberto had instilled in him the need for patience on such a links – 'attack and the course will kill you'. There is nothing like a 65, unless it is a 64, to make a man look more kindly on his fellow men. Where the previous evening Ballesteros had been visibly affected by Ken Brown's pace of play, now he was almost paternal, reflecting that he himself had had a tardy spell in his formative years. Trevino was not going to condemn Brown either, though he would admit, he shrugged, that he had had to shave twice during the round!

The overnight leader Longmuir had slipped to third after a gamely tenacious 74, but Tom Watson had closed to within four strokes of the lead, out in 32 in his 68, and requiring only a nine-iron for his second in his eagle at the 486-yard sixth. Nicklaus had moved up to equal fifth, a stroke behind Watson, after a second round 69 in which he was two and a half feet short with his six-iron to the short fifth where, the day before, he had had the 10th 'ace' of his career.

'Not enough club this time', he grumbled, straight-faced.

In a sentence, with the ring of Lord's cricket ground rather than Lytham, Irwin – only two under par after the third round when he had been six, but still two strokes clear of Ballesteros – declared that he had

Sympathy for Ben Crenshaw. He caught Ballesteros on the run-in, only to take six at the 17th hole.

made his 75 'mostly off the back foot'. In other words, he had had to work for his figures, never felt properly on form. He hates the cold, and over the closing holes the rain was spattering his glasses even beneath his protective visor.

Among those who helped to make the news on the penultimate day were three Britons. Back, a decade later, at the scene of his own Open triumph, Tony Jacklin, in his third round 76, called a penalty stroke upon himself when, noticed only by Jacklin, his ball moved as he addressed a putt on the ninth green.

With Wayne Player, the powerful and gifted 17-year-old son of Gary, failing to survive the 54-hole guillotine, England's Peter McEvoy, Amateur champion in 1977 and 1978, was assured of the Silver Medal, which goes to the leading amateur, for a second consecutive year. And Mark James, with a 69, joined Nicklaus on 214 to Irwin's 211, confessing that his secret possibly lay in his daily diet of raw meat. In the event James, by finishing fourth, was the leading home player for the second time in four years, having been fifth at Royal Birkdale in 1976.

It was possibly the nature of Seve's game as much as the state of his own which caused Irwin to look so disenchanted. Ballesteros's way is not his way, though Ballesteros at times might disconcert anyone short of the shade of Walter Hagen. In truth, he managed to look almost offended when he was asked if he had not felt a sudden panic when he saw his drive sailing away into the car park down the right of the 16th.

No, the very opposite, because the flag was on the left and the wind left-to-right. Yet the imagination boggles at what thoughts were seething through Irwin, playing with him, as the Spaniard blithely availed himself of the free lift and drop from the midst of the cars and walked away with a birdie.

That unforgettable final day witnessed the setting of a new record in respect of the total attendance for the week, the new figure being 135,000. It began with Hale Irwin out in front in his bid to join Bobby Jones, Gene Sarazen, Ben Hogan and Lee Trevino as the only men to win the US Open and our Open in the same year.

It was a day when Ben Crenshaw, so tantalisingly close to the title he unreservedly considers carries the most prestige in the world, was to take six at the 17th and so finish in second place in a major championship yet again. A day when Australia's nattily clad Rodger Davis discovered himself leading the Open with but five holes to play, bunkers fatally costing him four strokes in the space of three holes. A day when the defending champion, Jack Nicklaus, did not fade from the chase till he took three putts at both the 13th and 15th.

It included a point in the fortunes of the eventual champion when his caddie was moved to suggest that he shut his eyes and try having a small blindfold on the grounds that the result could not be much worse and might be a lot better. And it ended with the new champion, after shedding tears in fraternal arms as his three brothers, Baldomero, Manuel and Vincente enveloped him, apologising, with a typical twinkle, to the galleries for having so often had to move them out of their allotted pastures to make room to play his second.

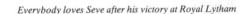

Everybody loves Seve after his victory at Royal Lytham

THE OPEN CHAMPIONSHIP

Royal Lytham & St Annes Golf Club, Lancashire   18–21 July 1979   Prize Money £155,000

Pos	Player						£
1	Severiano Ballesteros	73	65	75	70	283	15,000.00
2	Jack Nicklaus	72	69	73	72	286	11,250.00
	Ben Crenshaw	72	71	72	71	286	11,250.00
4	Mark James	76	69	69	73	287	7,500.00
5	Rodger Davis	75	70	70	73	288	6,500.00
6	Hale Irwin	68	68	75	78	289	6,000.00
7	Graham Marsh	74	68	75	74	291	5,000.00
	Isao Aoki	70	74	72	75	291	5,000.00
	Bob Byman	73	70	72	76	291	5,000.00
10	Bob Charles	78	72	70	72	292	4,000.00
	Masashi Ozaki	75	69	75	73	292	4,000.00
	Greg Norman	73	71	72	76	292	4,000.00
13	Wally Armstrong	74	74	73	72	293	3,125.00
	Terry Gale	71	74	75	73	293	3,125.00
	John O'Leary	73	73	74	73	293	3,125.00
	Simon Owen	75	76	74	68	293	3,125.00
17	Peter McEvoy*	71	74	72	77	294	–
	Lee Trevino	71	73	74	76	294	2,500.00
19	Ken Brown	72	71	75	77	295	1,810.00
	Nick Faldo	74	74	78	69	295	1,810.00
	Sandy Lyle	74	76	75	70	295	1,810.00
	Orville Moody	71	74	76	74	295	1,810.00
	Gary Player	77	69	75	74	295	1,810.00
24	Tony Jacklin	73	74	76	73	296	1,150.00
	Tohru Nakamura	77	75	67	77	296	1,150.00
26	Jerry Pate	69	74	76	78	297	880.00
	Ed Sneed	76	75	70	76	297	880.00
	Peter Thomson	76	75	72	74	297	880.00
	Tom Watson	72	68	76	81	297	880.00
30	Mark Hayes	75	75	77	71	298	713.00
	Simon Hobday	75	77	71	75	298	713.00
	Tom Kite	73	74	77	74	298	713.00
	Bill Longmuir	65	74	77	82	298	713.00
	Armando Saavedra	76	76	73	73	298	713.00
	Bobby Verwey	75	77	74	72	298	713.00
36	Peter Cowen	79	72	72	76	299	575.00
	Lee Elder	75	72	76	76	299	575.00
	Ray Floyd	76	73	71	79	299	575.00
	Mike King	75	70	73	81	299	575.00
	Christy O'Connor, Sr	79	73	71	76	299	575.00
41	Hugh Baiocchi	72	73	78	77	300	478.00
	Dennis Clark	72	69	76	83	300	478.00
	Martin Foster	77	75	74	74	300	478.00
	Hubert Green	77	71	73	79	300	478.00
	Peter Oosterhuis	75	74	73	78	300	478.00
	Noel Ratcliffe	79	73	72	76	300	478.00
	John Schroeder	74	75	74	77	300	478.00
	Philippe Toussaint	76	75	74	75	300	478.00
	Denis Watson	75	70	76	79	300	478.00
50	Brian Barnes	78	71	77	75	301	475.00
	Garry Cullen	72	74	77	78	301	475.00
	Carl Mason	77	72	76	76	301	475.00
	DeWitt Weaver	73	71	80	77	301	475.00
54	Geoff Parslow	75	75	76	76	302	450.00
	Ian Richardson	75	73	77	77	302	450.00
	Kosaku Shimada	75	74	75	78	302	450.00
57	Johnny Miller	77	73	77	76	303	450.00
	Jack Newton	76	73	78	76	303	450.00
	Guy Wolstenholme	77	75	71	80	303	450.00
	Yoshitaka Yamamoto	76	77	74	76	303	450.00
61	Robin Fyfe	74	73	79	81	307	450.00

*Amateur

THE US OPEN CHAMPIONSHIP 1979

Michael McDonnell

LO! THE HINKLE TREE

Pushing back the frontiers of knowledge is not the primary objective of any sport. Yet the American Open Championship at Inverness in Toledo, Ohio, managed to contribute a new arboreal specimen to the history of horticulture. It came to be known as the Hinkle Tree, though more serious students have identified it as a fine example of the 'Tatum dementia' species (after Sandy Tatum, President of the United States Golf Association), while the specimen itself was known for years to the locals as a Black Hills Spruce.

It has some startling characteristics. It springs up overnight to a height of 30 feet for the specific purpose of preventing golfers taking short cuts with their tee shots. It delights spectators, irks players, and makes the people who plant it look very silly. There is another characteristic about the Hinkle Tree. It doesn't work. Professionals still find a way round it.

With the best of, but ill-judged, intentions the United States Golf Association officials decided they had 'to protect the integrity of Inverness' (their words) after Lon Hinkle discovered in the first round that it was possible to shorten the playing distance of the eighth hole by some 75 yards by driving down the adjacent 17th fairway. It still left an extremely testing long iron to the green over dense forest and a gully, but it was well within range, and worth the risk as Hinkle proved by getting a birdie at the hole on his way to a share of that first-day lead.

Thus it came to pass that the USGA went out and bought a tree at a nearby nursery and caused it to be planted, just after dawn before the start of the second round, at what they assumed was the precise point between fairways to forestall more short-cut attempts. It was a great mistake because the tree was not tall enough, nor was it located properly, and moreover, it developed a very sad tilt which made the task of hitting a golf ball past it even less demanding.

But the greater error was that the Championship itself became of secondary interest in these early rounds to the sideshow of the eighth hole where pros, particularly Hinkle, were cajoled to 'have a go' and Chi Chi Rodriguez added to the circus mood by teeing his golf ball on a pencil before driving over the tree. The other aspect of this affair was that the USGA's action (changing the course once the contest was in progress by the addition of a tree) was unprecedented and open to legal, as well as ethical, argument by golf aficionados whose verdicts to this day are unresolved.

Indeed if golf can be said to have a 'silly season' then it peaked during this week in Toledo because even before the Hinkle Tree took root, the circus opened with the kind of gate-crashing trick that would have made those other famous rabbits, Maurice Flitcroft and Walter Danecki – who found a way to play in the British Open, even though neither could break 100 – extremely proud. Barry Bremen, a hacker who looked the part of a pro, managed to play half a practice round and get himself photographed on the practice ground with Jack Nicklaus before being rumbled by officials. Once caught, Barry left without a murmur, happy that his mission had been accomplished.

Cabaret time continued later with that daredevil amateur Bobby Clampett delighting the crowds by kneeling to play tee shots, hitting putts between his feet, and sometimes using a wedge to do it. His problem was that the USGA did not take too kindly to this talented young man acting the fool in their Championship and they accorded him an eternal niche in the history of the sport. He became the first golfer in the American Open – and probably anywhere else for that matter – to be ordered off the field in the midst of play in the style of a disgraced footballer. Why did he do it? The antics of this top US amateur were so out of character, and the mystery of it all was that he implored officials to let him play as a marker on the final day – when all this nonsense took place – after he had missed the 36-hole qualifying cut. Undoubtedly he thought it was harmless fun, but it proved to be neither the time nor the place, and he was despatched from the course.

All of which might have detracted from Hale Irwin's splendid victory, but didn't. It was his second US Open title, and confirmed him as a rightful member of that élite group who can be regarded as champions whether they possess a current title or not. Jack Nicklaus, Tom Watson, and Lee Trevino fall into that same small category.

Inverness is an uncompromising course, as forbidding as a cantankerous old uncle and part of golf history in the United States because it was here in 1920 that professionals were first allowed into the clubhouse, a social milestone that was to lead, albeit over many decades, to the millionaire superstars of the current era. In those days they were regarded as artisans, yet the transition to the status of highly paid entertainers was being led by the legendary Walter Hagen who played in that 1920 Championship and, with his colleagues, presented a long case clock to the Inverness club to mark the momentous occasion when they were at last treated as human beings.

Here too Harry Vardon lost that US Open to Ted Ray after being five strokes clear with seven holes to play. Thus, if the straightest hitter who ever lived could come to grief on Inverness, the power merchants of modern times were in for trouble. It can be an exasperating course for the challenger who tries to overpower it. Its small greens and narrow fairways carve a route through trees and are hemmed in by tangled, cloying grass. It was therefore an intimidating prospect for men who

*For Hale Irwin, victory at Inverness gave him his second US Open title in five years,
despite a double-bogey, bogey finish. (Golf Photography International)*

spend most of their year hammering the ball as far as they can to wide open spaces and getting away with murder with a pitch and a putt.

Inverness requires flawless repetitive technique governed, most importantly, by an unflappable temperament. Thus Irwin was qualified on all counts, and it is significant that two other campaigners notable for their self-control – Jerry Pate and Gary Player – also figured prominently at the finish. Indeed the claustrophobic aspect of Inverness brought Watson crashing down and dismissed him from the contest when it was half complete because his scores were not good enough to remain in play. He had taken 75 and 77 and his drives were so wayward there was little chance of survival very early in the Championship.

This sad and mystifying fall from form when only four weeks earlier he had played a truly historic round of golf in devastating conditions to win the Memorial Tournament suggests an almost artistic dimension to Watson's playing gift. His technique is not machine-like but, in the manner of all artistic talents, subject to violent variations.

He called his performance 'pathetic and careless' but there was just a hint of anxious awareness that the best players do not always win most titles and that Sam Snead, with no US Open to his name, and Arnold Palmer with no US PGA title in his collection, bear sad testimony to this truth. The irony is that the US Open seemed likely to be the first major title that Watson would win when he was out on his own at Winged Foot in 1974 but collapsed so that Irwin moved through to become champion. Now, two British Opens and an American Masters later, there is still no sign of a US Open medal in the Watson trophy case.

Yet Watson's early departure from Toledo served to confirm USGA officials about the correctness of the stern manner in which they had arranged the golf course, and Sandy Tatum, President of the USGA, said: 'We are not trying to catch out the best player. We are trying to seek him out.' The inference was that while week-to-week sponsors need the publicity of low scores and set their courses accordingly, the USGA wanted to find a true champion, testing every department of his skill and character in the process, regardless of the final score.

Not surprisingly they sprang therefore to the defence of Inverness with the Hinkle Tree when the pros were about to make it look easy. But their action was about as sensible as Olympic authorities building a brick wall across the track 'to protect the integrity of the 1,500 metres'. Yet in a perverse way the object of the Hinkle Tree worked on one man – the cause of it all. Hinkle became so obsessed with defeating the tree each day that he forgot about winning the tournament, and threw away a marvellous chance when in contention in the last round by tackling the tree and taking a double-bogey.

'It was a dumb thing to do', said Hinkle afterwards. Yet it contrasted sharply with his other clash with nature later in the year when he deliberately hit a ball so that it skipped across a pond at Akron on his way to winning the World Series. On that occasion there was simply no other shot.

Gary Player put in a great last round of 68 and failed by only two shots to catch the fading Irwin.

By Irwin's own reckoning he won the Open with his third round of 67 which was a masterpiece of opportunism, made all the more impressive because it matched stroke-for-stroke the efforts of challenger Tom Weiskopf who seemed to be setting the target. Weiskopf hammered a four-iron into the 523-yard 13th then sank the putt for an eagle three, while Irwin looked on. Not to be outdone, Irwin answered perfectly with a three-iron into the same green and a three-footer for his own eagle. So, even though Weiskopf finished with a 67, he was depressed to realise he had made no ground on Irwin who went into the last round with a three-stroke lead.

Irwin calculated in the final round that none of his close rivals would cut loose for fear of finding disaster on this narrow course. And the other challengers were just too far away from him to do serious damage even if they put together good last rounds. Sure enough Nicklaus erupted three days too late with a 68 to finish jointly in ninth place, while Gary Player made a better fist of it with his 68 which moved him into a share of second place with Jerry Pate. But everybody knew that Irwin would have to make a lot of errors for the outcome to change.

He almost obliged, for even though five strokes clear with two holes to play he was to win by only a two-stroke margin. He finished double-bogey, bogey, for a 75 and level-par 284. Was it nerves? Or the intelligent use of a lead by a clear-eyed professional, like a fisherman letting out as much of the line as was needed? It was both. Irwin said afterwards: 'It was a fight. I was choking from the first tee. It must have looked as though I couldn't get back to the barn quick enough, but I got there just in time. It's not my idea of championship golf to finish double-bogey, bogey, but it's two shots better than the next guy. That's all that counts.'

And that, too, was an echo from earlier times at Inverness. It was the great Hagen who said: 'It's not how. It's how many.' Which is true if your name is Hale Irwin – untrue if you're Bobby Clampett – and will earn you a transplant if you're a Hinkle Tree.

Jack Nicklaus erupted three days too late with a final round of 68.

THE UNITED STATES OPEN CHAMPIONSHIP

Inverness Golf Club, Toledo, Ohio 14–17 June 1979 Prize Money $325,000

Pos	Player					Total	$
1	Hale Irwin	74	68	67	75	284	50,000.00
2	Gary Player	73	73	72	68	286	22,250.00
	Jerry Pate	71	74	69	72	286	22,250.00
4	Bill Rogers	71	72	73	72	288	13,733.33
	Larry Nelson	71	68	76	73	288	13,733.33
	Tom Weiskopf	71	74	67	76	288	13,733.33
7	David Graham	73	73	70	73	289	10,000.00
8	Tom Purtzer	70	69	75	76	290	9,000.00
9	Jack Nicklaus	74	77	72	68	291	7,500.00
	Keith Fergus	70	77	72	72	291	7,500.00
11	Ed Sneed	72	73	75	73	293	4,340.00
	Andy North	77	74	68	74	293	4,340.00
	Ben Crenshaw	75	71	72	75	293	4,340.00
	Calvin Peete	72	75	71	75	293	4,340.00
	Lee Elder	74	72	69	78	293	4,340.00
16	Jim Simons	74	74	78	68	294	2,833.33
	Graham Marsh	77	71	72	74	294	2,833.33
	Bob Gilder	77	70	69	78	294	2,833.33
19	Lee Trevino	77	73	73	72	295	2,410.00
	D. A. Weibring	74	76	71	74	295	2,410.00
	Lanny Wadkins	73	74	71	77	295	2,410.00
	Bobby Walzel	74	72	71	78	295	2,410.00
	Al Geiberger	74	74	69	78	295	2,410.00
24	Hubert Green	77	74	73	72	296	2,200.00
25	Wayne Levi	77	73	75	72	297	2,000.00
	Mike Reid	74	75	74	74	297	2,000.00
	Lou Graham	70	75	75	77	297	2,000.00
	Bobby Nichols	76	75	71	75	297	2,000.00
	Bob Murphy	72	79	69	77	297	2,000.00
	Andy Bean	70	71	76	80	297	2,000.00
	Bob E. Smith	77	71	69	80	297	2,000.00
32	Lynn Janson	77	71	77	73	298	1,725.00
	Dale Douglass	72	76	76	74	298	1,725.00
	Howard Twitty	73	78	71	76	298	1,725.00
	ChiChi Rodriguez	73	76	71	78	298	1,725.00
36	Isao Aoki	73	77	76	73	299	1,560.00
	Jim Dent	75	76	75	73	299	1,560.00
	John Mahaffey	77	73	74	75	299	1,560.00
	Dave Stockton	75	70	78	76	299	1,560.00
	Bill Kratzert	77	72	78	72	299	1,560.00
41	Larry Ziegler	77	72	78	73	300	1,430.00
	Jack Renner	76	75	75	74	300	1,430.00
	Bruce Lietzke	74	77	73	76	300	1,430.00
	Jim Nelford	75	74	73	78	300	1,430.00
	Jim Colbert	71	74	78	77	300	1,430.00
	Dana Quigley	71	78	74	77	300	1,430.00
47	Forrest Fezler	76	77	73	75	301	1,360.00
48	Fred Couples*	76	74	80	72	302	–
	George Burns	74	73	78	77	302	1,312.50
	Greg Norman	76	74	74	78	302	1,312.50
	Frank Conner	73	78	73	78	302	1,312.50
	Rod Funseth	73	74	74	81	302	1,312.50
53	David Edwards	74	76	74	80	304	1,265.00
	Eddie Pearce	75	75	76	78	304	1,265.00
	Joe Inman	72	77	75	80	304	1,265.00
	Lon Hinkle	70	77	76	81	304	1,265.00
	John Cook*	71	80	77	76	304	–
	Joe Rassett*	75	75	77	77	304	–
59	Eric Batten	74	76	78	77	305	1,235.00
	Arnold Palmer	76	73	75	81	305	1,235.00
61	John Gentile	73	75	77	81	306	1,220.00
62	Mac McLendon	77	74	80	78	309	1,210.00
63	Tony Peterson	74	75	84	79	312	1,200.00

* Amateur

Stand square to the bar.
Take the base of the
glass firmly, but with a
relaxed grip.
Then without taking your
eyes off the ice cube,
bring the Martini up to
your lips in
one smooth action.

The right one

THE US MASTERS 1979

Michael Williams

FUZZY GIVES THANKS TO SNEED

The world does not necessarily remember only winners. Roberto de Vicenzo's momentary carelessness when he failed to notice a mistake on his scorecard in the 1968 Masters is still much more vividly recalled than the victory that year of Bob Goalby.

It is also possible that Ed Sneed's failure to grasp the 1979 Masters when it was his for the taking will be remembered just as much as the ultimate victory of Frank Urban Zoeller, whose initials inevitably gave him the nickname of 'Fuzzy'.

Both Vicenzo and Sneed won enormous public sympathy: the big, genial, Argentinian with his broken English, because he failed to notice a four against the 17th on his card when in fact he had scored a three; Sneed because he led by three strokes with three holes to play and still could not win. Zoeller, outgoing rather in the manner of Lee Trevino and with a style of play almost as individual, came from nowhere. He was three strokes behind after the first round, six behind after the second, still six after the third, four adrift with nine holes to play.

Moreover he had never played in the Masters before and therefore became the first man since Gene Sarazen in 1935 to be presented with the famous Augusta green jacket on his initial appearance. He made further history by being the first man to succeed in a sudden-death play-off. Ties had previously been decided over 18 holes.

Once given the chance, Zoeller took it eagerly. When he finished with a final round of 70, playing the back nine in 34, he could have had little idea that he would be involved in a play-off. But neither Sneed nor Tom Watson could beat his 72-hole total of 280 and it took Zoeller only two holes of sudden-death to get the birdie neither of the others could match.

Credit must always be given where credit is due but even when one looks back on the events of those four April days it was undoubtedly more a Masters that Sneed lost than a Masters that Zoeller won.

Sneed had commanded the richly colourful stage of Augusta almost from first to last. Only Bruce Lietzke was ahead of him after the first round. At half-way Sneed led jointly with Craig Stadler, three strokes clear of anybody else. With 18 holes to play he was in front on his own, a seemingly impregnable five shots to the good!

No one in the history of the Masters had ever lost such a lead. Once, in 1956, Ken Venturi had failed to protect a four-stroke lead from Jackie Burke, but never five. Nor, until those last dramatic holes when the sky suddenly caved in on him, did Sneed look like yielding. One can

Frank Urban (Fuzzy) Zoeller. He came from behind to win at Augusta after a play-off with Tom Watson and the luckless Ed Sneed. (Golf Photography International)

only say that afterwards he took it like a man, disappointed but never for a moment bitter.

Where then did he begin to go wrong? On the eve of that final round, Sneed was asked if he might be tempted to play conservatively and concentrate on protecting his substantial lead. 'I don't think so', he had replied. 'At the beginning of the round I'll play just as I have been playing. If I have a big lead on the back nine I won't do anything foolish on the water holes. But if my lead is only two or three shots, I can't play that safe. I would have to be more aggressive.'

In fact Sneed's lead was reduced to just such a margin. He dropped strokes at the two short holes, the fourth and sixth, where each time he underclubbed. So he went through the turn in 38 to Watson's 35 and he was only two ahead. If this was a potentially dangerous situation, I must say I was convinced that he would survive it. At the short 12th, where the wind plays such peculiar tricks that the whole art of playing the hole is to find the right club, he was bunkered behind the green. With water guarding the front of the shallow green, that is a terrifying recovery shot, but Sneed splashed out with nerveless aplomb to within inches of the hole. That was one crisis overcome and he abandoned any plans of aggression on the two famous par fives, the 13th and 15th.

Each time Sneed laid up short of the water. Each time he pitched up close. Each time he holed the putts for his birdie fours. That surely was it, though in fact the last of those two birdies could have been the one that put him in the wrong frame of mind. Still three strokes to the good, he may subconsciously have become defensive. 'I had control of the tournament. I didn't feel tight', he said afterwards. But he played away from danger at the short 16th and left his tee shot too far up the slope. From there he took three putts.

At the 17th, Sneed made sure of not being in the bunker short of the slightly raised green, was marginally too strong, and then took another three putts off the fringe at the back of the green. His lead was down to a single stroke. He took his spoon from the 18th tee and played his shot nicely to the centre of a fairway funnelled by trees. But his approach with a seven-iron lacked conviction and he ended up half in and half out of the bunker on the right.

In such a situation it was a horribly demanding shot, and Sneed did extremely well under the circumstances to get the ball to within six feet of the hole. So he had that for the Masters and, amid an awful silence, missed it. He thought, and his caddie thought, the putt broke right. But it did not and his ball stayed perched on the edge. All this was being watched from behind the green in the recorders' tent by Zoeller and Watson, hardly believing they were to be given another chance of winning a tournament both had given up for lost.

When Zoeller stood on the 16th tee from which Sneed began his slide, he was four strokes off the lead but not entirely without hope. Indeed he said later that he had just played 'the shot that was for me the turning point'. His drive at the 15th had left him with a second shot of 235 yards into the wind and that, he said, was 'as far as I can hit it'. In the air he did not think he had made it carry; but he did, and he got his birdie four. Then at the 17th he got another, pitching up to 10 feet and holing the putt.

It was only then that one seriously began to consider Zoeller as a contender, but even that chance seemed to have gone when he was short of the 18th in two. However he played a good pitch and sank the putt for his par, a round of 70 and a target of 280. Watson had the opportunity to win throughout the four days and never took it. For this I would blame some uncharacteristically poor play of the par fives. In the first round, when he had a 68, he went for the green at the 520-yard 15th with as little as a six-iron and put it in the water: six.

In the second round he had to play a three-wood for his second shot to the same hole and put that in the water as well. Though he still, in this case, saved his par, it was for him certainly a birdie opportunity spurned. In the third round, when he had a 70, Watson was in Rae's Creek with his second to the 13th and lost another chance of a birdie. When at last he did make the carry to the 15th, he took three putts. In essence, that was five strokes wasted.

Nor did anything go for him in the final round. He became locked in a run of pars, his putter repeatedly failing him as he missed again and again from inside 15 feet. It was a tantalising case of so near but yet so far. So it was also in the end for Jack Nicklaus. Though he had begun with a 69, he was five strokes behind after 36 holes and eight adrift going into the last round. Finally he cut loose with a 69 and it lifted him to within a stroke of Zoeller, Sneed and Watson.

Momentarily there was a chance that Nicklaus could even win. Out in

35 that final blustery afternoon, he had further birdies at the 10th and 13th. Then, after laying up short of the water at the 15th and seeing his third roll back into the shallows, he waded in after his ball, came out in a shower of spray, and still got his five. At the next he holed for a two which almost raised the roof, reminiscent as it was of the famous two he had made at the same hole in 1975 when he won by a hair's-breadth from Tom Weiskopf and Johnny Miller.

But just as Nicklaus's round seemed to be coming to another grand climax, so he was too strong with his approach to the 17th, ran through the green and took five. Already five times the Masters Champion, this was also the 13th time he had finished in the top half-dozen. So there it was, a play-off between Sneed, who only had a few minutes in which to compose himself after his enormous disappointment over the last three holes, the gregarious Zoeller, and Watson, now the favourite.

I must say I do not like sudden death play-offs but, for the two holes it lasted, it was absolutely captivating golf; in another gear, it seemed, to the tournament itself. All three hit colossal drives down the 10th. Watson and Sneed knocked in their second shots so close that Zoeller afterwards said that he didn't think he could 'find any room on the green' and all three missed for their birdies.

Three more mammoth drives disappeared down the 11th. Sneed was too strong with his approach but played such a wonderful bunker shot that he nearly holed it for a three. Watson had a putt for the birdie and missed it, and then Zoeller, from eight feet or so, holed. As the ball disappeared from view so Zoeller hurled his putter to the heavens. I am not sure that it ever came down.

A dismayed Ed Sneed watches his last putt for victory stop on the lip.

THE US MASTERS TOURNAMENT

Augusta National Golf Club, Augusta, Georgia   12–15 April 1979   Prize Money $299,625

Pos	Player					Total	$
1	Fuzzy Zoeller	70	71	69	70	280	50,000.00
2	Ed Sneed	68	67	69	76	280	30,000.00
	Tom Watson	68	71	70	71	280	30,000.00
	Zoeller won play-off at second extra hole						–
4	Jack Nicklaus	69	71	72	69	281	15,000.00
5	Tom Kite	71	72	68	72	283	13,000.00
6	Bruce Lietzke	67	75	68	74	284	11,500.00
7	Lanny Wadkins	73	69	70	73	285	9,000.00
	Leonard Thompson	68	70	73	74	285	9,000.00
	Craig Stadler	69	66	74	76	285	9,000.00
10	Hubert Green	74	69	72	71	286	6,500.00
	Gene Littler	74	71	69	72	286	6,500.00
12	Jack Newton	70	72	69	76	287	3,740.00
	Severiano Ballesteros	72	68	73	74	287	3,740.00
	Miller Barber	75	64	72	76	287	3,740.00
	Lee Trevino	73	71	70	73	287	3,740.00
	Andy North	72	72	74	69	287	3,740.00
17	Bill Kratzert	73	68	71	76	288	2,700.00
	Ray Floyd	70	68	73	77	288	2,700.00
	Gary Player	71	72	74	71	288	2,700.00
	Lee Elder	73	70	74	71	288	2,700.00
	Artie McNickle	71	72	71	74	288	2,700.00
22	J.C. Snead	73	71	72	73	289	2,400.00
23	Joe Inman	68	71	76	75	290	2,225.00
	Lou Graham	69	71	76	74	290	2,225.00
	Jim Simons	72	70	75	73	290	2,225.00
	Hale Irwin	72	70	74	74	290	2,225.00
	Bob Clampett*	73	71	73	73	290	–
28	Tommy Aaron	72	73	74	72	291	2,000.00
	Andy Bean	69	74	74	74	291	2,000.00
	Graham Marsh	71	72	73	75	291	2,000.00
31	Gil Morgan	72	69	71	80	292	1,975.00
	Victor Regalado	71	74	75	72	292	1,975.00
	Larry Nelson	70	75	70	77	292	1,975.00
34	Isao Aoki	71	72	72	78	293	1,950.00
	Bob Byman	71	73	75	74	293	1,950.00
	Scott Hoch*	72	73	74	74	293	–
	Charles Coody	71	72	74	76	293	1,950.00
	Peter Oosterhuis	73	72	73	75	293	1,950.00
39	John Cook*	72	72	75	76	295	–
40	Nick Faldo	73	71	79	73	296	1,875.00
41	Jerry Pate	72	70	75	80	297	1,850.00
	Tom Weiskopf	73	72	71	81	297	1,850.00
43	Billy Casper	73	70	80	76	299	1,800.00
44	Rod Funseth	69	73	78	80	300	1,775.00
45	Lindy Miller	73	67	75	86	301	1,750.00

* Amateur

SAM TORRANCE · SANDY LYLE · MIKE MILLER · JOHN MORGAN
VINCENTE FERNANDEZ · CARL MASON · TOMMY HORTON · BRIAN BARNES
DAVID INGRAM · MALCOLM GREGSON · EWEN MURRAY · MAURICE BEMBRIDGE

They fly British Caledonian from course to course, of course.

Above the "Golfing Lions." A formidable team of golfing talent, sponsored by the airline with a considerable commitment to golf and golfers–British Caledonian.

We'll carry you–and your clubs–to clubs all over Britain and Europe. And we're the only British Airline that flies to the major cities in South America, North, West and Central Africa, and to Houston–Texas and *Atlanta–Georgia.

So fly with us. Our lion is as good as an eagle.

*June 1st 1980.

British 🛡 **Caledonian**
We never forget you have a choice.

THE US PGA CHAMPIONSHIP 1979

George Simms

AGONY AT OAKLAND HILLS

They put up the 'Welcome Home' signs outside his home, The Hamlet, at Delray Beach, Florida, as an appropriate tribute to the Prince, when David Graham, 33-year-old winner of the United States PGA Championship, and 'one of us' to America despite his Australian nationality, returned to base from Michigan. He had just secured his first major victory, and ended the long wait for another Australian triumph in one of golf's accepted Grand Slam events – the last having been Peter Thomson's win in the Open Championship at Royal Birkdale, Lancashire, back in 1965.

Yet in 15 desperate minutes on the 72nd hole at Oakland Hills in suburban Detroit, Graham threw away the outright victory that was his for the taking, dissipated a winning lead, and then was compelled to survive a harrowing three-hole play-off with the luckless Ben Crenshaw. Only then did he claim the role of 61st PGA Champion, and the string of future exemptions that accompanied the honour.

It came out right in the end, for Graham was indeed the worthy winner of a title that fitted easily into a record embracing over a dozen wins since the lightly-built Australian had taken to the world's circuits a decade earlier. A professional from his mid-teens, he had been a frequent winner since leaving his native land in 1969 and making his first mark when losing a play-off for the Singapore Open.

Paradoxically in 1970, having failed to gain his Player's Card on the US Circuit, he teamed with Bruce Devlin to win the World Cup in Buenos Aires. That same year he won the Thailand Open, and gate-crashed Europe to capture the French Open title. He won his US credentials the following year and, apart from a modest season in 1973, had never been out of the top 50. His best year came in 1976 when he won the Westchester Classic and the American Golf Classic, the Chunichi Crowns in Japan, the World Match-Play Championship at Wentworth in England, and was eighth in the US Money List with $176,174. The following year he was to win his own Australian Open title, and the South African PGA Championship.

Off the course he had meanwhile built a reputation as a club designer, establishing along the way a close friendship with Jack Nicklaus who was among the first to congratulate him when he had survived the near-disasters of Detroit. Jack wired him: 'You showed what you are made of on the first two holes of the play-off. I'm proud of you. This is something you can be proud of the rest of your life.'

Certainly Graham will be unlikely to forget the play-off, and the circumstances that brought it about. Oakland Hills has a reputation of being among the toughest of Championship layouts. Ben Hogan, who won one of his four United States Open titles on it, described it as 'the monster'. But heavy rains in the days and weeks preceding the Championship took the venom out of the beast, softened the fairways, slowed the greens, and more than 60 scores were posted which bettered the par of 70 for the 7014-yard course.

Graham revelled in it – right up to the time he walked off the 71st green and headed for the 18th tee to play the final hole, two shots ahead of Crenshaw. He needed par at the 459-yard finishing stretch for a 63 which would have tied the Championship record set by his fellow-Australian Bruce Crampton at the Firestone Club in Akron, Ohio, in 1975. The same par four would also have given him a 10-under total of 270 and set a new record for the Championship since it switched from match-play in 1958.

He took six! Surging and jostling crowds seeking position for the last rites hampered his path to the 18th tee. Had it not been for his caddie using his golf bag as a ramrod, he said afterwards, he would not have got from the green to tee. 'I was pummelled, elbowed, whacked on the back, stepped on, and suddenly I was not keeping concentration on the job at hand, but trying to survive to the next tee.'

As he set himself up over the ball, the full realisation of the moment suddenly hit him. It came to him with impact that he was just a par four from one of the world's four major titles. He said later that he never felt comfortable as he addressed the ball, and such was apparent as he carved his tee shot way out to the right and over the galleries.

Jerry Pate, paired with him and Rex Caldwell, reckoned that David would find it in a good lie – and so it was. But the Australian, still surrounded by spectators, and with the gallery ranged between him and the fairway, could not check his yardage chart, did not seek the assistance of stewards, and in the clamour of the moment took a six-iron to the distant green when, as events proved, a seven-iron would have sufficed.

He went through the green, and now he had a bad lie. His chip out finished on the fringe, a downhill chip-and-run went five feet past, he missed the putt and had an 18-inch one back for his double-bogey six. Ben Crenshaw, Graham's old friend, couldn't believe it. He had put everything into a closing 67 to overhaul the third round leader Caldwell, but had been unable to shake the masterly Graham on the inward nine holes and could not believe that he would be given the chance of the 'major' victory he so wanted. Now here he was in a play-off to win it – courtesy of David Graham.

And win it the Texan so nearly did. At the first extra hole Graham pulled his drive and was short of the green in two. Crenshaw, on the front for two, ran the ball up close for an easy par four. It looked all over when Graham pitched to 25 feet, but the Australian saved his neck with an 'all the way' single putt. Again at the par-five second the odds were with Ben. His four-wood finished at the back of the green, five

For David Graham the US PGA Championship was his first 'major' triumph – but he had to survive a heart-thumping play-off.

yards past the pin. David was over the green, chipped to 10 feet and again holed it as they halved in birdie fours.

So to the vital par three third hole: and disaster for the luckless Crenshaw. His four-iron finished in a bunker, while with a similar club Graham put his tee shot to within 10 feet. Crenshaw failed with his putt for three from 15 feet and Graham, nerves now totally under control, ran down the putt for a winning birdie and the title. For Graham, elation. For poor Crenshaw, more sympathy. It was the fourth time in his last five tournaments to that point, including the Open Championship in Britain, that he had finished second. He was to do so again before the season's end.

To take nothing away from those who finally occupied centre stage, the 61st US PGA Championship was notable for the failure of the household names, Tom Watson apart, to make their impact on the proceedings. Hubert Green, Lee Trevino, Gary Player, and Ray Floyd all finished 'down the field': Hale Irwin failed to make the cut; while Nicklaus wound up in a tie for 65th place and in his much-restricted schedule wrote a new kind of personal record – the first year since joining the US Circuit in 1962 that he had not won an event.

It seemed that Watson might crown his finest year with his fourth 'major' when he went to the front in the opening round with a four-under-par 66. It put him a stroke ahead of Caldwell, and two in front of Ron Streck and Jay Haas. Graham was among a string of 69s. Crenshaw also opened with 69 and then went to the front at halfway with a 67, his 136 being a shot better than Caldwell, Haas, and Graham. Watson's driving deserted him, and after a second round of 72 he was never in a seriously challenging position.

The happy-go-lucky Caldwell, enjoying his finest year since joining the US Tour in 1975, eased his way into the 54-hole lead by matching Watson's opening 66, despite being interrupted for 45 minutes when a late afternoon thunderstorm and high winds forced suspension of play. The line-up for the final round was Caldwell 203, Crenshaw 205, Graham, Watson, and Pate 207.

Crenshaw made a tremendous start by birdying the first three holes to go eight under par. The Australian birdied the first and second to be five under. Caldwell birdied the third and went back again into the lead when Crenshaw dropped a shot at the sixth. Now Graham put in his surge. He birdied the seventh and eighth while Ben was rolling in a 15-yarder at the ninth.

The 10th was the critical hole. Here Crenshaw drove into a bunker and took two to get out, while Graham ran in a putt for a birdie three. That two-stroke swing put him in the lead for the first time in the Championship. He went nine under with another birdie at the 11th and was three ahead of Crenshaw who was again bunkered.

Crenshaw was not done. He birdied the 12th and 13th against the Australian's pars to get back to within a stroke of the leader, but when Graham hit a beautiful shot to the 15th to within a few inches of the flag for another birdie he was 10 under par and to most observers home and dry. He was still 10 under as the crowd engulfed him en route to the 18th tee.

When the loose ends were tidied up at the end of the four 1979 'majors', Watson, top of the US Money Winners' list for the third successive year, had gone two straight years without adding to his past tally of three major championship victories.

Crenshaw, steeped in the history of the game of golf, and longing for that first major title, was runner-up for one of them yet again, as he had been in two successive British Open Championships and a US Masters.

For Caldwell there was the satisfaction of his best-ever tour performance in his best-ever year. For Lee Elder there was the assurance of the 12th and last place in the Ryder Cup side, which would not have been his had one of the previously chosen 11 members of the US team won at Oakland Hills. For David Graham there was the satisfaction of knowing that his nerves had been sorely tried at a critical moment in his career, and had been found anything but wanting.

Compensation for the agony of it all was a cheque for $60,000; a 10-year exemption into all US sponsored tournaments; a five-year exemption to the United States Open Championship; a five-year exemption to the US Masters Tournament; and exemption for the rest of his life to the PGA Championship itself.

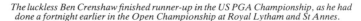

The luckless Ben Crenshaw finished runner-up in the US PGA Championship, as he had done a fortnight earlier in the Open Championship at Royal Lytham and St Annes.

THE US PGA CHAMPIONSHIP

Oakland Hills Country Club, Birmingham, Michigan   2–5 August 1979   Prize Money $350,000

Pos	Player	R1	R2	R3	R4	Total	$
1	David Graham	69	68	70	65	272	60,000.00
2	Ben Crenshaw	69	67	69	67	272	40,000.00
	Graham won play-off at third extra hole						
3	Rex Caldwell	67	70	66	71	274	25,000.00
4	Ron Streck	68	71	69	68	276	20,000.00
5	Gibby Gilbert	69	72	68	69	278	14,500.00
	Jerry Pate	69	69	69	71	278	14,500.00
7	Howard Twitty	70	73	69	67	279	9,200.00
	Jay Haas	68	69	73	69	279	9,200.00
	Don January	69	70	71	69	279	9,200.00
10	Gary Koch	71	71	71	67	280	6,750.00
	Lou Graham	69	74	68	69	280	6,750.00
12	Jerry McGee	73	69	71	68	281	5,250.00
	Andy Bean	76	69	68	68	281	5,250.00
	Jack Renner	71	74	66	70	281	5,250.00
	Tom Watson	66	72	69	74	281	5,250.00
16	Bob Gilder	73	71	68	70	282	3,780.00
	Hubert Green	69	70	72	71	282	3,780.00
	Graham Marsh	69	70	71	72	282	3,780.00
	Gene Littler	71	71	67	73	282	3,780.00
	Bruce Lietzke	69	69	71	73	282	3,780.00
21	John Schroeder	72	72	70	69	283	3,250.00
	Bob Byman	73	72	69	69	283	3,250.00
23	Rod Funseth	70	69	76	69	284	2,900.00
	Alan Tapie	73	65	76	70	284	2,900.00
	Frank Conner	71	73	69	71	284	2,900.00
	Gary Player	70	73	70	71	284	2,900.00
	Peter Jacobsen	73	74	67	70	284	2,900.00
28	Gil Morgan	72	73	70	70	285	2,300.00
	Larry Nelson	70	75	70	70	285	2,300.00
	Miller Barber	73	72	69	71	285	2,300.00
	Ed Sneed	77	67	70	71	285	2,300.00
	Mark McCumber	75	68	70	72	285	2,300.00
	Artie McNickle	69	70	72	74	285	2,300.00
	George Burns	71	74	67	73	285	2,300.00
35	Dave Stockton	70	75	72	70	287	1,600.00
	Lynn Janson	73	71	72	71	287	1,600.00
	Lee Trevino	70	73	72	72	287	1,600.00
	Bill Rogers	70	72	73	72	287	1,600.00
	Lee Elder	70	71	73	73	287	1,600.00
	Jim Masserio	69	73	71	74	287	1,600.00
	Tom Kite	72	72	69	74	287	1,600.00
42	Calvin Peete	75	71	70	72	288	1,050.00
	Sam Snead	73	71	71	73	288	1,050.00
	Jimmy Wright	72	69	72	75	288	1,050.00
	Kermit Zarley	73	69	71	75	288	1,050.00
46	Don Padgett	71	75	73	70	289	704.00
	Jim Simons	76	68	73	72	289	704.00
	Jim Colbert	73	73	72	71	289	704.00
	ChiChi Rodriguez	71	72	72	74	289	704.00
	Tommy Aaron	73	73	69	74	289	704.00
51	Rod Curl	72	72	73	73	290	600.00
	John Mahaffey	72	74	71	73	290	600.00
	Bob Mann	71	73	71	75	290	600.00
54	Fuzzy Zoeller	70	75	75	71	291	567.50
	Jim Dent	70	72	76	73	291	567.50
	Leonard Thompson	72	67	78	74	291	567.50
	Wally Armstrong	71	71	73	76	291	567.50
	DeWitt Weaver	73	73	71	74	291	567.50
	Dave Barber	74	69	71	77	291	567.50
60	Barry Jaeckel	71	73	75	73	292	547.50
	Keith Fergus	73	70	73	76	292	547.50
62	Mark Hayes	71	73	77	72	293	535.00
	Ray Floyd	74	70	77	72	293	535.00
	Rocky Thompson	72	72	73	76	293	535.00
65	Jack Nicklaus	73	72	78	71	294	515.00
	Scott Bess	73	72	75	74	294	515.00
	Al Geiberger	76	70	73	75	294	515.00
	Lon Hinkle	73	72	71	78	294	515.00
	Austin Straub	73	70	72	79	294	515.00
70	Lanny Wadkins	71	75	73	76	295	500.00
71	Bobby Wadkins	77	68	75	76	296	500.00
72	Dean Refram	75	69	79	75	298	500.00
73	Ronald Smoak	72	74	78	79	303	500.00
	Dennis Coscine	76	70	74	83	303	500.00

THE WORLD'S CIRCUITS
THE UNITED STATES

THE US TOURNAMENT CIRCUIT 1979
REPORT AND RESULTS

Tom Watson swept the US Tour's three top honours for the third successive year.

THE US TOURNAMENT CIRCUIT 1979

Tom Place
(Public Information Director of the US PGA Tour)

DEVASTATING WATSON HAD NO PEER

'There is a big difference in hoping to be a good player and really wanting to be a good player. You must have that burning desire. When I first started to watch Tom Watson a long time ago, even before he knew I existed other than by name, I knew he really wanted to be a good player. He had that burning desire.' (Byron Nelson)

Possibly more than anything else that has ever been said about Tom Watson, the words of Byron Nelson tell the story of why this young man is establishing marks unmatched in the United States PGA Tour history. Only time will tell if he goes on to approach the victory totals established by the likes of Sam Snead, Jack Nicklaus, and Ben Hogan. At his current pace, though, one has to believe that Watson will indeed find his name etched on the marble tablets for all time.

No-one had ever swept the game's three top honours – Player-of-the-Year, Vardon Trophy for low stroke average, and Leading Money-winner for two straight years. Tom accomplished that feat, in 1977 and 1978 and then in 1979 he made it three in a row. His game has been devastating, to say the least, but even more important is the man himself. He still is the same, friendly, freckle-faced redhead he was when his bright smile first appeared on the scene in 1972. He simply is a wonderful human being.

Tom established the Tour's record money mark in 1978 with $362,429. Last year, he increased that record by more than $100,000, with a total of $462,636. The surprising Larry Nelson finished second, $181,614 behind with $281,022. While accumulating a Tour high of five victories, four seconds and a third, Watson played 82 rounds with a stroke average of 70.27. Only one player has had a lower average in the last decade – and that was Tom himself with 70.16 in 1978.

There will be some who will look at Watson's record for 1979 and admit to it being impressive, but also assert that it was tarnished by the fact that he did not win one of the so-called majors. In only one did he come close to doing so – the Masters when he lost in a play-off to Fuzzy Zoeller. Under no circumstances, though, should that be considered as a detriment to his magnificent year. He merely was the best, and there were absolutely no challengers to his role.

There were surprises in 1979, such as the improved play of Nelson and veteran Lou Graham, but nothing could match the demise of Jack

Lanny Wadkins was the early winner of two events – at Los Angeles and at Sawgrass.
(Golf Photography International)

Nicklaus. Even though he only made 12 starts on the United States Tour, he fell all the way to 71st place on the Money List with $59,434. During the previous 17 years, he never was lower than fourth, and he was in that position only twice. Jack saved his best performances for the big ones, such as his tie for second in the Open at Royal Lytham; a solo fourth in the Masters, finishing just one stroke out of the Zoeller-Watson-Ed Sneed playoff; and a tie for ninth in the United States Open. In his last tournament of the year, he could do no better than tie for 65th in the PGA Championship.

During the year, Jack became tired of explaining what was wrong. He tried to cut back on his schedule, from between 16 and 20 tournaments to between 12 and 14 and still excel. He found it to be a most difficult task. People have been trying to compare Watson with Nicklaus, and this is unfair. It is unfair to compare any two greats in any sport, but, for the moment, Watson still has a few years to go before the comparisons truly can be made. In fact, there may never be another Nicklaus.

There is none the less one strong similarity. Tom seems to have the patience of Jack, not only on the golf course but off it as well.

There were a few other surprises in 1979, such as Tom Weiskopf and Jerry Pate going through the year without victories; and the awesome Andy Bean winning only once. Andy demonstrated in his victory at the Atlanta Classic just how good he can be, winning by eight strokes with a 23-under-par score of 265.

Lon Hinkle emerged as one of the brightest stars in the game; and there were some unusual happenings, such as Bill Rogers winning $230,500 *without* a victory in the United States, and Ben Crenshaw finishing second five times in six tournaments (including the Open at Lytham and the US PGA Championship).

Many people believe the outstanding accomplishment of the year happened on the final day at the Quad Cities Open in Moline, Illinois. Sam Snead at the age of 67, shot a 66. No one has ever done that on the PGA Tour. Two days earlier, he had a 67.

There was more than $13 million to be spread around the Tour's members in 1979 – an increase of nearly $3 million from 1978. As a result, there were 35 players who won at least $100,000 compared with 24 in 1978. Not too long ago, the century mark in dollars was a badge of distinction. It still is a nice figure to reach, but $200,000 is the new magic number. There were seven players who reached it in 1979 – Watson, Nelson, Lon Hinkle, Lee Trevino, Crenshaw, Rogers and Bean.

Possibly the major surprise of the year was provided by Nelson, the 32-year-old Georgian who leaped from the unheralded ranks to one of the fine players of the world. He won twice – the first victories of his career – in the Jackie Gleason-Inverrary Classic, and then defeated Crenshaw in a sudden-death play-off to win the Western Open. The previous week he had lost in a play-off to Gil Morgan in the Danny Thomas-Memphis Classic. He also tied for second in the World Series of Golf and was third twice. It surprised a few people when he distinguished himself in the Ryder Cup matches at the Greenbrier, going undefeated in five matches. He paired with Lanny Wadkins in the four team events, and then destroyed Severiano Ballesteros in the singles.

Lou Graham's performance in 1979 is still a mystery. Even Lou couldn't figure out what happened, except that he changed putters and made a few more putts than usual. Lou started on Tour in 1964 and by the end of 1978 had had a grand total of three victories. One of those was in the 1975 United States Open, edging John Mahaffey in a play-off. He played consistently well through those years, being named for three Ryder Cup teams, but going the distance was not his strong suit.

Early in 1979, he was playing badly, in fact very badly. He even hinted that maybe his time had come, and he should leave the Tour to the younger folks. A tie for 84th at the Western Open and a tie for 62nd at Milwaukee certainly didn't do anything to assure him things would get better. He took a week off while a number of his colleagues headed for Royal Lytham, and came back at Philadelphia in late July.

Somehow he felt better about his game, and on the final afternoon he burned the Whitemarsh Valley Country Club course with a brilliant 64 to tie with Bobby Wadkins. Then Lou won in a sudden death play-off. Through the next seven tournaments, he won two more – at the American Optical Classic and the San Antonio-Texas Open – had a tie for fifth in the Greater Hartford Open, and finished among the top 20 in the four. Why did he win only three times in 15 years and then suddenly win three times in 11 weeks? Lou would love to know the answer. All the veterans of the Tour would like to know where he found his Fountain of Youth.

There were six other players who won two events. Lanny Wadkins became the year's first double winner when he won the Glen Campbell-Los Angeles Open on the famed Riviera course, and then conquered the high winds at Sawgrass to win the Tournament Players' Championship. His final score in the TPC was five-under-par 283, and his closest challenger was Watson at even-par 288. The winds the final afternoon gusted to 45 miles per hour. He gave an incredible performance.

The weather was even worse the final day of the Andy Williams–San Diego Open when Fuzzy Zoeller came through for the first time.

The wind howled off the Pacific, and play even had to be delayed for 14 minutes due to a hailstorm. It was fierce, but Fuzzy won by five, and Watson was among those finishing in a tie for second.

Then came the Masters, and Zoeller won when least expected. Ed Sneed led by three with three to go, and bogeyed all three, letting Zoeller and Watson into the play-off. Fuzzy settled it on the second extra hole with a birdie.

Big Lon Hinkle had a very proud moment when he won the Bing Crosby National Pro-Amateur in a play-off over Mark Hayes and Andy Bean. Lon led by five entering the last day, and he faltered to a closing round of 77, so many wondered if he could hold together in the play-off. Bean slipped aside on the first extra hole, and Lon won it all with a birdie on the third. His year, financially, was made in late September when he won the rich World Series of Golf by a stroke over Nelson,

*Hubert Green scored a second successive victory in the Hawaiian Open, while another
in New Orleans took his career tournaments wins to 16.
(Golf Photography International)*

Rogers and Trevino. It was worth $100,000.

Hubert Green continued as one of the finest players in the game,
winning the Hawaiian Open in a driving rainstorm the last day, and his
victim at the finish was Zoeller. He also won the New Orleans Open,
giving him 16 triumphs for his career, and 15 in the last seven years.

Jerry McGee was having problems with his sponsor, and on two
occasions when he was scheduled to appear in court, he won the tournament the week before. It was the Kemper Open in June, as he edged
Jerry Pate by one; and the Sammy Davis Jr-Greater Hartford Open in
August, nosing out Jack Renner by one.

Hale Irwin remains one of the true stars of the game after his victory at Inverness in the United States Open. His victims were Pate and Player.

It was just a week after Hartford that Renner made up for his disappointment. He won the Westchester Classic and $72,000 in gaining his first Tour triumph – a nice way to do it, too!

John Fought, the former United States Amateur champion, was the only other multiple winner. He was a discouraged young man late in the summer, but he pulled everything together to win the Buick Open in a play-off over Jim Simons. That was while some of the super-stars were competing in the Ryder Cup. The next week John won again, with a birdie at the final hole to capture the Anheuser-Busch Classic by one. It was another disappointment for Bobby Wadkins. He tied for second and went another year without a US victory.

In a way, Ben Crenshaw was a double winner. He won the Phoenix Open, and that event was cut to 54 holes due to incessant rains and in the last event of the year, he teamed with George Burns to win the Walt Disney World National Team-Play Championship.

Ben also had a six-tournament stretch in which he finished second five times, twice losing play-offs. He lost one to Nelson at the Western, and also lost to David Graham in the tense PGA Championship. It was Graham's tournament to win, though, since he held the lead only to double-bogey the final hole. It went to the third hole before David finally clinched it with a birdie.

John Mahaffey has had his share of problems the last few years, and 1979 was included. He started with a victory in the Bob Hope Desert Classic. Three weeks later he injured his wrist coming out of a bunker, and it took him most of the year to recover.

There were other 'veterans' who managed to win, such as Bruce Lietzke in the Joe Garagiola-Tucson Open in which he led from start to finish and Watson was among those tying for second.

Raymond Floyd came from well back the last day to edge Gary Player and Burns in the Greater Greensboro Open. While the winners of the previous 12 months were in LaCosta watching Watson win another, Chi Chi Rodriguez came through in the Tallahassee Open. It was his first since the 1973 Greensboro.

Al Geiberger had physical problems, but he cured them on the difficult Colonial Country Club course in Fort Worth, winning the Colonial National Invitation over Gene Littler and Don January. Trevino enjoyed his biggest money year with $238,732 and his lone victory was in the Canadian Open. It was the third time he has won north of the border.

Among the other first-time winners, two had to go into overtime to enjoy the taste of victory. Bob Byman edged John Schroeder in Arnold Palmer's Bay Hill Classic; and Ed Fiori went to the second extra hole to nip Tom Weiskopf in the Southern Open.

The other first timers were Mark McCumber in the Doral-Eastern Open; Wayne Levi in the Houston Open; Calvin Peete in the Greater

Milwaukee Open; D.A. Weibring in the Quad Cities Open; Howard Twitty in the B. C. Open; and Curtis Strange in the final individual event of the year, the Pensacola Open.

Watson, though, was the true champion of the year. His 15 top-10 finishes in 21 starts proved that, and his five victories easily headed that category. He won convincingly, too: by five in the Heritage Classic, six in the Tournament of Champions, and three in The Memorial. Tom had to defeat Bill Rogers in the Byron Nelson Classic play-off; and Johnny Miller in the Colgate-Hall of Fame play-off.

In 15 years on the US Tour Lou Graham had won only three tournaments. In 1979 he won three more in the space of 11 weeks.

THE US FINAL MONEY WINNERS LIST FOR 1979

		$			$
1	Tom Watson	462,636	51	Mike Brannan	76,342
2	Larry Nelson	281,022	52	Joe Inman	75,035
3	Lon Hinkle	247,693	53	Gary Player	74,482
4	Lee Trevino	238,732	54	Andy North	73,873
5	Ben Crenshaw	236,770	55	Craig Stadler	73,392
6	Bill Rogers	230,500	56	Buddy Gardner	71,468
7	Andy Bean	208,253	57	D.A. Weibring	71,343
8	Bruce Lietzke	198,439	58	Al Geiberger	70,625
9	Fuzzy Zoeller	196,951	59	Gene Littler	70,522
10	Lanny Wadkins	195,710	60	Mark McCumber	67,886
11	Jerry Pate	193,707	61	Miller Barber	67,838
12	Lou Graham	190,827	62	Bob Murphy	66,916
13	Hubert Green	183,111	63	Kermit Zarley	66,414
14	Jack Renner	182,808	64	Lee Elder	65,247
15	Howard Twitty	179,619	65	Ed Fiori	64,428
16	David Graham	177,684	66	Mike Reid	64,046
17	Tom Kite	166,878	67	Brad Bryant	63,013
18	Jerry McGee	166,735	68	Tommy Aaron	62,814
19	Hale Irwin	154,168	69	Morris Hatalsky	61,962
20	Wayne Levi	141,612	70	Charles Coody	59,453
21	Curtis Strange	138,368	71	Jack Nicklaus	59,434
22	Bob Gilder	134,428	72	Chi Chi Rodriguez	58,225
23	Mark Hayes	130,878	73	Lindy Miller	57,704
24	J.C. Snead	129,585	74	Scott Simpson	53,084
25	Ed Sneed	123,606	75	Mark Lye	51,184
26	Ray Floyd	122,872	76	Bruce Devlin	50,997
27	Calvin Peete	122,481	77	Wally Armstrong	50,686
28	Bobby Wadkins	121,373	78	Peter Jacobsen	49,439
29	Gil Morgan	115,857	79	Johnny Miller	49,266
30	Tom Purtzer	113,270	80	Jim Thorpe	48,987
31	Grier Jones	111,501	81	Orville Moody	48,483
32	John Fought	108,427	82	Bobby Walzel	47,708
33	George Burns	107,830	83	Mike Morley	47,435
34	Jay Haas	102,515	84	Gary Koch	46,809
35	Bill Kratzert	101,628	85	Artie McNickle	46,746
36	Rex Caldwell	98,168	86	Barry Jaeckel	46,541
37	Keith Fergus	97,045	87	Frank Conner	46,020
38	Rod Curl	95,460	88	Dave Edwards	44,456
39	Bob Byman	94,243	89	Mike McCullough	43,664
40	Jim Colbert	91,139	90	Dave Eichelberger	43,187
41	Leonard Thompson	90,465	91	Eddie Pearce	43,120
42	Alan Tapie	88,113	92	Graham Marsh	41,620
43	Doug Tewell	84,500	93	Peter Oosterhuis	41,104
44	Victor Regalado	82,964	94	Terry Diehl	40,771
45	John Mahaffey	81,993	95	Jim Nelford	40,174
46	Don January	79,720	96	Jack Newton	38,904
47	John Schroeder	78,510	97	Mike Sullivan	38,596
48	Tom Weiskopf	76,999	98	Larry Ziegler	38,546
49	Gibby Gilbert	76,807	99	Ron Streck	38,484
50	Jim Simons	76,350	100	Dan Pohl	38,393

LEADING CAREER MONEY-WINNINGS ON THE US TOUR

		$				$
1	Jack Nicklaus	3,408,827	16	Lou Graham	1,149,972
2	Lee Trevino	2,088,178	17	Dave Stockton	1,068,402
3	Arnold Palmer	1,798,431	18	Dave Hill	1,065,458
4	Tom Weiskopf	1,741,155	19	Don January	1,024,951
5	Billy Casper	1,683,618	20	J.C. Snead	1,017,917
6	Tom Watson	1,671,433	21	Frank Beard	1,008,426
7	Gary Player	1,581,124	22	Julius Boros	1,004,861
8	Hale Irwin	1,580,064	23	George Archer	983,590
9	Gene Littler	1,509,870	24	Charles Coody	957,464
10	Miller Barber	1,418,892	25	Bob Murphy	949,407
11	Bruce Crampton	1,374,294	26	Bobby Nichols	944,651
12	Hubert Green	1,326,213	27	Ben Crenshaw	933,402
13	Ray Floyd	1,239,635	28	Lanny Wadkins	932,864
14	Johnny Miller	1,210,771	29	Tommy Aaron	871,151
15	Al Geiberger	1,169,074	30	ChiChi Rodriguez	834,649

Among the 1979 US Tour winners.

Ray Floyd.

John Mahaffey.

Jerry McGee.

Lee Trevino.

THE BOB HOPE DESERT CLASSIC

Bermuda Dunes Country Club, Indian Wells Country Club, La Quinta Country Club, Tamarisk Country Club 10–14 January 1979 Prize Money $275,500

								$
1	John Mahaffey	66	66	71	71	69	343	50,000.00
2	Lee Trevino	71	68	70	69	66	344	29,700.00
3	Mark Hayes	70	72	68	69	66	345	18,700.00
4	Grier Jones	70	68	71	69	68	346	13,200.00
5	Lanny Wadkins	71	66	74	69	68	348	10,450.00
	Keith Fergus	69	67	68	75	69	348	10,450.00
7	Bobby Wadkins	69	70	72	71	67	349	8,275.00
	Tom Purtzer	69	68	70	74	68	349	8,275.00
	Leonard Thompson	69	66	69	75	70	349	8,275.00
	Alan Tapie	71	71	68	68	71	349	8,275.00
11	Jerry Pate	71	72	70	69	68	350	6,325.00
	Jack Nicklaus	71	69	69	72	69	350	6,325.00
	Lon Hinkle	72	67	73	69	69	350	6,325.00
14	Don Bies	73	68	69	72	69	351	4,675.00
	Mark McCumber	70	73	70	70	68	351	4,675.00
	Butch Baird	72	72	71	67	69	351	4,675.00
	Andy Bean	72	68	74	68	69	351	4,675.00
	Orville Moody	71	70	68	73	69	351	4,675.00
19	Kermit Zarley	71	68	72	73	68	352	3,451.25
	Jim Colbert	72	72	70	69	69	352	3,451.25
	Wayne Levi	74	68	69	71	70	352	3,451.25
	Wally Armstrong	69	72	69	68	74	352	3,451.25
23	J.C. Snead	68	69	74	75	67	353	2,640.00
	Dave Hill	71	76	67	70	69	353	2,640.00
	Joe Inman	72	73	70	69	69	353	2,640.00

THE PHOENIX OPEN

Phoenix Country Club, Phoenix, Arizona 18–22 January 1979 Prize Money $187,500

						$
1	Ben Crenshaw	67	61	71	199	33,750.00
2	Jay Haas	65	67	68	200	20,250.00
3	Tom Kite	73	66	63	202	12,750.00
4	Pat McGowan	71	66	66	203	7,382.82
	Lon Hinkle	66	69	68	203	7,382.81
	Jerry Pate	66	66	71	203	7,382.81
	Andy Bean	66	66	71	203	7,382.81
8	Wayne Levi	71	68	66	205	5,250.00
	Joe Inman	69	68	68	205	5,250.00
	Phil Hancock	68	68	69	205	5,250.00
	Rod Funseth	70	66	69	205	5,250.00
12	Mike Reid	71	68	67	206	3,250.00
	Bob Gilder	69	70	67	206	3,250.00
	Mark Hayes	73	66	67	206	3,250.00
	Dave Stockton	71	66	69	206	3,250.00
	Bob Zender	71	66	69	206	3,250.00
	Dave Eichelberger	69	67	70	206	3,250.00
	George Burns	69	66	71	206	3,250.00
	Jim Nelford	70	65	71	206	3,250.00
	Bruce Lietzke	66	69	71	206	3,250.00
21	Mark McCumber	68	70	69	207	1,875.00
	Grier Jones	68	71	68	207	1,875.00
	Tom Purtzer	70	68	69	207	1,875.00
	Charles Coody	69	68	69	207	1,875.00
	Jim Colbert	66	70	71	207	1,875.00
	Keith Fergus	67	70	70	207	1,875.00

Tournament cut to 54 holes due to heavy rain

THE ANDY WILLIAMS–SAN DIEGO OPEN

Torrey Pines Golf Club, La Jolla, California   25–28 January 1979   Prize Money $250,000

Pos	Player					Total	$
1	Fuzzy Zoeller	76	67	72	67	282	45,000.00
2	Wayne Levi	79	68	72	68	287	16,500.00
	Tom Watson	74	70	71	72	287	16,500.00
	Artie McNickle	73	71	71	72	287	16,500.00
	Bill Kratzert	73	68	72	74	287	16,500.00
6	Victor Regalado	71	73	70	74	288	8,093.75
	Lee Trevino	75	69	72	72	288	8,093.75
	Jerry Pate	72	70	72	74	288	8,093.75
	Jerry McGee	71	67	74	76	288	8,093.75
10	Keith Fergus	74	73	72	70	289	6,000.00
	Howard Twitty	74	70	73	72	289	6,000.00
	Scott Simpson	73	73	71	72	289	6,000.00
	Larry Nelson	77	68	70	74	289	6,000.00
14	John Fought	78	70	69	73	290	4,000.00
	Randy Erskine	73	74	70	73	290	4,000.00
	Tom Weiskopf	74	70	73	73	290	4,000.00
	J.C. Snead	79	67	70	74	290	4,000.00
	Mark Hayes	77	69	70	74	290	4,000.00
	Tommy Aaron	69	70	75	76	290	4,000.00
	Tom Purtzer	78	66	70	76	290	4,000.00
21	Bob Gilder	74	71	70	76	291	2,700.00
	Jim Colbert	75	67	73	76	291	2,700.00
	Leonard Thompson	73	70	71	77	291	2,700.00
	Grier Jones	71	71	72	77	291	2,700.00

THE BING CROSBY NATIONAL PRO-AM

Pebble Beach Golf Links, Cypress Point Golf Club, Spyglass Hill Golf Club   1–4 February 1979   Prize Money $300,000

Pos	Player					Total	$
1	Lon Hinkle	70	68	69	77	284	54,000.00
2	Mark Hayes	73	73	66	72	284	26,400.00
	Andy Bean	72	73	70	69	284	26,400.00
	Hinkle won play-off at third extra hole						
4	Leonard Thompson	71	69	76	70	286	13,200.00
	Brad Bryant	71	70	73	72	286	13,200.00
6	Jim Nelford	72	74	70	71	287	10,425.00
	Jay Haas	68	77	74	68	287	10,425.00
8	Curtis Strange	70	70	74	74	288	8,700.00
	J.C. Snead	74	72	69	73	288	8,700.00
	Gibby Gilbert	72	73	70	73	288	8,700.00
11	Mark Pfeil	71	75	71	72	289	6,900.00
	Bobby Wadkins	75	70	73	71	289	6,900.00
	Lee Elder	73	70	75	71	289	6,900.00
14	Gil Morgan	69	73	72	76	290	5,550.00
	John Schroeder	70	71	75	74	290	5,550.00
16	Fuzzy Zoeller	72	72	73	74	291	4,350.00
	Grier Jones	75	70	69	77	291	4,350.00
	Jerry Heard	71	72	72	76	291	4,350.00
	Orville Moody	71	72	75	73	291	4,350.00
	Tommy Aaron	74	72	73	72	291	4,350.00
	Bruce Lietzke	73	75	72	71	291	4,350.00
22	Tom Watson	72	76	73	71	292	2,785.00
	Kermit Zarley	75	73	71	73	292	2,785.00
	Gene Littler	73	71	74	74	292	2,785.00
	Vance Heafner	72	77	73	70	292	2,785.00
	Mike Morley	71	76	73	72	292	2,785.00
	Tom Valentine	71	71	78	72	292	2,785.00

THE HAWAIIAN OPEN

Waialae Country Club, Honolulu   8–11 February 1979   Prize Money $300,000

Pos	Player					Total	$
1	Hubert Green	68	67	63	69	267	54,000.00
2	Fuzzy Zoeller	66	68	71	65	270	32,400.00
3	Larry Nelson	66	69	70	67	272	20,400.00
4	Charles Coody	66	72	66	69	273	12,400.00
	Miller Barber	71	68	65	69	273	12,400.00
	Lindy Miller	65	70	68	70	273	12,400.00
7	Don January	68	70	66	70	274	9,675.00
	Dan Halldorson	68	66	69	71	274	9,675.00
9	Hale Irwin	67	70	67	71	275	8,400.00
	George Burns	71	63	68	73	275	8,400.00
11	John Schroeder	68	73	70	65	276	7,200.00
	Tom Storey	68	70	66	72	276	7,200.00
13	Leonard Thompson	67	70	73	67	277	5,460.00
	Wayne Levi	66	73	71	67	277	5,460.00
	Jeff Mitchell	71	68	72	66	277	5,460.00
	Wally Armstrong	66	71	69	71	277	5,460.00
	Frank Conner	68	68	69	72	277	5,460.00
18	Bill Calfee	71	71	68	68	278	4,200.00
	Bill Rogers	70	72	68	68	278	4,200.00
	Andy Bean	66	71	72	69	278	4,200.00
21	Joe Hager	69	70	71	69	279	3,000.00
	Isao Aoki	72	68	70	69	279	3,000.00
	Bruce Lietzke	67	74	68	70	279	3,000.00
	Tom Chain	67	72	69	71	279	3,000.00
	Ed Sneed	71	71	69	68	279	3,000.00
	Lanny Wadkins	65	72	70	72	279	3,000.00

THE JOE GARAGIOLA–TUCSON OPEN

Randolph North Golf Club, Tucson, Arizona   15–18 February 1979   Prize Money $250,000

Pos	Player					Total	$
1	Bruce Lietzke	63	66	68	68	265	45,000.00
2	Tom Watson	67	66	66	68	267	18,666.67
	Jim Thorpe	67	65	67	68	267	18,666.67
	Buddy Gardner	69	66	67	65	267	18,666.66
5	Marty Fleckman	66	67	66	69	268	8,781.25
	Victor Regalado	66	68	67	67	268	8,781.25
	Curtis Strange	64	71	67	66	268	8,781.25
	Howard Twitty	69	68	66	65	268	8,781.25
9	Lee Trevino	67	68	66	68	269	7,000.00
	Dave Barr	69	67	66	67	269	7,000.00
11	Tommy Aaron	64	72	67	67	270	5,750.00
	Mark Hayes	69	65	66	70	270	5,750.00
	ChiChi Rodriguez	70	67	67	66	270	5,750.00
14	J.C. Snead	70	68	68	65	271	4,625.00
	Tom Purtzer	70	68	65	68	271	4,625.00
16	Mike Morley	70	69	66	67	272	3,750.00
	Jim Nelford	64	70	70	68	272	3,750.00
	Rod Funseth	71	67	66	68	272	3,750.00
	Jim Colbert	67	71	66	68	272	3,750.00
	Jeff Mitchell	69	70	66	67	272	3,750.00
21	Frank Beard	65	70	71	67	273	2,600.00
	Wayne Levi	67	68	69	69	273	2,600.00
	Bill Sander	70	64	69	70	273	2,600.00
	Tom Kite	68	69	68	68	273	2,600.00
	Bob Byman	72	67	67	67	273	2,600.00

THE GLEN CAMPBELL-LOS ANGELES OPEN
Riviera Country Club, Pacific Palisades, California   22–25 February 1979   Prize Money $250,000

								$
1	Lanny Wadkins	66	72	69	69	276		45,000.00
2	Lon Hinkle	67	69	71	70	277		27,000.00
3	Andy Bean	71	69	68	70	278		14,500.00
	Kermit Zarley	68	71	68	71	278		14,500.00
5	Ed Sneed	69	72	69	69	279		9,500.00
	Fuzzy Zoeller	70	67	72	70	279		9,500.00
7	Rod Curl	73	73	68	66	280		7,791.67
	Tommy Aaron	73	70	68	69	280		7,791.67
	Jim Colbert	73	67	71	69	280		7,791.66
10	Artie McNickle	71	69	72	69	281		6,750.00
11	Mike Reid	69	72	72	69	282		5,500.00
	Gary McCord	74	71	68	69	282		5,500.00
	Hale Irwin	68	73	70	71	282		5,500.00
	Tom Purtzer	73	69	70	70	282		5,500.00
15	Masashi Ozaki	76	68	73	66	283		4,500.00
16	Mark Lye	71	73	72	68	284		4,125.00
	Mike McCullough	73	72	68	71	284		4,125.00
18	Grier Jones	72	72	73	68	285		3,260.00
	Frank Conner	76	70	71	68	285		3,260.00
	Rik Massengale	74	77	66	70	285		3,260.00
	Charles Coody	69	77	66	73	285		3,260.00
	Dale Douglass	72	72	69	72	285		3,260.00
23	Bill Calfee	72	75	69	70	286		2,300.00
	Antonio Cerda	74	75	69	71	286		2,300.00
	Allen Miller	70	75	70	71	286		2,300.00
	Dave Eichelberger	71	73	68	74	286		2,300.00

THE BAY HILL CITRUS CLASSIC
Bay Hill Golf Club, Orlando, Florida   1–4 March 1979   Prize Money $250,000

								$
1	Bob Byman	67	70	70	71	278		45,000.00
2	John Schroeder	68	68	72	70	278		27,000.00
	Byman won play-off at second extra hole							
3	Bill Rogers	67	69	74	69	279		13,000.00
	Hale Irwin	69	70	72	68	279		13,000.00
	Andy Bean	64	69	76	70	279		13,000.00
6	Jerry Pate	68	68	77	70	283		7,562.50
	Alan Tapie	70	71	72	70	283		7,562.50
	Jay Haas	69	70	74	70	283		7,562.50
	Grier Jones	69	69	73	72	283		7,562.50
	Tom Watson	72	68	71	72	283		7,562.50
	David Edwards	68	70	71	74	283		7,562.50
12	Larry Ziegler	73	72	70	69	284		5,250.00
	Rik Massengale	71	67	72	74	284		5,250.00
	Rex Caldwell	70	70	68	76	284		5,250.00
15	Joe Hager	70	66	81	68	285		3,750.00
	Charles Coody	71	71	72	71	285		3,750.00
	Jim Colbert	65	73	75	72	285		3,750.00
	Andy North	71	70	72	72	285		3,750.00
	Joe Inman	73	67	73	72	285		3,750.00
	Tom Purtzer	73	70	69	73	285		3,750.00
	Fuzzy Zoeller	71	70	69	75	285		3,750.00
22	Wally Armstrong	72	71	73	71	286		2,700.00
	George Burns	70	73	71	72	286		2,700.00
24	John Fought	72	67	78	70	287		2,025.00
	Craig Stadler	71	71	74	71	287		2,025.00
	Don January	70	71	72	74	287		2,025.00
	Larry Nelson	72	66	75	74	287		2,025.00
	Ben Crenshaw	74	71	67	75	287		2,025.00
	Ed Sneed	66	69	73	79	287		2,025.00

THE JACKIE GLEASON-INVERRARY CLASSIC

Inverrary Golf Club, Lauderhill, Florida 8–11 March 1979 Prize Money $300,000

								$
1	Larry Nelson	67	69	67	71	274		54,000.00
2	Grier Jones	71	67	69	70	277		32,400.00
3	Hale Irwin	73	62	72	73	280		20,400.00
4	Lee Elder	72	71	68	70	281		13,200.00
	Tommy Aaron	66	69	74	72	281		13,200.00
6	Ray Floyd	69	72	67	74	282		10,800.00
7	Andy North	69	71	71	72	283		10,050.00
8	Pat McGowan	72	74	67	71	284		8,700.00
	Bob Gilder	67	69	68	71	284		8,700.00
	Charles Coody	68	69	74	73	284		8,700.00
11	Kermit Zarley	75	71	70	69	285		5,775.00
	Ben Crenshaw	72	72	69	72	285		5,775.00
	Lou Graham	72	70	71	72	285		5,775.00
	Jim King	72	73	68	72	285		5,775.00
	Howard Twitty	75	70	67	73	285		5,775.00
	Wayne Levi	66	73	72	74	285		5,775.00
	Mike McCullough	70	74	67	74	285		5,775.00
	Rod Curl	71	71	69	74	285		5,775.00
19	Wally Armstrong	73	70	72	71	286		3,765.00
	Frank Conner	72	73	70	71	286		3,765.00
	J.C.Snead	72	74	68	72	286		3,765.00
	Bill Rogers	72	67	73	74	286		3,765.00
23	Mike Hill	71	72	71	73	287		2,670.00
	Curtis Strange	71	69	71	76	287		2,670.00
	Don January	70	75	67	75	287		2,670.00
	Mark Lye	72	71	69	75	287		2,670.00
	DeWitt Weaver	71	71	69	76	287		2,670.00

THE DORAL-EASTERN OPEN

Doral Country Club, Blue Monster Course, Florida 15–18 March 1979 Prize Money $250,000

								$
1	Mark McCumber	67	71	69	72	279		45,000.00
2	Bill Rogers	70	68	70	72	280		27,000.00
3	Rod Curl	67	76	70	68	281		17,000.00
4	Mike McCullough	70	71	74	67	282		9,843.75
	Gibby Gilbert	67	77	70	68	282		9,843.75
	Kermit Zarley	73	72	66	71	282		9,843.75
	Alan Tapie	66	71	69	76	282		9,843.75
8	Bill Kratzert	67	69	75	72	283		7,750.00
9	Tom Kite	73	72	70	69	284		6,750.00
	Bobby Wadkins	73	70	71	70	284		6,750.00
	David Graham	69	72	73	70	284		6,750.00
12	Michael Brannan	74	71	72	68	285		5,500.00
	Andy Bean	69	71	73	72	285		5,500.00
14	Tommy Aaron	70	73	74	69	286		4,375.00
	J.C.Snead	73	73	72	68	286		4,375.00
	Wayne Levi	68	76	71	71	286		4,375.00
	Jim Dent	68	71	73	74	286		4,375.00
18	Jim Colbert	69	74	76	68	287		3,375.00
	Dick Mast	70	74	72	71	287		3,375.00
	Eddie Pearce	72	72	72	71	287		3,375.00
	Lou Graham	71	72	72	72	287		3,375.00
22	Lindy Miller	71	73	75	69	288		2,600.00
	Gil Morgan	75	69	73	71	288		2,600.00
	Wally Kuchar	70	73	73	72	288		2,600.00

THE TOURNAMENT PLAYERS' CHAMPIONSHIP
Sawgrass, Jacksonville, Florida   22–25 March 1979   Prize Money $437,292

							$
1	Lanny Wadkins	67	68	76	72	283	72,000.00
2	Tom Watson	70	72	75	71	288	43,200.00
3	Jack Renner	73	70	71	75	289	27,200.00
4	Phil Hancock	69	73	75	74	291	19,200.00
5	Wayne Levi	69	72	77	75	293	14,600.00
	Bill Kratzert	69	70	75	79	293	14,600.00
	Lee Trevino	70	69	75	79	293	14,600.00
8	Andy Bean	72	73	74	75	294	12,400.00
9	Tom Kite	72	73	75	75	295	10,800.00
	Jack Newton	69	74	77	75	295	10,800.00
	Jay Haas	71	74	74	76	295	10,800.00
12	Mike McCullough	71	73	79	73	296	8,800.00
	Gil Morgan	68	77	76	75	296	8,800.00
14	Ray Floyd	71	72	80	74	297	6,600.00
	Peter Jacobsen	74	72	76	75	297	6,600.00
	Graham Marsh	72	75	75	75	297	6,600.00
	Ed Fiori	69	71	79	78	297	6,600.00
	Victor Regalado	70	74	73	80	297	6,600.00
	George Burns	72	66	76	83	297	6,600.00
20	Rex Caldwell	70	76	78	74	298	4,035.00
	Hubert Green	73	72	78	75	298	4,035.00
	Tim Simpson	69	73	80	76	298	4,035.00
	Larry Nelson	72	75	74	77	298	4,035.00
	Jerry Pate	69	73	77	79	298	4,035.00
	Andy North	67	74	76	81	298	4,035.00
	Howard Twitty	75	67	76	80	298	4,035.00
	Gary Koch	70	72	74	82	298	4,035.00

THE SEA PINES HERITAGE CLASSIC
Harbour Town Golf Links, Hilton Head Island, South Carolina   29 March–1 April 1979   Prize Money $300,000

							$
1	Tom Watson	65	65	69	71	270	54,000.00
2	Ed Sneed	69	69	71	66	275	32,400.00
3	Mike Morley	69	68	72	70	279	17,400.00
	Tom Kite	69	68	71	71	279	17,400.00
5	Bill Rogers	69	68	72	71	280	11,400.00
	Ray Floyd	72	68	69	71	280	11,400.00
7	Bob Murphy	71	67	74	69	281	9,675.00
	George Burns	67	72	72	70	281	9,675.00
9	Don January	72	70	69	71	282	8,400.00
	Lanny Wadkins	66	67	74	75	282	8,400.00
11	Jerry Pate	67	72	76	69	284	6,900.00
	Joe Inman	72	70	72	70	284	6,900.00
	Hubert Green	71	71	67	75	284	6,900.00
14	Rod Curl	73	70	73	69	285	5,400.00
	Bob Gilder	71	70	75	69	285	5,400.00
	Craig Stadler	70	70	74	71	285	5,400.00
17	Larry Nelson	75	69	73	69	286	3,795.00
	Bobby Walzel	72	67	75	72	286	3,795.00
	Gene Littler	69	73	72	72	286	3,795.00
	Miller Barber	68	73	73	72	286	3,795.00
	Jack Newton	74	70	69	73	286	3,795.00
	Allen Miller	72	71	70	73	286	3,795.00
	Tom Purtzer	71	73	69	73	286	3,795.00
	Lee Trevino	73	67	71	75	286	3,795.00
25	Mike Reid	74	67	74	72	287	2,392.50
	Tim Simpson	68	73	74	72	287	2,392.50
	Victor Regalado	74	69	69	75	287	2,392.50
	Gary Koch	69	71	72	75	287	2,392.50

THE GREATER GREENSBORO OPEN

Forest Oaks Country Club, Greensboro, North Carolina 5–8 April 1979 Prize Money $250,000

Pos	Player	R1	R2	R3	R4	Total	$
1	Ray Floyd	73	71	71	67	282	45,000.00
2	George Burns	73	71	69	70	283	22,000.00
	Gary Player	70	71	71	71	283	22,000.00
4	Bobby Wadkins	70	73	67	74	284	12,000.00
5	Rex Caldwell	70	74	71	72	287	10,000.00
6	Doug Tewell	72	74	71	71	288	8,375.00
	Lee Elder	73	73	69	73	288	8,375.00
	Tom Purtzer	70	71	72	75	288	8,375.00
9	Bobby Walzel	68	75	74	72	289	6,750.00
	Curtis Strange	71	75	71	72	289	6,750.00
	Jack Renner	68	71	70	80	289	6,750.00
12	Severiano Ballesteros	72	74	74	70	290	4,750.00
	Fuzzy Zoeller	70	74	74	72	290	4,750.00
	Leonard Thompson	73	76	70	71	290	4,750.00
	Bob Eastwood	69	77	72	72	290	4,750.00
	Bob Gilder	71	74	71	74	290	4,750.00
	Jim Thorpe	68	75	71	76	290	4,750.00
18	Jay Haas	76	70	76	69	291	2,937.50
	Jim Chancey	73	71	76	71	291	2,937.50
	Bobby Nichols	71	76	72	72	291	2,937.50
	Marty Fleckman	73	70	75	73	291	2,937.50
	Miller Barber	70	73	74	74	291	2,937.50
	Craig Stadler	72	74	72	73	291	2,937.50
	Joe Inman	71	72	74	74	291	2,937.50
	Tommy Valentine	73	72	71	75	291	2,937.50

MONY TOURNAMENT OF CHAMPIONS

LaCosta Country Club, Rancho LaCosta, California 19–22 April 1979 Prize Money $300,000

Pos	Player	R1	R2	R3	R4	Total	$
1	Tom Watson	69	66	70	70	275	54,000.00
2	Jerry Pate	72	71	65	73	281	29,500.00
	Bruce Lietzke	72	66	70	73	281	29,500.00
4	Gary Player	71	69	74	68	282	18,000.00
5	Lee Trevino	72	68	72	72	284	15,000.00
	Larry Nelson	74	69	69	72	284	15,000.00
7	Tom Kite	76	69	68	72	285	12,000.00
8	Ben Crenshaw	75	71	75	67	288	10,625.00
	Lee Elder	72	73	68	75	288	10,625.00
10	Andy Bean	75	72	71	73	291	8,750.00
	Lon Hinkle	75	70	73	73	291	8,750.00
	Hubert Green	73	71	73	74	291	8,750.00
13	Lanny Wadkins	79	70	71	73	293	7,250.00
	Jim Simons	73	72	75	73	293	7,250.00
15	Jack Nicklaus	72	72	77	73	294	6,250.00
	Ray Floyd	71	74	75	74	294	6,250.00
17	Gil Morgan	71	72	76	78	297	5,600.00
18	Ron Streck	70	78	75	75	298	5,150.00
	Andy North	75	76	71	76	298	5,150.00
20	Fuzzy Zoeller	77	72	74	76	299	4,500.00
	Bob Byman	80	71	75	73	299	4,500.00
	Victor Regalado	71	76	75	77	299	4,500.00
	Mac McLendon	73	76	74	76	299	4,500.00
24	Rod Funseth	77	78	73	76	300	4,000.00
25	Jack Newton	72	78	78	73	301	3,800.00
26	Barry Jaeckel	78	73	78	74	303	3,700.00
27	Mark McCumber	78	78	75	78	309	3,600.00
28	Jerry Heard	79	76	83	75	313	3,500.00

THE TALLAHASSEE OPEN
Killearn Golf & Country Club, Tallahassee, Florida   19–22 April 1979   Prize Money $100,000

Pos	Player					Total	$
1	ChiChi Rodriguez	66	69	67	67	269	18,000.00
2	Lindy Miller	65	72	67	68	272	10,800.00
3	Bobby Wadkins	68	69	65	72	274	6,800.00
4	Rex Caldwell	69	67	68	71	275	4,950.00
5	Billy Casper	68	71	70	67	276	3,660.00
	Gary Koch	68	68	71	69	276	3,660.00
	Bobby Walzel	70	68	68	70	276	3,660.00
	Bob Eastwood	68	69	70	69	276	3,660.00
	Bob Mann	64	71	70	71	276	3,660.00
10	Bob E. Smith	71	70	68	68	277	2,600.00
	Jim Thorpe	68	69	69	71	277	2,600.00
	Wayne Levi	67	69	68	73	277	2,600.00
13	John Lister	69	67	73	69	278	1,925.00
	Tim Simpson	67	68	72	71	278	1,925.00
	Bill Rogers	71	69	67	71	278	1,925.00
	Allen Miller	70	69	67	72	278	1,925.00
17	Barney Thompson	74	67	72	66	279	1,550.00
	Jim Chancey	70	69	70	70	279	1,550.00
19	Buddy Gardner	73	68	72	67	280	1,210.00
	Mark Lye	68	72	71	69	280	1,210.00
	Don Iverson	69	71	71	69	280	1,210.00
	Doug Tewell	69	69	72	70	280	1,210.00
	Bob Murphy	67	71	70	72	280	1,210.00

THE FIRST NBC NEW ORLEANS OPEN
Lakewood Country Club, New Orleans, Louisiana   26–29 April 1979   Prize Money $250,000

Pos	Player					Total	$
1	Hubert Green	69	67	69	68	273	45,000.00
2	Bruce Lietzke	68	70	69	67	274	16,500.00
	Steve Melnyk	68	68	70	68	274	16,500.00
	Frank Conner	65	71	68	70	274	16,500.00
	Lee Trevino	68	67	69	70	274	16,500.00
6	Calvin Peete	70	67	69	69	275	8,375.00
	Curtis Strange	66	70	67	72	275	8,375.00
	Bob Gilder	71	73	62	69	275	8,375.00
9	Jim Colbert	66	71	71	68	276	7,250.00
10	Leonard Thompson	72	68	69	68	277	6,500.00
	Doug Tewell	66	72	68	71	277	6,500.00
12	Gary Koch	69	71	72	66	278	5,500.00
	Bob Shearer	69	68	69	72	278	5,500.00
14	Lon Hinkle	69	72	73	65	279	4,500.00
	Mike Morley	69	73	70	67	279	4,500.00
	Mike Sullivan	71	70	67	71	279	4,500.00
17	Roger Calvin	71	70	73	66	280	3,750.00
	Bob E. Smith	69	70	69	72	280	3,750.00
	Jim Dent	69	72	68	71	280	3,750.00
20	Tom Watson	71	73	70	67	281	2,708.34
	Homero Blancas	72	72	68	69	281	2,708.34
	Billy Casper	71	72	68	70	281	2,708.33
	Gibby Gilbert	69	69	72	71	281	2,708.33
	Joe Inman	70	71	69	71	281	2,708.33
	Allen Miller	67	75	66	73	281	2,708.33

THE HOUSTON OPEN

Woodlands Country Club, Woodlands, Texas 3–6 May 1979 Prize Money $300,000

							$
1	Wayne Levi	69	65	63	71	268	54,000.00
2	Mike Brannan	68	66	66	70	270	32,400.00
3	Orville Moody	72	64	67	69	272	14,400.00
	Hale Irwin	69	64	71	68	272	14,400.00
	Bob Gilder	70	64	70	68	272	14,400.00
	Sammy Rachels	68	65	68	71	272	14,400.00
7	Bill Rogers	67	69	69	68	273	9,675.00
	Calvin Peete	70	70	68	65	273	9,675.00
9	John Schroeder	68	66	70	70	274	8,400.00
	Dave Stockton	72	66	67	69	274	8,400.00
11	Rod Curl	69	70	66	70	275	6,360.00
	Jim Colbert	66	70	69	70	275	6,360.00
	Buddy Gardner	69	67	69	70	275	6,360.00
	Leonard Thompson	66	68	70	71	275	6,360.00
	David Edwards	68	70	68	69	275	6,360.00
16	Scott Simpson	69	67	70	70	276	4,500.00
	Mike Reid	70	70	69	67	276	4,500.00
	J.C. Snead	70	66	69	71	276	4,500.00
	Barney Thompson	67	70	73	66	276	4,500.00
	Grier Jones	71	67	68	70	276	4,500.00
21	Lon Hinkle	70	70	68	69	277	2,816.25
	Tom Purtzer	70	66	72	69	277	2,816.25
	Mike Sullivan	70	70	68	70	277	2,816.25
	Lee Trevino	69	66	69	73	277	2,816.25
	Doug Tewell	68	68	70	71	277	2,816.25
	Jerry McGee	70	67	71	69	277	2,816.25
	Mike Morley	70	68	70	69	277	2,816.25
	Tom Kite	72	67	68	70	277	2,816.25

THE BYRON NELSON GOLF CLASSIC

Preston Trail Golf Club, Dallas, Texas 10–13 May 1979 Prize Money $300,000

							$
1	Tom Watson	64	72	69	70	275	54,000.00
2	Bill Rogers	68	73	68	66	275	32,400.00
	Watson won play-off at first extra hole						
3	Larry Nelson	65	68	74	69	276	20,400.00
4	Jerry Pate	69	70	67	72	278	14,400.00
5	Jerry McGee	71	72	69	67	279	10,537.50
	Michael Brannan	69	73	69	68	279	10,537.50
	Calvin Peete	68	70	73	68	279	10,537.50
	Morris Hatalsky	67	71	72	69	279	10,537.50
9	Brad Bryant	67	73	73	67	280	8,400.00
	Gene Littler	69	72	71	68	280	8,400.00
11	Gary Koch	70	72	70	69	281	6,900.00
	Larry Ziegler	69	74	69	69	281	6,900.00
	George Burns	66	68	71	76	281	6,900.00
14	Alan Tapie	71	70	70	71	282	5,250.00
	Jay Haas	72	69	70	71	282	5,250.00
	Lee Trevino	70	72	69	71	282	5,250.00
	Ed Sneed	70	70	71	71	282	5,250.00
18	Curtis Strange	68	76	70	69	283	4,500.00
19	Grier Jones	70	73	73	68	284	3,636.00
	Johnny Miller	70	71	72	71	284	3,636.00
	Lanny Wadkins	67	67	78	72	284	3,636.00
	Scott Simpson	70	71	72	71	284	3,636.00
	Rod Curl	70	69	73	72	284	3,636.00

THE COLONIAL NATIONAL INVITATION TOURNAMENT
Colonial Country Club, Fort Worth, Texas 17–20 May 1979 Prize Money $300,000

Pos	Name					Total	$
1	Al Geiberger	68	69	64	73	274	54,000.00
2	Don January	72	70	68	65	275	26,400.00
	Gene Littler	70	70	67	68	275	26,400.00
4	Tom Watson	71	73	65	67	276	13,200.00
	Jim Colbert	70	73	64	69	276	13,200.00
6	Fuzzy Zoeller	70	68	70	70	278	10,425.00
	Leonard Thompson	65	68	73	72	278	10,425.00
8	Bruce Lietzke	66	73	74	66	279	8,100.00
	Lindy Miller	68	74	70	67	279	8,100.00
	Ed Sneed	69	74	69	67	279	8,100.00
	Jack Renner	70	74	66	69	279	8,100.00
	Wayne Levi	68	71	71	69	279	8,100.00
13	D. A. Weibring	70	69	69	72	280	6,000.00
	Gil Morgan	69	67	71	73	280	6,000.00
15	Bob Shearer	73	71	69	68	281	4,800.00
	Ben Crenshaw	70	70	70	71	281	4,800.00
	Keith Fergus	71	69	70	71	281	4,800.00
	Howard Twitty	72	68	69	72	281	4,800.00
	Barry Jaeckel	70	67	68	76	281	4,800.00
20	Lee Elder	73	72	70	67	282	3,250.00
	Buddy Gardner	71	72	71	68	282	3,250.00
	Alan Tapie	74	70	69	69	282	3,250.00
	Bob Clampett *	71	72	69	70	282	–
	Bruce Devlin	70	69	71	72	282	3,250.00
	Hale Irwin	70	72	69	71	282	3,250.00
	Grier Jones	67	69	72	74	282	3,250.00

* Amateur

THE MEMORIAL TOURNAMENT
Muirfield Village Golf Club, Dublin, Ohio 24–27 May 1979 Prize Money $329,885

Pos	Name					Total	$
1	Tom Watson	73	69	72	71	285	54,000.00
2	Miller Barber	74	73	71	70	288	32,400.00
3	Bob Gilder	74	80	68	69	291	20,400.00
4	Lanny Wadkins	69	79	73	71	292	13,200.00
	Tom Kite	74	72	74	72	292	13,200.00
6	Ed Sneed	71	78	75	69	293	10,800.00
7	Howard Twitty	75	76	74	69	294	9,350.00
	Jim Colbert	73	78	73	70	294	9,350.00
	Bill Rogers	77	75	71	71	294	9,350.00
10	George Burns	76	78	73	68	295	7,800.00
	Jay Haas	73	78	73	71	295	7,800.00
12	Fuzzy Zoeller	79	74	71	72	296	6,075.00
	Hubert Green	75	77	72	72	296	6,075.00
	Hale Irwin	73	80	76	67	296	6,075.00
	Bruce Lietzke	75	74	72	75	296	6,075.00
16	Terry Diehl	79	71	74	73	297	4,350.00
	Alan Tapie	75	76	73	73	297	4,350.00
	Tom Weiskopf	76	73	74	74	297	4,350.00
	Barry Jaeckel	76	77	76	68	297	4,350.00
	Lon Hinkle	75	73	72	77	297	4,350.00
	Lee Elder	75	76	77	69	297	4,350.00
22	John Mahaffey	78	78	72	70	298	2,880.00
	Jim Nelford	73	78	75	72	298	2,880.00
	J. C. Snead	76	73	77	72	298	2,880.00
	Bobby Walzel	73	78	75	72	298	2,880.00
	Leonard Thompson	78	75	72	73	298	2,880.00

THE KEMPER OPEN
Quail Hollow Country Club, Charlotte, North Carolina 31 May–3 June 1979 Prize Money $350,000

	Name						$
1	Jerry McGee	61	74	69	68	272	63,000.00
2	Jerry Pate	71	70	64	68	273	37,800.00
3	Andy Bean	69	68	72	68	277	20,300.00
	J. C. Snead	71	65	71	70	277	20,300.00
5	Ray Floyd	70	68	68	72	278	14,000.00
6	Mark Hayes	69	71	68	71	279	12,600.00
7	Homero Blancas	71	68	72	69	280	10,185.00
	Bill Rogers	69	71	70	70	280	10,185.00
	Victor Regalado	71	66	72	71	280	10,185.00
	Bobby Walzel	68	71	69	72	280	10,185.00
	Craig Stadler	62	69	73	76	280	10,185.00
12	Mark Lye	71	69	71	70	281	6,450.00
	Tom Purtzer	70	69	71	71	281	6,450.00
	Fred Marti	68	72	70	71	281	6,450.00
	Gary McCord	67	73	69	72	281	6,450.00
	Jim Thorpe	69	72	68	72	281	6,450.00
	Rod Funseth	70	68	71	72	281	6,450.00
	John Schroeder	72	72	70	67	281	6,450.00
19	Mike Hill	71	71	71	69	282	3,950.00
	Rex Caldwell	70	68	73	71	282	3,950.00
	Bobby Wadkins	67	73	70	72	282	3,950.00
	Lanny Wadkins	72	68	70	72	282	3,950.00
	ChiChi Rodriguez	72	69	69	72	282	3,950.00
	Bob Gilder	69	69	70	74	282	3,950.00
	Dennis Sullivan	70	72	72	68	282	3,950.00

THE ATLANTA CLASSIC
Atlanta Country Club, Marietta, Georgia 7–10 June 1979 Prize Money $300,000

	Name						$
1	Andy Bean	70	67	61	67	265	54,000.00
2	Joe Inman	71	64	68	70	273	32,400.00
3	David Graham	71	70	67	68	276	17,400.00
	Grier Jones	68	68	70	70	276	17,400.00
5	Fuzzy Zoeller	68	71	64	74	277	12,000.00
6	Wally Armstrong	71	70	69	67	279	10,800.00
7	Doug Tewell	72	70	69	69	280	9,350.00
	Hubert Green	69	71	70	70	280	9,350.00
	Jack Renner	68	71	70	71	280	9,350.00
10	Bob Murphy	68	71	74	68	281	7,200.00
	Curtis Strange	70	71	70	70	281	7,200.00
	Ed Dougherty	71	73	65	72	281	7,200.00
	Barry Jaeckel	67	72	68	74	281	7,200.00
14	Peter Oosterhuis	68	72	73	69	282	5,250.00
	Ed Fiori	67	74	72	69	282	5,250.00
	Larry Ziegler	70	74	66	72	282	5,250.00
	Mark Lye	63	75	71	73	282	5,250.00
18	Bob Byman	69	74	70	70	283	3,651.43
	Hale Irwin	71	69	71	72	283	3,651.43
	Leonard Thompson	69	73	70	71	283	3,651.43
	Mike Reid	70	71	69	73	283	3,651.43
	Ben Crenshaw	71	69	70	73	283	3,651.43
	Mike Hill	71	70	68	74	283	3,651.43
	Morris Hatalsky	71	68	68	76	283	3,651.42

THE CANADIAN OPEN

Glen Abbey Golf Club, Oakville, Ontario 21–24 June 1979 Prize Money $350,000

Pos	Player	R1	R2	R3	R4	Total	$
1	Lee Trevino	67	71	72	71	281	63,000.00
2	Ben Crenshaw	70	70	73	71	284	37,800.00
3	Tom Watson	66	69	72	78	285	23,800.00
4	Bob Gilder	70	70	76	70	286	16,800.00
5	Howard Twitty	69	76	73	69	287	12,775.00
	Bruce Lietzke	71	74	72	70	287	12,775.00
	David Graham	72	70	74	71	287	12,775.00
8	Jim Nelford	71	72	73	72	288	10,850.00
9	Eddie Pearce	74	72	72	71	289	9,100.00
	Keith Fergus	70	75	71	73	289	9,100.00
	Johnny Miller	67	73	75	74	289	9,100.00
	D. A. Weibring	68	72	77	72	289	9,100.00
13	Gil Morgan	69	72	77	72	290	6,562.50
	Tommy Aaron	75	70	73	72	290	6,562.50
	Barry Jaeckel	70	74	72	74	290	6,562.50
	Jack Newton	64	74	73	79	290	6,562.50
17	Bobby Wadkins	71	75	72	73	291	5,075.00
	Mike Reid	69	71	76	75	291	5,075.00
	Morris Hatalsky	77	68	72	74	291	5,075.00
	Hale Irwin	72	73	71	75	291	5,075.00
21	Curtis Strange	72	69	73	78	292	4,200.00
22	Bob Lunn	68	72	78	75	293	3,640.00
	Bob Murphy	68	77	75	73	293	3,640.00
	Jack Nicklaus	70	75	71	77	293	3,640.00
25	Wayne Levi	72	73	78	71	294	2,671.67
	Victor Regalado	71	74	77	72	294	2,671.67
	Bob Byman	73	73	75	73	294	2,671.67
	Bruce Devlin	72	69	78	75	294	2,671.67
	Dave Stockton	72	73	74	75	294	2,671.66
	Bob Eastwood	71	75	71	77	294	2,671.66

THE DANNY THOMAS MEMPHIS CLASSIC

Colonial Country Club, Cordova, Tennessee 28 June–1 July 1979 Prize Money $300,000

Pos	Player	R1	R2	R3	R4	Total	$
1	Gil Morgan	72	71	69	66	278	54,000.00
2	Larry Nelson	72	71	70	65	278	32,400.00
	Morgan won play-off at second extra hole						
3	Tom Kite	71	70	69	70	280	20,400.00
4	Bruce Lietzke	71	73	72	66	282	11,812.50
	J. C. Snead	69	70	76	67	282	11,812.50
	Mark Hayes	71	70	74	67	282	11,812.50
	Graham Marsh	72	70	70	70	282	11,812.50
8	Tom Purtzer	74	72	70	67	283	8,100.00
	Bob Byman	71	69	75	68	283	8,100.00
	Andy Bean	71	74	68	70	283	8,100.00
	Peter Jacobsen	71	71	69	72	283	8,100.00
	Cesar Sanudo	72	68	71	72	283	8,100.00
13	Gary Player	69	75	70	70	284	5,800.00
	Rod Curl	70	75	67	72	284	5,800.00
	Wally Armstrong	69	73	69	73	284	5,800.00
16	George Burns	73	69	76	67	285	4,350.00
	Morris Hatalsky	71	74	72	68	285	4,350.00
	Stan Lee	75	70	71	69	285	4,350.00
	Gibby Gilbert	73	70	71	71	285	4,350.00
	Brad Bryant	69	72	68	76	285	4,350.00
	Jim Simons	70	72	69	74	285	4,350.00
22	Rex Caldwell	75	69	73	69	286	2,880.00
	Jack Newton	70	68	76	72	286	2,880.00
	Gary Koch	68	76	71	71	286	2,880.00
	George Johnson	70	70	74	72	286	2,880.00
	Larry Ziegler	71	70	71	74	286	2,880.00
27	Hale Irwin	72	72	72	69	287	2,265.00
	Jack Renner	74	69	71	73	287	2,265.00

THE WESTERN OPEN
Butler National Golf Club, Oak Brook, Illinois 5–8 July 1979 Prize Money $300,000

							$
1	Larry Nelson	71	69	70	76	286	54,000.00
2	Ben Crenshaw	75	69	71	71	286	32,400.00
	Nelson won play-off at first extra hole						
3	Dan Pohl	71	72	71	73	287	17,400.00
	Bruce Devlin	69	71	76	71	287	17,400.00
5	Bruce Lietzke	73	73	73	69	288	12,000.00
6	John Schroeder	75	73	74	67	289	9,712.50
	Jim Simons	69	76	72	72	289	9,712.50
	Mark Hayes	75	71	72	71	289	9,712.50
	Tom Watson	70	73	68	78	289	9,712.50
10	Graham Marsh	72	74	75	69	290	7,500.00
	Calvin Peete	70	75	74	71	290	7,500.00
	Bobby Wadkins	75	72	70	73	290	7,500.00
13	Gibby Gilbert	73	74	75	69	291	5,625.00
	Howard Twitty	74	74	72	71	291	5,625.00
	John Fought	70	73	74	74	291	5,625.00
	Jim Colbert	71	74	73	73	291	5,625.00
17	Curtis Strange	78	71	75	68	292	4,500.00
	Tim Simpson	74	71	77	70	292	4,500.00
	Tom Jenkins	72	70	76	74	292	4,500.00
20	Ed Sneed	75	74	73	71	293	3,750.00
	Andy North	74	75	72	72	293	3,750.00
22	Peter Oosterhuis	74	76	74	70	294	2,880.00
	Tom Weiskopf	71	78	73	72	294	2,880.00
	George Burns	72	75	75	72	294	2,880.00
	Mike Sullivan	73	76	73	72	294	2,880.00
	Barney Thompson	74	76	70	74	294	2,880.00

THE GREATER MILWAUKEE OPEN
Tuckaway Country Club, Franklin, Wisconsin 12–15 July 1979 Prize Money $200,000

							$
1	Calvin Peete	69	67	68	65	269	36,000.00
2	Jim Simons	68	68	71	67	274	14,933.34
	Victor Regalado	66	68	69	71	274	14,933.33
	Lee Trevino	70	68	66	70	274	14,933.33
5	John Lister	67	69	71	68	275	7,600.00
	Ed Dougherty	67	66	70	72	275	7,600.00
7	Brad Bryant	69	70	70	67	276	6,450.00
	David Graham	68	67	71	70	276	6,450.00
9	Rex Caldwell	71	71	69	66	277	5,400.00
	Grier Jones	69	67	71	70	277	5,400.00
	Jim Dent	70	67	70	70	277	5,400.00
12	ChiChi Rodriguez	70	68	75	65	278	3,685.72
	Wayne Levi	70	70	71	67	278	3,685.72
	Johnny Miller	68	68	73	69	278	3,685.72
	Hubert Green	70	69	69	70	278	3,685.71
	Kermit Zarley	68	67	72	71	278	3,685.71
	Bill Kratzert	69	68	70	71	278	3,685.71
	Andy North	66	70	69	73	278	3,685.71
19	Bob Mann	68	67	74	70	279	2,424.00
	Jack Ferenz	72	68	70	69	279	2,424.00
	Dave Eichelberger	68	69	71	71	279	2,424.00
	Bobby Wadkins	69	70	70	70	279	2,424.00
	Mike Reid	66	69	69	75	279	2,424.00

THE ED McMAHON QUAD CITIES OPEN
Oakwood Country Club, Coal Valley, Illinois 19–22 July 1979 Prize Money $200,000

Pos	Player					Total	$
1	D.A. Weibring	67	65	69	65	266	36,000.00
2	Calvin Peete	68	70	67	63	268	21,600.00
3	Ken Still	67	68	67	68	270	13,600.00
4	Craig Stadler	70	66	66	69	271	9,600.00
5	Victor Regalado	64	70	72	66	272	7,300.00
	Ed Sabo	71	66	69	66	272	7,300.00
	Lon Nielsen	66	69	68	69	272	7,300.00
8	Brad Bryant	70	70	69	64	273	5,000.00
	Dan Pohl	68	70	70	65	273	5,000.00
	Mike Morley	70	68	69	66	273	5,000.00
	Curtis Strange	69	70	66	68	273	5,000.00
	Morris Hatalsky	66	71	67	69	273	5,000.00
	Rod Curl	67	65	70	71	273	5,000.00
	Dan Halldorson	65	68	67	73	273	5,000.00
15	Dennis Sullivan	65	68	73	68	274	2,813.34
	Jeff Mitchell	66	67	72	69	274	2,813.34
	Roger Maltbie	69	68	69	68	274	2,813.34
	George Cadle	63	74	68	69	274	2,813.33
	Peter Jacobsen	66	72	67	69	274	2,813.33
	Mike Reid	68	69	68	69	274	2,813.33
	Bob Gilder	67	67	70	70	274	2,813.33
	Keith Fergus	68	66	70	70	274	2,813.33
	Lindy Miller	71	68	65	70	274	2,813.33

THE IVB-PHILADELPHIA GOLF CLASSIC
Whitemarsh Valley Country Club, Lafayette Hill, Pennsylvania 26–29 July 1979 Prize Money $250,000

Pos	Player					Total	$
1	Lou Graham	68	70	71	64	273	45,000.00
2	Bobby Wadkins	67	69	67	70	273	27,000.00
	Graham won play-off at first extra hole						
3	Jack Nicklaus	72	70	67	65	274	13,000.00
	J.C. Snead	68	64	73	69	274	13,000.00
	Mark Hayes	68	70	67	69	274	13,000.00
6	Bill Kratzert	69	72	68	66	275	8,687.50
	David Graham	65	69	70	71	275	8,687.50
8	Jerry Pate	69	71	70	66	276	7,250.00
	Ray Floyd	71	68	70	67	276	7,250.00
	Ben Crenshaw	69	66	72	69	276	7,250.00
11	Bob Byman	67	69	71	69	277	6,250.00
12	Dave Stockton	68	72	69	69	278	5,750.00
13	Morris Hatalsky	67	73	72	67	279	4,550.00
	Barry Jaeckel	69	72	69	69	279	4,550.00
	Jeff Mitchell	68	71	70	70	279	4,550.00
	Andy Bean	68	68	72	71	279	4,550.00
	Doug Tewell	71	71	65	72	279	4,550.00
18	Lanny Wadkins	70	71	72	67	280	3,500.00
	Jay Sigel*	71	72	69	68	280	–
	Howard Twitty	71	69	69	71	280	3,500.00
	Gene Littler	72	70	65	73	280	3,500.00
22	Wally Armstrong	71	71	70	69	281	2,346.88
	Tom Purtzer	71	72	69	69	281	2,346.88
	Kermit Zarley	70	70	70	71	281	2,346.88
	Mike Reid	68	72	70	71	281	2,346.88
	Tommy Valentine	67	69	72	73	281	2,346.87
	Steve Veriato	68	73	68	72	281	2,346.87
	Forrest Fezler	67	72	69	73	281	2,346.87
	Calvin Peete	70	70	68	73	281	2,346.87

* Amateur

THE SAMMY DAVIS-GREATER HARTFORD OPEN

Wethersfield Country Club, Wethersfield, Connecticut 9–12 August 1979 Prize Money $300,000

								$
1	Jerry McGee	68	67	67	65	267		54,000.00
2	Jack Renner	68	67	66	67	268		32,400.00
3	Curtis Strange	70	66	69	65	270		17,400.00
	George Cadle	62	73	66	69	270		17,400.00
5	Mark Hayes	66	66	73	66	271		10,950.00
	Lou Graham	69	69	67	66	271		10,950.00
	J. C. Snead	65	66	71	69	271		10,950.00
8	Hubert Green	67	71	68	66	272		9,000.00
	Michael Brannan	67	67	70	68	272		9,000.00
10	Dave Eichelberger	69	71	67	66	273		7,200.00
	Victor Regalado	69	70	67	67	273		7,200.00
	Ray Floyd	70	69	67	67	273		7,200.00
	Peter Oosterhuis	67	68	69	69	273		7,200.00
14	Bob Murphy	68	68	72	66	274		5,250.00
	Keith Fergus	66	69	71	68	274		5,250.00
	John Fought	68	67	69	70	274		5,250.00
	Joe Inman	67	68	68	71	274		5,250.00
18	Don Bies	70	70	69	66	275		4,350.00
	Morris Hatalsky	73	67	66	69	275		4,350.00
20	D. A. Weibring	68	73	70	65	276		3,026.25
	Kermit Zarley	71	69	68	68	276		3,026.25
	Alan Tapie	67	72	69	68	276		3,026.25
	Lee Elder	69	71	68	68	276		3,026.25
	Tom Purtzer	70	69	68	69	276		3,026.25
	Craig Stadler	68	68	70	70	276		3,026.25
	Pat McGowan	66	71	71	68	276		3,026.25
	Rod Curl	67	69	69	71	276		3,026.25

THE MANUFACTURERS HANOVER WESTCHESTER CLASSIC

Westchester Country Club, Harrison, New York 16–19 August 1979 Prize Money $400,000

								$
1	Jack Renner	69	71	70	67	277		72,000.00
2	Howard Twitty	70	70	71	67	278		35,200.00
	David Graham	65	73	69	71	278		35,200.00
4	Peter Oosterhuis	70	75	71	63	279		17,600.00
	Scott Simpson	70	68	70	71	279		17,600.00
6	Tom Kite	69	67	74	70	280		14,400.00
7	George Burns	69	70	72	70	281		12,466.67
	J. C. Snead	73	68	71	69	281		12,466.67
	Bob Murphy	73	68	69	71	281		12,466.66
10	Gil Morgan	71	68	76	67	282		10,000.00
	Tom Watson	69	75	70	68	282		10,000.00
	Lon Hinkle	69	69	72	71	282		10,000.00
13	Alan Tapie	73	69	72	69	283		7,500.00
	Rex Caldwell	77	68	69	69	283		7,500.00
	Mike Hill	74	71	68	70	283		7,500.00
	Hubert Green	73	69	70	71	283		7,500.00
17	Andy North	73	71	73	67	284		5,413.34
	Greg Powers	73	71	71	69	284		5,413.34
	ChiChi Rodriguez	73	71	71	69	284		5,413.33
	Bob Eastwood	69	74	71	70	284		5,413.33
	Jerry McGee	71	67	74	72	284		5,413.33
	Leonard Thompson	72	70	70	72	284		5,413.33
23	Charles Coody	72	73	72	68	285		3,371.43
	Bob Byman	69	71	75	70	285		3,371.43
	Fred Marti	70	69	76	70	285		3,371.43
	Bob Gilder	72	73	70	70	285		3,371.43
	Ed Dougherty	76	68	71	70	285		3,371.43
	Jim Simons	74	70	70	71	285		3,371.43
	Bruce Lietzke	76	68	69	72	285		3,371.42

THE COLGATE HALL OF FAME CLASSIC

Pinehurst No. 2, Pinehurst, North Carolina   23–26 August 1979   Prize Money $250,000

							$
1	Tom Watson	70	68	65	69	272	45,000.00
2	Johnny Miller	69	63	70	70	272	27,000.00
	Watson won play-off at second extra hole						
3	Keith Fergus	68	68	67	71	274	17,000.00
4	Danny Edwards	67	68	69	71	275	12,000.00
5	Andy North	69	70	67	70	276	10,000.00
6	Bill Rogers	74	66	69	69	278	9,000.00
7	Bob Zender	73	71	69	66	279	8,062.50
	Michael Braman	67	68	74	70	279	8,062.50
9	Lyn Lott	72	70	72	66	280	6,750.00
	Bruce Devlin	70	67	70	73	280	6,750.00
	Kermit Zarley	68	70	70	72	280	6,750.00
12	Charles Coody	70	69	70	72	281	5,250.00
	Larry Nelson	70	69	69	73	281	5,250.00
	Tommy Aaron	69	66	71	75	281	5,250.00
15	Bob Eastwood	72	71	68	71	282	3,875.00
	Lou Graham	67	74	71	70	282	3,875.00
	Bobby Baker	71	68	71	72	282	3,875.00
	Cesar Sanudo	68	72	70	72	282	3,875.00
	Craig Stadler	67	73	69	73	282	3,875.00
	Bob Murphy	71	70	68	73	282	3,875.00
21	Allen Miller	71	71	71	70	283	3,000.00
22	Hubert Green	72	71	72	69	284	2,500.00
	Bob Mann	70	71	71	72	284	2,500.00
	Curtis Strange	69	70	72	73	284	2,500.00
	Dana Quigley	63	74	73	74	284	2,500.00

THE BC OPEN

EnJoie Golf Club, Endicott, New York   30 August–2 September 1979   Prize Money $275,000

							$
1	Howard Twitty	69	70	64	67	270	49,500.00
2	Tom Purtzer	70	67	68	66	271	29,700.00
3	Doug Tewell	67	69	66	70	272	18,700.00
4	Rod Curl	70	66	70	68	274	12,100.00
	Tom Kite	72	68	67	67	274	12,100.00
6	Brad Bryant	67	67	68	73	275	9,900.00
7	Jay Haas	71	66	68	71	276	8,850.00
	Curtis Strange	64	73	68	71	276	8,850.00
9	Peter Jacobsen	68	69	75	65	277	6,600.00
	Grier Jones	71	68	70	68	277	6,600.00
	ChiChi Rodriguez	70	69	70	68	277	6,600.00
	Craig Stadler	69	70	69	69	277	6,600.00
	Jerry Pate	72	66	69	70	277	6,600.00
	Parker Moore	69	72	66	70	277	6,600.00
15	Lindy Miller	71	72	70	65	278	4,125.00
	Alan Tapie	65	67	76	70	278	4,125.00
	Gary Koch	69	68	71	70	278	4,125.00
	Bill Rogers	71	69	68	70	278	4,125.00
	Dave Eichelberger	71	69	68	70	278	4,125.00
	John Mazza	72	67	67	72	278	4,125.00
	Mike Reid	69	69	66	73	278	4,125.00
22	Tommy Valentine	67	68	76	68	279	2,860.00
	Buddy Gardner	70	70	67	72	279	2,860.00
	Don Iverson	69	67	69	74	279	2,860.00

THE AMERICAN OPTICAL CLASSIC

Pleasant Valley Country Club, Sutton, Massachusetts   6–9 September 1979   Prize Money $250,000

Pos	Name						$
1	Lou Graham	68	67	71	69	275	45,000.00
2	Ben Crenshaw	67	71	68	70	276	27,000.00
3	Terry Diehl	66	71	69	72	278	17,000.00
4	Jeff Mitchell	70	70	67	72	279	12,000.00
5	Rod Curl	74	68	69	70	281	8,475.00
	Bruce Devlin	70	70	69	72	281	8,475.00
	Rex Caldwell	69	71	72	69	281	8,475.00
	Tim Simpson	70	70	69	72	281	8,475.00
	David Eger	69	69	70	73	281	8,475.00
10	Jeff Thomsen	70	71	71	70	282	6,250.00
	Larry Ziegler	71	73	71	67	282	6,250.00
	David Edwards	72	67	66	77	282	6,250.00
13	John Lister	69	74	71	69	283	4,416.67
	Bob Byman	71	72	69	71	283	4,416.67
	Bruce Lietzke	70	75	70	68	283	4,416.67
	George Archer	70	67	71	75	283	4,416.67
	Al Geiberger	69	68	72	74	283	4,416.66
	Ron Terry	68	70	72	73	283	4,416.66
19	Dana Quigley	73	70	70	71	284	3,250.00
	Bob Zender	70	69	70	75	284	3,250.00
	Tom Weiskopf	74	71	69	69	284	3,250.00
22	Jack Renner	72	70	73	70	285	2,320.84
	Jim Thorpe	70	71	72	72	285	2,320.84
	Leonard Thompson	70	75	70	70	285	2,320.83
	Gibby Gilbert	68	71	75	71	285	2,320.83
	Dave Stockton	74	71	67	73	285	2,320.83
	Mark Lye	69	70	74	72	285	2,320.83

THE BUICK-GOODWRENCH OPEN

Warwick Hills Country Club, Grand Blanc, Michigan   13–16 September 1979   Prize Money $150,000

Pos	Name						$
1	John Fought	71	72	68	69	280	27,000.00
2	Jim Simons	72	71	70	67	280	16,200.00
	Fought won play-off at second extra hole						
3	Dave Eichelberger	68	72	72	71	281	10,200.00
4	Jim Colbert	69	72	72	69	282	7,425.00
5	Bob Eastwood	68	75	74	66	283	6,000.00
	Lon Hinkle	73	69	73	68	283	6,000.00
	Bill Kratzert	71	71	70	70	283	6,000.00
8	Lindy Miller	71	71	75	67	284	4,075.00
	David Edwards	72	70	71	71	284	4,075.00
	David Graham	68	74	70	72	284	4,075.00
	George Burns	68	72	72	72	284	4,075.00
	Tom Weiskopf	69	74	70	71	284	4,075.00
	Dana Quigley	70	71	70	73	284	4,075.00
14	Tommy Valentine	73	72	72	68	285	2,421.43
	Steve Melnyk	70	73	74	68	285	2,421.43
	Terry Diehl	69	72	71	70	285	2,421.43
	Bob Zender	70	71	74	70	285	2,421.43
	Bob E. Smith	73	68	72	72	285	2,421.43
	Jeff Mitchell	70	73	68	74	285	2,421.43
	George Archer	68	72	71	74	285	2,421.42
21	Dan Halldorson	71	70	71	74	286	1,725.00
	Mike Hill	69	73	69	75	286	1,725.00

THE ANHEUSER-BUSCH CLASSIC
Silverado Country Club, Napa, California   20–23 September 1979   Prize Money $300,000

								$
1	John Fought	69	68	71	69	277	54,000.00
2	Alan Tapie	68	75	69	66	278	22,400.00
	Bobby Wadkins	66	72	71	69	278	22,400.00
	Buddy Gardner	68	72	68	70	278	22,400.00
5	Bill Rogers	68	71	72	68	279	12,000.00
6	Andy North	71	69	71	69	280	10,050.00
	Mark Lye	66	72	67	75	280	10,050.00
	Lon Hinkle	69	66	70	75	280	10,050.00
9	Rod Curl	73	69	73	66	281	7,800.00
	Bruce Lietzke	71	68	71	71	281	7,800.00
	Mike Sullivan	70	70	70	71	281	7,800.00
	Bob Gilder	69	68	70	74	281	7,800.00
13	Tom Weiskopf	71	72	70	69	282	5,800.00
	J.C.Snead	71	70	69	72	282	5,800.00
	Lou Graham	68	66	72	76	282	5,800.00
16	Pat McGowan	73	69	72	69	283	4,950.00
	Jerry McGee	69	74	72	68	283	4,950.00
18	Dave Eichelberger	72	72	70	70	284	3,651.43
	Craig Stadler	70	73	72	69	284	3,651.43
	Jack Renner	72	69	72	71	284	3,651.43
	Tom Kite	70	72	74	68	284	3,651.43
	Steve Melnyk	72	69	70	73	284	3,651.43
	Rod Funseth	73	68	68	75	284	3,651.43
	Tim Simpson	70	71	67	76	284	3,651.42

THE WORLD SERIES OF GOLF
Firestone Country Club, Akron, Ohio   27–30 September 1979   Prize Money $400,000

								$
1	Lon Hinkle	67	67	71	67	272	100,000.00
2	Bill Rogers	69	67	68	69	273	37,266.67
	Larry Nelson	68	67	68	70	273	37,366.67
	Lee Trevino	67	68	72	66	273	37,366.66
5	Hale Irwin	69	70	70	65	274	15,000.00
	Tom Watson	68	65	72	69	274	15,000.00
7	Tom Kite	67	68	70	70	275	12,800.00
8	Howard Twitty	69	67	71	69	276	11,600.00
9	Bob Gilder	74	67	67	70	278	10,400.00
10	Bruce Lietzke	71	68	71	69	279	9,400.00
	Andy Bean	64	75	70	70	279	9,400.00
12	John Mahaffey	74	68	68	71	281	8,200.00
	Jerry Pate	68	72	65	76	281	8,200.00
14	J.C.Snead	66	70	73	73	282	7,000.00
	Fuzzy Zoeller	69	69	71	73	282	7,000.00
16	Tohru Nakamura	70	71	70	72	283	6,100.00
17	Ben Crenshaw	73	69	73	69	284	5,800.00
18	John Fought	73	68	76	68	285	5,200.00
	David Graham	72	73	70	70	285	5,200.00
	Lou Graham	73	70	70	72	285	5,200.00
21	Graham Marsh	66	74	71	75	286	4,450.00
	Lanny Wadkins	72	71	70	73	286	4,450.00
23	Isao Aoki	71	70	77	69	287	3,850.00
	Dale Hayes	72	74	70	71	287	3,850.00
25	Gil Morgan	71	71	72	74	288	3,350.00
	Ed Sneed	70	72	76	70	288	3,350.00
27	Bobby Wadkins	74	74	70	71	289	3,060.00
28	Hubert Green	74	69	75	72	290	2,700.00
	Ray Floyd	82	71	68	69	290	2,700.00
	Mark Hayes	70	73	75	72	290	2,700.00
31	Greg Norman	73	73	75	70	291	2,340.00
32	Mark O'Meara*	74	74	70	74	292	–
	Jerry McGee	71	75	75	71	292	2,160.00
34	Jay Sigel*	76	73	72	73	294	–
35	Wayne Levi	77	78	74	68	297	2,025.00
	Jack Renner	73	75	73	76	297	2,025.00
37	Lu Hsi-Chuen	76	78	78	69	301	1,890.00
38	Hsu Chi-San	78	72	77	80	307	1,800.00

* Amateur

THE SAN ANTONIO–TEXAS OPEN

Oak Hills Country Club, San Antonio, Texas 4–7 October 1979 Prize Money $250,000

Pos	Name						$
1	Lou Graham	69	64	69	66	268	45,000.00
2	Doug Tewell	66	68	63	72	269	18,666.67
	Bill Rogers	72	68	62	67	269	18,666.67
	Eddie Pearce	69	65	65	70	269	18,666.67
5	Gary McCord	70	69	67	65	271	8,781.25
	Keith Fergus	69	65	69	68	271	8,781.25
	Ben Crenshaw	70	65	68	68	271	8,781.25
	Lee Trevino	68	65	69	69	271	8,781.25
9	Bob Gilder	72	68	67	65	272	7,000.00
	Mike Sullivan	68	69	68	67	272	7,000.00
11	Rex Caldwell	69	72	68	64	273	5,500.00
	Calvin Peete	71	67	68	67	273	5,500.00
	Bob Murphy	69	69	67	68	273	5,500.00
	John Mahaffey	71	64	67	71	273	5,500.00
15	Scott Simpson	72	69	66	67	274	4,375.00
	Bill Kratzert	69	70	65	70	274	4,375.00
17	Orville Moody	69	69	70	67	275	3,750.00
	Gibby Gilbert	66	71	68	70	275	3,750.00
	Tom Weiskopf	71	67	67	70	275	3,750.00
20	Dale Douglass	72	66	70	68	276	2,912.50
	Curtis Strange	69	69	69	69	276	2,912.50
	Mark McCumber	69	69	69	69	276	2,912.50
	Marty Fleckman	72	68	67	69	276	2,912.50
24	Mark Pfeil	68	75	66	68	277	2,200.00
	Jim Colbert	71	68	69	69	277	2,200.00
	Ed Fiori	68	72	68	69	277	2,200.00

THE SOUTHERN OPEN

Green Island Country Club, Columbus, Georgia 11–14 October 1979 Prize Money $200,000

Pos	Name						$
1	Ed Fiori	69	72	65	68	274	36,000.00
2	Tom Weiskopf	69	67	68	70	274	21,600.00
	Fiori won play-off at second extra hole						
3	Artie McNickle	70	68	68	69	275	10,400.00
	Calvin Peete	69	67	67	72	275	10,400.00
	Mike Reid	67	69	68	71	275	10,400.00
6	Barney Thompson	69	70	68	69	276	7,200.00
7	David Edwards	72	69	67	69	277	6,450.00
	Gibby Gilbert	69	66	71	71	277	6,450.00
9	Michael Brannan	68	69	72	69	278	5,600.00
	Jerry Pate	66	69	69	74	278	5,600.00
11	Hubert Green	70	70	73	66	279	4,600.00
	Dan Pohl	69	67	73	70	279	4,600.00
	George Burns	70	69	67	73	279	4,600.00
14	Eddie Pearce	66	74	72	68	280	3,300.00
	Ben Crenshaw	67	70	71	72	280	3,300.00
	Mike Nicolette	71	72	66	71	280	3,300.00
	Doug Tewell	70	69	70	71	280	3,300.00
	Dale Douglass	70	68	70	72	280	3,300.00
	Mike Hill	69	72	68	71	280	3,300.00
20	Bill Kratzert	69	72	71	69	281	2,248.00
	Butch Baird	70	68	71	72	281	2,248.00
	Mike Sullivan	72	68	71	70	281	2,248.00
	Brad Bryant	70	68	72	71	281	2,248.00
	Mike McCullough	65	69	73	74	281	2,248.00

THE PENSACOLA OPEN

Perdido Bay Golf Club, Pensacola, Florida   18–21 October 1979   Prize Money $200,000

							$
1	Curtis Strange	69	71	62	69	271	36,000.00
2	Bill Kratzert	64	70	70	68	272	21,600.00
3	Morris Hatalsky	64	69	72	69	274	11,600.00
	John Mahaffey	67	67	70	70	274	11,600.00
5	Don January	70	67	68	70	275	7,025.00
	Keith Fergus	69	69	68	69	275	7,025.00
	Terry Diehl	67	71	69	68	275	7,025.00
	Orville Moody	68	67	68	72	275	7,025.00
9	Bob Murphy	70	69	69	68	276	5,600.00
	Dan Pohl	68	69	67	72	276	5,600.00
11	ChiChi Rodriguez	73	68	68	68	277	4,800.00
	Peter Jacobsen	70	71	68	68	277	4,800.00
13	Mark Lye	69	72	70	67	278	3,533.34
	Doug Tewell	69	70	70	69	278	3,533.34
	Tom Purtzer	68	71	69	70	278	3,533.33
	Mike Sullivan	71	68	69	70	278	3,533.33
	Wally Armstrong	70	72	66	70	278	3,533.33
	Mike Nicolette	67	73	64	74	278	3,533.33
19	Mike Hill	72	70	69	68	279	2,700.00
	Tom Weiskopf	73	68	69	69	279	2,700.00
21	Rex Caldwell	73	69	71	67	280	2,080.00
	Bob Wynn	71	67	73	69	280	2,080.00
	Frank Beard	70	71	69	70	280	2,080.00
	Robert Donald	71	71	68	70	280	2,080.00
	Jeff Mitchell	68	71	69	72	280	2,080.00

WALT DISNEY WORLD NATIONAL TEAM CHAMPIONSHIP

Walt Disney World, Lake Buena Vista, Florida   25–28 October 1979   Prize Money $250,000

							$
1	George Burns & Ben Crenshaw	62	66	62	65	255	22,500.00
2	Peter Jacobsen & D.A. Weibring	64	64	68	62	258	10,500.00
	Scott Bess & Dan Halldorson	66	66	64	62	258	10,500.00
	Jeff Hewes & Sammy Rachels	65	65	64	64	258	10,500.00
5	Forrest Fezler & Larry Ziegler	61	68	68	62	259	5,350.00
	Brad Bryant & Joe Hager	67	65	65	62	259	5,350.00
7	Wayne Levi & Bob Mann	65	67	65	63	260	3,725.00
	Jim Colbert & Mike Sullivan	62	65	69	64	260	3,725.00
	Terry Diehl & Ken Venturi	66	67	64	63	260	3,725.00
	Miller Barber & Don January	64	66	65	65	260	3,725.00
	Gibby Gilbert & Grier Jones	64	68	62	66	260	3,725.00
	Gary Koch & Curtis Strange	62	67	65	66	260	3,725.00
13	Mark Hayes & Gil Morgan	67	66	66	62	261	2,700.00
	Bruce Fleisher & Tom Jenkins	64	64	66	67	261	2,700.00
15	Morris Hatalsky & Don Pooley	67	66	64	65	262	2,500.00
16	Mark Lye & Tommy Valentine	66	64	67	64	263	2,250.00
	Dave Hill & Mike Hill	66	66	67	64	263	2,250.00
	Tom Chain & Jack Ferenz	69	63	66	65	263	2,250.00
	Barry Jaeckel & Gary McCord	66	65	65	67	263	2,250.00
20	Dave Barr & Ed Fiori	67	65	67	65	264	1,700.00
	Joe Carr & Tom Shaw	67	66	66	65	264	1,700.00
	Roger Maltbie & Lee Mikles	67	65	66	66	264	1,700.00
	Tom Purtzer & Howard Twitty	63	64	70	67	264	1,700.00
	Don Iverson & Bob Zender	65	67	66	66	264	1,700.00
	Bruce Devlin & Jerry McGee	64	65	68	67	264	1,700.00
	George Archer & Jim Simons	63	67	66	68	264	1,700.00

Above: Jack Nicklaus holed this one in the British Open, but on the US Tour his restricted appearances led to a slump to 71st place. (Phil Sheldon)

Below: Bill Rogers won over $230,000 in America but notched his one victory in the World Match-Play at Wentworth, Surrey.

THE 1980 UNITED STATES TOURNAMENT SCHEDULE

Date	Event	Venue	Prize Money
January			
9–13	Bob Hope Desert Classic	Indian Wells CC, Bermuda Dunes CC, El Dorado CC, La Quinta CC, Palm Desert, Cal	$304,500
17–20	Phoenix Open	Phoenix CC, Phoenix, Ariz	$300,000
24–27	Andy Williams-San Diego Open	Torrey Pines GC, La Jolla, Cal	$250,000
31–3 Feb	Bing Crosby National Pro-Am.	Pebble Beach GL, Spyglass Hill GC, Cypress Point GC, Pebble Beach, Cal	$300,000
February			
7–10	Hawaiian Open	Waialae CC, Honolulu	$325,000
14–17	Joe Garagiola-Tucson Open	Tucson National GC, Tucson, Ariz	$300,000
21–24	Glen Campbell-Los Angeles Open	Riviera CC, Pacific Palisades, Cal	$250,000
28–2 March	Bay Hill Classic	Bay Hill Club and Lodge, Orlando	$300,000
March			
6–9	Jackie Gleason-Inverrary Classic	Inverrary G & CC, Lauderhill, Fl	$300,000
13–16	Doral-Eastern Open	Doral CC, Miami, Fl	$250,000
20–23	Tournament Players' Championship	Sawgrass, Ponte Vedra Beach, Fl	$440,000+
27–30	Sea Pines Heritage Classic	Harbour Town GL, Hilton Head Island, SC	$300,000
April			
3–6	Greater Greensboro Open	Forest Oaks CC, Greensboro, NC	$250,000
10–13	The Masters Tournament	Augusta National CC, Augusta, Ga	Undecided
17–20	Mony Tournament of Champions	La Costa CC, Carlsbad, Cal	$300,000
17–20	Tallahassee Open	Killearn G & CC, Tallahassee, Fl	$100,000
24–27	New Orleans Open	Lakewood CC, New Orleans, La	$250,000
May			
1–4	Michelob Houston Open	Woodlands CC, Houston, Texas	$350,000
8–11	Byron Nelson Classic	Preston Trail GC, Dallas, Texas	$300,000
15–18	Colonial National Invitation	Colonial CC, Fort Worth, Texas	$300,000
22–25	Memorial Tournament	Muirfield Village GC, Dublin, Ohio	$300,000+
29–1 June	Kemper Open	Congressional CC, Bethesda, Md	$400,000
June			
5–8	Atlanta Golf Classic	Atlanta CC, Atlanta, Ga	$300,000
12–15	United States Open Champ.	Baltusrol GC, Springfield, NJ	Undecided
19–22	Canadian Open Champ.	Royal Montreal GC, Quebec	$350,000
26–29	Danny Thomas-Memphis Classic	Colonial CC, Cordova, Tenn	$300,000
July			
3–6	Western Open	Butler National GC, Oak Brook, Ill	$300,000
10–13	Greater Milwaukee Open	Tuckaway CC, Franklin, Wisconsin	$300,000
17–20	Quad Cities Open	Oakwood CC, Coal Valley, Ill	$200,000
24–27	Sammy Davis-Greater Hartford Open	Wethersfield CC, Wethersfield, Conn	$300,000
31–3 Aug	IVB-Philadelphia Classic	Whitemarsh Valley CC, Lafayette Hill, Pa	$250,000
August			
7–10	US PGA Championship	Oak Hills CC, Rochester, NY	Undecided
14–17	Manufacturers Hanover-Westchester Classic	Westchester CC, Rye, NY	$400,000
21–24	World Series of Golf	Firestone CC, Akron, Ohio	Undecided
21–24	Buick-Goodwrench Open	Warwick Hills CC, Grand Blanc, Mich	Undecided
28–31	BC Open	En-Joie GC, Endicott, NY	$275,000
September			
4–7	Pleasant Valley Classic	Pleasant Valley CC, Sutton, MA	$300,000
11–14	Hall of Fame Tournament	Pinehurst CC, Pinehurst, NC	$250,000
18–21	San Antonio-Texas Open	Oak Hills CC, San Antonio, Texas	$250,000
25–28	Anheuser-Busch Classic	Silverado CC, Napa, CA	$300,000
October			
2–5	Southern Open	Green Island CC, Columbus, Ga	$200,000
9–12	Pensacola Open	Perdido Bay CC, Pensacola, Fl	$200,000
16–19	Walt Disney World Team Championship	Magnolia, Palm and Buena Vista Courses, Lake Buena Vista, Fl	$350,000

THE WORLD'S CIRCUITS EUROPE

THE EUROPEAN TOURNAMENT CIRCUIT 1979
REPORT AND RESULTS

Sandy Lyle European Open Champion, Scandinavian Open Champion, winner of the British Airways/Avis tournament, and number one in Europe in 1979. (Golf Photography International)

THE EUROPEAN TOURNAMENT CIRCUIT 1979

George Simms

SANDY ENDS THE SEVE MONOPOLY

Sandy Lyle had the right pedigree when he decided to join the professional ranks towards the end of 1977. His father, Alex Lyle, was the highly-respected professional, at the Hawkstone Park club in Shropshire; he had won international recognition by England at all levels at the age of 16; had twice won the English stroke-play title and a British Youths' title; and at 19 had gained Walker Cup honours.

At the end of his first year as a professional, having finished top of the essential Qualifying School before setting out, he could look back with satisfaction. He had won the Nigerian Open, including an eye-catching round of 61; had finished in the top 20 of tournaments here and there; had finished 49th in the Order of Merit; and had been voted 'Rookie of the Year'.

At the end of his second year as a professional he could look back not so much with satisfaction as with astonishment!

Still only a ripe young age of 21, he had won the European Open Championship; won the Scandinavian Open Championship; won the British Airways/Avis tournament; won the Scottish Professional Championship; added a Ryder Cup badge to his Walker Cup honours; topped the European Order of Merit; and ended Severiano Ballesteros' dominance in Europe.

Ballesteros, who had headed the Order of Merit for the previous three years, did not surrender his crown without a fight. It was his ambition to match the record of four years in a row as number one, set up by Peter Oosterhuis in the years 1971–74. But Lyle overtook him in the finishing stretch with his victory at Turnberry and its valuable first prize of £17,500, and although Seve made a late bid for the top with an 11th-hour entry for the Dunlop Masters, Lyle never relaxed his grip.

Ballesteros, of course, won the greater prize, and rightly the greater acclaim, with his swashbuckling victory in the Open Championship at Lytham, but by his own standards of the preceding two years it was, for him, an inconsistent year. It had the benefit of a purple patch coming at the right time when he won the Lada English Classic, finished second in the Scandinavian Open behind Lyle, and then carried off the Open title, all in the space of three consecutive tournaments.

Unquestionably Lyle, Mark James and Ken Brown will continue to press Ballesteros hard in the coming years for a bigger share of the limelight, as will Nick Faldo whose indifferent performance in 1979, after the rich promise of the previous two years, was surely only a temporary lapse. His contribution with Oosterhuis in the Ryder Cup matches was proof of that, if such was needed.

The publicity accorded to Brown and James was not always of the kind calculated to show them in the best light, but it was of their own doing and one can but hope that maybe wise counsel, and the disciplinary measures imposed at the end of the season, will have had the desired effect. Both are far too proficient and have much to offer to themselves and to the game, for them to be embroiled in the avoidable controversies of 1979.

Lyle was not the only former Walker Cup player to 'come good' in 1979. Michael King, having worked his way steadily up the ladder since turning professional in 1975, produced his finest year at the right time. He won the SOS Talisman Tournament Players' Championship at Moor Park, to cap a year of 11 top 10 finishes and near misses, all of which had earned him a Ryder Cup place and fifth spot in the Order of Merit with best-ever winnings of around £30,000.

The season began traditionally with the Portuguese Open in the Algarve in mid-April, and ended six months later at the picturesque Woburn Golf & Country Club where the Dunlop Masters broke new ground. Including the World Match-Play Championship, which then followed at Wentworth, Surrey, it was possible to play for over £1¼ million in total prize money, pre-supposing that one was invited to the World Match-Play, was eligible for the over-50s and under-25s events, and played in everything that was going, including the Pro-Amateur tournaments! With something like £400,000 also available in regional events within the six areas administered by the General Division of the PGA, the rewards for playing golf at the best level were enormous.

Brian Barnes, who had made a conspicuous start the previous year in winning the Spanish Open and finishing second in Portugal, went one better with victory at Vilamoura, little knowing that the season would be virtually over before the prize money for one and all seeped through from Portugal and allowed him to bank his first prize cheque!

He lost his Spanish title at Torrequebrada to South Africa's Dale Hayes, who not only repeated his victory of eight years earlier but served notice that he would again be a scourge to his fellow-professionals in Europe, as he had been the previous year after giving up the demanding US circuit. After an interlude in Madrid where Simon Hobday broke a three-year victory drought, Barnes and Hayes were head-on again at Monticello where after a number of past near misses the big Scot finally won the Italian Open title, but only after a four holes play-off.

Scotland also provided the French Open champion in Bernard Gallacher, and Barnes should have won the PGA title at St Andrews but let it slip into the grateful and nerveless hands of Argentine's Vicente Fernandez. Like Hayes, Fernandez had battled in vain in the United States for a couple of years and, again like Hayes, he had returned to Europe to become an immediate winner.

Australia's Greg Norman repeated his 1977 Martini victory, Lyle won in Jersey, new South African professional Gavin Levenson captured the Belgian Open title, James won a spectator-impoverished Welsh Classic, and another South African Mark McNulty won the Greater Manchester. About which time Ballesteros returned to the fold to begin at The Belfry a top-class stretch which ended in his triumph at Lytham.

Graham Marsh won in the Netherlands and Maurice Bembridge got back on to the victory rostrum in Cornwall before the event which everyone had been waiting for since 1974 finally happened. Tony Jacklin emerged triumphant in a 'big one' again. The former Open and US Open Champion, after years of self-doubt, recrimination, and experimentation, won the German Open at Frankfurt which, with eight other top 10 finishes, served notice that he was far from spent.

Enormous crowds in Dublin saw Mark James equal the course record to win the Irish Open, Baiocchi won at Crans, Lyle wrapped up the Order of Merit with his victory at Turnberry, and after King had won at Moor Park, Marsh produced the finish of the year with a three-wood to within 10 feet of the pin at the 514 yards 72nd at Woburn to get the birdie he needed for his first Dunlop Masters victory. Of the 22 events played, British players won 11, South Africans four, Australians three, and Zimbabwe-Rhodesia, Argentina, Spain, and Ireland, one apiece.

Sad note of the year was the death of Spain's Salvador Balbuena on the eve of the French Open Championship. The former winner of the Portuguese Open and Moroccan Grand Prix collapsed and died while dining with fellow Spanish professionals in a restaurant in Lyon.

There were two milestones. Neil Coles, whose first tournament victory was back in 1961 in the Ballantine's event at Wentworth, in finishing fourth in the European Open at Turnberry, passed the £200,000 mark in tournament winnings. Only once since 1961 had he finished outside the top 10 in the Order of Merit – and that was in 1977. That year he finished 11th!

For the other milestone, nostalgia takes this particular writer back to 1951 when he went to a London West End hotel to be the first to interview a promising 21-year-old newly-turned professional on his initial visit to Britain from Australia under the watchful eye of his travelling companion Norman von Nida. If memory after all these years serves aright, they had stopped off en route from Australia to play in the Egyptian Open. I remember interviewing him amidst a small mountain of tinned Australian fruit they had intuitively and wisely brought with them into a still-rationed Britain!

Peter Thomson has since then graced the professional game with his expertise, courtesy, and dignity, these last three decades. His five Open Championship victories are unlikely to be matched in this modern era, and it was a sentimental moment at Lytham when he bowed out on the 72nd green of the Open for the last time to a standing ovation.

We, and that includes Arnold Palmer, welcome him to the over 50s.

THE PORTUGUESE OPEN CHAMPIONSHIP

Vilamoura Golf Club, Algarve   12–15 April 1979   Prize Money £28,810

Another Ryder Cup year, over a million pounds to play for, and defeat by a shot 12 months earlier, was sufficient incentive for Brian Barnes to open the European season on a high note. Having won the Zambian Open a couple of weeks earlier he was in the right frame of mind, and timed his surge to the front for the final round for a two-strokes victory over Spain's Francisco Abreu. The early spotlight shone on Ireland's Des Smyth who set a new course record with a six-under-par opening 67 and was still in front at halfway. Abreu took over in front when Smyth slumped to a third round 79. Three birdies in the last five holes gave Barnes compensation for his 1978 second place.

Pos	Player						£
1	Brian Barnes	69	75	71	72	287	4,801.96
2	Francisco Abreu (S)	71	70	73	75	289	3,196.09
3	Dale Hayes (SA)	73	77	69	72	291	1,807.34
4	Mark James	74	73	75	70	292	1,329.10
	Eamonn Darcy (IRE)	71	75	75	71	292	1,329.10
6	Antonio Garrido (S)	73	72	76	72	293	1,017.11
7	Tommy Horton	76	75	71	73	295	743.28
	Sandy Lyle	77	71	71	76	295	743.28
	Tony Jacklin	74	73	72	76	295	743.28
10	Ken Brown	76	70	76	74	296	542.79
	Simon Hobday (ZIM)	73	75	74	74	296	542.79
12	Baldovino Dassu (I)	78	76	72	71	297	474.33
	Des Smyth (IRE)	67	71	79	80	297	474.33
14	Harold Henning (SA)	75	76	76	71	298	396.78
	Manuel Pinero (S)	76	71	77	74	298	396.78
	John Morgan	76	74	73	75	298	396.78
	Manuel Ballesteros (S)	80	73	70	75	298	396.78
	German Garrido (S)	77	73	72	76	298	396.78
	José Cabo (S)	73	75	73	77	298	396.78
	Noel Hunt	74	73	70	81	298	396.78
21	Angel Gallardo (S)	76	72	76	75	299	342.30
	Salvador Balbuena (S)	76	75	72	76	299	342.30
	Martin Poxon	72	77	71	79	299	342.30
24	Michael King	75	75	76	74	300	303.18
	Tony Price	77	76	73	74	300	303.18
	Jeff Hawkes (SA)	72	75	79	74	300	303.18
	David Vaughan	75	74	74	77	300	303.18
	Nick Job	75	74	73	78	300	303.18
29	Manuel Montes (S)	76	75	74	76	301	264.06
	Patricio Garrido (S)	73	72	78	78	301	264.06
	Charles Dernie	75	74	73	79	301	264.06
32	Sam Torrance	76	73	78	75	302	244.50
33	Steve Wildman	73	78	76	76	303	203.75
	Malcolm Gregson	76	73	78	76	303	203.75
	Howard Clark	79	74	74	76	303	203.75
	Gordon Brand	77	76	74	76	303	203.75
	Roberto Bernardini (I)	79	71	76	77	303	203.75
	David Chillas	74	76	74	79	303	203.75
	Bill Lockie	78	74	72	79	303	203.75
	Philip Elson	73	79	72	79	303	203.75
	Vince Baker (SA)	76	76	71	80	303	203.75
42	Massimo Mannelli (I)	73	80	77	74	304	171.15
	Warren Humphreys	77	77	75	75	304	171.15
	Bob Verwey (SA)	75	76	72	81	304	171.15
45	José-Maria Canizares (S)	75	77	77	76	305	161.37
46	Ian Mosey	75	76	79	76	306	141.80
	Guy Hunt	75	79	76	76	306	141.80
	Peter Townsend	77	76	76	77	306	141.80
	Garry Cullen	76	77	75	78	306	141.80
	Gar Hamilton (C)	75	75	77	79	306	141.80
	Manuel Calero (S)	72	75	71	78	80	306	141.80

	Player						£
	Manuel Garcia (S)	75	77	74	80	306	141.80
53	Armando Saavedra (ARG)	71	79	82	75	307	119.80
	Jan Sonnevi (SW)	77	77	73	80	307	119.80
55	Carl Mason	73	79	78	78	308	107.58
	Steve Martin	76	77	76	79	308	107.58
	Bill McColl	74	74	78	82	308	107.58
	Tim Giles	75	71	85	78	309	92.91
58	Lionel Platts	72	79	79	79	309	92.91
	Robbie Stewart (SA)	80	74	73	82	309	92.91
	P. Curry*	76	77	77	79	309	–
61	Trevor Powell	77	77	75	81	310	83.13
62	Michel Tapia (F)	76	77	76	82	311	78.24
63	Manuel Sanchez (S)	80	74	80	78	312	72.86
64	Francisco Hernandez (S)	77	75	81	81	314	66.25
	Karl-Heinz Gogele (G)	79	74	80	81	314	66.25

*Amateur

Previous Winners

Year	Winner	Venue	Score
1953	E.C. Brown	Estoril	260
1954	A. Miguel	Estoril	263
1955	F. Van Donck	Estoril	267
	After a tie with A. Miguel		
1956	A. Miguel	Estoril	268
1957	Not Played		
1958	P. Alliss	Estoril	264
1959	S. Miguel	Estoril	265
1960	K. Bousfield	Estoril	268
1961	K. Bousfield	Estoril	263
1962	A. Angelini	Estoril	269
1963	R. Sota	Estoril (54 holes)	204
1964	A. Miguel	Estoril	279
	After a tie with R. Sota		
1965	Not played		
1966	A. Angelini	Estoril	273
1967	A. Gallardo	Estoril (54 holes)	214
1968	M. Faulkner	Estoril	273
1969	R. Sota	Estoril	270
1970	R. Sota	Estoril	274
1971	L. Platts	Estoril	277
1972	G. Garrido	Estoril (54 holes)	196
1973	J. Benito	Penina	294
	After a tie with B. Gallacher		
1974	B. Huggett	Estoril	272
1975	H. Underwood	Penina	292
1976	S. Balbuena	Vale do Lobo	283
1977	M. Ramos	Penina	287
1978	H. Clark	Penina	291

THE SPANISH OPEN CHAMPIONSHIP

Torrequebrada Golf Club, near Torremolinos   19–22 April 1979   Prize Money £35,000

Back in 1971 a slim 18-year-old South African by the name of Dale Hayes surprised the professional world by winning the Spanish Open in Barcelona. But it was no surprise when he won it again in 1979, for since returning to the European circuit from the heartbreaks of the American tour Hayes had been dominant. Runner-up to Seve Ballesteros in the 1979 Order of Merit, he was quickly into his stride at the new Torrequebrada course with a two-shots victory over the in-form holder Barnes. Eight strokes behind Martin

Poxon and José Canizares after 36 holes, Dale swept to victory on a tremendous 67–66 finish, equalling the record in the last round. Ballesteros blew his chances with a nine in an opening 81, and missed the cut despite a second round 70.

Pos	Player						£
1	Dale Hayes (SA)	70	75	67	66	278	5,788.65
2	Brian Barnes	69	73	66	72	280	3,862.41
3	Bernard Gallacher	74	70	69	68	281	1,956.03
	José-Maria Canizares (S)	67	70	73	71	281	1,956.03
5	Baldovino Dassu (I)	71	71	68	72	282	1,474.47
6	John Morgan	74	71	70	68	283	1,042.55
	Martin Poxon	67	70	76	70	283	1,042.55
	Sandy Lyle	70	72	71	72	283	1,042.55
9	Antonio Garrido (S)	74	71	70	69	284	737.23
	Nick Price (SA)	74	68	70	72	284	737.23
11	David Jones	73	69	68	75	285	645.39
12	Ernesto Acosta (MEX)	69	72	71	74	286	605.67
13	Michael King	70	72	75	70	287	546.10
	Francisco Abreu (S)	70	73	73	71	287	546.10
	Mark James	69	70	75	73	287	546.10
16	Angel Gallardo (S)	77	71	71	69	288	456.74
	Gordon Brand	75	71	72	70	288	456.74
	Tony Price	74	68	73	73	288	456.74
	Manuel Ballesteros (S)	77	68	69	74	288	456.74
20	Eddie Polland	73	73	73	70	289	397.16
	Tony Jacklin	70	76	73	70	289	397.16
	German Garrido (S)	72	72	72	75	289	397.16
	Trevor Johnson	71	71	71	76	289	397.16
	Tommy Horton	68	75	74	72	289	397.16
25	Des Smyth (IRE)	79	72	69	70	290	342.55
	Brian Huggett	72	75	73	70	290	342.55
	Philip Elson	73	70	76	71	290	342.55
	Manuel Montes (S)	73	76	70	71	290	342.55
	John Bland (SA)	72	74	72	72	290	342.55
	Hugh Baiocchi (SA)	67	72	72	79	290	342.55
31	Armando Saavedra (ARG)	77	73	70	71	291	297.87
	Peter Dawson	76	69	71	75	291	297.87
	Salvador Balbuena (S)	71	73	70	77	291	297.87
34	John O'Leary (IRE)	75	73	76	68	292	253.19
	Harold Henning (SA)	74	74	72	72	292	253.19
	Bernhard Langer (G)	76	72	72	72	292	253.19
	Jeff Hawkes (SA)	69	78	69	76	292	253.19
	Nick Job	72	73	72	75	292	253.19
40	Gavin Levenson (SA)	69	74	71	78	292	253.19
	Gar Hamilton (C)	73	75	73	74	293	210.17
	Garry Cullen	73	74	73	73	293	210.17
	Jamie Benito (S)	73	74	74	72	293	210.17
43	Bob Wynn	71	77	75	71	294	186.17
	J. Jiminez (S)	75	74	72	73	294	186.17
	José Rivero (S)	72	73	75	74	294	186.17
	Manuel Pinero (S)	73	73	74	74	294	186.17
	Ian Mosey	76	67	75	76	294	186.17
	J. Mangas (S)	74	74	69	77	294	186.17
49	José Cabo (S)	73	77	73	72	295	153.90
	Manuel Ramos (S)	74	75	72	74	295	153.90
	David Vaughan	73	73	73	76	295	153.90
	Garry Harvey	71	75	73	76	295	153.90
	Derrick Cooper	74	68	72	81	295	153.90
	Manuel Cabrera (S)	73	76	73	73	295	153.90
	Bill Longmuir	74	72	75	74	295	153.90
56	Peter Townsend	74	74	75	73	296	129.08
	Manuel Calero (S)	74	70	73	79	296	129.08
	Eamonn Darcy	71	72	78	75	296	129.08
	Tommy Horton	76	74	73	73	296	129.08
59	Tienie Britz (SA)	76	74	73	74	297	116.67
	Peter Berry	71	77	75	74	297	116.67
61	Sam Torrance	75	72	77	74	298	106.74
	Valentin Barrios (S)	73	74	75	76	298	106.74
63	Guy Hunt	74	75	70	81	300	96.81
	Emilio Rodriguez (S)	72	74	73	81	300	96.81
65	Patricio Garrido (S)	74	76	74	79	303	44.68
	Vince Baker (SA)	74	74	77	78	303	44.68
67	Juan Anglada (S)	79	71	80	75	305	–
68	Gunnar Mueller (SWE)	73	77	76	82	308	–
69	David Chillas	76	74	80	87	317	–

Previous winners

Year	Winner	Venue
1951	M. Provencio	Madrid
1952	M. Faulkner	Madrid
1953	M. Faulkner	Madrid
1954	S. Miguel	Madrid
1955	H. de Lamaze	Madrid
1956	P. Alliss	Barcelona
1957	M. Faulkner	Madrid
1958	P. Alliss	Madrid
1959	P.W. Thomson	Barcelona
1960	S. Miguel	Madrid
1961	A. Miguel	Madrid
1962	No championship	
1963	R. Sota	Barcelona
1964	A. Miguel	Santa Cruz

Year	Winner	Venue
1965	No championship	
1966	R. de Vicenzo	Sotogrande
1967	S. Miguel	Barcelona
1968	R. Shaw	Bilbao
1969	J. Garaialde	Madrid
1970	A. Gallardo	Neuva Andalucia
1971	D. Hayes	Barcelona
1972	A. Garrido	Gerona
1973	N. Coles	La Manga
1974	J. Heard	La Manga
1975	A. Palmer	La Manga
1976	E. Polland	La Manga
1977	B.J. Gallacher	La Manga
1978	B.W. Barnes	Barcelona

THE MADRID OPEN CHAMPIONSHIP

Real Club de la Puerta de Hierro, Madrid 26–29 April 1979 Prize Money £33,000

Simon Hobday was a start-to-finish leader in Madrid where he recorded his first victory in Europe since the 1976 German Open. With his British winnings frozen by the Bank of England, the Rhodesian's victory on the Continent was timely. He shared the first round lead with Bernard Gallacher and Hugh Baiocchi, the second round with the Spaniards Abreu and Montes, and after three rounds was two shots clear of Michael King. After having missed the cut the previous week in the Spanish Open, Ballesteros was in close contention throughout, but was unable to produce a really telling round. Gordon Brand's joint-second with Abreu was his best since he turned professional in 1976.

							£
1	Simon Hobday (ZIM)	67	73	71	74	285	5,514.71
2	Gordon Brand	69	73	76	69	287	2,463.24
	Tienie Britz(SA)	73	76	69	69	287	2,463.24
	Francisco Abreu(S)	70	70	74	73	287	2,463.24
5	Bernard Gallacher	67	76	73	72	288	1,404.41
6	Salvador Balbuena(S)	75	77	70	67	289	992.65
	Hugh Baiocchi(SA)	67	74	75	73	289	992.65
	Michael King	70	72	71	76	289	992.65

							£
9	José-Maria Canizares(S)	74	74	71	71	290	661.76
	Antonio Garrido(S)	73	74	68	75	290	661.76
12	Severiano Ballesteros(S)	73	74	68	75	290	661.76
	Manuel Montes (S)	71	69	81	70	291	513.24
	Vince Baker(SA)	73	73	73	72	291	513.24
	Nick Job	72	72	74	73	291	513.24

						£
Manuel Calero(S)	72	74	71	74	291	513.24
Vicente Fernandez(ARG)	74	74	68	75	291	513.24
17 Ken Brown	69	75	74	74	292	448.53
18 Valentin Barrios(S)	73	78	73	69	293	404.41
Maurice Bembridge	72	79	72	70	293	404.41
Gavin Levenson(SA)	74	75	70	74	293	404.41
Malcolm Gregson	74	75	68	76	293	404.41
22 Gunnar Mueller(SWE)	72	77	77	70	294	351.73
Philip Elson	75	77	71	71	294	351.73
Sam Torrance	77	74	70	73	294	351.73
Dale Hayes(SA)	69	79	72	74	294	351.73
Peter Townsend	70	79	70	75	294	351.73
José Rivero(S)	73	74	71	76	294	351.73
28 Bobby Verwey(SA)	75	74	73	73	295	305.15
Manuel Ramos(S)	72	75	74	74	295	305.15
Gar Hamilton(C)	75	77	69	74	295	305.15
Jeff Hall	74	77	70	74	295	305.15
32 Bernhard Langer(G)	76	73	75	72	296	275.74
Nick Price(SA)	74	73	75	74	296	275.74
John Fourie(SA)	72	77	73	74	296	275.74
Peter Dawson	76	72	72	76	296	275.74
36 Garry Cullen	74	77	76	70	297	253.68
John Bland(SA)	77	74	71	75	297	253.68
38 Martin Poxon	74	72	74	78	298	242.65
39 Manuel Ballesteros(S)	72	76	80	72	300	221.51

						£
Garry Harvey	72	81	72	75	300	221.51
Bill Longmuir	72	80	75	73	300	221.51
Rafe Botts(USA)	73	74	75	78	300	221.51
43 Nigel Blenkarne	77	76	77	71	301	191.18
Jaime Benito(S)	75	75	76	75	301	191.18
Howard Clark	75	77	72	77	301	191.18
Martin Foster	74	77	74	77	301	191.18
48 Armando Saavedra(ARG)	76	77	74	74	302	153.82
Manuel Sanchez(S)	77	76	81	73	302	153.82
Donald Armour	72	81	74	75	302	153.82
Keith Waters	76	75	75	76	302	153.82
Derrick Cooper	75	76	75	76	302	153.82
German Garrido(S)	72	77	76	77	302	153.82
Harold Henning(SA)	74	76	73	79	303	132.35
54 Manuel Garcia(S)	75	76	75	77	304	114.89
José Blas(S)	75	78	74	77	304	114.89
55 John O'Leary(IRE)	71	76	79	78	304	114.89
Bill McColl	78	76	77	73	304	114.89
Jimmy Heggarty	72	76	77	79	304	114.89
59 Horacio Carbonetti(ARG)	78	75	75	75	305	102.94
60 Ian Mosey	72	76	81	77	306	99.26
61 Michael Miller	78	74	81	74	307	91.91
James Edman(USA)	77	74	77	79	307	91.91
Robbie Stewart(SA)	77	76	74	80	307	91.91
64 J. Simarro(S)	76	75	79	78	308	84.56

Previous Winners

Year	Winner	Venue	Score
1968	G. Garrido	Madrid	279
1969	R. Sota	Madrid	278
1970	M. Cabrera	Madrid	286
1971	V. Barrios	Madrid	286
1972	J. Kinsella	Madrid	283
1973	G. Garrido	Madrid	287

Year	Winner	Venue	Score
1974	M. Pinero	Madrid	283
	After a tie with V. Barrios		
1975	R. Shearer	Madrid	135
	Rain restricted to 36 holes		
1976	F. Abreu	Madrid	275
1977	A. Garrido	Madrid	278
1978	H. Clark	Madrid	282

THE ITALIAN OPEN CHAMPIONSHIP

Monticello Golf Club, Como   3–6 May 1979   Prize Money £33,500

If patience was one of Brian Barnes's virtues it was well rewarded when the Italian Open returned to Monticello, for it was there he finished second to Billy Casper in 1975 and lost a play-off with Angel Gallardo for first place in 1977. This time he needed another play-off before justice was finally done. But he was taken to the fourth extra hole by South Africa's Dale Hayes before ensuring the first prize of £5,500. Three birdies and an eagle in the last seven holes highlighted Barnes's final round of 67 and a seven-under 281, while Hayes three-putted 17 when eight under. Michael King, leading for three rounds, had his best tournament since turning professional.

Pos	Player					Total	£
1	Brian Barnes	73	70	71	67	281	5,582.39
2	Dale Hayes(SA)	73	69	71	68	281	3,724.43

Barnes won play-off at fourth extra hole

Pos	Player					Total	£
3	Sam Torrance	72	73	69	70	284	1,886.36
	Vicente Fernandez(ARG)	72	74	67	71	284	1,886.36
5	Severiano Ballesteros(S)	73	72	68	72	285	1,109.52
	Antonio Garrido(S)	73	73	68	71	285	1,109.52
	Tony Jacklin	79	67	68	71	285	1,109.52
	Ben Crenshaw(USA)	74	70	68	73	285	1,109.52
9	Brian Waites	72	71	71	72	286	711.08
	Michael King	70	71	71	74	286	711.08
11	Delio Lovato(I)	71	72	71	73	287	622.16
12	Malcolm Gregson	75	70	69	75	289	555.30
	Gar Hamilton(C)	73	75	70	71	289	555.30
	Sandy Lyle	71	76	70	72	289	555.30
15	Gordon Brand	73	74	74	69	290	483.52
	Garry Cullen	72	74	74	70	290	483.52
17	Massimo Mannelli(I)	70	77	73	71	291	445.46
18	Baldovino Dassu(I)	75	72	75	70	292	410.51
	Harold Henning(SA)	76	69	75	72	292	410.51
	Silvano Locatelli(I)	73	72	74	73	292	410.51
	Roberto Bernardini(I)	76	73	70	73	292	410.51
22	Eddie Polland	73	74	70	73	293	359.09
	John O'Leary(IRE)	76	73	73	71	293	359.09
	Manuel Pinero(S)	78	71	72	72	293	359.09
	Nick Price(SA)	78	69	74	72	293	359.09
	Noel Ratcliffe(AUS)	77	72	71	73	293	359.09
28	Robbie Stewart(SA)	74	74	71	74	294	311.08
	Simon Hobday(ZIM)	76	73	73	72	294	311.08
	Juan Anglada(S)	71	72	76	75	294	311.08
	Salvador Balbuena(S)	72	73	73	76	294	311.08
	Denis Watson(SA)	73	73	72	76	294	311.08
32	Glenn Ralph	74	75	76	70	295	258.52
	Dennis Durnian	77	74	72	72	295	258.52
	Angel Gallardo(S)	75	72	74	74	295	258.52
	John Colwell(C)	73	76	72	74	295	258.52
	Bobby Verwey(SA)	75	74	71	75	295	258.52
	John Bland(SA)	77	71	72	75	295	258.52
	Bill Longmuir	72	73	72	78	295	258.52
39	E. Della Torre(I)	77	73	75	71	296	203.98
	James Edman(USA)	76	70	76	74	296	203.98
	John Fourie(SA)	72	73	76	75	296	203.98
	Geromalo Delfino(I)	72	75	73	76	296	203.98
	Hugh Baiocchi(SA)	77	77	69	77	296	203.98
44	Tommy Horton	74	77	74	72	297	182.01
	Nick Faldo	73	76	75	73	297	182.01
	David A. Russell	74	72	78	73	297	182.01
47	Keith Waters	75	72	79	72	298	165.06

	Name					Total	£
	Manuel Ramos(S)	75	75	77	71	298	165.06
	Nick Job	76	72	76	74	298	165.06
	Manuel Calero(S)	72	71	77	78	298	165.06
51	Peter Senior(AUS)	79	69	79	72	299	150.86
	Gunnar Mueller(SWE)	75	76	73	75	299	150.86
53	Pietro Molteni(I)	76	75	77	72	300	134.09
	Anthony Charnley	72	78	75	75	300	134.09
	Ian Woosnam	76	74	75	75	300	134.09
	Bernhard Langer(G)	78	69	77	76	300	134.09
	Rafe Botts(USA)	76	71	73	80	300	134.09

	Name					Total	£
58	Donald Armour	78	71	74	78	301	114.96
	Luciano Grappasonni(I)	74	75	73	79	301	114.96
61	Ian Mosey	77	72	72	80	301	114.96
	Vince Baker(SA)	76	71	79	76	302	105.11
62	Trevor Powell	75	75	80	73	303	98.30
	Vance Waters	76	74	75	78	303	98.30
64	David Vaughan	73	75	81	75	304	90.91
65	Philip Kilgour	77	74	79	77	307	86.36
66	Bassili Karatzas(GR)	72	77	81	80	310	–

Previous Winners

Year	Winner	Venue	Score
1947	F. van Donck	San Remo	263
1948	A. Casera	San Remo	267
1949	H. Hassanein	Villa d'Este	263
1950	U. Grappasonni	Rome	281
	After a tie with A. Angelini		
1951	J. Adams	Milan	289
1952	E.C. Brown	Milan	273
1953	F. van Donck	Como	267
1954	U. Grappasonni	Villa d'Este	272
	After a tie with J.R.M. Jacobs		
1955	F. van Donck	Venice	287
1956	A. Cerda	Monza	–
	After a tie with F. van Donck		
1957	H. Henning	Villa d'Este	273
1958	P. Alliss	Varese	282
1959	P.W. Thomson	Villa d'Este	269
1960	B.B.S. Wilkes	Venice	285
	Discontinued until 1971		
1971	R. Sota	Garlenda	282
1972	N. Wood	Villa d'Este	271
1973	A. Jacklin	Rome	284
1974	P. Oosterhuis	Venice (63 holes)	249
1975	B. Casper	Como	286
1976	B. Dassu	Sardinia	280
1977	A. Gallardo	Como	286
1978	D. Hayes	Sardinia	293

THE FRENCH OPEN CHAMPIONSHIP

Golf Club de Lyon   10–13 May 1979   Prize Money £33,500

The Championship was overshadowed by the death of Spain's Salvador Balbuena at the age of only 29. On the eve of the event the former winner of the Portuguese Open and Moroccan Grand Prix collapsed and died in a Lyon restaurant. Vicente Fernandez, a fugitive from the US tour, dominated the early stages with an improving Tony Jacklin, but it was a Scot who eventually won the day, this time Bernard Gallacher who notched his first big win since the 1977 Spanish Open. He was pressed home by another Scot, Willie Milne whose hole-in-one at the 15th eventually earned him a Mercedes car which, according to the programme, was his due.

Pos	Name					Total	£
1	Bernard Gallacher	71	69	74	70	284	5,945.37
2	Willie Milne	76	70	67	72	285	3,960.42
3	Severiano Ballesteros (S)	73	74	71	68	286	2,008.08
	Hugh Baiocchi (SA)	73	69	69	75	286	2,008.08
5	Bill Longmuir	71	69	78	70	288	1,278.33
	Nick Faldo	72	72	73	71	288	1,278.33
	David Chillas	76	72	68	72	288	1,278.33
8	Eamonn Darcy (IRE)	74	69	71	75	289	891.86
9	Dale Hayes (SA)	73	74	73	70	290	673.35
	Garry Cullen	74	70	75	71	290	673.35
	Noel Ratcliffe (AUS)	75	72	71	72	290	673.35
	Tony Jacklin	70	70	77	73	290	673.35
	Gary Player (SA)	75	68	73	74	290	673.35
14	Manuel Calero (S)	73	74	72	72	291	503.45
	Angel Gallardo (S)	73	73	72	73	291	503.45
	Tienie Britz (SA)	73	68	76	74	291	503.45
	Bobby Verwey (SA)	74	74	68	75	291	503.45
	Vicente Fernandez (ARG)	70	69	75	77	291	503.45
19	Gordon Brand	78	71	74	69	292	415.27
	Jeff Hall	77	70	74	71	292	415.27
	John Fourie (SA)	73	73	74	72	292	415.27
	Francisco Abreu (S)	74	71	74	73	292	415.27
	John Bland (SA)	73	70	75	74	292	415.27
	Terry Kendall (NZ)	74	70	74	74	292	415.27
	Eddie Polland	74	72	71	75	292	415.27
26	Garry Harvey	74	72	76	71	293	350.33
	Peter Townsend	75	71	75	72	293	350.33
	Robbie Stewart (SA)	76	71	73	73	293	350.33
	Noel Hunt	76	70	72	75	293	350.33
30	Bernard Pascassio (F)	76	73	73	72	294	309.36
	Greg Norman (AUS)	71	71	77	75	294	309.36
	Nick Price (SA)	75	66	78	75	294	309.36
33	Wayne Grady (AUS)	78	70	73	74	295	269.78
	Jan Sonnevi (SWE)	75	72	73	75	295	269.78
	Philippe Toussaint (B)	74	73	73	75	295	269.78
	Joe Higgins	73	71	73	78	295	269.78
37	Ewen Murray	75	74	71	76	296	247.21
	Keith Waters	72	74	72	78	296	247.21
39	Malcolm Gregson	72	76	76	73	297	217.18
	Michael King	77	72	74	73	297	217.18
	Sam Torrance	78	72	74	73	297	217.18
	Mark James	72	72	75	74	297	217.18
	Juan Anglada (S)	73	75	75	74	297	217.18
	Manuel Ballesteros (S)	75-	73	74	75	297	217.18
	Michel Damiano (F)	76	74	71	76	297	217.18
	Gavin Levenson (SA)	75	73	72	77	297	217.18
47	Rafe Botts (USA)	76	70	77	75	298	180.74
	Horacio Carbonetti (ARG)	77	68	77	76	298	180.74
	Ken Brown	73	75	74	76	298	180.74
	Donald Armour	74	76	71	77	298	180.74
51	Ian Mosey	75	72	79	73	299	157.32
	Bernhard Langer (G)	77	71	75	76	299	157.32
	Tony Charnley	76	73	73	76	299	157.32
	R. Darrieumerlou (F)	74	72	71	82	299	157.32
55	Tommy Horton	75	75	75	75	300	139.63
	Peter Cowen	76	74	74	76	300	139.63
57	Mike Miller	72	75	79	75	301	122.07
	Stephen Cipa*	76	74	75	76	301	–
	Dennis Durnian	71	79	75	76	301	122.07
	Mike Inglis	74	72	78	77	301	122.07
	Vaughan Somers (AUS)	75	69	74	83	301	122.07
61	Glenn Ralph	76	72	79	75	302	101.63
	John Whitehead	75	75	75	77	302	101.63
	Manuel Garcia (S)	75	74	74	79	302	101.63
64	L. Capoccia (F)	77	73	74	79	303	87.23
	Gery Watine (F)	75	73	75	80	303	87.23
66	José Hunchak (ARG)	76	74	77	77	304	–
	Andrew Chandler	76	72	77	79	304	–
68	Michael Daly (C)	76	74	74	83	307	–
69	G. Boucher (F)	74	76	80	81	311	–

*Amateur

Previous Winners

Year	Winner	Venue	Score
1951	H. Hassanein	St Cloud	273
1952	A.D. Locke	St Germain	268
1953	A.D. Locke	La Boulie	276
1954	F. van Donck	St Cloud	275
1955	B. Nelson	La Boulie	271
1956	A. Miguel	Deauville	277
1957	F. van Donck	St Cloud	266
1958	F. van Donck	St Germain	276
After a tie with H. Henning			
1959	D.C. Thomas	La Boulie	276
1960	R. de Vicenzo	St Cloud	275
1961	K.D.G. Nagle	La Boulie	271
1962	A. Murray	St Germain	274
1963	B. Devlin	St Cloud	273
1964	R. de Vicenzo	Chantilly	272
After a tie with C.L. Le Grange			
1965	R. Sota	St Nom-la-Breteche	268
1966	D.J. Hutchinson	La Boulie	274
1967	B.J. Hunt	St Germain	271
1968	P.J. Butler	St Cloud	272
1969	J. Garaialde	St Nom-la-Breteche	277
After a tie with R. de Vicenzo			
1970	D. Graham	Chantaco	268
1971	Lu Liang-Huan	Biarritz	262
1972	B. Jaeckel	La Nivelle and Biarritz	265
1973	P. Oosterhuis	La Vallee and La Foret, Paris	280
1974	P. Oosterhuis	Chantilly	284
1975	B. Barnes	La Boulie	281
1976	V. Tshabalala	Le Touquet	272
1977	S. Ballesteros	Le Touquet	282
1978	D. Hayes	La Baule	269

THE COLGATE PGA CHAMPIONSHIP

The Old Course, St Andrews, Scotland   17–20 May 1979   Prize Money £50,000

After an abortive attempt to make an impact on the US circuit, the diminutive Vicente Fernandez from Argentina emulated South Africa's Dale Hayes and returned to become a winner again in Europe. PGA Champion seemed a title no one wanted to win. The holder Nick Faldo soared into the first-round lead with a record-equalling 65 and had four shots in hand at midway. He fell away in difficult third round conditions and was caught by Fernandez, a shot behind US Open Champion Andy North, Gordon Brand and Ireland's Des Smyth. A bleak cold windy final day saw Gary Player make a steady but vain bid for the title while Faldo, North, and Co. disappeared into the high 70s. Barnes had the best chance but finished with three fives, and Vicente's 75 won the day with a level-par 288.

Pos	Name					Total	£
1	Vicente Fernandez (ARG)	71	70	72	75	288	8,330.00
2	Gary Player (SA)	73	72	71	73	289	4,340.00
	Baldovino Dassu (I)	71	70	74	74	289	4,340.00
4	Brian Barnes	71	71	72	76	290	2,310.00
	Gordon Brand	68	74	70	78	290	2,310.00
6	Raymond Floyd (USA)	74	75	71	71	291	1,405.00
	Philip Elson	70	71	76	74	291	1,405.00
	Andy North (USA)	69	70	73	79	291	1,405.00
	Des Smyth (IRE)	70	70	79	72	291	1,405.00
10	Neil Coles	71	73	76	72	292	870.00
	Severiano Ballesteros (S)	70	72	75	75	292	870.00
	Greg Norman (AUS)	72	70	75	75	292	870.00
	Eddie Polland	70	72	72	78	292	870.00
	Nick Faldo	65	70	78	79	292	870.00
15	Brian Huggett	74	71	76	73	294	690.00
	John Morgan	73	73	74	74	294	690.00
	Garry Cullen	69	77	73	75	294	690.00
	Howard Clark	72	74	70	78	294	690.00
19	Martin Poxon	73	72	76	74	295	586.00
	Nick Job	68	78	75	74	295	586.00
	Peter Oosterhuis	74	75	72	74	295	586.00
	Vince Baker (SA)	73	75	70	77	295	586.00
	John Fowler	71	75	71	78	295	586.00
24	Michael King	74	73	73	76	296	525.00
	Sandy Walker	73	70	75	78	296	525.00
	John Fourie (SA)	72	71	75	78	296	525.00
27	Doug McClelland	73	74	77	73	297	457.50
	Willie Milne	74	71	75	77	297	457.50
	Rodger Davis (AUS)	71	73	78	75	297	457.50
	Tienie Britz (SA)	72	74	74	77	297	457.50
	Ken Brown	75	71	73	78	297	457.50
	Ewen Murray	72	74	73	78	297	457.50
33	Hugh Baiocchi (SA)	72	74	74	78	298	395.00
	David A. Russell	75	74	75	74	298	395.00
	Donald Armour	71	76	76	75	298	395.00
	Bob Charles (NZ)	71	77	71	79	298	395.00
37	Dennis Durnian	73	75	79	72	299	335.00
	Tommy Horton	74	75	75	75	299	335.00
	John Bland (SA)	71	73	77	78	299	335.00
	Bobby Verwey (SA)	74	74	73	78	299	335.00
	Peter Townsend	74	75	72	78	299	335.00
	Francisco Abreu (S)	74	74	72	79	299	335.00
	Peter Cowen	73	73	73	80	299	335.00
	David Jagger	71	75	73	80	299	335.00
45	Angel Gallardo (S)	74	75	78	73	300	275.00
	Andrew Chandler	75	74	78	73	300	275.00
	Noel Hunt	74	72	75	79	300	275.00
	Bernhard Langer (G)	74	73	73	80	300	275.00
49	Dale Hayes (SA)	72	74	79	76	301	220.00
	Peter Senior (AUS)	72	77	75	77	301	220.00
	Mark James	72	75	80	74	301	220.00
	Sam Torrance	70	79	76	76	301	220.00
	Simon Owen (NZ)	71	74	78	78	301	220.00
	Denis Watson (SA)	76	73	74	78	301	220.00
	Robin Fyfe	74	75	72	80	301	220.00
56	Bernard Gallacher	73	72	77	80	302	175.00
	David Ingram	73	74	75	80	302	175.00
58	Alan Mew (TRI)	75	73	78	77	303	152.50
	Peter Headland (AUS)	73	78	76	76	303	152.50
	Maurice Bembridge	73	73	77	80	303	152.50
	David Vaughan	74	74	74	81	303	152.50
62	Robbie Stewart (SA)	72	75	79	78	304	88.33
	Garry Harvey	77	69	78	80	304	88.33
	Gavin Levenson (SA)	73	75	76	80	304	88.33
	John O'Leary (IRE)	74	76	74	80	304	88.33
	David Chillas	72	76	75	81	304	88.33
	Alastair Thomson	76	72	74	82	304	88.33
68	Simon Cox	70	72	77	86	305	—
69	Peter Butler	73	75	79	79	306	—
	Butch Baird (USA)	72	74	78	82	306	—
71	Juan Cabrera (ARG)	72	74	80	81	307	—
72	Jeff Hall	74	71	81	82	308	—
	Harold Henning (SA)	73	72	81	82	308	—
74	Stuart Brown	71	76	77	86	310	—
75	Alistair McLean	73	75	79	84	311	—
76	Gregor Jamieson	72	77	80	85	314	—
77	Basilio Hunchak (ARG)	75	74	82	85	316	—

For previous winners of the PGA title see Championship Rolls

Golf's most coveted award

All over the world, this beautiful prize is awarded by golfers to other golfers at the 19th hole.
All you have to do to win one, is to finish your round.

The right one MARTINI

ROSSO·EXTRA DRY·BIANCO·ROSÉ

THE MARTINI INTERNATIONAL TOURNAMENT

NORMAN SAYS 'SAME AGAIN'

A break with tradition took the long-established Martini International Tournament back to Wentworth in Surrey, scene of Christy O'Connor's victory in 1964. It was the first time that the event, launched in 1961, had been staged twice at one venue.

It proved to be another Norman Conquest for Australia when Greg Norman, the six-foot blond Queenslander, took the title for the second time in three years. Greg, who had won at Blairgowrie in Scotland in 1977, won a nerve-stretching victory over Antonio Garrido and John Morgan by the narrowest of one-shot margins. His was the sixth Australian victory in the tournament. Peter Thomson had won in 1962 and 1970, Stewart Ginn in 1974, and Ian Stanley had shared first place in 1975.

Morgan, enjoying a rewarding season which had already included victories in the Nigeria and Lusaka Opens, but without a victory in Europe, blazed the early trail with an opening 69. It was a mixture of the good and the bad, containing as it did seven birdies and four bogeys, and gave him a stroke lead over the newly-turned professional Robbie Stewart from South Africa, with Terry Kendall of New Zealand and Ken Brown a further stroke away. Norman was back on 75.

Bank Holiday Saturday was rewarded with torrential and persistent rain which meant the second round had to be abandoned at mid-day. Spectators were generously refunded their admission money, but the only really happy man around was Martin Foster who had holed in one at the fifth, moments before the abandonment. For Foster a case of champagne! Norman began his charge when play resumed the following day. Out early, he swept round in a five-under-par 67, getting home in 32 with an eagle three at the 12th and birdies at the 13th and 18th.

Morgan held on to his lead covering the last nine holes in 34 after a nervous outward 38, and his halfway 141 led by one stroke from Norman and two from Brown.

Two rounds on the scheduled final day meant a 6.45am start to the third round – and a two-strokes penalty for Brian Barnes for being late on the tee. The news, given verbally to the big Scot on the fourth tee, coincided a moment later with the disappearance into an adjacent garden of the tee box!

Norman's par-72 in the wind and the rain and with the West Course 'Burma Road' playing to its full length, was sound enough to give him the mid-day lead, but he had to battle to hold on in the afternoon. He was bunkered and took five at the seventh, and had an unplayable lie at the ninth for a six, but he finished on a high note with a birdie at the 18th and a level-par winning total of 288 after Garrido had set the target at one shot higher.

THE MARTINI INTERNATIONAL TOURNAMENT

Wentworth Golf Club, Surrey   25–28 May 1979   Prize Money £42,000

								£
1	Greg Norman (AUS)	75	67	74	72	288		7,000.00
2	Antonio Garrido (S)	73	71	73	72	289		3,645.00
	John Morgan	69	72	74	74	289		3,645.00
4	Tienie Britz (SA)	75	71	69	76	291		1,783.33
	Vicente Fernandez (ARG)	73	71	74	73	291		1,783.33
	Ken Brown	71	72	73	75	291		1,783.33
7	Severiano Ballesteros (S)	75	75	70	72	292		1,155.00
	Mark James	74	70	72	76	292		1,155.00
9	Michael King	73	76	72	72	293		940.00
10	Nick Job	75	73	73	73	294		786.66
	Brian Barnes	75	69	79	71	294		786.66
	Tommy Horton	74	70	75	75	294		786.66
13	Rodger Davis (AUS)	78	72	72	73	295		622.00
	Harold Henning (SA)	80	69	74	72	295		622.00
	Nick Price (SA)	72	76	74	73	295		622.00
	Garry Cullen	74	74	74	73	295		622.00
	Gavin Levenson (SA)	75	70	74	76	295		622.00
18	Robbie Stewart (SA)	70	76	77	73	296		540.00
	Warren Humphreys	72	72	76	76	296		540.00
20	Guy Hunt	75	73	74	75	297		490.00
	Dale Hayes (SA)	75	72	74	76	297		490.00
	David Jagger	76	69	78	74	297		490.00
23	John Fourie (SA)	78	72	73	75	298		431.00
	Peter Tupling	76	74	73	75	298		431.00
	David Good (AUS)	73	71	76	78	298		431.00
	Tony Jacklin (GB)	75	69	77	77	298		431.00
	Andries Oosthuizen (SA)	73	71	74	79	298		431.00
28	Brian Waites	74	74	74	77	299		375.00
	Neil Coles	74	74	76	75	299		375.00
	Peter Butler	73	75	74	77	299		375.00
	Manuel Ballesteros (S)	74	73	76	76	299		375.00
	Manuel Pinero (S)	72	74	70	83	299		375.00
	Peter Berry	75	70	78	76	299		375.00
34	Sam Torrance	78	70	76	76	300		340.00
35	Eamonn Darcy (IRE)	77	72	75	77	301		320.00
	Vaughan Somers (AUS)	75	74	75	77	301		320.00
	Malcolm Gregson	76	72	74	79	301		320.00
38	Hugh Baiocchi (SA)	75	73	76	78	302		300.00
39	Brian Huggett	76	73	79	75	303		285.00
	Martin Foster	74	75	79	75	303		285.00
41	Maurice Bembridge	74	73	78	79	304		260.00
	Peter Cowen	72	75	78	79	304		260.00
	Ian Mosey	74	73	77	80	304		260.00
44	Robin Mann	75	72	79	79	305		240.00
45	Anthony Charnley	77	72	81	76	306		230.00
46	Juan Cabrera (ARG)	77	72	70	78	307		220.00
47	Derrick Cooper	74	76	79	79	308		205.00
	Bob Charles (NZ)	73	76	83	76	308		205.00
49	Simon Owen (NZ)	75	75	84	75	309		195.00
50	Philip Loxley	76	75	82	78	310		190.00
51	John Fowler	76	73	79	85	313		185.00

Previous Winners

Year	Winner	Venue	Score
1961	B. J. Hunt	Sundridge Park	270
	After a tie with G. W. Low		
1962	P. Thomson	St Andrews	275
1963	C. O'Connor	Hoylake	298
	N. C. Coles		
1964	C. O'Connor	Wentworth	286
1965	P. J. Butler	Little Aston	275
1966	P. Alliss	Long Ashton	275
	W. Large		
1967	M. E. Gregson	Fulford	279

Year	Winner	Venue	Score
1968	B. C. G. Huggett	Southerndown	278
1969	B. C. G. Huggett	Queens Park	282
	G. Henning		
	A. Caygill		
1970	P. Thomson	Conway	284
	D. Sewell		
1971	B. Gallacher	Royal Norwich	282
1972	B. Barnes	Abridge	277
1973	M. Bembridge	Barnton	279
1974	S. Ginn	Pannal	286
1975	I. E. Stanley	Westward Ho!	279
	C. O'Connor Jr		
1976	S. Torrance	Ashburnham	280
1977	G. Norman	Blairgowrie	277
1978	S. Ballesteros	RAC Epsom	270

THE BRITISH AIRWAYS/AVIS OPEN

La Moye Golf Club, Jersey   31 May–3 June 1979   Prize Money £30,000

Sandy Lyle, only a little over 21, registered his first big win as a professional in sunny Jersey, lurking constantly behind early leaders Tony Jacklin and Bernard Gallacher and surging to a three-shots victory with a closing 68 for a winning aggregate of 13-under-par. But it was a third round of 66 that put the former Walker Cup international, English Stroke-Play, and British Youths' champion on the road to victory. It cut Bernard Gallacher's four-stroke halfway lead to a single margin, and in the vital last round Bernard never recovered from dropping three shots in the first four holes. Sandy was to taste more success as the season unfolded.

Pos	Player	R1	R2	R3	R4	Total	£
1	Sandy Lyle	66	71	66	68	271	5,000.00
2	Howard Clark	70	68	69	67	274	3,300.00
3	Sam Torrance	69	69	72	65	275	1,425.00
	Tony Jacklin	64	75	68	68	275	1,425.00
	Bernard Gallacher	64	69	69	73	275	1,425.00
	Michael King	69	70	67	69	275	1,425.00
7	Hugh Baiocchi (SA)	68	71	71	66	276	773.33
	Noel Ratcliffe (AUS)	70	70	70	66	276	773.33
	Bob Charles (NZ)	72	68	69	67	276	773.33
10	Peter Cowen	70	72	71	64	277	600.00
11	Brian Huggett	69	69	72	68	278	535.00
	Manuel Pinero (S)	73	70	66	69	278	535.00
13	Jeff Hawkes (SA)	68	71	69	71	279	490.00
14	Peter Headland (AUS)	72	72	68	68	280	409.28
	Eddie Polland	67	73	71	69	280	409.28
	James Edman (USA)	70	74	67	69	280	409.28
	Baldovino Dassu (I)	66	70	70	71	280	409.28
	Gavin Levenson (SA)	66	71	72	71	280	409.28
	Peter Townsend	69	71	69	71	280	409.28
	Willie Milne	68	69	68	75	280	409.28
21	Robin Mann	73	71	72	65	281	345.00
	Des Smyth (IRE)	69	74	69	69	281	345.00
	Rodger Davis (AUS)	69	71	72	69	281	345.00
	Peter Tupling	69	70	69	73	281	345.00
25	Eamonn Darcy (IRE)	66	76	71	69	282	305.00
	Mark McNulty (SA)	68	70	74	70	282	305.00
	Dale Hayes (SA)	69	68	74	71	282	305.00

							£
	Christy O'Connor Jr (IRE)	67	73	70	72	282	305.00
29	Greg Norman (AUS)	72	71	70	70	283	280.00
30	John Hay	68	72	74	70	284	260.00
	John Fourie (SA)	75	69	69	71	284	260.00
	John Morgan	72	70	70	72	284	260.00
33	Malcolm Gregson	71	71	73	70	285	235.00
	Jeff Hall	73	71	70	71	285	235.00
35	Nick Price (SA)	71	75	72	68	286	212.50
	Ian Mosey	73	73	71	69	286	212.50
	Glenn Ralph	70	72	75	69	286	212.50
	Carl Mason	70	73	70	73	286	212.50
39	Guy Hunt	72	72	72	71	287	192.50
	Keith Waters	71	74	72	70	287	192.50
	David Good (AUS)	70	75	71	71	287	192.50
	Nick Job	72	68	74	73	287	192.50
43	Rafe Botts (USA)	69	77	72	70	288	165.00
	Martin Foster	70	70	71	77	288	165.00
	Stephen Rolley	73	71	73	71	288	165.00
	Maurice Bembridge	73	72	71	72	288	165.00
	Garry Harvey	71	72	72	73	288	165.00
	Bobby Verwey (SA)	71	71	73	73	288	165.00
	Bobby Lincoln (SA)	72	72	68	76	288	165.00
50	John Fowler	74	71	72	72	289	142.50
	Brian Waites	72	73	72	72	289	142.50
52	Peter Senior (AUS)	71	71	78	70	290	122.50
	Horacio Carbonetti (ARG)	73	72	75	70	290	122.50
	David Robertson	67	77	74	72	290	122.50
	Adan Sowa (ARG)	70	73	75	72	290	122.50
	David A. Russell	75	74	71	73	290	122.50
	Trevor Powell	70	74	70	76	290	122.50
58	Christopher Moody	74	71	74	72	291	97.50
	Craig Defoy	69	75	76	71	291	97.50
	Juan Cabrera (ARG)	73	72	79	67	291	97.50
	Richard Eyles	73	73	70	75	291	97.50
62	Peter Dawson	70	74	74	74	292	82.50
	Vin Baker (SA)	73	70	75	74	292	82.50
64	Tienie Britz (SA)	70	72	77	74	293	36.25
	Gary Potter	72	70	80	71	293	36.25
	Andries Oosthuizen (SA)	69	77	77	70	293	36.25
	Peter Wilcock	73	72	71	77	293	36.25
68	Michael Gallagher	72	73	74	76	295	–
69	Peter Seal	71	74	77	75	297	–
70	Roy Stephenson	76	70	74	78	298	–
71	Charles Dernie	74	71	76	78	299	–
72	Philip Morley	75	71	81	74	301	–

Previous Winner

Year	Winner	Venue	Score
1978	B.G.C. Huggett	Jersey	271

THE BELGIAN OPEN CHAMPIONSHIP

Royal Waterloo Golf Club, Brussels   7–10 June 1979   Prize Money £32,300

Gavin Levenson turned professional in November 1978 soon after finishing second to Hugh Baiocchi in his native South African Open Championship, and had to wait only seven months for his first big win. Levenson, with 11 amateur tournament victories under his belt, led from start to finish, climaxing his 13-under-par 279 with three closing birdies. He had shared the first round lead with Tony Jacklin – having a much-improved 1979 season – was in a triple tie with Mark James and Baldovino Dassu of Italy after two rounds, but a third round of 68 put him three strokes clear – a margin he held to the end. Equally happy was Peter Barber with a £14,000 car for a hole in one!

Pos	Player	R1	R2	R3	R4	Score	£
1	Gavin Levenson (SA)	68	71	68	72	279	5,382.19
2	Michael King	70	73	71	68	282	2,411.35
	Bobby Cole (SA)	71	71	71	69	282	2,411.35
	Nick Faldo	69	72	70	71	282	2,411.35
5	Baldovino Dassu (I)	73	66	71	73	283	1,252.96
	Jeff Hall	69	74	73	67	283	1,252.96
7	Simon Owen (NZ)	70	74	69	71	284	890.46
	Mark James	71	68	73	72	284	890.46
9	Ken Brown	72	70	72	71	285	685.58
	Tony Jacklin	68	72	71	74	285	685.58
11	Robin Fyfe	71	74	66	75	286	605.20
12	Don Levin* (USA)	73	72	71	71	287	–
	Peter Townsend	71	74	70	72	287	550.83
	Eddie Polland	72	74	68	73	287	550.83
14	Bob Charles (NZ)	71	76	73	68	288	468.09
	Nick Job	75	69	74	70	288	468.09
	Gordon Brand	69	74	74	71	288	468.09
	Vaughan Somers (AUS)	74	70	73	71	288	468.09
18	Peter Headland (AUS)	73	73	73	70	289	408.98
	Adan Sowa (ARG)	69	73	74	73	289	408.98
20	Peter Cowen	69	72	78	71	290	373.52
	Howard Clark	73	72	73	72	290	373.52
	Mark McNulty (SA)	69	73	73	75	290	373.52
23	David Robertson	75	70	74	72	291	345.94
	David Chillas	70	72	73	76	291	345.94
25	Donald Armour	72	75	75	70	292	307.33
	Bill Longmuir	73	75	72	72	292	307.33
	Carl Mason	74	71	74	73	292	307.33
	Sandy Lyle	76	72	71	73	292	307.33
	Ian Mosey	75	71	72	74	292	307.33
	Bobby Lincoln (SA)	74	72	70	76	292	307.33
31	Steve Martin	71	75	74	73	293	263.99
	Bernhard Langer (G)	76	75	67	75	293	263.99
	Armando Saavedra (ARG)	76	73	73	71	293	263.99
	Ewen Murray	73	73	76	71	293	263.99
35	Peter Senior (AUS)	73	79	71	71	294	240.35
	Noel Ratcliffe (AUS)	73	79	69	73	294	240.35

Pos	Player	R1	R2	R3	R4	Score	£
37	Maurice Bembridge	76	70	76	73	295	223.80
	Warren Humphreys	73	75	74	73	295	233.80
	Robin Mann	75	73	71	76	295	223.80
40	Chris Moody	75	72	75	76	296	208.04
	Martin Poxon	73	72	77	76	296	208.04
42	Nigel Blenkarne	72	77	76	72	297	186.29
	Massimo Mannelli (I)	71	77	77	73	297	186.29
	Ross Drummond	74	74	77	72	297	186.29
	Peter Barber	75	76	73	73	297	186.29
	Richard Eyles	74	78	72	73	297	186.29
47	John Morgan	75	73	78	72	298	163.12
	Philippe Toussaint (B)	74	76	72	75	298	163.12
	Mike Inglis	77	73	72	75	298	163.12
	Andrew Chandler	77	73	73	75	298	163.12
51	Rafe Botts (USA)	76	72	75	76	299	148.94
	Sam Torrance	75	77	71	76	299	148.94
53	Trevor Powell	71	77	78	74	300	137.12
	Juan Cabrera (ARG)	74	76	76	74	300	137.12
	Gunnar Mueller (SWE)	73	73	79	75	300	137.12
56	Rodger Davis (AUS)	71	76	79	75	301	125.30
	Karl-Heinz Gogele (G)	76	74	72	79	301	125.30
58	Tony Charnley	77	75	77	74	303	115.81
	Thierry Goossens* (B)	75	73	78	77	303	–
	John O'Leary (IRE)	76	76	73	78	303	115.81
60	Torsten Denward (C)	77	72	80	75	304	106.38
	Jeff Hawkes (SA)	76	75	75	78	304	106.38
62	José Basilio Hunchak (ARG)	76	76	79	74	305	99.29
63	Glenn Ralph	75	70	75	86	306	92.20
	Philip Morley	71	78	74	83	306	92.20
65	Jan Sonnevi (SWE)	74	72	79	76	307	42.85
	Julio Orrillo (ARG)	75	75	78	79	307	42.85
67	Tony Minshall	75	77	78	79	309	–
68	Peter Seal	79	72	77	82	310	–
69	Marcel Vercruyce (B)	77	74	80	83	314	–

*Amateur

Previous Winners (Championship revived in 1978 after 20 years)

Year	Winner	Venue	Score
1978	N. Ratcliffe	Brussels	280

THE WELSH GOLF CLASSIC

Wenvoe Castle Golf Club, near Cardiff   14–17 June 1979   Prize Money £30,000

The UK segment of the European circuit welcomed a new tournament with the multi-sponsored Welsh Classic. So did the Sun Alliance European Match-play Champion Mark James who took the inaugural title after a play-off with Eddie Polland and Scotland's Mike Miller. It was a splendid performance by Miller who turned professional in 1978 after being one of four amateurs to reach the final round of the Open Championship. Pip Elson, having set a course record with an opening seven-under 64, drifted out in round three where James went to the front. Miller caught him with a final 69, as did Polland who got home in 31. Polland left the play-off at the second hole, and James won at the third when Miller was bunkered.

							£
1	Mark James	72	68	68	70	278	5,000.00
2	Eddie Polland	66	73	72	67	278	2,605.00
	Michael Miller	72	68	69	69	278	2,605.00
	James won play-off at third extra hole						
4	Sandy Lyle	69	72	72	66	279	1,385.00
	Bob Charles (NZ)	73	69	69	68	279	1,385.00
6	Howard Clark	70	72	68	70	280	1,050.00
7	Philip Elson	64	74	75	68	281	773.33
	Neil Coles	76	67	69	69	281	773.33
	Ken Brown	69	72	70	70	281	773.33
10	Nick Faldo	74	70	73	65	282	600.00
11	Malcolm Gregson	71	73	71	68	283	550.00
12	Nick Job	69	75	69	71	284	520.00
13	Ewen Murray	72	71	71	71	285	490.00
	Don Levin* (USA)	75	72	70	68	285	—
14	Vaughan Somers (AUS)	74	74	70	68	286	441.66
	Des Smyth (IRE)	70	72	75	69	286	441.66
	Gary Birch	72	71	73	70	286	441.66
17	Christy O'Connor Jr (IRE)	73	78	70	66	287	375.00
	John Morgan	72	71	76	68	287	375.00
	Brian Waites	72	75	72	68	287	375.00
	Mike Krantz (USA)	72	72	69	69	287	375.00
	Massimo Mannelli (I)	77	70	68	72	287	375.00
	Tony Jacklin	71	69	73	74	287	375.00
23	Vicente Fernandez (ARG)	71	75	72	70	288	325.00
	Bill Longmuir	70	74	74	70	288	325.00
	Anthony Charnley	72	75	71	70	288	325.00
	Simon Owen (NZ)	76	72	70	70	288	325.00
27	Jeff Hawkes (SA)	69	75	75	70	289	295.00
	Martin Poxon	73	74	71	71	289	295.00
29	Brian Barnes	75	75	73	67	290	255.00
	Bobby Verwey (SA)	77	74	70	69	290	255.00
	Bernard Gallacher	75	72	73	70	290	255.00
	Gavin Levenson (SA)	73	69	77	71	290	255.00
	Steve Martin	74	72	70	74	290	255.00
	Robin Fyfe	75	73	70	72	290	255.00
35	Willie Milne	74	75	75	67	291	202.50
	Peter Berry	75	74	74	68	291	202.50
	Mike Inglis	75	73	73	70	291	202.50
	Eamonn Darcy (IRE)	74	77	70	70	291	202.50
	Warren Humphreys	77	74	69	71	291	202.50
	Guy Hunt	74	75	71	71	291	202.50
	Ian Mosey	73	74	71	73	291	202.50
	Michael King	71	76	73	71	291	202.50
43	Keith Benson	73	72	76	71	292	177.50
	Gordon Brand	78	72	71	71	292	177.50
45	Richard Fish	72	75	75	71	293	167.50
	Carl Mason	76	71	71	75	293	167.50
47	Noel Ratcliffe (AUS)	73	77	73	71	294	150.00

Pos	Name	R1	R2	R3	R4	Total	£
	Jeff Hall	79	69	73	73	294	150.00
	Dennis Durnian	76	74	70	74	294	150.00
	Tommy Horton	77	71	71	75	294	150.00
	Juan Cabrera (ARG)	75	72	72	75	294	150.00
52	David Robertson	74	74	76	71	295	132.50
	Craig Defoy	76	73	74	72	295	132.50
54	Peter Barber	77	72	75	72	296	120.00
	Michael Gallagher	75	74	76	71	296	120.00
	Norman Wood	77	72	72	75	296	120.00
57	Keith Waters	73	78	76	70	297	100.00
	Tim Giles	77	74	71	75	297	100.00
	Stuart Brown	77	73	71	76	297	100.00
	David Regan	74	76	71	76	297	100.00
	Peter Headland (AUS)	77	73	70	77	297	100.00
62	Andrew Murray	74	73	76	75	298	85.00
63	Robin Mann	76	73	76	75	300	80.00
64	David A. Russell	76	75	73	77	301	72.50
	Ross Drummond	73	76	76	76	301	72.50
66	David Vaughan	76	74	76	76	302	–
	Charles Dernie	74	77	78	73	302	–
68	Trevor Powell	76	73	80	75	304	–
69	Don Jones	76	72	89	74	311	–

* Amateur

THE GREATER MANCHESTER OPEN

Wilmslow Golf Club, Cheshire   21–24 June 1979   Prize Money £30,000

Mark McNulty, in only his second professional season, became the fourth South African to win in Europe in 1979, leading from start to finish to take the multi-sponsored Greater Manchester Open. He equalled the course record with a first round of 64 to take a one-shot lead over PGA Champion Fernandez, and a second round of 66 put him four clear of the field. Manuel Pinero made a third round surge in an effort to close the gap, but the 25-years-old former amateur international, who had finished 43rd in the previous year's Order of Merit, closed everyone out with a final 66 and a winning 13-under-par total of 267. Pinero was second with Brian Waites a creditable third via four sub-par rounds.

Pos	Name	R1	R2	R3	R4	Total	£
1	Mark McNulty (SA)	64	66	71	66	267	5,000.00
2	Manuel Pinero (S)	69	69	66	68	272	3,330.00
3	Brian Waites	69	67	69	68	273	1,880.00
4	Des Smyth (IRE)	70	69	66	69	274	1,385.00
	Neil Coles	68	66	71	69	274	1,385.00
6	Ken Brown	70	69	70	66	275	1,050.00
7	Antonio Garrido (S)	68	72	69	67	276	825.00
	Sandy Lyle	66	72	67	71	276	825.00
9	David Jagger	71	71	68	67	277	635.00
	Brian Barnes	70	71	67	69	277	635.00
11	Mike Ingham	70	71	69	68	278	480.83
	Bill Lockie	68	70	71	69	278	480.83
	Jeff Hall	73	68	68	69	278	480.83
	Howard Clark	67	71	70	70	278	480.83
	Vicente Fernandez (ARG)	65	70	72	71	278	480.83
	Robin Mann	68	69	71	70	278	480.83
17	Martin Poxon	70	72	71	66	279	365.00
	Greg Norman (AUS)	70	68	73	68	279	365.00
	Vaughan Somers (AUS)	72	69	69	69	279	365.00
	Nick Job	69	71	69	70	279	365.00
	Martin Foster	68	73	68	70	279	365.00
	Doug McClelland	70	71	68	70	279	365.00

Pos	Player	R1	R2	R3	R4	Total	£
	Michael Gallagher	72	67	68	72	279	365.00
	Michael King	70	72	65	72	279	365.00
25	José Maria Canizares (S)	71	73	69	67	280	310.00
	Terry Gale (AUS)	72	68	71	69	280	310.00
	Mike Slater	73	69	68	70	280	310.00
28	Peter Tupling	70	71	71	69	281	265.00
	Bill Longmuir	67	73	71	70	281	265.00
	Mark James	68	68	73	72	281	265.00
	Ewen Murray	73	69	67	72	281	265.00
	Bob Charles (NZ)	72	70	67	72	281	265.00
	David Vaughan	72	70	66	73	281	265.00
34	Steve Martin	75	62	64	71	282	221.66
	Philip Elson	71	69	69	73	282	221.66
	Christy O'Connor Jr (IRE)	69	68	71	74	282	221.66
37	Craig Defoy	69	74	70	70	283	205.00
	Peter Cowen	72	70	69	72	283	205.00
	Gavin Levenson (SA)	72	69	69	73	283	205.00
40	Juan-Carlos Martin (ARG)	70	73	71	70	284	185.00
	Warren Humphreys	71	71	70	72	284	185.00
	Garry Cullen	70	68	72	74	284	185.00
	Sam Torrance	71	66	73	74	284	185.00
45	Peter Senior (AUS)	72	70	66	76	284	185.00
	Keith Waters	69	71	74	71	285	162.50
	Michael Miller	71	68	72	74	285	162.50
	Manuel Calero (S)	69	69	71	76	285	162.50
	John O'Leary (IRE)	70	72	67	76	285	162.50
49	Ross Drummond	73	70	75	68	286	137.50
	Juan Cabrera (ARG)	75	67	72	72	286	137.50
	Graham Burroughs	70	70	72	74	286	137.50
	Stuart Brown	72	71	69	74	286	137.50
	John Fowler	69	74	68	75	286	137.50
	Eamonn Darcy (IRE)	73	71	66	76	286	137.50
55	Glenn Ralph	74	68	74	71	287	117.50
	Kim Dabson	71	71	71	74	287	117.50
57	David A. Russell	72	70	75	71	288	105.00
	Tony Price	69	73	73	73	288	105.00
	Gary Birch	73	69	69	77	288	105.00
60	David Ingram	72	69	75	73	289	92.50
	Horacio Carbonetti (ARG)	70	74	72	73	289	92.50
62	Jaime Gonzalez (BZ)	73	71	74	72	290	82.50
	Noel Ratcliffe (AUS)	71	69	75	75	290	82.50
64	Gaylord Burrows (USA)	72	72	73	75	292	75.00
65	Lloyd Freeman	70	68	74	76	293	70.00
66	Tim Giles	71	71	77	83	302	–

Previous Winners

Year	Winner	Venue	Score
1976	J. O'Leary	Wilmslow	276
1977	E. Darcy	Wilmslow	269
1978	B.W. Barnes	Wilmslow	275

THE LADA ENGLISH GOLF CLASSIC

The Belfry, Sutton Coldfield, West Midlands   28 June–1 July 1979   Prize Money £50,000

The English Classic, like the Welsh a new event on the calendar, had the importers of the Soviet-made Lada cars as its chief sponsors, with other companies combining in a multi-sponsored event. It was the tournament in which Severiano Ballesteros 'came good' for the first time in 1979, his victory being his first since winning the Japanese Open in November. Australia's Rodger Davis led for two rounds, but the

Spaniard went to the front in round three, was the only one under par, and nobody put him under pressure in the final round when he coasted home to a six shots victory. His previous best to that point had been third place in the French Open.

Pos	Name						£
1	Severiano Ballesteros (S)	73	71	71	71	286	8,330.00
2	Neil Coles	73	77	72	70	292	4,340.00
	Simon Hobday (ZIM)	73	71	73	75	292	4,340.00
4	Sandy Lyle	76	70	75	72	293	2,310.00
	Nick Faldo	72	71	77	73	293	2,310.00
6	Greg Norman (AUS)	74	73	73	74	294	1,500.00
	Brian Huggett	71	77	72	74	294	1,500.00
	Hugh Baiocchi (SA)	72	75	73	74	294	1,500.00
9	Eddie Polland	73	73	79	71	296	1,013.33
	Tommy Horton	80	71	72	73	296	1,013.33
	Manuel Pinero (S)	71	76	75	74	296	1,013.33
12	Bobby Verwey (SA)	74	75	74	74	297	791.25
	Hugh Boyle	76	74	73	74	297	791.25
	Brian Barnes	79	73	71	74	297	791.25
	Armando Saavedra (ARG)	73	74	73	77	297	791.25
16	Peter Senior (AUS)	74	74	80	70	298	690.00
	Francisco Abreu (S)	73	74	73	78	298	690.00
18	Vaughan Somers (AUS)	72	77	78	72	299	604.00
	Bob Charles (NZ)	78	71	78	72	299	604.00
	David Dunk	78	73	75	73	299	604.00
	Graham Burroughs	71	72	77	79	299	604.00
	Ken Brown	72	74	76	77	299	604.00
23	Martin Poxon	73	75	78	74	300	510.00
	Rodger Davis (AUS)	69	73	83	75	300	510.00
	Steve Martin	74	77	75	74	300	510.00
	Antonio Garrido (S)	75	77	74	74	300	510.00
	George Will	75	76	74	75	300	510.00
	Carl Mason	71	78	72	79	300	510.00
	Brian Waites	75	74	72	79	300	510.00
30	Dale Hayes (SA)	75	77	77	72	301	417.50
	Jeff Hawkes (SA)	77	74	74	76	301	417.50
	Howard Clark	79	73	75	74	301	417.50
	Guy Hunt	74	76	76	75	301	417.50
	Mike Krantz (USA)	73	74	77	77	301	417.50
	Vin Baker (SA)	75	77	75	74	301	417.50
36	Anthony Charnley	74	77	75	76	302	360.00
	Martin Foster	76	72	78	76	302	360.00
	David Vaughan	76	75	74	77	302	360.00
	Michael King	74	74	77	77	302	360.00
	Bill Longmuir	76	74	73	79	302	360.00
41	David Good (AUS)	76	76	75	76	303	320.00
	Baldovino Dassu (I)	73	74	76	80	303	320.00
	David Jagger	75	74	70	84	303	320.00
44	Ewen Murray	73	77	78	76	304	290.00
	Trevor Johnson	76	74	77	77	304	290.00
	Peter Townsend	74	77	76	77	304	290.00
47	Mark McNulty (SA)	72	79	79	75	305	260.00
	Noel Ratcliffe (AUS)	76	75	76	78	305	260.00
	David Jones	74	74	76	81	305	260.00
50	Bernhard Langer (G)	77	73	79	77	306	220.00
	John Hay	75	77	77	77	306	220.00
	David Regan	75	74	79	78	306	220.00
	Maurice Bembridge	75	75	77	79	306	220.00
	Willie Milne	75	75	73	83	306	220.00
55	Chris Tickner (AUS)	78	74	78	77	307	175.00
	Nick Job	81	71	79	76	307	175.00
	Peter Tupling	71	81	79	76	307	175.00
	Harold Henning (SA)	74	78	79	76	307	175.00
59	Dennis Durnian	76	76	77	79	308	152.50
	Vicente Fernandez (ARG)	77	75	75	81	308	152.50
61	David A. Russell	74	77	77	81	309	140.00
	Jeff Hall	71	78	76	84	309	140.00
	Gary Birch	77	74	74	84	309	140.00
64	Bill McAdams	78	72	80	80	310	127.50
	Keith Waters	76	76	81	77	310	127.50
66	David Chillas	78	74	79	80	311	–
67	Warren Humphreys	77	75	84	80	316	–

THE SCANDINAVIAN OPEN CHAMPIONSHIP
Vasatorps Golf Club, Helsingborg, Sweden 5–8 July 1979 Prize Money £35,000

Sandy Lyle continued establishing himself as one of the best young professionals in Europe when he added the Scandinavian title to his victory in the British Airways/Avis event. He won in Sweden with a 12-under-par total of 276, three ahead of the back-in-form Ballesteros, shooting three sub-par rounds after an indifferent opening. It included a third round of 65 when paired with the Spaniard, built on an inward half of 30 that contained six birdies. Nick Faldo and Australia's Michael Ferguson had led the first round, but both fell away thereafter. Mike Krantz of America, an experienced Asia Circuit performer, also shot a third round of 65 and went on to finish in lone third place.

							£
1	Sandy Lyle	73	69	65	69	276	5,300.82
2	Severiano Ballesteros (S)	70	72	68	69	279	3,530.35
3	Mike Krantz (USA)	71	72	65	73	281	1,993.12
4	Ken Brown	71	70	72	71	284	1,468.33
	Dale Hayes (SA)	70	72	71	71	284	1,468.33
6	Eamonn Darcy (IRE)	70	73	74	68	285	1,033.66
	Michael King	73	71	69	72	285	1,033.66
8	Terry Gale (AUS)	72	72	74	70	288	681.15
	Eddie Polland	71	73	71	73	288	681.15
	Armando Saavedra (ARG)	71	72	70	75	288	681.15
	Peter Townsend	70	73	70	75	288	681.15
12	Mark McNulty (SA)	75	74	72	68	289	495.10
	Peter Senior (AUS)	72	76	69	72	289	495.10
	Baldovino Dassu (I)	74	74	68	73	289	495.10
	Tommy Horton	71	75	70	73	289	495.10
	José-Maria Canizares (S)	70	73	75	71	289	495.10
17	Mike Ferguson (AUS)	69	75	73	73	290	424.07
18	Hugh Baiocchi (SA)	71	76	74	70	291	408.16
	Robbie Stewart (SA)	72	74	74	71	291	408.16
20	Nick Faldo	69	78	74	71	292	371.06
	Peter Headland (AUS)	73	72	76	71	292	371.06
	Gordon Brand	73	72	75	72	292	371.06
	Simon Hobday (SA)	77	68	75	72	292	371.06
	Garry Cullen	72	74	74	72	292	371.06
25	Brian Jones (AUS)	72	78	74	69	293	323.35
	Guy Wolstenholme (AUS)	75	74	71	73	293	323.35
	Steve Martin	72	78	69	74	293	323.35
	Simon Owen (NZ)	72	78	76	73	293	323.35
29	Gavin Levenson (SA)	74	78	76	66	294	291.54
	Gary Hallberg* (USA)	74	74	77	69	294	–
	Vin Baker (SA)	75	76	72	71	294	291.54
31	Carl Mason	74	72	79	70	295	270.34
	Martin Foster	76	72	74	73	295	270.34
	Mikael Sorling* (SWE)	74	76	73	73	296	–
33	Dennis Durnian	76	70	77	74	297	254.44
34	Denis Clark (NZ)	77	75	75	71	298	235.04
	Chris Tickner (AUS)	73	78	73	74	298	235.04
	Mark James	76	74	73	75	298	235.04
37	Jaime Gonzalez (BZ)	78	75	77	69	299	212.03
	Tohru Nakamura (J)	78	76	75	70	299	212.03
	Mike Inglis	80	74	71	74	299	212.03
	Per Andersson* (SWE)	78	75	71	75	299	–
	Rick Mallicoat (USA)	74	75	74	76	299	212.03
	Jan Sonnevi (SWE)	80	76	67	76	299	212.03
42	Bernhard Langer (G)	76	76	76	72	300	180.23
	Philip Morley	73	80	74	73	300	180.23
	Gunnar Mueller (SWE)	77	76	74	73	300	180.23
	Gar Hamilton (C)	78	77	73	72	300	180.23
	Jeff Hawkes (SA)	78	75	71	76	300	180.23
	Maurice Bembridge	73	74	76	77	300	180.23

Pos	Player						£
	John Benda (USA)	75	74	74	77	300	180.23
	Olle Dahlgren* (SWE)	71	77	74	78	300	–
	Dag Aurell* (SWE)	74	74	76	77	301	–
49	Peter Lindwall (SWE)	80	73	74	75	302	153.72
	Juan Cabrera (ARG)	77	72	76	77	302	153.72
	David Vaughan	72	77	75	78	302	153.72
52	Adan Sowa (ARG)	75	78	78	72	303	140.47
	David Nicholson	76	80	74	73	303	140.47
54	Hans Hedjerson (SWE)	78	78	77	73	304	132.53
	Krister Kinell* (SWE)	77	78	72	77	304	–
	Bjorn Svedin* (SWE)	74	78	73	79	304	–
55	Bob Beattie	78	75	75	78	306	124.57
	Dietrich Geise (G)	75	78	71	82	306	124.57
57	Julio Orillo (ARG)	78	78	73	78	307	116.62
	Jan Rube* (SWE)	74	78	76	79	307	–
58	Gary Birch	77	78	80	73	308	106.02
	Pat Dunleavy (USA)	75	80	78	75	308	106.02
	Robert Heyman (SWE)	78	70	80	80	308	106.02
61	Sayed Cherif (SWE)	77	79	76	77	309	90.11
	Robert Kristensen (DEN)	79	75	78	77	309	90.11
	Bill Longmuir	72	77	82	78	309	90.11
64	Juan-Carlos Martin (ARG)	77	75	81	77	310	76.86
	Ingemar Christersson (SWE)	82	74	79	75	310	76.86
	Anders Starkman* (SWE)	77	78	76	79	310	–
66	José-Basilio Hunchak (ARG)	76	77	78	80	311	–
	Goran Knutsson* (SWE)	77	79	83	73	312	–
67	Lars Thonning (SWE)	77	78	83	83	321	–

*Amateur

Previous Winners

Year	Winner	Venue	Score
1973	R.J. Charles	Stockholm	278
1974	A. Jacklin	Malmo	279
1975	G. Burns	Malmo	279
1976	H. Baiocchi	Drottningholm	271
1977	B. Byman	Drottningholm	275
1978	S. Ballesteros	Helsingborg	279

After a tie with G. Marsh

THE EXPRESS/CAMBRIDGE PGA SENIORS' CHAMPIONSHIP

Cambridgeshire Hotel Golf Course, Cambridge 5–8 July 1979 Prize Money £8,000

Christy O'Connor, who had won the National and the World Seniors' titles in 1976 and 1977 came spectacularly from behind to win at home for the third time. All the early glory belonged to Roberto de Vicenzo. He was denied a new course record with his opening 65 with preferred lies being played, and was seven shots ahead of the Irishman at halfway. But Roberto fell to pieces in the third round, slipped a shot behind, caught O'Connor again in the last round, and then lost the play-off at the second extra hole.

Pos	Player					Total	£
1	Christy O'Connor (Royal Dublin)	71	67	70	72	280	2,000.00
2	Roberto de Vicenzo (ARG)	65	66	78	71	280	1,000.00
	O'Connor won play-off at second extra hole						
3	John Panton (Glenbervie)	70	75	73	75	293	750.00
4	Jimmy Martin (Wicklow)	73	76	72	73	294	350.00
	Paddy Skerritt (St Annes)	69	74	77	74	294	350.00
6	Syd Scott (Roehampton)	72	71	74	79	296	250.00
7	Ken Bousfield (Coombe Hill)	73	74	75	76	298	200.00
8	Malcolm Leeder (Sheringham)	76	73	78	75	302	150.00
9	Bobby Locke (SA)	78	75	73	75	303	125.00
10	Ted Large (Great Hay)	76	76	74	79	305	97.50
	Harold Lees (Dore & Totley)	78	76	72	79	305	97.50

THE SLAZENGER-PGA CLUB PROFESSIONALS' CHAMPIONSHIP

Pannal Golf Club, Harrogate, Yorkshire   24–27 July 1979   Prize Money £12,000

Pos	Player					Total	£
1	D. Jones (Bangor)	70	70	72	66	278	2,000.00
2	M. Steadman (Cleeve Hill Municipal)	70	76	68	67	281	1,500.00
3	G. Will (Sundridge Park)	71	68	74	70	283	725.00
	P.J. Butler (RAC, Epsom)	70	74	69	70	283	725.00
	D.J. Ridley (Oxton)	72	70	70	71	283	725.00
	B.J. Waites (Notts)	70	74	69	70	283	725.00
7	J. Morgan (Royal Liverpool)	69	77	71	67	284	375.00
	D. Huish (North Berwick)	72	75	68	69	284	375.00
	P. Leonard (Killymoon)	75	70	71	69	285	300.00
9	J.C. Farmer (Duddingston)	69	73	71	73	286	205.00
	A. Bickerdike (Crosland Heath)	72.	73	70	71	286	205.00
10	G. Townhill (Hull)	72	74	72	68	286	205.00
	J. Fowler (Mid-Herts)	72	75	70	69	286	205.00

Previous Winners

Year	Winner	Venue	Score
1973	D.N. Sewell	Calcot Park	276
1974	W.B. Murray	Calcot Park	275
1975	D.N. Sewell	Calcot Park	276
1976	W.J. Ferguson	Moortown	283
1977	D. Huish	Notts, Hollinwell	284
1978	D. Jones	Pannal	281

From 1973-75 sponsored by MacGregor. In 1976 jointly-sponsored by Rank Xerox and Slazenger.

THE DUTCH OPEN CHAMPIONSHIP

Noordwijk Golf Club, near Leiden   26–29 July 1979   Prize Money £35,000

A victory drought stretching back to his peak year of 1977 finally ended for Graham Marsh in the Netherlands where the Australian came from behind in the wind and the rain to capture a championship in which he had twice finished second. It was the 31st victory of his distinguished career. Some accurate work on the greens gave Jeff Hall from Bristol the early lead with a five-under 67, but he was caught in the second round by John Bland of South Africa with a 66 – a new course record. Bland was two shots clear and five ahead of Marsh going into the last round, but he took seven at the par-5 ninth, bogeyed the next, and with Marsh picking up birdies at the 11th and 14th the Australian was set for victory.

Pos						Total	£
1	Graham Marsh (AUS)	71	70	70	74	285	5,015.01
2	Malcolm Gregson	72	71	69	74	286	2,615.05
	Antonio Garrido (S)	73	71	70	72	286	2,615.05
4	Manuel Pinero (S)	70	73	73	71	287	1,391.40
	John Bland (SA)	72	66	72	77	287	1,391.40
6	Denis Watson (SA)	74	74	68	72	288	846.24
	Rodger Davis (AUS)	72	72	72	72	288	846.24
	Michael King	70	72	74	72	288	846.24
	Nick Job	71	71	72	74	288	846.24
10	Bobby Verwey (SA)	73	70	74	72	289	580.65
	Geoffrey Parslow (AUS)	74	73	66	76	289	580.65
12	Ken Brown	70	76	74	70	290	498.92
	David Ingram	71	77	68	74	290	498.92
	Jeff Hall	67	71	77	75	290	498.92
15	Noel Ratcliffe (AUS)	71	76	72	72	291	434.41
	Brian Barnes	74	71	72	74	291	434.41
17	Terry Gale (AUS)	69	77	71	75	292	387.10
	Maurice Bembridge	68	78	70	76	292	387.10
	Eamonn Darcy (IRE)	71	73	72	76	292	387.10
20	Sandy Lyle	72	71	80	70	293	339.78
	Robbie Stewart (SA)	73	75	74	71	293	339.78
	Eddie Polland	76	75	68	74	293	339.78
	Vicente Fernandez (ARG)	71	78	69	75	293	339.78
	David Vaughan	76	70	71	76	293	339.78
	Tommy Horton	71	72	70	80	293	339.78
26	Philip Elson	76	74	72	72	294	288.17

Pos						Total	£
	Gavin Levenson (SA)	75	73	73	73	294	288.17
	Guy Wolstenholme (AUS)	74	70	75	75	294	288.17
	Christy O'Connor Jnr (IRE)	73	72	73	76	294	288.17
	Gar Hamilton (C)	75	67	76	76	294	288.17
	Sam Torrance	73	67	78	76	294	288.17
32	Garry Cullen	74	74	73	74	295	245.16
	Vaughan Somers (AUS)	74	76	69	76	295	245.16
	Doug McClelland	76	74	69	76	295	245.16
	Gary Logan	75	74	68	78	295	245.16
36	Bill Loeffler (USA)	73	78	71	74	296	202.15
	Noel Hunt	77	72	73	74	296	202.15
	Martin Poxon	77	73	71	75	296	202.15
	Mark McNulty (SA)	72	74	75	75	296	202.15
	John O'Leary (IRE)	74	72	70	80	296	202.15
	Carl Mason	69	75	72	80	296	202.15
42	Armando Saavedra (ARG)	72	72	78	75	297	169.89
	Simon Hobday (ZIM)	73	75	72	77	297	169.89
	Mike Inglis	74	76	68	79	297	169.89
	Peter Cowen	73	73	72	79	297	169.89
46	Martin Foster	76	75	74	73	298	146.24
	Willie Milne	75	75	72	76	298	146.24
	Mitch Adcock (USA)	80	71	71	76	298	146.24
	Bill Longmuir	76	72	74	76	298	146.24
	Peter Senior (AUS)	77	71	74	76	298	146.24
	Mark James	72	73	76	77	298	146.24
	Robin Mann	78	70	70	80	298	146.24

							£
53	Nick Price (SA)	74	75	75	75	299	124.73
	Howard Clark	75	73	74	77	299	124.73
	Alan Mew (TRI)	72	76	74	77	299	124.73
56	Nigel Blenkarne	71	81	76	72	300	109.68
	Jamie Edman (USA)	75	74	77	74	300	109.68
	Jeff Hawkes (SA)	72	73	78	77	300	109.68
	Vin Baker (SA)	76	73	73	78	300	109.68
60	Garry Harvey	72	75	76	78	301	98.92
61	Steve Martin	74	76	74	78	302	94.62
62	Harold Henning (SA)	75	77	75	76	303	90.32
63	Anthony Charnley	75	77	79	73	304	86.02
64	Jan Dorrestein (NLD)	77	75	76	77	305	79.57
	Gordon Brand	72	73	75	85	305	79.57
66	Patrick Lemair (F)	78	74	77	77	306	–

Previous Winners

Year	Winner	Venue	Score
1951	F. van Donck	Kennemer	281
1952	C. Denny	Hilversum	284
1953	F. van Donck	Eindhoven	286
1954	U. Grappasonni	The Hague	295
	After a tie with Gerard de Wit		
1955	A. Angelini	Zandvoort	280
	After a tie with Gerard de Wit		
1956	A. Cerda	Eindhoven	277
1957	J. Jacobs	Hilversum	284
1958	D. Thomas	Zandvoort	277
1959	S. Sewgolum	The Hague	283
1960	S. Sewgolum	Eindhoven	280
1961	B.B.S. Wilkes	Zandvoort	279
1962	B. Huggett	Hilversum	274
1963	R. Waltman	Wassenaar	279
1964	S. Sewgolum	Eindhoven	275
1965	A. Miguel	Breda	278
	After a tie with J. Benito		
1966	R. Sota	Zandvoort	276
1967	P. Townsend	The Hague	282
1968	J. Cockin	Hilversum	292
1969	G. Wolstenholme	Utrecht	277
1970	V. Fernandez	Eindhoven	279
1971	R. Sota	Zandvoort	277
1972	J. Newton	The Hague	277
1973	D. McClelland	The Hague	279
1974	B. Barnes	Hilversum (54 holes)	211
1975	H. Baiocchi	Hilversum	279
1976	S. Ballesteros	Zandvoort	275
1977	B. Byman	Zandvoort	278
1978	B. Byman	Noordwijk (54 holes)	214

For the second time in three years Australia's Greg Norman won the Martini title.
(Golf Photography International)

THE SUN ALLIANCE EUROPEAN MATCH-PLAY CHAMPIONSHIP

SMYTH SEALS RYDER CUP PLACE

When Des Smyth set out on the 1979 trail it was highly unlikely that he foresaw by the conclusion of it the capture of the PGA's oldest championship title plus a place in Europe's Ryder Cup side against the United States. But such was the achievement of the Irish tournament professional from Laytown & Bettystown who carried off the Sun Alliance European Match-Play Championship at Fulford, York. Moreover he did so after pre-qualifying for a place in the field. The Championship is the modern version of the former PGA Match-Play event which has enjoyed sponsorship by the Sun Alliance Insurance Group since 1975.

Smyth, 26 years old, rolled some notable heads on his way to the final in which he met and defeated South Africa's Nick Price with a birdie on the 18th green. Along the way he beat the Ryder Cup player Norman Wood, Martin Green, the formidable Spaniard Manuel Pinero, South Africa's Bobby Verwey, the strongly-fancied former winner Brian Barnes, and Carl Mason. Price, the 1974 World Junior champion, who with Verwey represented South Africa in the 1978 World Cup event, had disposed of an even more impressive opposition comprising PGA Champion Vicente Fernandez, Bernhard Langer, Ian Mosey, Bernard Gallacher, Brian Waites, and Antonio Garrido.

Match-play over 18 holes is a great leveller, as Tony Jacklin and Nick Faldo well knew when they joined Fernandez among the first round casualties. Jacklin went under by the big margin of five and four to Yorkshire's Stephen Rolley – an unkind cut by a fellow resident Channel Islander – while Faldo fell to a municipal club professional in Michael Steadman from Cleeve Hill, in Gloucestershire, who had won nothing until a cheque for £1,500 the previous week for second place in the Club Professionals' championship.

Mark James, defending the title he had won at Dalmahoy, Edinburgh, played some of the day's best golf in round one, but the following day joined the sidelines with Lyle and Clark after losing two and one to the 'unknown' Yorkshire Open champion Alec Bickerdike. Garrido's fine golf, which had been too much for Clark, installed him as a favourite for the title, but Price's birdie on the 17th in the semi-final ended the Spaniard's run.

Smyth dominated the final for 15 holes. He won the third, fourth and fifth to go two up, lost the 11th to Price's birdie, but himself birdied the 15th to be two up and three to play. At which point Price ran down a 20ft putt for a birdie three at the 16th, and squared the match at the next when Smyth missed from around three feet. Came Smyth's glorious two shots to the heart of the home hole and an eagle putt from 10 feet which earned for the former Irish amateur international his first big win since he turned professional in 1973.

There was a nostalgic conclusion when Lady Heathcoat-Amory, who as Joyce Wethered was the finest golfer of her time, presented the prizes.

Des Smyth with the Sun Alliance trophy. (Press Agency, Yorkshire)

THE SUN ALLIANCE EUROPEAN MATCH-PLAY CHAMPIONSHIP

Fulford Golf Club, York   2–5 August 1979   Prize Money £40,000

Final
D. Smyth (IRE) (£6,660) beat N. Price (SA) (£4,450) 1 hole

Semi-final
Smyth beat C. Mason 1 hole
Price beat A. Garrido (S) 2 and 1

Play-off for 3rd and 4th places
Garrido (£2,500) beat Mason (£2,100) 20th hole

Play-off for 5th and 6th places
B.J. Waites (£1,800) beat J.M. Canizares (S) (£1,550) 1 hole

Play-off for 7th and 8th places
B. Barnes (£1,340) beat H. Henning (SA) (£1,200) 1 hole

Quarter-finals
Smyth beat Barnes 3 and 2; Price beat Waites 4 and 3; Garrido beat Henning 6 and 5; Mason beat Canizares 1 hole.

For previous winners of the PGA Match-Play title see Championship Rolls

Fourth Round (Losers each received £700)
Smyth beat R. Verwey (SA) 3 and 2
Price beat B.J. Gallacher 20th hole
Mason beat M. Foster 1 hole
Garrido beat A. Sowa (ARG) 5 and 4
Waites beat T. Horton 21st hole
Barnes beat D. Watson (SA) 4 and 3
Canizares beat K. Brown 25th hole
Henning beat S. Rolley 2 holes

Third Round (Losers each received £400)
Smyth beat M. Pinero (S) 1 hole; Price beat I. Mosey 5 and 4; Mason beat J. Bland (SA) 3 and 1; Garrido beat W. Humphreys 5 and 4; Waites beat P. Cowen 21st hole; Barnes beat E. Polland 4 and 3; Canizares beat I. Woosnam 2 and 1; Henning beat A. Bickerdike 4 and 3; Verwey beat M. Steadman 3 and 2; Gallacher beat A. Caygill 2 holes; Foster beat S. Owen (NZ) 5 and 4; Sowa beat S. Hobday (SA) 1 hole; Horton beat D. McClelland 1 hole; Watson beat N. Ratcliffe (AUS) 3 and 2; Brown beat P.M.P. Townsend 1 hole; Rolley beat G. Hunt 19th hole.

THE BENSON AND HEDGES INTERNATIONAL OPEN

St Mellion Golf & Country Club, Cornwall   9–12 August 1979   Prize Money £60,000

The tournament broke a long association with the Fulford club in York to 'go west' for the first time, and chose the new complex near the Tamar Estuary as their venue. It was a successful move, not only for the sponsors but also for Maurice Bembridge who ended four years in the wilderness in Europe with his first win since his victory in the German Open in 1975. Bembridge led from start to finish, holding off a determined challenge throughout by Ken Brown. Bembridge's £10,000 winner's cheque put him into 10th place in the Ryder Cup points table, while the ever-improving Jacklin made a significant move with his three successive 67s and fifth finishing place.

Pos	Player					Total	£
1	Maurice Bembridge	67	67	69	69	272	10,000.00
2	Ken Brown	71	65	70	68	274	6,660.00
3	Sam Torrance	73	68	69	66	276	3,380.00
3	Jaime Gonzalez (BZ)	72	71	67	66	276	3,380.00
5	Tony Jacklin	76	69	67	65	277	2,540.00
6	José-Maria Canizares (S)	74	71	67	66	278	1,800.00
6	Michael King	72	73	65	68	278	1,800.00
6	Harold Henning (SA)	74	65	70	69	278	1,800.00
9	David Ingram	72	69	71	67	279	1,213.33
9	Brian Huggett	71	67	70	71	279	1,213.33
9	David J. Russell	76	69	70	64	279	1,213.33
12	Nick Faldo	75	71	66	68	280	934.00
12	Jeff Hall	68	72	71	69	280	934.00
12	Baldovino Dassu (I)	74	68	68	70	280	934.00
12	Hugh Baiocchi (SA)	73	67	69	71	280	934.00
12	Nick Job	73	68	67	72	280	934.00
17	Manuel Ballesteros (S)	76	68	70	67	281	790.00
17	Brian Barnes	69	73	70	69	281	790.00
19	Christy O'Connor Jnr (IRE)	73	72	70	67	282	700.00
19	Gavin Levenson (SA)	73	70	71	68	282	700.00
19	Ian Mosey	77	68	69	68	282	700.00
19	Dale Hayes (SA)	73	72	68	69	282	700.00
19	Mark James	76	68	69	69	282	700.00
19	Lee Trevino (USA)	75	68	71	68	282	700.00
19	Peter Berry	76	68	66	72	282	700.00
26	Ross Drummond	73	69	70	71	283	580.00
26	Bernard Gallacher	74	69	70	70	283	580.00
26	Simon Hobday (ZIM)	74	69	70	70	283	580.00
26	Peter Townsend	72	69	71	71	283	580.00
26	Vin Baker (SA)	73	68	70	72	283	580.00
31	Garry Cullen	73	70	75	66	284	451.11
31	John O'Leary (IRE)	75	71	72	66	284	451.11
31	Sandy Lyle	71	73	72	68	284	451.11
	Manuel Pinero (S)	73	71	70	70	284	451.11
	Des Smyth (IRE)	72	68	73	71	284	451.11
	Doug McClelland	71	75	68	70	284	451.11
	Simon Owen (NZ)	74	69	70	71	284	451.11
	Carl Mason	70	75	68	71	284	451.11
	Brian Waites	74	70	69	71	284	451.11
40	Philip Elson	76	68	72	69	285	385.00
	George Will	75	69	70	71	285	385.00
42	Jamie Edman (USA)	74	70	72	70	286	345.00
	Howard Clark	72	72	72	70	286	345.00
	Malcolm Gregson	74	71	71	70	286	345.00
	Richard Fish	76	67	72	71	286	345.00
	Massimo Mannelli (I)	73	72	70	71	286	345.00
	Bernhard Langer (G)	74	71	68	73	286	345.00
48	Peter Butler	73	69	74	71	287	295.00
	Tommy Horton	74	69	73	71	287	295.00
	David Jagger	72	71	73	71	287	295.00
	Bobby Verwey (SA)	74	70	70	73	287	295.00
52	Tony Charnley	74	71	73	70	288	250.00
	Keith Waters	73	72	72	71	288	250.00
	Denis Watson (SA)	76	69	72	71	288	250.00
	Tienie Britz (SA)	78	68	70	72	288	250.00
	Rodger Davis (AUS)	72	71	69	76	288	250.00
57	Andrew Murray	74	70	75	70	289	210.00
	Ron Wood (AUS)	77	68	72	72	289	210.00
	Severiano Ballesteros (S)	75	68	72	74	289	210.00
60	John Fourie (SA)	74	72	73	71	290	175.00
	Jeff Hawkes (SA)	79	67	71	73	290	175.00
	David A. Russell	75	70	71	74	290	175.00
	John Yeo	72	74	68	76	290	175.00
64	Graham Burroughs	74	71	69	77	291	150.00
65	John Morgan	76	69	75	74	294	140.00

Previous winners

Year	Winner	Venue	Score
1971	A. Jacklin	Fulford	279
	After a tie with P.J. Butler		
1972	J. Newton	Fulford	281
1973	V. Baker	Fulford	276
1974	P. Toussaint	Fulford	276
1975	V. Fernandez	Fulford	266
1976	G. Marsh	Fulford	272
1977	A. Garrido	Fulford	280
1978	L. Trevino	Fulford	274

NEWS OF THE WORLD PGA UNDER-23 MATCH-PLAY CHAMPIONSHIP

Scarborough South Cliff Golf Club, Yorkshire   16–18 August 1979   Prize Money £10,000

Final
I.H. Woosnam (Oswestry) (£1,000) beat J. Hay (Waterlooville) (£500) 4 and 3

Semi-finals
Woosnam beat J.G. Bond (Knole Park) (£350) 4 and 2
Hay beat M. Thomas (Gloucester) (£350) 6 and 5

Quarter-finals
Woosnam beat J. Nelson (Oxton) (£250) 1 hole
Hay beat S.F. Bishop (West Herts) (£250) 1 hole
Bond beat P.J. Glozier (Ruislip) (£250) 3 and 1
Thomas beat C. Potts (Wentworth) (£250) 5 and 3

Previous winner

Year	Winner	Runner-up	Venue
1978	T.W. Rastall	W.J. McAdams	The Belfry

THE GERMAN OPEN CHAMPIONSHIP

Frankfurt Golf Club   16–19 August 1979   Prize Money £32,000

At last! Tony Jacklin's long wait for further glory finally ended in Frankfurt where he clinched his first major win in five years. The former British and US Open Champion had last tasted a big win back in 1974 in the Scandinavian Open. His seven-under-par score of 277 gave him a two-shots win over Antonio Garrido and Lanny Wadkins, both of whom put him under tremendous pressure in the final round. These two came back in 32, but, with a putter borrowed from Ben Crenshaw, Jacklin survived the ordeal and his win carried him into a virtually unassailable Ryder Cup place. Thus ended Tony's self-doubts which, he said, at one time even had him considering giving up the game.

							£
1	Tony Jacklin	68	68	70	71	277	5,665.00
2	Antonio Garrido (S)	70	71	71	67	279	2,961.82
	Lanny Wadkins (USA)	71	71	71	66	279	2,961.82
4	Simon Hobday (ZIM)	71	74	69	68	282	1,699.51
5	Howard Clark	69	71	70	73	283	1,428.57
6	James Edman (USA)	68	76	72	68	284	857.96
	Hugh Baiocchi (SA)	69	74	73	68	284	857.96
	David Ingram	75	73	68	68	284	857.96
	John Bland (SA)	73	69	72	70	284	857.96
	Maurice Bembridge	70	72	71	71	284	857.96

Pos	Player					Total	£
12	José-Maria Canizares (S)	69	73	69	73	284	857.96
	Jeff Hall	75	70	67	73	285	543.41
	Bob Charles (NZ)	72	74	70	69	285	543.41
	Martin Foster	69	71	71	74	285	543.41
	Mark McNulty (SA)	72	72	70	71	285	543.41
16	Severiano Ballesteros (S)	70	74	71	71	286	467.98
17	Nick Price (SA)	76	69	73	69	287	437.19
	Dale Hayes (SA)	71	70	75	71	287	437.19
	John Fourie (SA)	69	73	73	72	287	437.19
20	Vance Haefner (USA)	72	75	73	68	288	397.78
	Sam Torrance	74	70	73	71	288	397.78
	Gordon Brand	74	69	73	72	288	397.78
23	Baldovino Dassu (I)	74	73	71	71	289	378.08
24	Vicente Fernandez (ARG)	77	70	74	69	290	344.83
	Pip Elson	75	72	73	70	290	344.83
	Alan Mew (TRI)	72	75	72	71	290	344.83
	Nick Job	74	73	72	71	290	344.83
	Bernard Gallacher	76	69	73	72	290	344.83
	Steve Martin	76	72	68	74	290	344.83
30	Bernard Langer (G)	70	76	73	72	291	296.80
	Wayne Grady (AUS)	71	75	73	72	291	296.80
	Simon Owen (NZ)	74	74	75	68	291	296.80
	Nick Faldo	72	75	73	71	291	296.80
34	Eamonn Darcy (IRE)	73	70	71	78	292	245.69
	Gary Cullen	73	75	68	76	292	245.69
	Karl-Heinz Gogele (G)	71	75	75	71	292	245.69
	Mitch Adcock (USA)	76	72	73	71	292	245.69
	Francisco Abreu (S)	72	73	75	72	292	245.69
	Gavin Levenson (SA)	72	75	73	72	292	245.69
	Arnold Palmer (USA)	75	72	73	72	292	245.69
42	Vaughan Somers (AUS)	70	73	76	73	292	245.69
	Vin Baker (SA)	74	73	76	70	293	200.74
	Eddie Polland	71	72	78	72	293	200.74
	Richard Eyles	78	68	75	72	293	200.74
	Peter Dawson	72	70	78	73	293	200.74
46	Michael King	76	72	75	71	294	182.27
47	Massimo Mannelli (I)	72	76	77	71	296	174.88
48	Denis Watson (SA)	71	79	74	73	297	163.79
	Robbie Stewart (SA)	74	74	74	75	297	163.79
50	Wolfgang Jersombeck (G)	77	75	70	78	298	155.17
51	Juan Anglada (S)	74	75	75	78	299	137.93
	Patrick Lemaire (F)	77	73	78	71	299	137.93
	Willi Hofmann (G)	74	74	77	74	299	137.93
	Philip Simmons (SA)	75	74	75	75	299	137.93
	Willie Milne	74	74	74	77	299	137.93
	Manuel Garcia (S)	73	74	76	76	299	137.93
57	David A. Russell	74	72	80	74	300	115.76
	Vance Waters	73	74	75	78	300	115.76
	Roddy Carr (IRE)	76	73	74	77	300	115.76
60	Trevor Powell	74	75	77	75	301	103.45
	Jeff Hawkes (SA)	76	72	76	77	301	103.45
62	Uwe Nievert (G)	70	78	79	75	302	93.60
	David Chillas	72	75	79	76	302	93.60
64	Patrick Bagnoud (SZ)	67	77	83	76	303	86.21
65	John Benda (USA)	76	74	78	77	305	40.64
	Siegfried Vollrath (G)	76	72	79	78	305	40.64
67	Manuel Ramos (S)	74	75	78	79	306	–
68	Ron Wood (AUS)	75	74	78	81	309	–
69	Gary Potter	74	76	80	82	312	–
70	Thomas Hubner* (G)	74	76	83	81	314	–

*Amateur

Previous Winners

Year	Winner	Venue	Score
1951	A. Cerda	Hamburg	286
1952	A. Cerda	Hamburg	283
1953	F. van Donck	Frankfurt	271
1954	A.D. Locke	Krefeld	279

After a tie with D.J. Rees

Year	Winner	Venue	Score
1955	K. Bousfield	Hamburg	279
1956	F. van Donck	Frankfurt	277
	After a tie with E. C. Brown		
1957	H. Weetman	Cologne	279
1958	F. de Luca	Krefeld	275

Year	Winner	Venue	Score
1959	K. Bousfield	Hamburg	271
1960	P.W. Thomson	Cologne	281
1961	B.J. Hunt	Krefeld	272
1962	R. Verwey	Hamburg	276
1963	B.G.C. Huggett	Cologne	278
1964	R. de Vicenzo	Krefeld	275
1965	H.R. Henning	Hamburg	274
1966	R. Stanton	Frankfurt	274
1967	D. Swaelens	Krefeld	273
1968	B. Franklin	Cologne	285
1969	J. Garaialde	Frankfurt	272
1970	J. Garaialde	Krefeld	276
1971	N.C. Coles	Bremen	279
1972	G. Marsh	Frankfurt	271
1973	F. Abreu	Dusseldorf	276
1974	S. Owen	Krefeld	276
1975	M. Bembridge	Bremen	285
1976	S. Hobday	Frankfurt	266
1977	T. Britz	Dusseldorf	275
1978	S. Ballesteros	Cologne	268

THE CARROLLS IRISH OPEN CHAMPIONSHIP

Portmarnock Golf Club, Dublin   23–26 August 1979   Prize money £60,000

Not only the first prize of £10,000 was commanding the thoughts of several of the field when they lined up at Portmarnock. For Howard Clark and Michael King in particular this was to be the last-ditch chance for a place in the Ryder Cup side to be announced at the end of the tournament. Clark made a brave bid, leading at the end of the second and third rounds, but slumped to a 75 while Mark James was surging to victory in the last round, and the Yorkshireman failed to make the team. King did enough to secure his place. For James it was his second victory of the year. His nerves withstood the challenge of Ed Sneed, who also shot a final 65.

						£
1	Mark James	73	75	69	65	282	10,000.00
2	Ed Sneed (USA)	75	72	71	65	283	6,660.00
3	Mark McCumber (USA)	75	71	70	69	285	3,760.00
4	José-Maria Canizares (S)	73	73	73	68	287	2,546.66
	Brian Barnes	81	69	67	70	287	2,546.66
	Simon Hobday (ZIM)	73	74	67	73	287	2,546.66
7	Howard Clark	71	69	73	75	288	1,650.00
	Tony Jacklin	73	69	72	74	288	1,650.00
9	Michael King	73	71	75	70	289	1,213.33
	Guy Hunt	73	72	73	71	289	1,213.33
	Philip Elson	76	70	71	72	289	1,213.33
12	Al Geiberger (USA)	75	70	75	70	290	934.00
	John O'Leary (IRE)	78	72	70	70	290	934.00
	Doug McClelland	78	67	74	71	290	934.00
	John Bland (SA)	69	75	74	72	290	934.00
	David Jones	71	73	72	74	290	934.00
17	Christy O'Connor Jnr (IRE)	76	74	71	70	291	760.00
	Severiano Ballesteros (S)	77	74	70	70	291	760.00
	Bill Longmuir	74	71	73	73	291	760.00
	Rodger Davis (AUS)	78	67	72	74	291	760.00

Pos	Player	R1	R2	R3	R4	Score	£
22	Bernard Gallacher	76	69	71	75	291	760.00
	Dale Hayes (SA)	78	73	72	69	292	670.00
	David Ingram	76	74	72	70	292	670.00
	John Morgan	77	72	70	73	292	670.00
	Sandy Lyle	76	69	72	75	292	670.00
26	Maurice Bembridge	80	71	73	69	293	570.00
	Garry Cullen	79	71	74	69	293	570.00
	Manuel Pinero (S)	79	72	69	73	293	570.00
	John Mahaffey (USA)	74	75	70	74	293	570.00
	Robbie Stewart (SA)	77	71	70	75	293	570.00
	Nick Faldo	78	71	69	75	293	570.00
32	Mike Miller	73	74	76	71	294	480.00
	Bob Charles (NZ)	75	75	72	72	294	480.00
	Tommy Halpin (IRE)	76	71	71	76	294	480.00
35	Nick Price (SA)	76	74	73	72	295	430.00
	Christy O'Connor, Snr (IRE)	76	73	73	73	295	430.00
	Eddie Polland	75	74	73	73	295	430.00
38	Antonio Garrido (S)	73	77	75	71	296	395.00
	Des Smyth (IRE)	73	73	74	76	296	395.00
	Tienie Britz (SA)	79	71	74	72	296	395.00
	Jaime Gonzalez (BZ)	77	72	74	73	296	395.00
42	Tommy Horton	77	74	77	69	297	350.00
	Sam Torrance	75	74	75	73	297	350.00
	Ken Brown	75	76	73	73	297	350.00
	Noel Ratcliffe (AUS)	73	76	72	76	297	350.00
	Harold Henning (SA)	75	71	74	77	297	350.00
47	Jimmy Heggarty (IRE)	82	69	77	70	298	305.00
	Neil Coles	77	74	73	74	298	305.00
	Steve Martin	75	73	74	76	298	305.00
	Alan Mew (TRI)	78	70	73	77	298	305.00
51	Gordon Brand	71	77	77	74	299	260.00
	Orville Moody (USA)	75	72	77	75	299	260.00
	Ernie Jones	74	76	74	75	299	260.00
	John Benda (USA)	73	76	73	77	299	260.00
	Simon Owen (NZ)	73	76	71	79	299	260.00
56	Ewen Murray	76	75	73	76	300	225.00
	Ross Drummond	81	70	71	78	300	225.00
58	Martin Foster	77	73	74	77	301	195.00
	Peter Townsend	75	75	74	77	301	195.00
	John Downie	72	78	74	77	301	195.00
	Manuel Garcia (S)	78	71	74	78	301	195.00
	Arthur Pierse* (IRE)	74	75	78	74	301	–
63	Peter Butler	80	71	76	75	302	165.00
	Hugh Baiocchi (SA)	71	74	79	78	302	165.00
65	Peter Cowen	73	78	77	75	303	150.00
66	Francisco Abreu (S)	77	74	78	75	304	70.00
	David J. Russell	77	73	75	79	304	70.00
	David Long* (IRE)	76	75	73	80	304	–
69	Phil Simmons (SA)	77	74	80	74	305	–
70	David Chillas	78	73	78	78	307	–
71	Tom Melville	74	77	81	79	311	–
72	Raymond Kane* (IRE)	75	76	82	81	314	–

*Amateur

Previous winners

Year	Winner	Venue	Score
1963	B.J. Hunt	Woodbrook	270
1964	C. O'Connor	Woodbrook	268
	After a tie with R. de Vicenzo		
1965	N.C. Coles	Little Island, Cork	269
1966	C. O'Connor	Royal Dublin	272
1967	C. O'Connor	Woodbrook	277
1968	J. Martin	Woodbrook	281
1969	R.D.B.M. Shade	Woodbrook	289
1970	B.G.C. Huggett	Woodbrook	279
1971	N.C. Coles	Woodbrook	276
1972	C. O'Connor	Woodbrook	284
1973	P. McGuirk	Woodbrook	277
1974	B. Gallacher	Woodbrook	279
1975	C. O'Connor Jr	Woodbrook	275
1976	B. Crenshaw	Portmarnock	284
1977	H. Green	Portmarnock	283
1978	K. Brown	Portmarnock	281

THE SWISS OPEN CHAMPIONSHIP

Crans-sur-Sierre Golf Club   30 August–2 September 1979   Prize money £48,400

Hugh Baiocchi has always been something of a Continental specialist, having in the past won the Dutch, Scandinavian, and Swiss titles, and at Crans he came to the front at the right time with a closing 67 to capture again the Swiss crown. It was the South African Open Champion's first win in Europe since his victory in the Sun Alliance Match-Play in 1977. Three shots behind Italy's Delio Lovato after 54 holes, Baiocchi's confident putting took him to the turn in 31 and he went on to an impressive five-shots victory. Lovato had been the surprise of the Championship – virtually unknown despite holding his country's professional title.

							£
1	Hugh Baiocchi (SA)	68	67	73	67	275	8,064.52
2	Antonio Garrido (S)	69	71	72	68	280	3,607.53
	Dale Hayes (SA)	68	71	68	73	280	3,607.53
	Delio Lovato (I)	67	70	68	75	280	3,607.53
5	Ken Brown	72	70	71	68	281	1,731.18
	Bernhard Langer (G)	72	69	70	70	281	1,731.18
	Mitch Adcock (USA)	66	72	72	71	281	1,731.18
8	Ewen Murray	73	67	68	74	282	1,209.68
9	Tienie Britz (SA)	72	70	73	68	283	943.55
	Manuel Pinero (S)	73	68	71	71	283	943.55
	Rafe Botts (USA)	68	67	75	73	283	943.55
	Al Geiberger (USA)	69	68	72	74	283	943.55
13	Vicente Fernandez (ARG)	70	72	73	69	284	731.85
	Jean Garaialde (F)	70	70	74	70	284	731.85
	Robbie Stewart (SA)	75	68	71	70	284	731.85
	Manuel Ballesteros (S)	71	71	69	73	284	731.85
17	Angel Gallardo (S)	73	73	69	70	285	629.03
	Mark James	75	71	69	70	285	629.03
	Bernard Pascassio (F)	68	74	72	71	285	629.03
20	Luciano Grappasonni (I)	72	73	72	69	286	540.32
	James Edman (USA)	73	70	73	70	286	540.32
	Juan Anglada (S)	71	72	73	70	286	540.32
	Gavin Levenson (SA)	74	70	72	70	286	540.32
	Nick Job	73	68	74	71	286	540.32
	David Ingram	72	70	73	71	286	540.32
	Garry Cullen	70	72	73	71	286	540.32
	R. Adham* (USA)	72	72	71	71	286	–
	Jeff Hawkes (SA)	72	73	69	72	286	540.32
	Vin Baker (SA)	67	71	77	72	287	411.29
29	Trevor Johnson	70	75	72	70	287	411.29
	Tommy Horton	72	69	74	72	287	411.29
	Maurice Bembridge	72	71	72	72	287	411.29
	Manuel Garcia (S)	72	73	70	72	287	411.29
	Alberto Croce (I)	69	76	70	72	287	411.29
	P. Hessemer (USA)	71	73	70	73	287	411.29
	Massimo Manelli (I)	70	71	72	74	287	411.29
37	Gordon Brand	72	71	74	71	288	326.61
	Geromalo Delfino (I)	71	72	74	71	288	326.61
	Evan Williams (USA)	71	73	73	71	288	326.61
	Silvano Locatelli (I)	74	71	71	72	288	326.61
	Peter Cowen	73	69	73	73	288	326.61
	Harold Henning (SA)	67	75	71	75	288	326.61
43	Warren Humphreys	70	73	74	72	289	282.26
	John Benda (USA)	72	71	73	73	289	282.26
	Manuel Calero (S)	72	74	70	73	289	282.26
	Vaughan Somers (AUS)	69	72	73	75	289	282.26
	Roberto Campagnoli (I)	72	70	70	77	289	282.26
48	Pietro Molteni (I)	74	70	78	69	291	237.90
	Rodger Davis (AUS)	69	71	78	73	291	237.90
	Peter Dawson	72	69	77	73	291	237.90
	Bobby Verwey (SA)	71	72	74	74	291	237.90
	Tony Price	71	69	77	74	291	237.90

							£
54	Ossie Gartenmaier (A)	71	69	76	75	291	237.90
	Denis Watson (SA)	72	74	76	71	293	201.61
	Ian Mosey	71	73	74	75	293	201.61
	Manuel Gallardo (S)	73	71	74	75	293	201.61
57	Des Smyth (IRE)	74	71	77	73	295	181.45
	Clive Bonner	74	69	77	75	295	181.45
59	Noel Ratcliffe (AUS)	70	75	79	72	296	157.26
	Mike Inglis	75	71	76	74	296	157.26
63	Gery Watine (F)	72	74	75	75	296	157.26
64	John Hay	73	72	76	75	296	157.26
	David J. Russell	77	69	79	72	297	137.10
	David Watkinson	72	72	75	79	298	129.03
65	Paul McGarry	73	70	77	79	299	120.97
66	Tim Giles	76	70	81	78	305	112.90
67	Keith Waters	74	72	84	78	308	–

*Amateur

Previous winners

Year	Winner	Venue	Score
1957	A. Angelini	Crans-sur-Sierre	270
1958	K. Bousfield	Crans-sur-Sierre	272
1959	D. J. Rees	Crans-sur-Sierre	274
1960	H. Henning	Crans-sur-Sierre	270
1961	K. D. G. Nagle	Crans-sur-Sierre	268
1962	R. J. Charles	Crans-sur-Sierre	272
	After a tie with P. J. Butler and F. van Donck		
1963	D. J. Rees	Crans-sur-Sierre	278
	After a tie with H. R. Henning		
1964	H. R. Henning	Crans-sur-Sierre	276
1965	H. R. Henning	Crans-sur-Sierre	208
		(54 holes)	
1966	A. Angelini	Crans-sur-Sierre	271
1967	R. Vines	Crans-sur-Sierre	272
1968	R. Bernardini	Crans-sur-Sierre	272
1969	R. Bernardini	Crans-sur-Sierre	277
1970	G. Marsh	Crans-sur-Sierre	274
1971	P. M. P. Townsend	Crans-sur-Sierre	270
1972	G. Marsh	Crans-sur-Sierre	270
1973	H. Baiocchi	Crans-sur-Sierre	278
1974	R. J. Charles	Crans-sur-Sierre	275
1975	D. Hayes	Crans-sur-Sierre	273
1976	M. Pinero	Crans-sur-Sierre	274
1977	S. Ballesteros	Crans-sur-Sierre	273
1978	S. Ballesteros	Crans-sur-Sierre	272

THE EUROPEAN OPEN CHAMPIONSHIP

Ailsa Course, Turnberry Hotel, Ayrshire   6–9 September 1979   Prize Money £105,000

The European Open Championship in its second year might not have had the big international entry that greeted its inauguration at Walton Heath, but America's Bobby Wadkins defended and their second leading money-winner Larry Nelson had a tilt at the title, as did Australia's David Graham fresh from his US PGA victory. But it was a Briton, Sandy Lyle, with his ever-maturing game, who spreadeagled them all with a great seven-shots victory. Lyle, Ballesteros, and Brown were the 36-holes leaders, but James and Coles shot to the front with splendid third rounds – James's 64 being only a stroke outside the Open Championship record of 63. Lyle's fourth round composure was majestic as he birdied six of the first seven holes and, after some wayward shots in between, finished with birdies at the last two holes. It was his third victory of the season and his winner's cheque for £17,500 took him past Ballesteros to the top of the Order of Merit.

Pos	Player						£
1	Sandy Lyle	71	67	72	65	275	17,500.00
2	Dale Hayes (SA)	72	72	70	68	282	9,025.00
	Peter Townsend	72	68	70	72	282	9,025.00
4	Tommy Horton	74	72	71	66	283	4,227.50
	Neil Coles	73	70	66	74	283	4,227.50
6	Sam Torrance	69	72	71	70	284	2,233.33
	Severiano Ballesteros (S)	69	69	75	71	284	2,233.33
	Mark James	73	72	64	75	284	2,233.33
9	Howard Clark	74	71	67	73	285	1,675.00
	José-Maria Cañizares (S)	70	70	72	73	285	1,675.00
11	Ken Brown	70	68	74	75	287	1,500.00
12	Bill Longmuir	73	73	72	70	288	1,400.00
	Des Smyth (IRE)	73	68	76	71	288	1,400.00
	Gordon Brand	75	66	74	73	288	1,400.00
15	Larry Nelson (USA)	77	70	74	68	289	1,143.75
	Noel Ratcliffe (AUS)	75	68	77	69	289	1,143.75
	Robin Fyfe	75	70	75	69	289	1,143.75
	Robbie Stewart (SA)	77	70	72	70	289	1,143.75
	Bobby Wadkins (USA)	75	71	71	72	289	1,143.75
	Brian Waites	72	72	73	72	289	1,143.75
	John Morgan	75	70	70	74	289	1,143.75
	Manuel Pinero (S)	74	72	70	73	289	1,143.75
23	Trevor Johnson	71	77	72	70	290	945.00
	Tienie Britz (SA)	77	69	69	74	290	945.00
25	David Jagger	75	73	74	69	291	862.50
	David Huish	73	73	73	72	291	862.50
	Peter Cowen	76	71	70	74	291	862.50
	James Farmer	75	69	73	74	291	862.50
29	Michael King	74	71	74	73	292	763.75
	Bob Charles (NZ)	70	70	77	75	292	763.75
	Nick Faldo	70	74	73	75	292	763.75
	Garry Cullen	70	74	69	79	292	763.75
33	Brian Barnes	75	67	80	71	293	660.00
	Ewen Murray	74	73	73	73	293	660.00
	Tony Jacklin	73	73	74	73	293	660.00
	Bill Murray	74	72	74	73	293	660.00
	Christy O'Connor Jnr (IRE)	75	71	72	75	293	660.00
	Jeff Hall	71	73	74	75	293	660.00
39	Nick Price (SA)	73	74	73	74	294	556.00
	Malcolm Gregson	73	71	75	75	294	556.00
	Vin Baker (SA)	69	74	75	76	294	556.00
	Rodger Davis (AUS)	73	74	71	76	294	556.00
	Tony Charnley	68	76	74	76	294	556.00
44	Doug McClelland	74	72	76	71	295	470.00
	Martin Foster	74	72	76	73	295	470.00
	Bernard Gallacher	73	75	73	74	295	470.00
	John Bland (SA)	74	70	76	75	295	470.00
	Carl Mason	75	73	71	76	295	470.00
	Baldovino Dassu (I)	74	67	78	76	295	470.00
	Graham Burroughs	74	74	74	76	295	470.00
	Antonio Garrido (S)	80	68	71	76	295	470.00
	Angel Gallardo (S)	73	71	74	77	295	470.00
53	David J. Russell	77	71	77	71	296	410.00
	Hugh Baiocchi (SA)	74	70	75	77	296	410.00
	Denis Watson (SA)	78	68	72	78	296	410.00
56	Vaughan Somers (AUS)	73	74	76	74	297	375.00
	David Graham (AUS)	73	73	73	78	297	375.00
	Norman Wood	72	71	76	78	297	375.00
	Jamie Edman (USA)	72	73	74	78	297	375.00
60	David Watkinson	75	75	72	77	299	350.00
61	David Vaughan	74	71	75	80	300	340.00
62	Mitch Adcock (USA)	73	74	82	72	301	325.00
	Eamonn Darcy (IRE)	78	70	77	76	301	325.00
64	Simon Hobday (ZIM)	75	72	78	77	302	305.00
	Peter Butler	72	75	75	80	302	305.00

Previous winner

Year	Winner	Venue	Score
1978	B. Wadkins (USA)	Walton Heath, Surrey	283

THE TOURNAMENT PLAYERS' CHAMPIONSHIP

Moor Park Golf Club, Rickmansworth, Herts   20–23 September 1979   Prize Money £50,000

The new sponsorship of the Championship by the SOS Talisman company proved a lucky charm for Mike King who recorded his first victory since joining the professional ranks five years previously. His consistent 'so near and yet so far' season had earned him Ryder Cup honours to go with his Walker Cup distinction, and although he played in only one match in West Virginia he came straight back to victory at Moor Park. Scotland's Ewen Murray was the clear leader for two rounds and was then joined by King with a round to go. But it was defending champion Brian Waites who with four birdies and an eagle in eight holes made the final challenge.

							£
1	Michael King	71	67	72	71	281	8,330.00
2	Brian Waites	75	69	70	68	282	5,550.00
3	Ewen Murray	68	68	74	74	284	3,130.00
4	Gary Player (SA)	72	72	68	74	286	2,500.00
5	Bernard Gallacher	74	71	73	69	287	2,120.00
6	Neil Coles	74	70	75	69	288	1,500.00
	Peter Townsend	70	73	72	73	288	1,500.00
	Des Smyth (IRE)	74	68	72	74	288	1,500.00
9	Sam Torrance	75	69	75	71	290	1,060.00
	Peter Dawson	73	73	69	75	290	1,060.00
11	Christy O'Connor Jnr (IRE)	75	74	73	69	291	837.50
	Greg Norman (AUS)	75	70	75	71	291	837.50
	Mark James	71	74	70	76	291	837.50
	Bill Longmuir	71	74	70	76	291	837.50
15	David Graham (AUS)	75	71	76	70	292	663.33
	John O'Leary (IRE)	71	77	73	71	292	663.33
	Brian Marchbank	75	71	72	74	292	663.33
	Bob Charles (NZ)	75	69	74	74	292	663.33
	Nick Price (SA)	73	73	72	74	292	663.33
	John Bland (SA)	74	68	71	79	292	663.33
21	Howard Clark	72	75	72	74	293	577.50
	Sandy Lyle	74	72	72	75	293	577.50
23	Nick Faldo	72	72	78	72	294	555.00
24	Rafe Botts (USA)	76	75	74	70	295	502.50
	Simon Hobday (ZIM)	75	72	76	72	295	502.50

							£
	Andrew Chandler	78	74	72	71	295	502.50
	Stephen Rolley	72	73	77	73	295	502.50
	Nick Job	73	73	75	74	295	502.50
	Mark McNulty (SA)	71	73	73	78	295	502.50
30	Manuel Calero (S)	77	74	75	70	296	435.00
	Warren Humphreys	74	74	72	76	296	435.00
	Garry Cullen	74	74	71	77	296	435.00
33	Geoff Tickell	73	76	72	76	297	395.00
	Derrick Cooper	75	74	74	74	297	395.00
	Michael Miller	72	77	74	74	297	395.00
37	Denis Watson (SA)	75	71	76	75	298	365.00
	Charles Dernie	77	72	76	73	298	365.00
39	Graham Burroughs	74	71	75	78	299	330.00
	Malcolm Gregson	74	75	81	69	299	330.00
	Philip Loxley	74	78	74	73	299	330.00
	Brian Barnes	77	70	77	75	299	330.00
	Bernhard Langer (G)	79	71	73	76	299	330.00
	Ken Brown	69	76	76	78	299	330.00
44	Brian Evans	75	73	76	76	300	295.00
	Carl Mason	77	71	76	76	300	295.00
46	Peter Tupling	80	70	76	75	301	265.00
	David Ingram	77	72	77	75	301	265.00
	Norman Wood	79	72	74	76	301	265.00
	Peter Cowen	77	73	72	79	301	265.00
50	Richard Eyles	76	74	74	73	302	210.00

Pos	Player						£
	Brian Huggett	77	75	75	75	302	210.00
	Gordon Brand	77	73	76	76	302	210.00
	Bill McColl	78	74	74	76	302	210.00
	José-Maria Canizares (S)	76	73	76	77	302	210.00
	Michael Steadman	76	71	73	82	302	210.00
	David J. Russell	72	69	77	84	302	210.00
57	Tommy Horton	75	75	74	79	303	170.00
58	Noel Ratcliffe (AUS)	78	74	78	74	304	145.00
	David Dunk	81	71	76	76	304	145.00
	Dale Hayes (SA)	78	73	78	75	304	145.00
	Joe Higgins	75	73	78	78	304	145.00
	Philip Elson	76	76	75	77	304	145.00
	John Fowler	75	75	75	79	304	145.00
65	Tienie Britz (SA)	80	72	73	79	304	145.00
66	David Talbot	76	75	79	75	305	125.00
	Tim Rastall	72	79	79	76	306	–
68	Mitch Adcock (USA)	77	73	80	77	307	–
	Peter Butler	77	75	79	76	307	–
	Manuel Pinero (S)	74	75	78	80	307	–
	Jeff Hall	74	77	78	78	307	–
	Ian Mosey	74	78	73	82	307	–
72	Hugh Jackson	78	73	77	80	308	–
73	Keith Waters	76	75	80	78	309	–
74	Mike Ingham	78	74	80	78	310	–
75	Martin Foster	74	76	81	82	313	–
	Ross Whitehead	79	73	82	79	313	–

Previous winners

Year	Winner	Venue	Score
1977	N.C. Coles	Foxhills	288
1978	B.J. Waites	Foxhills	286

CACHAREL WORLD UNDER-25 CHAMPIONSHIP

Club de Campagne, Nîmes, France   27–30 September 1979   Prize Money £20,000

	Player					Total
1	Bernard Langer (G)	73	67	67	67	274
2	Jim Nelford (C)	70	75	75	71	291
	Denis Watson (SA)	70	72	78	71	291
4	Martin Poxon	74	73	70	75	292
5	Mitch Adcock (USA)	73	72	78	71	294
6	Jeff Hall	73	77	71	74	295
7	Steve Martin	77	69	73	77	296
8	Gordon Brand	80	78	69	71	298
9	Nick Faldo	73	79	73	75	300
	Nick Price (SA)	75	76	73	76	300

THE DUNLOP MASTERS

Woburn Golf & Country Club, Bucks   3–6 October 1979   Prize Money £60,000

Europe's final major stroke-play event of the season produced two definitive results. Graham Marsh won it with probably the finest 72nd-hole birdie of the year, and Sandy Lyle clinched top place in the Order of Merit in only his second full year on the circuit. Ballesteros was an 11th-hour contestant in a bid to retain the number one spot for the fourth successive year, but was never in the hunt. Tony Jacklin and Tienie Britz were the early threats on the magnificent new par-72 Woburn course, but Marsh led into the third round and clinched a one-shot victory with a superb three-wood to within 10 feet of the flag at the 514yd 18th to snuff out the play-off hopes of Aoki and Coles and spectacularly earn the £10,000 first prize.

	Name						£
1	Graham Marsh (AUS)	70	68	72	73	283	10,000.00
2	Isao Aoki (J)	73	73	68	70	284	5,210.00
	Neil Coles	72	68	71	73	284	5,210.00
4	Tony Jacklin	69	69	74	74	286	3,000.00
5	Michael King	69	77	73	68	287	2,540.00
6	Roger Maltbie (USA)	73	71	75	69	288	2,020.00
	Malcolm Gregson	74	70	72	72	288	2,020.00
8	Ken Brown	75	75	69	70	289	1,416.66
	Fuzzy Zoeller (USA)	71	74	71	73	289	1,416.66
	Nick Price (SA)	71	73	71	74	289	1,416.66
11	José-Maria Canizares (S)	74	71	73	72	290	1,170.00
12	Bob Shearer (AUS)	74	73	72	72	291	1,080.00
	Sam Torrance	72	71	72	76	291	1,080.00
14	Philip Elson	69	76	75	72	292	953.33
	Bob Charles (NZ)	72	71	76	73	292	953.33
	Eddie Polland	71	74	74	73	292	953.33
17	Mark McNulty (SA)	73	74	73	73	293	860.00
	Tienie Britz (SA)	69	67	77	80	293	860.00
19	Sandy Lyle	71	76	80	67	294	790.00
	Nick Faldo	71	76	75	72	294	790.00
	Bernard Gallacher	76	71	75	72	294	790.00
	Peter Townsend	72	72	74	76	294	790.00
	Brian Waites	71	79	66	78	294	790.00
24	Simon Owen (NZ)	71	78	75	71	295	730.00
25	Severiano Ballesteros (S)	73	75	78	70	296	690.00
	Tohru Nakamura (J)	70	78	75	73	296	690.00
28	Tommy Horton	77	71	75	73	296	690.00
	Brian Barnes	74	74	73	73	297	630.00
	Bill Longmuir	80	71	68	75	297	630.00
	Brian Huggett	74	71	73	79	297	630.00
31	Antonio Garrido (S)	70	78	76	74	298	570.00
	Simon Hobday (ZIM)	75	75	71	77	298	570.00
	David Jones	73	74	73	78	298	570.00
34	Gordon Brand	72	76	78	73	299	520.00
	Baldovino Dassu (I)	78	74	73	74	299	520.00
36	Gavin Levenson (SA)	78	78	70	74	300	495.00
	Maurice Bembridge	73	73	78	76	300	495.00
38	John Morgan	79	74	74	74	301	470.00
	Nick Job	77	74	72	78	301	470.00
	John O'Leary (IRE)	70	73	76	82	301	470.00
41	Garry Cullen	73	76	75	80	304	450.00
42	Manuel Pinero (S)	72	77	77	79	305	435.00
	Howard Clark	76	77	74	78	305	435.00
44	Hubert Green (USA)	74	77	80	76	307	415.00
	Des Smyth (IRE)	70	77	82	78	307	415.00
46	Ian Woosnam	74	78	80	76	308	400.00
47	Mark James	70	80	77	84	311	390.00
48	Guy Hunt	80	76	78	78	312	380.00
49	Willie Milne	84	76	77	80	317	365.00
	Gaylord Burrows (USA)	81	77	78	81	317	365.00

For previous winners of the Dunlop Masters see Championship Rolls

Wentworth Golf Club, Surrey 11–14 October 1979   Prize Money £110,000

One of the finest 36-hole finals in the long history of the Championship rewarded the event's new sponsors Suntory, the Japanese whisky company, the American Bill Rogers defeating the holder Isao Aoki on the 36th green. Compensation for Aoki, now established as one of the world's foremost players, was a record £73,000 – £18,000 as the runner-up and £55,000 as the value of a furnished apartment at Gleneagles in Scotland for holing his tee shot with a seven-iron at the second during his match against David Graham! Rogers was the 'outsider' of the 12 competitors, but upset the form book in unarguable style. He beat the European number one Sandy Lyle, the US Open champion and favourite Hale Irwin, and the US Masters winner Fuzzy Zoeller, before capturing the title and the £30,000 winner's cheque with a 36th-hole birdie which made him 28-under-par for his four victories. Aoki had a classic semi-final with Severiano Ballesteros, recovering from three down after 25 holes to square at the 35th and going on to win at the 40th hole.

Final

W. Rogers (USA) (£30,000) beat I. Aoki (J) (£18,000)   1 hole

Semi-final

Rogers beat F. Zoeller (USA)   2 holes
Aoki beat S. Ballesteros (S)   40th hole

Play-off

Zoeller (£12,500) beat Ballesteros (£9,500)   1 hole

Second round

Rogers beat H. Irwin (USA) (£6,000)   3 and 2
Aoki beat D. Graham (AUS) (£6,000)   3 and 1
Zoeller beat G. Player (SA) (£6,000)   1 hole
Ballesteros beat L. Wadkins (USA) (£6,000)   3 and 1

First round

Graham beat M. James (GB) (£4,000)   3 and 2
Wadkins beat V. Fernandez (ARG) (£4,000)   3 and 1
Rogers beat S. Lyle (GB) (£4,000)   4 and 2
Player beat T. Nakamura (J) (£4,000)   2 holes

For previous winners of the World Match-Play title see Championship Rolls

THE LANCÔME TROPHY

St Nom-la-Brétèche, Paris 25–28 October 1979   Prize Money £25,000

	Player						£
1	Johnny Miller (USA)	70	71	69	71	281	10,000.00
2	Lee Trevino (USA)	74	72	68	70	284	3,500.00
	Sandy Lyle (GB)	71	71	72	70	284	3,500.00
4	Ray Floyd (USA)	72	65	74	74	285	1,750.00
5	Bill Rogers (USA)	72	71	73	71	287	1,375.00
	Mark James (GB)	69	75	73	70	287	1,375.00
7	Tony Jacklin (GB)	72	67	74	75	288	1,000.00
8	Arnold Palmer	72	75	73	72	292	800.00
9	Dale Hayes (SA)	77	71	70	76	294	600.00
	Brian Barnes (GB)	75	76	72	71	294	600.00
11	Jean Garaïalde (F)	74	73	71	79	297	500.00
12	Bobby Clampett (USA)*	74	75	79	70	298	–

*Amateur

TOP 60 – 1979 ORDER OF MERIT

(Confined to players who contested five or more Order of Merit Tournaments)

		OM Points	OM Tmts	Tmts Plyd	Strokes	Rds	Avge	Prize Money £
1	Sandy Lyle	39,807.67	20	22	5,044	70	72.05	49,232.63
2	Severiano Ballesteros (S)	37,026.02	16	17	4,190	58	72.24	47,411.00
3	Mark James	32,493.98	20	22	5,083	70	72.61	38,534.09
4	Dale Hayes (SA)	30,031.05	17	18	4,779	66	72.40	32,540.33
5	Michael King	26,283.29	22	22	6,070	84	72.26	29,724.59
6	Brian Barnes	26,218.24	16	17	4,345	60	72.41	28,203.51
7	Ken Brown	22,990.89	20	20	5,361	74	72.44	25,406.78
8	Antonio Garrido (S)	21,825.02	15	15	3,907	54	72.35	24,664.80
9	Tony Jacklin	20,504.91	18	19	4,479	62	72.24	22,178.61
10	Neil Coles	19,185.83	11	11	2,739	38	72.07	21,350.99
11	Simon Hobday (ZIM)	18,565.70	17	17	4,103	56	73.26	21,218.21
12	Hugh Baiocchi (SA)	18,033.01	17	17	4,505	62	72.66	20,265.30
13	Bernard Gallacher	17,283.14	16	16	3,913	54	72.46	20,047.76
14	Peter Townsend	15,886.70	17	17	4,246	58	73.20	18,972.96
15	Vicente Fernandez (ARG)	15,811.17	18	19	3,948	54	73.11	20,933.05
16	Des Smyth (IRE)	15,553.60	17	17	3,707	51	72.68	17,447.89
17	Greg Norman (AUS)	15,361.86	10	10	2,461	34	72.38	16,465.67
18	Maurice Bembridge	14,747.29	18	18	4,586	62	73.96	15,616.79
19	Sam Torrance	14,314.73	21	21	5,263	72	73.09	19,132.25
20	Brian Waites	13,928.44	14	14	3,343	46	72.67	16,665.26
21	Nick Faldo	13,899.80	17	18	4,372	60	72.86	14,910.79
22	Howard Clark	13,412.58	21	21	5,140	70	73.42	16,919.84
23	Jose-Maria Canizares (S)	13,393.88	15	15	3,634	50	72.68	16,754.58
24	Manuel Pinero (S)	11,730.18	18	18	4,542	62	73.25	16,178.97
25	Tommy Horton	11,725.74	20	20	5,223	71	73.56	13,093.44
26	Bob Charles (NZ)	11,499.24	14	14	3,925	54	72.68	12,945.22
27	Baldovino Dassu (I)	11,478.73	18	18	4,088	56	73.00	11,990.87
28	Rodger Davis (AUS)	11,409.94	14	14	3,514	48	73.20	12,391.87
29	Gavin Levenson (SA)	10,971.30	23	23	5,284	72	73.38	12,798.4
30	Gordon Brand	10,913.13	22	23	5,370	73	73.56	13,970.9
31	Nick Price (SA)	10,593.83	17	18	3,958	54	73.29	11,524.6
32	Eddie Polland	9,874.96	21	21	4,749	65	73.06	13,566.6
33	John Morgan	9,196.20	19	19	4,205	57	73.77	11,875.8
34	Mark McNulty (SA)	9,102.04	16	16	3,367	46	73.19	12,336.4
35	Tienie Britz (SA)	8,898.99	14	14	3,665	50	73.30	12,666.5
36	Malcolm Gregson	8,551.69	19	19	4,347	59	73.67	12,474.5
37	Nick Job	8,339.81	21	21	5,420	74	73.24	15,842.3
38	Garry Cullen	7,994.11	21	21	5,520	75	73.60	11,658.8
39	Francisco Abreu (S)	7,961.39	11	11	2,725	37	73.64	8,572.2
40	Bill Longmuir	7,745.94	21	21	5,104	69	73.97	8,338.5
41	Ewen Murray	7,738.38	18	18	3,762	51	73.76	11,684.00
42	Simon Owen (NZ)	7,366.72	16	16	3,609	49	73.65	9,627.5
43	John O'Leary (IRE)	7,319.40	20	20	4,623	62	74.56	11,145.5
44	Philip Elson	6,801.68	17	17	4,106	56	73.32	9,858.8
45	John Bland (SA)	6,621.71	15	15	3,531	48	73.56	9,518.8
46	Willie Milne	6,456.37	16	16	2,976	40	74.40	7,816.3
47	Harold Henning (SA)	6,028.23	15	15	3,715	50	74.30	7,160.7
48	Brian Huggett	5,755.88	12	12	2,722	37	73.56	7,049.2
49	Noel Ratcliffe (AUS)	5,716.82	17	17	4,279	58	73.77	8,559.5
50	Eamonn Darcy (IRE)	5,706.49	18	18	4,131	56	73.76	11,241.8
51	Bobby Verwey (SA)	5,670.51	19	19	4,434	60	73.90	8,956.8
52	Jeff Hall	5,615.54	21	22	4,497	61	73.72	6,579.6
53	Carl Mason	5,556.01	20	20	4,394	59	74.47	8,674.4
54	Robbie Stewart (SA)	4,879.90	18	18	4,014	54	74.33	4,954.9
55	David Ingram	4,863.03	15	15	3,332	45	74.04	6,644.5
56	Bernhard Langer (G)	4,662.54	16	17	3,856	52	74.15	7,972.2
57	Peter Cowen	4,662.15	18	18	4,295	58	74.05	6,039.1
58	Terry Gale (AUS)	4,503.25	5	5	1,307	18	72.61	4,503.2
59	Jaime Gonzalez (BZ)	4,243.53	11	11	1,847	25	73.88	4,514.4
60	Martin Foster	4,168.95	21	21	4,782	64	74.71	6,232.8

TOP 20 LEADING MONEY-WINNERS 1979

		£
1	Sandy Lyle	49,232.63
2	Severiano Ballesteros	47,411.00
3	Mark James	38,534.09
4	Dale Hayes	32,540.33
5	Bill Rogers*	31,403.32
6	Michael King	29,724.59
7	Isao Aoki*	28,350.00
8	Brian Barnes	28,203.51
9	Ken Brown	25,406.78
10	Antonio Garrido	24,664.80
11	Tony Jacklin	22,178.61
12	Neil Coles	21,350.99
13	Simon Hobday	21,218.21
14	Vicente Fernandez	20,993.05
15	Hugh Baiocchi	20,265.76
16	Graham Marsh*	20,158.52
17	Bernard Gallacher	20,047.76
18	Sam Torrance	19,132.25
19	Peter Townsend	18,972.96
20	Des Smyth	17,447.89

* Not in ETPD Order of Merit Top 60

POST-WAR COMPOSITE MONEY-WINNING LEADERS

		£
1	Neil Coles	209,918
2	Severiano Ballesteros	195,608
3	Brian Barnes	157,095
4	Tony Jacklin	152,736
5	Dale Hayes	136,835
6	Gary Player	133,752
7	Christy O'Connor	127,239
8	Bernard Gallacher	120,404
9	Graham Marsh	119,915
10	Tommy Horton	119,650
11	Bob Charles	119,364
12	Peter Oosterhuis	111,830
13	Hugh Baiocchi	109,120
14	Brian Huggett	103,637
15	Peter Butler	100,511
16	Manuel Pinero	94,120
17	Peter Townsend	91,811
18	Eddie Polland	87,854
19	Mark James	85,940
20	Jack Nicklaus	81,331

LEADING PGA MONEY-WINNERS 1963–1979

		£			£
1963	Bernard Hunt	7,209	1972	Bob Charles	18,538
1964	Neil Coles	7,890	1973	Tony Jacklin	24,839
1965	Peter Thomson	7,011	1974	Peter Oosterhuis	32,127
1966	Bruce Devlin	13,205	1975	Dale Hayes	20,507
1967	Gay Brewer	20,235	1976	Severiano Ballesteros	39,503
1968	Gay Brewer	23,107	1977	Severiano Ballesteros	46,435
1969	Billy Casper	23,483	1978	Severiano Ballesteros	54,348
1970	Christy O'Connor	31,532	1979	Sandy Lyle	49,232
1971	Gary Player	11,281			

THE HARRY VARDON TROPHY

Awarded annually to the leading player in the PGA Order of Merit

Year	Winner	Club	Year	Winner	Club
1937	C.A. Whitcombe	Crews Hill	1961	C. O'Connor	Royal Dublin
1938	T.H. Cotton	Royal Mid-Surrey	1962	C. O'Connor	Royal Dublin
1939	R.A. Whitcombe	Parkstone	1963	N.C. Coles	Coombe Hill
1940–45	*In abeyance*		1964	P. Alliss	Parkstone
1946	A.D. Locke	South Africa	1965	B.J. Hunt	Hartsbourne
1947	N.G. Von Nida	Australia	1966	P. Alliss	Parkstone
1948	C.H. Ward	Little Aston	1967	M.E. Gregson	Dyrham Park
1949	C.H. Ward	Little Aston	1968	B.G.C. Huggett	Betchworth Park
1950	A.D. Locke	South Africa	1969	B. Gallacher	Ifield
1951	J. Panton	Glenbervie	1970	N.C. Coles	Coombe Hill
1952	H. Weetman	Croham Hurst	1971	P.A. Oosterhuis	Dulwich and Sydenham
1953	F. van Donck	Belgium	1972	P.A. Oosterhuis	Pacific Harbour, Fiji
1954	A.D. Locke	South Africa	1973	P.A. Oosterhuis	Pacific Harbour, Fiji
1955	D.J. Rees	South Herts	1974	P.A. Oosterhuis	Pacific Harbour, Fiji
1956	H. Weetman	Croham Hurst	1975	D. Hayes	St Pierre and South Africa
1957	E.C. Brown	Buchanan Castle	1976	S. Ballesteros	Spain
1958	B.J. Hunt	Hartsbourne	1977	S. Ballesteros	Spain
1959	D.J. Rees	South Herts	1978	S. Ballesteros	Spain
1960	B.J. Hunt	Hartsbourne	1979	A.W.B. Lyle	Hawkstone Park

THE 1979 EUROPEAN TOURNAMENT SCHEDULE

Date	Event	Venue	Prize Money
April			
17–20	Italian Open Championship	Rome Golf Club (Acquasanta)	£35,000
24–27	Madrid Open Championship	Real Club de la Puerta de Hierro	£40,000 (To be confirmed)
May			
1–4	Spanish Open Championship	El Escorpian, Valencia	£42,000
8–11	French Open Championship	St Cloud, Paris	£40,000
15–18	Martini International Tournament	Wentworth Club, Surrey	£54,000
23–26	Sun Alliance PGA Championship	Royal St George's, Sandwich	£70,000
29–1 June	Avis-Jersey Open	La Moye, Jersey	£35,000
June			
5–8	Newcastle '900' Open	Northumberland Club, Newcastle	£42,000
19–22	Greater Manchester Open	Wilmslow Golf Club, Cheshire	£35,000
26–29	Coral Welsh Classic	Royal Porthcawl Golf Club, Mid-Glamorgan	£35,000
July			
3–6	Scandinavian Enterprises Open Championship	Vasatorps Golf Club, Helsingborg, Sweden	£46,000
9–12	English Golf Classic	The Belfry, Sutton Coldfield	£54,000
17–20	109th Open Golf Championship	Muirfield, East Lothian	£200,000
24–27	Dutch Open Championship	Hilversum	£35,000
August			
7–10	Benson and Hedges International Open	Fulford Golf Club, York	£80,000
14–17	Carrolls Irish Open Championship	Portmarnock Golf Club, near Dublin	Undecided
21–24	German Open Championship	Berlin	£50,000
28–31	Swiss Open Championship	Crans-sur-Sierre	£57,000
September			
4–7	European Open Golf Championship	Walton Heath Golf Club, Tadworth, Surrey	£105,000
11–13	Merseyside Open (54 holes)	Royal Liverpool Golf Club	£18,000
12–14	The Hennessy Cognac Cup Matches	Sunningdale Golf Club, Berkshire	£50,000
18–21	The Tournament Players' Championship	To be announced	£55,000
25–28	The Bob Hope British Classic	RAC G & CC, Epsom, Surrey	£100,000
October			
1–4 or 2–5	Dunlop Masters	St Pierre G & CC, Chepstow	Undecided
To be scheduled	The Suntory World Match Play Championship	Wentworth Club, Surrey	£110,000
To be scheduled	Lancôme Invitational	St-Nom-La-Brètêche, Paris	£30,000

THE WORLD'S CIRCUITS
JAPAN, ASIA
SOUTH AFRICA
AUSTRALASIA

REPORTS AND RESULTS

Isao Aoki retained four of the Japanese titles he had won in 1978.

THE JAPANESE CIRCUIT 1979

KUO VADIS

While Isao Aoki again enhanced his name and prowess abroad, his fellow professionals saw to it that he did not have things entirely his own way at home, as he did in 1978 when he won five domestic titles. In 1979 they were more evenly shared. Aoki managed to acquire four of them, with three going to Tohru Nakamura and Taiwan's Kuo Chie-Hsiung who is as much at home in Japan as he is in his own country.

Kuo in fact had the most spectacular time, winning the Japanese Open Championship, the Golf Digest Tournament, and the Jun Classic in the space of five weeks. He captured the $40,000 first prize in the Japanese Open at Hino only after a four-way play-off with Yoshitaka Yamamoto, Koichi Uehara, and Aoki himself, and finally got home at the fourth extra hole. It was a sad finale for Uehara who had come from the pack with a seven-under-par 65 to earn the play-off.

Kuo's other two victories came in events truncated by rain. Even so he was involved in another lengthy play-off, this time in the Jun Classic in which he was level, after the prescribed 63 holes, with Ikuhiro Funatogawa and then won at the fifth extra hole. He had three shots in hand, however, in winning the 54-hole Golf Digest tournament. For his three victories Chie-Hsiung banked $100,000.

Remarkably, all four of Aoki's victories were repeats of 1978 successes. He again won the Chunichi Crowns, this time by a shot from Nakamura and Yasuda, and retained his native PGA Match-Play title with a one-hole victory over Taiwan's Hsieh Min-Nan. He had five shots in hand in winning the Kanto PGA, while he won the Japan Series by a mammoth 13 shots. He easily topped the Order of Merit.

Tohru Nakamura had his best year since turning professional in 1968 – at 18 the youngest pro in Japan at that time. He has come to his peak in the last half-dozen years since the Hiroshima Open gave him his first tour victory back in 1973. He has been a regular winner since, and went into 1979 with his tournament tally at 10.

That figure increased to 13 as he reeled off the Mitsubishi Galant and the Tohuku Classic in successive weeks, and only a few weeks later added the Kansai professional title. Hsieh Min-Nan, beaten by Aoki in the PGA Match-Play final, was on the losing end of a play-off with Nakamura for the Tohuku first prize. But the Taiwanese World Cup star found compensation in his victory in the Japan PGA Championship which he won by a shot, helped by a six-under third round of 66.

It was a good season, too, for the experienced Masaji Kusakabe who won two tournaments within the space of three weeks. He took yet another rain-affected event, the KBC Augusta, and then edged Mr Lu Liang-Huan by a stroke in winning the first prize of $40,000 in the

Tohru Nakamura had his finest year since turning pro in 1968. (Ken Prince)

$200,000 Suntory Open. Kusakabe had numerous other high finishes as well.

The Taiheiyo Pacific Masters, second in importance only to the Japanese Open, went to Norio Suzuki who finished proudly two shots ahead of the powerful American trio of Tom Watson, Bill Rogers, and Rod Curl.

THE SHIZUOKA OPEN

Shizuoka Country Club, Ogasa   29 March–1 April 1979   Prize Money $125,000

1	Akira Yabe	71	75	71	217	$25,000.00
2	Kikuo Arai	71	79	69	219	9,500.00
2	Shigeru Noguchi	71	73	75	219	9,500.00
4	Yoshitaka Yamamoto	76	77	67	220	5,000.00
	Masashi Ozaki	71	78	71	220	5,000.00
	Koichi Uehara	66	77	77	220	5,000.00
7	Haruo Yasuda	74	76	71	221	$4,000.00
8	Yoshihisa Iwashita	73	80	70	223	3,250.00
	Katsuji Hasegawa	72	80	71	223	3,250.00
	Seiichi Kanai	73	77	73	223	3,250.00

(The tournament was reduced to three rounds because of rain)

THE CHUNICHI CROWNS CLASSIC

Nagoya Country Club   26–29 April 1979   Prize Money $300,000

1	Isao Aoki	67	73	69	70	279	$60,000.00
2	Tohru Nakamura	71	77	65	67	280	26,250.00
	Haruo Yasuda	69	71	70	70	280	26,250,00
4	Lu Hsi-Chuen (TAI)	69	73	71	70	283	13,500.00
5	Namio Takasu	73	73	69	69	284	10,750.00
7	Kenji Mori	67	74	69	74	284	$10,750.00
	Lu Liang-Huan (TAI)	68	72	69	76	285	8,500.00
	Graham Marsh (AUS)	69	71	71	74	285	8,500.00
9	Yoshikazu Yokoshima	70	74	73	69	286	7,250.00
	Hsu Sheng-San (TAI)	71	76	70	69	286	7,250.00

THE FUJI-SANKEI CLASSIC

Higashi Matsuyama Country Club   10–13 May 1979   Prize Money $150,000

1	Shoichi Sato	68	71	75	69	283	$30,000.00
2	Isao Aoki	69	70	71	74	284	15,000.00
3	Tohru Nakamura	73	71	74	68	286	10,000.00
4	Toshiharu Kawada	75	70	73	69	287	7,500.00
5	Masashi Ozaki	70	74	69	75	288	4,750.00
	Hiroshi Ishii	72	71	73	72	288	4,750.00
7	Kosaku Shimada	71	74	71	73	289	$3,750.00
	Akira Yabe	71	72	73	73	289	3,750.00
	Hseih Min-Nan (TAI)	73	71	73	72	289	3,750.00
10	Kikuo Arai	72	69	76	73	290	3,000.00
	Toshiaki Sekimizu	77	70	74	69	290	3,000.00
	Lu Hsi-Chuen (TAI)	75	72	72	71	290	3,000.00

THE JAPANESE PGA MATCH-PLAY CHAMPIONSHIP

Totsuka Country Club, Kanagawa, Yokohoma   17–20 May 1979   Prize Money $150,000

Final

Isao Aoki ($30,000) beat Hseih Min-Nan (TAI) ($15,000)   1 hole

Semi-finals

Aoki beat Kosaku Shimada ($10,000)   1 hole
Hsieh beat Yoshitaka Yamamoto ($7,500)   2 and 1

Quarter-finals

Aoki beat Tohru Nakamura ($5,000)   1 hole
Shimada beat Koichi Uehara ($4,000)   3 and 1
Hsieh beat Naomichi Ozaki ($6,000)   3 and 2
Yamamoto beat Seiji Kusakabe ($3,000)   1 hole
(Prize money of losers decided by play-off for final placings)

THE YOMIURI OPEN

Osaka Yomiuri Country Club   24–27 May 1979   Prize Money $150,000

	Player	R1	R2	R3	R4	Total	Money
1	Teruo Sugihara	72	71	71	73	287	$30,000.00
2	Masashi Ozaki	72	71	72	72	287	16,500.00

Sugihara won play-off at second extra hole

	Player	R1	R2	R3	R4	Total	Money
3	Lu Liang-Huan (TAI)	76	69	72	71	288	10,000.00
4	Hsieh Yung-Yo (TAI)	74	72	72	71	289	7,500.00
5	Akira Yabe	73	76	70	72	291	5,000.00
	Kikuo Arai	72	73	73	73	291	5,000.00
	Seiichi Kanai	71	77	71	72	291	5,000.00
	Kenji Mori	73	73	74	71	291	5,000.00
	Kuo Chie-Hsiung (TAI)	76	73	70	72	291	5,000.00
	Lu Hsi-Chuen (TAI)	72	73	74	72	291	5,000.00

THE MITSUBISHI GALANT TOURNAMENT

Oharai Golf Club   31 May–3 June 1979   Prize Money $150,000

	Player	R1	R2	R3	R4	Total	Money
1	Tohru Nakamura	74	72	71	68	285	$30,000.00
2	Yoshio Kusayanagi	72	69	75	70	286	15,500.00
3	Masashi Ozaki	70	72	77	68	287	7,665.00
	Miller Barber (USA)	75	67	73	72	287	7,665.00
	Masaji Kusakabe	71	73	73	70	287	7,665.00
6	Isao Aoki	72	71	77	68	288	$5,000.00
7	Lu Hsi-Chuen (TAI)	70	75	75	69	289	4,500.00
8	Yasuhiro Miyamoto	77	73	68	72	290	3,750.00
	Kikuo Arai	75	67	73	75	290	3,750.00
	Fujio Kobayashi	71	73	73	73	290	3,750.00

THE TOHOKU CLASSIC TOURNAMENT

Nishisendai Country Club, Sendai, Miyagi   7–10 June 1979   Prize Money $125,000

	Player	R1	R2	R3	R4	Total	Money
1	Tohru Nakamura	73	67	69	69	278	$25,000.00
2	Hsieh Min-Nan (TAI)	69	71	66	72	278	13,500.00

Nakamura won play-off at second extra hole

	Player	R1	R2	R3	R4	Total	Money
3	Hiroshi Ishii	69	67	69	74	279	7,500.00
4	Yoshitaka Yamamoto	68	71	71	71	281	5,000.00
5	Haruo Yasuda	71	71	71	70	283	4,000.00
6	Yoshihisa Iwashita	69	74	71	69	283	$4,000.00
	Chen Tze-Ming (TAI)	67	72	73	71	283	4,000.00
8	Shoichi Saito	73	70	68	73	284	3,000.00
9	Kikuo Arai	76	71	70	68	285	2,500.00
	Teruo Sugihara	71	74	69	71	285	2,500.00
	Akio Kanamoto	67	70	73	75	285	2,500.00

THE SAPPORO TOKYU OPEN

Sapporo Kokusai Country Club, Hokkaido   14–17 June 1979   Prize Money $125,000

	Player	R1	R2	R3	R4	Total	Money
1	Yasuhiro Miyamoto	69	67	71	73	280	$25,000.00
2	Teruo Sugihara	68	73	71	70	282	14,000.00
3	Hisashi Suzumura	70	70	73	70	283	7,125.00
	Masaji Kusakabe	72	69	70	72	283	7,125.00
5	Norio Suzuki	71	69	75	69	284	5,000.00
6	Kenji Mori	71	74	71	69	285	$4,000.00
	Kazuo Yoshikawa	71	75	69	70	285	4,000.00
	Lu Liang-Huan (TAI)	69	72	70	74	285	4,000.00
9	Haruo Yasuda	70	73	73	70	286	3,000.00
	Satsuki Takahashi	70	71	71	74	286	3,000.00

THE PEPSI-WILSON TOURNAMENT
Hachinohe Country Club   21–24 June 1979   Prize Money $125,000

						Total	Money
1	Mya Aye (BUR)	64	69	67	74	274	$25,000.00
2	Hiroshi Ishii	70	68	68	71	277	12,500.00
3	Ben Arda (PI)	70	64	74	70	278	7,500.00
4	Lu Liang-Huan (TAI)	67	68	71	73	279	4,665.00
	Koichi Inoue	71	68	67	73	279	4,665.00
	Isao Aoki	66	70	69	74	279	4,665.00
7	Shinsaku Maeda	72	64	73	71	280	$3,250.00
	Teruo Sugihara	71	68	66	75	280	3,250.00
9	Fujio Kobayashi	69	71	71	70	281	2,750.00
10	Kuo Chie-Hsiung (TAI)	67	70	69	76	282	2,400.00
	Namio Takasu	72	66	70	74	282	2,400.00
	Tohru Nakamura	70	68	67	77	282	2,400.00

THE KANTO PGA CHAMPIONSHIP
Higashi-Tsukuba Country Club   28 June–1 July 1979   Prize Money $100,000

						Total	Money
1	Isao Aoki	68	66	72	73	279	$15,000.00
2	Seiichi Kanai	72	70	71	71	284	6,750.00
	Toshiharu Kawada	73	68	71	72	284	6,750.00
4	Katsuji Hasegawa	74	71	71	72	288	4,250.00
	Masashi Ozaki	67	75	71	75	288	4,250.00
	Kenichi Yamada	70	71	72	75	288	4,250.00
	Fumio Hitachi	71	74	68	75	288	4,250.00
8	Masayuki Imai	75	74	72	68	289	$2,380.00
	Hsieh Min-Nan (TAI)	73	74	70	72	289	2,380.00
	Hsieh Yung-Yo (TAI)	73	69	74	73	289	2,380.00
	Katsuji Kikuchi	68	73	75	73	289	2,380.00
	Tsuneyuki Nakajima	70	77	70	72	289	2,380.00
	Wataru Horiguchi	69	73	73	74	289	2,380.00

THE KANSAI PGA CHAMPIONSHIP
Tokinodai Country Club   28 June–1 July 1979   Prize Money $60,000

						Total	Money
1	Tohru Nakamura	69	66	68	70	273	$10,000.00
2	Yasuhiro Miyamoto	69	67	70	71	277	5,500.00
	Shigeru Uchida	65	72	72	68	277	5,500.00
4	Norio Suzuki	70	68	69	72	279	3,500.00
5	Koichi Inoue	71	71	70	68	280	2,750.00
	Yoshitaka Yamamoto	68	71	70	71	280	2,750.00
7	Kazuo Yoshikawa	69	72	70	70	281	$1,875.00
	Hiroshi Ishii	65	76	69	71	281	1,875.00
9	Eitaro Deguchi	69	69	73	71	282	1,250.00
	Isao Ohba	72	71	67	72	282	1,250.00
	Tsutomu Irie	68	72	69	73	282	1,250.00

THE NIHON KOKUDO KEIKAKU SUMMERS TOURNAMENT
Shirasagi Country Club, Kawachi, Tochigi   2–5 August 1979   Prize Money $150,000

						Total	Money
1	Norio Mikami	73	70	66	70	279	$30,000.00
2	Kenji Mori	71	71	69	71	282	15,000.00
	Kazuo Yoshikawa	73	71	68	71	282	15,000.00
4	Minoru Hiyoshi	69	72	68	74	283	7,500.00
5	Lu Liang-Huan (TAI)	68	71	72	73	284	3,350.00
	Yoshitaka Yamamoto	71	72	70	71	284	$3,350.00
	Kikuo Arai	73	68	73	70	284	3,350.00
	Hsieh Min-Nan (TAI)	70	72	74	68	284	3,350.00
	Shigeru Noguchi	71	69	73	71	284	3,350.00
10	Tohru Nakamura	69	76	70	70	285	2,000.00

THE MIZUNO TOURNAMENT

Tokinodai Country Club, Ishikawa 9–12 August 1979 Prize Money $100,000

1	Mituhiro Kitta	67	70	68	67	272	$20,000.00
2	Ichiro Terada	70	65	67	72	274	8,750.00
	Teruo Sugihara	66	67	71	70	274	8,750.00
4	Kazuo Yoshikawa	71	67	66	72	276	5,000.00
5	Kohsaku Shimada	72	69	71	65	277	3,250.00
	Kikuo Arai	67	71	72	67	277	3,250.00
	Shinsaku Maeda	74	64	70	69	277	3,250.00
	Norio Suzuki	69	67	71	70	277	3,250.00
9	Yoshitaka Yamamoto	69	71	71	67	278	1,800.00
	Masahiko Yamamoto	72	69	66	71	278	1,800.00
	Kenji Mori	69	67	70	72	278	1,800.00
	Yasuhiro Miyamoto	70	69	69	72	278	1,800.00
	Shigeru Uchida	70	67	69	72	278	1,800.00

THE KBC AUGUSTA TOURNAMENT

Fukuoka Country Club, Fukuoka 23–26 August 1979 Prize Money $160,000

1	Masaji Kusakabe	67	71	68	34	240	$30,000.00
2	Kuo Chie-Hsiung (TAI)	67	66	71	39	243	15,000.00
3	Shigeru Uchida	69	68	71	36	244	10,000.00
4	Norio Suzuki	71	68	70	36	245	5,500.00
	Kenji Mori	72	69	71	33	245	5,500.00
	Fujio Kobayashi	69	67	70	39	245	5,500.00
7	Teruo Sugihara	71	67	69	39	246	3,750.00
	Shinsaku Maeda	68	72	71	35	246	$3,750.00
	Hsieh Yung-Yo (TAI)	71	70	69	36	246	3,750.00
10	Takahiro Takeyasu	71	68	73	35	247	2,650.00
	Graham Marsh (AUS)	73	68	70	36	247	2,650.00
	Akio Kanamoto	73	68	69	37	247	2,650.00
	George Yokoi	69	72	67	39	247	2,650.00

(The tournament was reduced to 63 holes because of rain)

THE ANA SAPPORO OPEN

Sapporo Country Club, Hokkaido 30 August–2 September 1979 Prize Money $150,000

1	Graham Marsh (AUS)	71	73	68	72	284	$30,000.00
2	Kikuo Arai	73	71	71	71	286	15,000.00
3	Isao Aoki	69	72	77	69	287	8,750.00
	Lu Liang-Huan (TAI)	68	70	73	76	287	8,750.00
5	Masashi Ozaki	68	74	74	72	288	6,000.00
6	Teruo Sugihara	71	70	72	76	289	$5,500.00
7	Tsuneyuki Nakajima	71	72	75	73	291	4,500.00
	Norio Suzuki	72	72	71	76	291	4,500.00
	Yasuhiro Miyamoto	68	71	74	78	291	4,500.00
10	Fujio Kobayashi	70	76	70	76	292	3,500.00

THE SUNTORY OPEN

Narashino Country Club, Chiba 6–9 September 1979 Prize Money $200,000

1	Masaji Kusakabe	66	73	69	69	277	$40,000.00
2	Lu Liang-Huan (TAI)	71	69	69	69	278	21,250.00
3	Yoshihisa Iwashita	66	76	66	71	279	13,500.00
4	Tateo Ozaki	69	76	70	65	280	7,200.00
	Isao Aoki	68	72	73	67	280	7,200.00
	Hubert Green (USA)	65	75	70	70	280	7,200.00
	Haruo Yasuda	71	72	67	70	280	$7,200.00
	Katsuji Hasegawa	70	70	71	69	280	7,200.00
9	Kohsaku Shimada	69	71	71	70	281	4,500.00
	Ho Ming-Chung (TAI)	73	70	68	70	281	4,500.00
11	Graham Marsh (AUS)	69	70	75	68	282	3,625.00
	Ikuhiro Minatogawa	73	71	69	69	282	3,625.00

THE JAPAN PGA CHAMPIONSHIP

Asami Country Club 13–16 September 1979 Prize Money $125,000

1	Hsieh Min-Nan (TAI)	67	68	66	71	272	$20,000.00
2	Teruo Sugihara	69	67	70	67	273	10,000.00
3	Masaji Kusakabe	71	68	69	66	274	7,500.00
4	Tsuneyuki Nakajima	70	69	68	68	275	6,500.00
5	Toshiharu Kawada	70	69	68	69	276	5,250.00
	Tohru Nakamura	69	72	67	68	276	$5,250.00
7	Hiroshi Ishii	69	73	68	69	279	4,250.00
	Masami Kawamura	73	68	67	71	279	4,250.00
9	Yoshitaka Yamamoto	69	69	72	71	281	3,375.00
	Fujio Kobayashi	70	70	71	70	281	3,375.00

THE KANSAI OPEN

Rokko Kokusai Country Club 20–23 September 1979 Prize Money $75,000

1	Yasuhiro Miyamoto	70	74	72	67	283	$20,000.00
2	Tohru Nakamura	70	72	72	70	284	10,000.00
3	Fuminori Sano*	67	73	73	75	286	–
	Masanori Miura	70	73	71	72	286	5,000.00
5	Teruo Sugihara	74	71	70	72	287	3,750.00
	Hisashi Morioka	73	74	67	73	287	3,750.00
7	Shinichi Hayashi	72	71	74	71	288	$2,500.00
	Shinsaku Maeda	73	73	71	71	288	2,500.00
	Kohsaku Shimada	70	73	73	72	288	2,500.00
	Yoshitaka Yamamoto	74	71	71	72	288	2,500.00
	Tsutomu Irie	70	72	73	73	288	2,500.00

* Amateur

THE KANTO OPEN

Ikaho Country Club 20–23 September 1979 Prize Money $100,000

1	Masaru Amano	68	76	69	65	278	$20,000.00
2	Masashi Ozaki	70	70	68	72	280	7,815.00
	Kikuo Arai	71	68	72	69	280	7,815.00
	Kenji Mori	74	73	66	67	280	7,815.00
5	Haruo Yasuda	70	74	67	70	281	5,000.00
6	Isao Aoki	71	68	72	71	282	$3,750.00
	Masaji Kusakabe	72	68	69	73	282	3,750.00
8	Yoshikazu Yokoshima	69	70	75	70	284	3,000.00
9	Fujio Kobayashi	66	70	75	74	285	2,500.00
10	Satsuki Takahashi	71	71	71	73	286	2,000.00

THE HIROSHIMA OPEN

Hiroshima Country Club 27–30 September 1979 Prize Money $100,000

1	Yoshitaka Yamamoto	67	70	67	66	270	$20,000.00
2	Haruo Yasuda	70	66	71	71	278	8,750.00
	Yoshikazu Yokoshima	65	73	69	71	278	8,750.00
4	Chen Tze-Ming (TAI)	70	70	65	74	279	5,500.00
	Mya Aye (BUR)	69	66	70	74	279	5,500.00
6	Tadami Ueno	71	73	71	65	280	4,000.00
7	Tsutomu Irie	66	73	74	68	281	3,000.00
	Ho Ming-Chung (TAI)	66	72	72	71	281	$3,000.00
	Koichi Inoue	75	67	67	72	281	3,000.00
10	Tsuneyuki Nakajima	71	71	69	71	282	1,850.00
	Yoshiharu Takai	69	75	72	66	282	1,850.00
	Fumio Hitachi	69	72	72	70	282	1,850.00
	Seiichi Kanai	70	73	69	70	282	1,850.00

THE JUN CLASSIC
Jun Classic Country Club, Tochigi 4–7 October 1979 Prize Money $175,000

1	Kuo Chie-Hsiung (TAI)	68	73	69	38	248	$35,000.00
2	Ikuhiro Funatogawa	70	69	74	35	248	17,500.00
	Kuo won play-off at fifth extra hole						
3	Hiroshi Ishii	71	71	70	37	249	12,500.00
4	Tsuneyuki Nakajima	69	72	69	40	250	7,665.00
	Haruo Yasuda	71	68	73	38	250	7,665.00
	Fujio Kobayashi	69	71	70	40	250	7,665.00
7	Yoshitaka Yamamoto	68	72	71	40	251	$4,500.00
	Naomichi Ozaki	72	73	68	38	251	4,500.00
	Seiji Ebihara	72	74	69	36	251	4,500.00
10	Hsieh Min-Nan (TAI)	71	70	75	37	253	3,500.00
11	Satsuki Takahashi	68	73	73	40	254	3,125.00
	Norio Suzuki	71	72	71	40	254	3,125.00

(The tournament was reduced to 63 holes because of rain)

THE TOHKAI CLASSIC
Miyoshi Country Club, Nishikamo 11–14 October 1979 Prize Money $167,500

1	Tsutomu Irie	70	69	68	68	275	$35,000.00
2	Hsieh Min-Nan (TAI)	67	72	71	70	280	14,500.00
	Masaji Kusakabe	69	71	68	72	280	14,500.00
4	Ben Arda (PI)	70	67	74	70	281	7,500.00
5	Toshiharu Kawada	72	69	71	70	282	5,750.00
	Tadashi Kitta	70	70	70	72	282	5,750.00
	Andy Bean (USA)	69	69	72	72	282	5,750.00
8	Lu Liang-Huan (TAI)	73	70	71	69	283	$4,000.00
	Tsuneyuki Nakajima	71	71	71	70	283	4,000.00
	Norio Suzuki	71	72	68	72	283	4,000.00
11	Teruo Sugihara	70	70	72	72	284	2,750.00
	Yutaka Suzuki	71	68	73	72	284	2,750.00
	Shigeru Uchida	70	71	70	73	284	2,750.00

THE GOLF DIGEST TOURNAMENT
Tomei Country Club, Susonoshi, Shizuoka 18–21 October 1979 Prize Money $125,000

1	Kuo Chie-Hsiung (TAI)	69	68	69	206	$25,000.00
2	Fujio Kobayashi	64	70	75	209	12,500.00
3	Namio Takasu	68	72	70	210	7,500.00
4	Tsuneyuki Nakajima	71	68	72	211	5,500.00
	Lu Hsi-Chuen (TAI)	72	71	68	211	5,500.00
6	Saburo Fujiki	70	70	72	212	4,500.00
7	Masaji Kusakabe	72	67	74	213	$3,750.00
	Hsieh Min-Nan (TAI)	72	71	70	213	3,750.00
9	Tsutomu Irie	72	74	68	214	2,615.00
	Takaaki Kono	77	65	72	214	2,615.00
	Ho Ming-Chung (TAI)	72	70	72	214	2,615.00

(The tournament was reduced to three rounds because of rain)

THE BRIDGESTONE TOURNAMENT
Sodegaura Country Club, Chiba 25–28 October 1979 Prize Money $150,000

1	Lanny Wadkins (USA)	66	71	69	71	277	$30,000.00
2	Yoshikazu Yokoshima	67	68	71	72	278	15,000.00
3	Seiichi Kanai	72	72	71	68	281	7,830.00
	Norio Suzuki	70	72	68	71	281	7,830.00
	Ikuhiro Funatogawa	72	69	68	72	281	7,830.00
6	Fujio Kobayashi	72	73	70	67	282	4,700.00
7	Kenichi Yamada	73	71	67	71	282	$4,700.00
	Kuo Chie-Hsiung (TAI)	72	70	72	68	282	4,700.00
9	Shinsaku Maeda	72	71	69	69	283	3,625.00
	Masaji Kusakabe	69	72	71	71	283	3,625.00
11	Masashi Ozaki	72	71	72	69	284	2,950.00

THE JAPANESE OPEN CHAMPIONSHIP

Hino Golf Club, Gamo 1–4 November 1979 Prize Money $250,000

Pos	Player	R1	R2	R3	R4	Total	Money
1	Kuo Chie-Hsiung (TAI)	71	70	70	74	285	$40,000.00
2	Yoshitaka Yamamoto	73	71	67	74	285	17,150.00
	Isao Aoki	75	73	66	71	285	17,150.00
	Koichi Uehara	74	72	74	65	285	17,150.00
Kuo won play-off at fourth extra hole							
5	Shigeru Uchida	71	74	69	72	286	8,250.00
	Lon Hinkle (USA)	71	74	68	73	286	8,250.00
7	Teruo Sugihara	73	69	72	73	287	6,000.00
	Haruo Yasuda	71	74	71	71	287	6,000.00
	Severiano Ballesteros (S)	74	71	73	69	287	6,000.00
10	Yoshikazu Yokoshima	76	71	72	69	288	$4,750.00
	Masaji Kusakabe	73	74	71	70	288	4,750.00
	Norio Suzuki	74	72	70	72	288	4,750.00
13	Tohru Nakamura	71	75	73	70	289	3,500.00
	Kohsaku Shimada	74	74	69	72	289	3,500.00
	Tadami Ueno	70	69	75	75	289	3,500.00
	Shigeru Uchida	71	69	70	79	289	3,500.00
	Tadashi Kitta	73	72	75	69	289	3,500.00
	Teruo Suzumura	71	72	72	74	289	3,500.00
	Lu Liang-Huan (TAI)	72	75	70	72	289	3,500.00

JAPAN v THE UNITED STATES OF AMERICA (Annual International Match)

Sports Shinko Country Club, Kobe 8–11 November 1979 Prize Money $117,300

Japan beat the US by 2,306 strokes to 2,311 for the sixth time in the ninth international match between the two countries.

Individual scores

Pos	Player	R1	R2	R3	R4	Total	Money
1	Tom Purtzer (USA)	69	67	68	72	276	$25,000.00
2	Bill Rogers (USA)	73	73	69	71	286	12,500.00
3	Isao Aoki	71	72	72	72	287	4,445.00
	Fujio Kobayashi	73	71	71	72	287	4,445.00
	Yoshitaka Yamamoto	71	70	74	72	287	4,445.00
6	Ray Floyd (USA)	66	74	73	76	289	2,395.00
	Masashi Ozaki	71	76	70	72	289	2,395.00
8	Andy North (USA)	76	71	72	71	290	1,979.00
	Tsuneyuki Nakajima	73	70	73	74	290	1,979.00
10	Kohsaku Shimada	75	72	74	70	291	$1,562.00
	Tohru Nakamura	71	73	74	73	291	1,562.00
12	Lee Trevino (USA)	73	74	77	69	293	1,320.00
	Ed Sneed (USA)	70	72	77	74	293	1,320.00
	Dave Stockton (USA)	71	75	73	74	293	1,320.00
15	Teruo Sugihara	72	72	80	70	294	1,041.00
16	Haruo Yasuda	75	72	75	73	295	1,041.00
17	Bruce Lietzke (USA)	75	74	75	72	296	937.00
18	Bob Byman (USA)	73	73	77	76	299	937.00

THE TAIHEIYO CLUB (PACIFIC) MASTERS

Taiheiyo Golf Club, Gotenba 15–18 November 1979 Prize Money $300,000

Pos	Player	R1	R2	R3	R4	Total	Money
1	Norio Suzuki	73	69	67	71	280	$65,000.00
2	Tom Watson (USA)	73	69	68	72	282	22,524.00
	Rod Curl (USA)	71	72	67	72	282	22,524.00
	Bill Rogers (USA)	69	71	69	73	282	22,524.00
5	Masaru Amano	66	72	73	72	283	11,012.00
6	Fujio Kobayashi	73	72	70	69	284	8,008.00
7	Naomichi Ozaki	79	68	68	70	285	6,355.00
	Bruce Lietzke (USA)	70	77	67	71	285	6,355.00
9	Masashi Ozaki	75	71	70	70	286	$4,507.00
	Shigeru Uchida	72	71	72	71	286	4,507.00
	Hiroshi Ishii	71	73	71	71	286	4,507.00
	John Fought (USA)	72	69	73	72	286	4,507.00
	Lon Hinkle (USA)	70	71	72	73	286	4,507.00
	Lu Liang-Huan (TAI)	68	71	72	75	286	4,507.00
	Gil Morgan (USA)	72	71	68	75	286	4,507.00

THE DUNLOP PHOENIX TOURNAMENT

Phoenix Country Club, Miyazaki   22–25 November 1979   Prize Money $250,000

1	Bobby Wadkins (USA)	73	67	71	73	284	$41,666.00
2	Namio Takasu	69	70	73	75	287	20,833.00
	Lu Liang-Huan (TAI)	72	72	74	69	287	20,833.00
4	Takahiro Takeyasu	68	75	70	75	288	11,458.00
	Sandy Lyle (GB)	70	72	70	76	288	11,458.00
6	Bob Byman (USA)	73	73	72	71	289	8,542.00
	Tom Watson (USA)	73	75	67	74	289	$8,542.00
8	Masashi Ozaki	75	72	74	69	290	6,320.00
	Tohru Nakamura	71	72	73	74	290	6,320.00
	Lon Hinkle (USA)	76	71	72	71	290	6,320.00
11	Hubert Green (USA)	73	72	74	72	291	5,416.00
12	Masaji Kusakabe	75	71	75	71	292	5,000.00

THE JAPAN SERIES OF GOLF

Osaka Yomiuri CC and Tokyo Yomiuri CC   28 November–2 December 1979   Prize Money $60,000

1	Isao Aoki	68	71	66	71	276	$20,000.00
2	Tohru Nakamura	71	75	73	70	289	7,600.00
	Kikuo Arai	73	71	71	74	289	7,600.00
4	Fujio Kobayashi	71	76	68	75	290	3,600.00
5	Norio Suzuki	71	71	73	77	292	3,200.00
6	Masashi Ozaki	81	69	70	73	293	2,600.00
	Kuoh Chie-Hsiung (TAI)	73	72	72	76	293	2,600.00
8	Teruo Suguhara	76	71	67	80	294	$2,000.00
9	Yasuhiro Miyamoto	77	72	74	72	295	1,840.00
	Haruo Yasuda	75	74	73	73	295	1,840.00
	Hsieh Min-Nan (TAI)	71	73	73	78	295	1,840.00
12	Masaru Amano	74	72	75	76	297	1,520.00
	Namio Takasu	74	74	75	74	297	1,520.00

Prize money equated throughout from yen to US dollars.

THE ASIAN CIRCUIT 1979

MASTER LU BOWS IN

Mister Lu needs no introduction to world golf galleries – particularly in Britain where he will be remembered forever as the happy hat-doffing deadly-putting Taiwanese who finished just a stroke behind Lee Trevino in the 1971 Open Championship at Royal Birkdale, Lancashire.

Master Lu caused a certain amount of head-scratching – that is, until 1979. Then Lu Hsi-Chuen, 26-year-old nephew of Lu Liang-Huan, burst on the Asian scene with all the self-confidence and not a little of the ability of his famous uncle, won three of the Circuit's 10 Championships, and romped away with the top spot in the Order of Merit. Lu turned professional only in the October preceding the tour, having won 13 titles in an impressive amateur career. But few predicted what was to come.

After joint 12th place in the opening Philippine Championship, won by home hero Ben Arda, and a tie for second behind Australia's Greg Norman in Hong Kong, Master Lu walked off successively with the Singapore and Malaysia Open titles. He survived a play-off with fellow-countryman Hsu Sheng-San to win the first, but ran away to a seven-shot victory in Kuala Lumpur with an 11-under-par 277, including a hole-in-one in his closing round.

Lu's third victory came in Jakarta where he was behind all the way until a final round of 68 gave him a one-shot win over Burma's World Cup veteran Mya Aye who had led for three rounds. He had to give way to age and family experience in his native Taiwan Open, won by his uncle Lu Liang-Huan despite an indifferent last round, but he tied for third in Korea and ended his first professional tour with over $40,000 in prize money, plus a further $10,000 for heading the Order.

Second in the Final Order was Hsu Chi-San who, like Lu, had seven top 10 finishes, but he did not win a title, while his brother Hsu Sheng-San occupied third spot. Apart from the young Lu, there was another notable debut by the Taiwanese Chen Tze-Ming who in 1976 shared the individual title with Scotland's Ian Hutcheon when Britain won the Eisenhower Trophy in Portugal. Chen turned professional in December, had three second-place finishes, and finished sixth in the Order of Merit.

Two of the 10 Championships, with prize money totalling $600,000, were won by American professionals minus US Tour cards. Gaylord Burrows won the India Open in New Delhi to put with the Indonesian Open he won in 1977, while another Asian Circuit regular Mike Krantz won in Bangkok after a play-off with Jaime Gonzales of Brazil.

PHILIPPINE OPEN CHAMPIONSHIP

Wack Wack Golf and Country Club, Manila   15–18 February 1979   Prize Money US$100,000

Pos	Player	R1	R2	R3	R4	Total	Prize
1	Ben Arda (PI)	69	71	71	75	286	$25,000.00
2	Hung Fa (TAI)	72	72	70	75	289	11,250.00
	Hsu Sheng-San (TAI)	72	70	74	73	289	11,250.00
4	Mya Aye (BUR)	77	73	68	72	290	5,100.00
	Yoshikazu Yokoshima (J)	71	71	78	70	290	5,100.00
	Kuo Chie-Hsiung (TAI)	74	67	77	72	290	5,100.00
7	Hsu Chi-San (TAI)	73	73	69	76	291	4,100.00
8	Hsieh Yung-Yo (TAI)	71	73	75	73	292	3,600.00
9	Tsutomu Irie (J)	69	74	72	78	293	$3,100.00
10	Paterno Braza (PI)	71	75	73	75	294	2,425.00
	Ireneo Legaspi (PI)	73	73	75	73	294	2,425.00
12	Lu Liang-Huan (TAI)	72	73	79	71	295	1,650.00
	Lim Kian Tiong (SING)	76	76	71	72	295	1,650.00
	Rudolf Lavares (PI)	75	72	73	75	295	1,650.00
	Lu Hsi-Chuen (TAI)	72	74	69	80	295	1,650.00
	Takashi Kurihara (J)	73	76	71	75	295	1,650.00

HONG KONG OPEN CHAMPIONSHIP

Royal Hong Kong Golf Club   22–25 February 1979   Prize Money US$100,000

Pos	Player	R1	R2	R3	R4	Total	Prize
1	Greg Norman (AUS)	70	66	69	68	273	$20,000.00
2	Lu Hsi-Chuen (TAI)	65	68	69	74	276	8,500.00
	Chen Tze-Ming (TAI)	69	67	70	70	276	8,500.00
	Hsu Chi-San (TAI)	66	67	69	74	276	8,500.00
5	Hisashi Suzumura (J)	67	68	73	71	279	3,500.00
	Yoshikazu Yokoshima (J)	69	68	69	73	279	3,500.00
7	Chen Chien-Chin (TAI)	73	68	72	68	281	3,000.00
	Kosaku Shimada (J)	67	71	69	74	281	3,000.00
	Graham Marsh (AUS)	65	66	74	76	281	$3,000.00
10	Minoru Nakamura (J)	69	74	71	68	282	2,300.00
	Kurt Cox (USA)	70	67	73	72	282	2,300.00
	Hsu Sheng-San (TAI)	69	67	71	75	282	2,300.00
	Ireneo Legaspi (PI)	69	68	70	75	282	2,300.00
14	Mya Aye (BUR)	70	66	74	73	283	1,700.00
	Don Klenk (USA)	71	70	70	72	283	1,700.00

SINGAPORE OPEN CHAMPIONSHIP

Bukit Course, Singapore Island Country Club   1–4 March 1979   Prize Money US$60,000

Pos	Player	R1	R2	R3	R4	Total	Prize
1	Lu Hsi-Chuen (TAI)	71	70	70	69	280	$10,000.00
2	Hsu Sheng-San (TAI)	72	71	68	69	280	6,000.00
3	Hsieh Min-Nam (TAI)	69	70	72	70	281	3,666.60
	Kazunari Takahashi (J)	75	68	68	70	281	3,666.60
	Walter Godfrey (NZ)	69	74	68	70	281	3,666.60
6	George Serhan (AUS)	72	69	71	70	282	2,500.00
7	Kuo Chie-Hsiung (TAI)	71	71	73	69	284	2,250.00
8	Michael Soli (USA)	74	69	71	71	285	1,875.00
	Kevin Jones (UK)	70	71	72	72	285	$1,875.00
10	Ho Ming Chung (TAI)	74	69	74	69	286	1,375.00
	Masakichi Toda (J)	72	70	75	69	286	1,375.00
12	James Booros (USA)	70	74	74	69	287	993.50
	Martin Bohen (USA)	74	69	73	71	287	993.50
	Yurio Akitomi (J)	71	73	71	72	287	993.50
	Lim Swee Chew (SING)	72	70	71	74	287	993.50

Lu won play-off at the second extra hole

MALAYSIA OPEN CHAMPIONSHIP
Royal Selangor Golf Club, Kuala Lumpur, 8–11 March 1979, Prize Money US$60,000

Pos	Player	R1	R2	R3	R4	Total	Prize
1	Lu Hsi-Chuen (TAI)	69	71	67	70	277	$10,000.00
2	Ron Milanovich (USA)	68	75	71	70	284	5,000.00
	Tsutomu Irie (J)	73	67	73	71	284	5,000.00
	Chen Chien-Chin (TAI)	70	71	72	71	284	5,000.00
5	Kuo Chie-Hsiung (TAI)	75	67	74	69	285	3,250.00
	Hal Underwood (USA)	69	77	70	69	285	3,250.00
7	Kurt Cox (USA)	73	72	73	68	286	1,741.50
	Hsieh Min-Nan (TAI)	73	70	74	69	286	1,741.50
	Bruce Douglass (USA)	70	72	74	70	286	$1,741.50
	George Serhan (AUS)	70	72	72	72	286	1,741.50
	Maria Ramayah (MAL)	69	74	71	72	286	1,741.50
	Michael Soli (USA)	71	68	74	73	286	1,741.50
13	Sukree Onsham (THAI)	73	73	71	70	287	1,150.00
	Gar Hamilton (C)	74	69	73	71	287	1,150.00
	Chang Chung-Fa (TAI)	74	70	70	73	287	1,150.00

THAILAND OPEN CHAMPIONSHIP
Royal Thai Air Force Golf Club, Don Muang, Bangkok, 15–18 March 1979, Prize Money US$40,000

Pos	Player	R1	R2	R3	R4	Total	Prize
1	Mike Krantz (USA)	71	70	74	67	282	$6,400.00
2	Jaime Gonzalez (BZ)	74	69	68	71	282	3,600.00

Krantz won play-off at first extra hole

Pos	Player	R1	R2	R3	R4	Total	Prize
3	Kurt Cox (USA)	69	73	72	69	283	2,350.00
	Hahn Chang Sang (SK)	74	69	70	70	283	2,350.00
5	Lim Kian Tiong (SING)	71	72	70	71	284	1,733.00
	Norio Mikami (J)	76	71	67	70	284	1,733.00
	Ron Milanovich (USA)	70	74	68	72	284	1,733.00
8	Hsu Chi-San (TAI)	67	74	74	70	285	$1,450.00
	George Serhan (AUS)	72	71	68	74	285	1,450.00
10	Chen Tze-Ming (TAI)	73	78	67	68	286	1,150.00
	Bruce Douglass (USA)	72	73	66	75	286	1,150.00
	Pradhana Ngamphrom (THAI)	73	70	70	73	286	1,150.00
	Ireneo Legaspi (PI)	70	70	70	76	286	1,150.00
14	Mya Aye (BUR)	70	78	69	70	287	925.00
	Ho Ming-Chung (TAI)	73	75	69	70	287	925.00

INDIA OPEN CHAMPIONSHIP
New Delhi Golf Club, 22–25 March 1979, Prize Money US$30,000

Pos	Player	R1	R2	R3	R4	Total	Prize
1	Gaylord Burrows (USA)	73	70	71	70	284	$5,225.00
2	Hsu Chi-San (TAI)	75	68	67	75	285	3,325.00
3	Mike Krantz (USA)	67	69	76	75	287	2,280.00
4	Kazunari Takahashi (J)	71	72	71	74	288	1,757.00
	Peter Thomson (AUS)	73	68	74	73	288	1,757.00
6	Brian Jones (AUS)	69	79	70	71	289	1,520.00
7	Minoru Kumabe (J)	73	75	72	70	290	1,377.00
	Mya Aye (BUR)	75	71	72	72	290	1,377.00
9	Lu Hsi-Chuen (TAI)	76	73	74	70	293	1,187.00
	Jaime Gonzalez (BZ)	73	74	71	75	293	$1,187.00
11	Michael Sholdar (USA)	73	76	74	74	297	1,045.00
12	Ashok Malik (IN)*	72	79	72	75	298	–
	Noni (IN)	72	77	77	72	298	950.00
14	Lance Ten Broeck (USA)	76	75	75	77	299	855.00
	Shen Chang-Shyan (TAI)	69	75	82	73	299	855.00
	Martin Bohen (USA)	72	73	74	80	299	855.00

* Amateur

INDONESIA OPEN CHAMPIONSHIP

Jakarta Golf Club 29 March–1 April 1979 Prize Money US$50,000

1	Lu Hsi-Chuen (TAI)	67	67	70	68	272	$6,800.00
2	Mya Aye (BUR)	63	70	69	71	273	3,900.00
3	Sukree Onsham (THAI)	71	71	67	70	279	2,550.00
	Don Klenk (USA)	70	71	70	68	279	2,550.00
5	Mark Hillsinger (USA)	74	67	68	71	280	2,000.00
6	Hsu Chi-San (TAI)	71	68	70	72	281	1,750.00
	Shen Chung-Shyan (TAI)	65	73	71	72	281	1,750.00
8	Gaylord Burrows (USA)	69	73	71	69	282	$1,550.00
	Lance Ten Broeck (USA)	70	73	69	70	282	1,550.00
10	Ryuzo Yamaguchi (J)	72	69	72	71	283	1,200.00
	Sandy Galbraith (USA)	73	68	70	71	283	1,200.00
	Bob Henderson (USA)	70	67	69	77	283	1,200.00
	Maria Ramayah (MAL)	68	71	71	73	283	1,200.00
	Brian Jones (AUS)	74	74	67	68	283	1,200.00

TAIWAN OPEN CHAMPIONSHIP

Peitou Kuo Hua Golf & Country Club, Taipeh 5–8 April 1979 Prize Money US$50,000

1	Lu Liang-Huan (TAI)	70	72	71	74	287	$10,000.00
2	Chen Tze-Ming (TAI)	77	68	74	70	289	5,250.00
3	Hsu Chi-San (TAI)	72	72	71	75	290	3,250.00
4	Hsieh Min-Nan (TAI)	75	72	73	71	291	2,500.00
5	Hsu Sheng-San (TAI)	72	74	73	74	293	2,250.00
6	Kuo Chie-Hsiung (TAI)	71	76	74	73	294	2,000.00
7	Tsuneyuki Nakajima (J)	72	75	72	77	296	1,625.00
	Hsieh Yung-Yo (TAI)	75	73	73	75	296	1,625.00
	Lu Hsi-Chuen (TAI)	76	75	75	70	296	$1,625.00
10	Mike Krantz (USA)	76	75	76	71	298	1,375.00
11	Ho Ming-Chung (TAI)	78	75	75	71	299	1,111.00
	Chen Chien-Chin (TAI)	76	72	75	76	299	1,111.00
	Masakichi Toda (J)	74	73	76	76	299	1,111.00
	Shen Chung-Shyan (TAI)	74	78	76	71	299	1,111.00
	Hal Underwood (USA)	73	76	77	73	299	1,111.00

KOREAN OPEN CHAMPIONSHIP

Seoul Country Club, Seoul 12–15 April 1979 Prize Money US$60,000

1	Shen Chung-Shyan (TAI)	70	71	72	76	289	$11,000.00
2	Chen Tze-Ming (TAI)	69	71	73	78	291	5,700.00
3	Kuo Chie-Hsiung (TAI)	68	75	78	72	293	3,166.00
	Lu Hsi-Chuen (TAI)	70	73	78	72	293	3,166.00
	Hsu Sheng-San (TAI)	69	76	75	73	293	3,166.00
6	Kim Suk Bong (SK)	70	80	75	70	295	2,300.00
7	Ho Ming-Chung (TAI)	72	76	76	72	296	2,000.00
	Hsu Chi-San (TAI)	71	74	79	72	296	2,000.00
	Bruce Douglass (USA)	73	78	76	69	296	$2,000.00
10	Jerry Minor (USA)	72	77	75	74	298	1,700.00
11	Cho Tae Woon (SK)	72	75	79	73	299	1,550.00
12	Tatsuo Fujima (J)	75	79	74	72	300	1,375.00
	Sei-Ha Chin (TAI)	73	76	75	76	300	1,375.00
	Chang Teh-Kwei (TAI)	72	78	74	76	300	1,375.00
	Son Heung Soo (SK)	75	80	75	70	300	1,375.00

Lu Hsi-Chuen, nephew of 'Mr Lu', won three titles in his first year as a professional.

THE DUNLOP INTERNATIONAL OPEN
Ibaraki Golf Club, Tokyo 19–22 April 1979 Prize Money US$100,000

1	Hiroshi Ishii (J)	70	68	70	70	278	$20,000.00
2	Seiji Ebihara (J)	70	74	73	64	281	8,500.00
	Tateo Ozaki (J)	70	71	72	68	281	8,500.00
	Kazunari Takahashi (J)	72	70	68	71	281	8,500.00
5	Lu Liang-Huan (TAI)	71	69	69	73	282	3,666.67
	Mya Aye (BUR)	71	69	72	70	282	3,666.67
	Isao Aoki (J)	70	73	72	67	282	3,666.67
8	Michael Soli (USA)	71	68	72	73	284	2,250.00
	Taichi Nakagawa (J)	72	72	73	67	284	2,250.00
10	Kurt Cox (USA)	72	69	70	74	285	1,450.00
	Tadami Ueno (J)	73	73	66	73	285	1,450.00
12	Masashi Ozaki (J)	69	67	74	76	286	1,200.00
	Kazuo Yoshikawa (J)	71	71	73	71	286	1,200.00
	Yoshitaka Yamamoto (J)	72	69	76	69	286	1,200.00
15	Greg Norman (AUS)	73	73	71	70	287	980.00
	Haruo Yasuda (J)	73	71	72	71	287	980.00
	Namio Takasu (J)	73	70	70	74	287	980.00

LEADERS IN THE 1979 ASIAN CIRCUIT ORDER OF MERIT

		Circuit Points	Grand Circuit Prize Money US$	Prize Money US$
1	Lu Hsi-Chuen (TAI)	141½	10,000	43,670.00
2	Hsu Chi-San (TAI)	109	7,500	25,242.50
3	Hsu Sheng-San (TAI)	84	5,000	26,686.50
4	Kuo Chie-Hsiung (TAI)	83	2,500	18,396.00
5	Mya Aye (BUR)	78⅜		17,881.17
6	Chen Tze-Ming (TAI)	69		22,150.00
7	Mike Krantz (TAI)	55⅝		12,365.00
8	Kazunari Takahashi (J)	54		15,648.50
	Kurt Cox (USA)	54		9,689.00
10	Hsieh Min-Nan (TAI)	45¼		8,658.00

THE SOUTH AFRICAN CIRCUIT 1979

A PLAYER SPECTACULAR

The officially-styled Sunshine Circuit was sunshine all the way for South Africa's most famous golfing son Gary Player. The incredible little world star, who first won his country's own Open title back in 1956, won it again for the 12th time at Houghton, Johannesburg, to crown a spectacular season in which he also captured the South African PGA, the Masters title and the Sun City Classic.

He took the PGA Championship at the Wanderers club, Johannesburg, being a shot ahead with a 54-hole total of 203 when rain caused cancellation of the last round. Player had been seven shots behind Dale Hayes on the opening day – Hayes opening with 64 – but two 66s shot Gary to the front, when the weather called a halt.

When the tour moved on to Milnerton, Cape Town, it was Calvin Peete who opened with a 64, with Player three shots back. But Gary caught the American with six birdies and an eagle three in a second round of 65, only to be caught himself at 54 holes by Ireland's John O'Leary. No one matched the South African's final 68, which gave him the Masters title by six shots with an 18-under-par aggregate of 270.

The Open Championship at Houghton was a tragedy for Britain's Ian Mosey from Manchester, and a triumph for the dogged resolution of the never-give-up Player. Ian, a former English amateur international, third in the South African Open in 1978, had never won a tournament since turning professional in 1972. He trailed the three-times British Open Champion by a single shot after the opening round, but found himself a stroke ahead of Allan Henning after round two in which Player fell away with a 75.

When he went two clear of Simon Hobday with 18 holes to play, and with Player 'back in the pack' joint-sixth and six strokes adrift, the title was Ian's for the taking. But Gary Player is never done. A typical last-round charge of 66, six under par and built on birdies at the first three holes still left the 28-year-old Mosey with a par four at the 18th for the first British victory in the South African Open since Tommy Horton won in 1970. But Mosey took a tragic six, including three putts – the second only 18 inches – and Player's hat-trick of major domestic titles was complete. The next week he crowned a superb run with victory in the Sun City, on the course he had created.

The Sunshine Circuit proved good to Nick Faldo who got recompense for a poor season in Europe by winning the ICL International at Kensington, while Simon Hobday celebrated being voted Rhodesia's Sportsman of the Year by winning the Zimbabwe-Rhodesian Open title.

THE ZIMBABWE-RHODESIAN OPEN CHAMPIONSHIP

Henry Chapman Golf Club, Salisbury 7–10 November 1979 Prize Money R30,000

1	Simon Hobday (ZIM)	69	71	65	70	275	R4,500.00
2	Denis Watson	67	68	71	69	275	2,750.00
	Hobday won play-off at second extra hole						
3	Mark McNulty	69	68	73	67	277	2,185.00
4	Alan Henning	74	69	70	66	279	1,700.00
5	John Bland	71	71	67	71	280	1,400.00
6	Nick Price	73	68	68	73	282	1,200.00
7	Cobie LeGrange	66	73	72	72	283	1,100.00
8	Tienie Britz	74	73	69	68	284	R883.34
	Gavin Levenson	71	70	73	70	284	883.33
	Bobby Verwey	66	73	69	76	284	883.33
11	Bill Longmuir (GB)	73	72	68	72	285	750.00
	Harold Henning (GB)	69	72	68	76	285	750.00
13	John Fourie	70	71	71	74	286	637.50
	Jeff Hawkes	71	74	72	69	286	637.50

THE ICL INTERNATIONAL TOURNAMENT

Kensington Golf Club, Johannesburg 14–17 November 1979 Prize Money R40,000

1	Nick Faldo (GB)	68	66	69	65	268	R6,000.00
2	Alan Henning	69	69	66	67	271	4,000.00
3	Harold Henning	67	69	69	68	273	1,937.50
	George Harvey (ZIM)	70	66	67	70	273	1,937.50
	Denis Watson	67	65	65	76	273	1,937.50
	John Fourie	66	68	67	72	273	1,937.50
7	Nick Price	68	69	66	71	274	1,250.00
8	Nick Job (GB)	66	69	68	72	275	1,100.00
9	Tertius Claassens	72	67	69	69	277	1,000.00
10	Mark McNulty	73	66	68	71	278	R925.00
	Bobby Cole	66	71	70	71	278	925.00
12	Vince Baker	69	74	70	66	279	850.00
13	Tienie Britz	74	70	67	69	280	775.00
	Jeff Hawkes	68	73	67	72	280	775.00
	Philip Jonas *	73	68	67	72	280	–
	Philip Simmons	73	69	65	73	280	775.00
	Amateur						

THE LEXINGTON SOUTH AFRICAN PGA CHAMPIONSHIP

Wanderers Golf Club, Joannesburg 21–24 November 1979 Prize Money R83,000

1	Gary Player	71	66	66	203	R12,450.00
2	Harold Henning	69	70	65	204	5,363.87
	Denis Watson	66	71	67	204	5,363.87
	Bobby Cole	67	69	68	204	5,363.87
	Nick Price	68	68	68	204	5,363.87
6	Nick Job (GB)	68	68	69	205	3,154.00
	Dale Hayes	64	70	71	205	3,154.00
8	Mark McNulty	69	68	69	206	2,573.00
	Alan Henning	71	66	69	206	2,573.00
10	Hugh Baiocchi	68	69	70	207	R2,199.50
	Jimmy Johnson (USA)	67	68	72	207	2,199.50
12	Ian Mosey (GB)	70	69	69	208	1,763.75
	Noel Hunt (GB)	70	67	71	208	1,763.75
14	John Bland	71	70	68	209	1,294.80
	John Fourie	67	78	70	209	1,294.80
	Calvin Peete (USA)	67	72	70	209	1,294.80
	Jannie LeGrange	69	69	71	209	1,294.80
	Bill Longmuir (GB)	69	68	72	209	1,294.80

(Tournament reduced to 54 holes because of rain)

I struck the blows and did it my way! Gary Player won the South African PGA, South African Masters, South African Open and Sun City titles in a spectacular four weeks.

THE KRONENBRAU SOUTH AFRICAN MASTERS

Milnerton Golf Club, Cape Town   28 November–1 December 1979   Prize Money R83,000

1	Gary Player	67	65	70	68	270	R12,450.00
2	John O'Leary (IRE)	68	66	68	74	276	8,300.00
3	Des Smyth (IRE)	68	65	70	74	277	5,395.00
4	Calvin Peete (USA)	64	68	74	72	278	4,150.00
5	Bobby Verwey	72	68	69	70	279	3,610.00
6	John Mahaffey (USA)	66	67	75	72	280	2,988.00
	John Bland	66	71	69	74	280	2,988.00
	Hugh Baiocchi	68	69	68	75	280	R2,988.00
9	Nick Faldo (GB)	65	70	70	76	281	2,490.00
10	Mike King (GB)	65	70	71	76	282	2,199.50
	Ken Brown (GB)	68	69	76	69	282	2,199.50
12	Don Bies (USA)	68	68	68	75	283	1,673.83
	Mark McNulty	70	68	70	75	283	1,673.83
	Harold Henning	70	69	70	74	283	1,673.83

THE SOUTH AFRICAN OPEN CHAMPIONSHIP

Houghton Golf Club, Johannesburg   5–8 December 1979   Prize Money R65,000

1	Gary Player	67	75	71	66	279	R9,780.00
2	Ian Mosey (GB)	68	70	69	73	280	6,390.00
3	Simon Hobday (ZIM)	71	69	69	73	282	3,636.67
	Allan Henning	71	68	72	71	282	3,636.67
	Jeff Hawkes	69	73	70	70	282	3,636.67
6	Bobby Cole	71	71	71	70	283	2,710.00
7	Hugh Baiocchi	70	73	71	70	284	2,110.00
	Des Smyth (IRE)	72	73	69	70	284	2,110.00
	Mark McNulty	70	70	71	73	284	R2,110.00
10	Robbie Stewart	68	77	70	70	285	1,485.00
	John Bland	72	70	72	71	285	1,485.00
	Nick Price	71	75	68	71	285	1,485.00
13	Philip Jonas*	72	72	72	70	286	–
	Bobby Verwey	70	73	72	71	286	1,096.67
	Ken Brown (GB)	74	75	67	70	286	1,096.67
	James Edman (USA)	74	72	71	69	286	1,096.67

Amateur

Sponsored by Yellow Pages/British Airways

THE SUN CITY CLASSIC

Pilansberg Golf Club, Bophuthatswana, near Johannesburg   12–16 December 1979   Prize Money R100,000

1	Gary Player	70	71	67	70	278	R15,000.00
2	Bobby Verwey	68	71	71	72	282	9,900.00
3	Nick Price	73	73	70	68	284	6,400.00
4	Des Smyth (IRE)	73	73	73	67	286	4,416.67
	Dennis Watson	72	70	75	69	286	4,416.67
	Tertius Claassens	73	70	70	73	286	4,416.66
7	Bobby Cole	70	73	70	74	287	R3,350.00
	Jim Thorpe (USA)	74	71	67	73	287	3,350.00
9	Mark Hayes (USA)	72	75	71	70	288	2,850.00
	Noel Hunt (GB)	68	72	75	73	288	2,850.00
11	Arnold Palmer (USA)	69	76	73	71	289	2,450.00

THE AUSTRALASIAN CIRCUIT 1979

JACK'S ALL RIGHT

Greg Norman watched in anguish as his putt of four feet curled around the hole on the 72nd green. In the gallery Jack Newton's sigh of relief was almost audible, and his joy unbounded. He had won the Australian Open Championship which had been something of a dream since he began playing golf at the age of 12. Jack had had his disappointments in his time, not the least of them the losing play-off with Tom Watson for the 1975 Open Championship at Carnoustie, but here was compensation indeed at Melbourne's Metropolitan Golf Club.

Newton, a shot behind Norman going into the last round, had an adventurous par-72 among the trees and bunkers, but he holed a chip at the 15th, and had pars at the last three holes for a total of 288. Norman's missed putt for the play-off dropped him into a share of second place with Graham Marsh, who was left regretting an opening 76.

It was a happy homecoming for the 29-year-old Sydney-born Newton, who won tournaments in Europe before trying his luck in America where, in 1978, he won the Buick-Goodwrench Open. Prior to his victory at the Metropolitan he had won the New South Wales Open by the massive margin of nine shots, playing some of the finest golf of the Australian season.

But he was among those trying not to have red faces when the experienced Australian amateur from Queensland, Jeff Senior, won the Dunhill Queensland Open by two shots with a nine-under-par score of 279! Newton had led until halfway through the final round. Jeff's brother Peter, a professional, had won the Dunhill South Australian Open at the end of the 1978–79 season.

Ruefully surveying what might have been was Stewart Ginn, born in Melbourne but now based in Tasmania. Stewart, who in the early 1970s campaigned in Europe, won two tournaments and lost two play-offs!

His victories came in the Australian PGA Championship at Royal Melbourne, where he won by three shots from Bob Shearer and Bob Charles, and in the New South Wales PGA Championship which he won by eight shots.

Ginn lost a play-off with Mike Ferguson in the Gold Coast Tweed event, and was later beaten over extra holes after he had tied with Ian Stanley in the Garden State PGA.

When the circuit moved to New Zealand, Ginn had further success with victory in the New Zealand Open.

THE NEW SOUTH WALES PGA CHAMPIONSHIP

Penrith Golf Club, NSW   6–9 September 1979   Prize Money A$15,000

							A$
1	Stewart Ginn	68	71	69	67	275	3,000.00
2	Richard Coombes (NZ)	71	69	73	70	283	1,800.00
3	Rob McNaughton	71	71	75	67	284	945.00
	Colin Bishop	72	72	71	69	284	945.00
5	Kel Nagle	70	75	72	69	286	570.00
	George Serhan	70	73	70	73	286	570.00
7	Bryan Smith	76	68	70	73	287	480.00
8	Tom Linskey	74	73	68	73	288	405.00
	Bob Shaw	73	74	66	75	288	405.00
10	Richard Lee	72	74	72	71	289	330.00
	Doug Merriman	72	70	73	74	289	330.00
	Ted Ball	72	71	70	76	289	330.00
13	Ian Stanley	73	71	72	74	290	288.00

THE WIN TV ILLAWARRA OPEN

Grange Golf Club, Port Kembla   20–23 September 1979   Prize Money A$20,000

							A$
1	Mike Ferguson	70	69	76	73	288	4,000.00
2	Chris Tickner	69	73	73	74	289	1,950.00
	Tom Linskey	68	71	73	77	289	1,950.00
4	Randall Vines	73	72	72	73	290	795.00
	Stewart Ginn	72	69	77	72	290	795.00
	George Serhan	74	72	69	75	290	795.00
	Billy Dunk	74	66	73	77	290	795.00
8	Ted Ball	73	72	73	74	292	560.00
9	Terry Kendall (NZ)	71	73	73	77	294	520.00
10	Peter Fowler	74	72	76	73	295	480.00
11	Ray Hore	71	73	79	73	296	408.00
	Colin Mellish	77	74	72	73	296	408.00
	George Bell	76	77	69	74	296	408.00

THE GOLD COAST TWEED CLASSIC

Coolangatta-Tweed Heads Golf Club, NSW   27–20 September 1979   Prize Money A$20,000

							A$
1	Mike Ferguson	71	67	71	72	281	4,000.00
2	Stewart Ginn	69	65	78	69	281	2,400.00

Ferguson won play-off at third extra hole

							A$
3	Randall Vines	72	68	76	68	284	1,260.00
	Bob Shaw	73	66	73	72	284	1,260.00
5	Terry Gale	71	71	71	72	285	800.00
6	Ray Hore	69	73	75	69	286	680.00
	Wayne Grady	70	74	72	70	286	680.00
8	Barry Vivian (NZ)	71	72	74	71	288	560.00
9	Sam Snead (USA)	69	74	72	74	289	500.00
	Billy Dunk	71	69	73	76	289	500.00
11	Colin Bishop	73	76	71	70	290	408.00
	Allan Cooper	73	71	75	71	290	408.00
	Vaughan Somers	76	72	70	72	290	408.00

THE DUNHILL QUEENSLAND OPEN CHAMPIONSHIP
Indooroopilly Golf Club, Brisbane   4–7 October 1979   Prize Money A$30,000

							A$
1	Jeff Senior*	68	71	73	67	279	–
2	Jack Newton	66	68	75	72	281	6,000.00
3	Vaughan Somers	73	69	70	71	283	3,600.00
4	Billy Dunk	68	72	68	76	284	2,250.00
5	Stuart Reese (NZ)	72	68	70	75	285	1,365.00
	Terry Gale	69	67	75	74	285	1,365.00
7	David Good	70	71	72	73	286	960.00
	Ian Stanley	67	73	74	72	286	960.00
	Art Russell (USA)	69	70	74	73	286	960.00
	Glen Cogill*	74	64	75	73	286	–
11	Brandon Coleman	72	72	70	73	287	690.00
	Ted Ball	73	74	69	71	287	690.00
	Greg Norman	71	71	72	73	287	690.00
	Randall Vines	75	71	69	72	287	690.00

* Amateur

THE CITIZEN WATCHES SENIORS' CHAMPIONSHIP
Manly Golf Club, NSW   5–7 October 1979   Prize Money A$25,000

						A$
1	Tommy Bolt (USA)	68	72	74	214	5,000.00
2	Jack Fleck (USA)	72	71	72	215	3,000.00
3	Jimmy Martin (IRE)	71	72	74	217	1,875.00
4	George Bayer (USA)	71	77	70	218	1,137.50
	Dow Finsterwald (USA)	68	77	73	218	1,137.50
6	Kel Nagle (AUS)	70	75	74	219	900.00
7	Art Wall (USA)	76	73	72	221	750.00
	Tomoo Ishii (J)	76	67	78	221	750.00
9	Christy O'Connor (IRE)	74	71	78	223	650.00
10	Sam Snead (USA)	73	78	73	224	600.00

THE GARDEN STATE PGA CHAMPIONSHIP
Woodlands Golf Club, Melbourne   11–14 October 1979   Prize Money A$50,000

							A$
1	Ian Stanley	71	70	73	72	286	10,000.00
2	Stewart Ginn	72	73	69	72	286	6,000.00

Stanley won play-off at second extra hole

							A$
3	Bob Shearer	69	74	74	72	289	3,750.00
4	Greg Norman	69	78	71	72	290	2,275.00
	Terry Kendall (NZ)	70	73	73	74	290	2,275.00
6	Mike Ferguson	73	72	70	77	292	1,800.00
7	Bobby Wadkins (USA)	71	73	79	70	293	1,600.00
8	Terry Gale	71	76	74	73	294	1,160.00
	Rob McNaughton	76	73	72	73	294	1,160.00
	Bob Beauchemin	70	77	72	75	294	1,160.00
	Stuart Reese (NZ)	73	74	73	74	294	1,160.00
	Mike Cahill	72	72	76	74	294	1,160.00
	Billy Dunk	74	72	74	74	294	1,160.00
14	Bill Britten	74	75	74	72	295	875.00
	Vaughan Somers	73	75	70	77	295	875.00

THE CBA WEST LAKES CLASSIC
Grange Golf Club, Adelaide   25–28 October 1979   Prize Money A$65,000

Pos	Player						A$
1	David Graham	72	70	71	72	285	13,000.00
2	Gary Vanier (USA)	71	74	75	67	287	6,337.50
	Bob Shearer	69	72	73	73	287	6,337.50
4	Guy Wolstenhome	71	72	77	68	288	2,583.75
	Greg Norman	73	74	69	72	288	2,583.75
	Mike Ferguson	70	72	71	75	288	2,583.75
	Christy O'Connor (IRE)	70	76	69	73	288	2,583.75
8	Terry Kendall (NZ)	69	74	75	71	289	1,755.00
	Randall Vines	72	76	66	75	289	1,755.00
10	Bob Charles (NZ)	74	75	71	72	292	1,430.00
	Stewart Ginn	74	73	72	73	292	1,430.00
	Barry Vivian (NZ)	75	70	72	75	292	1,430.00
13	Walter Godfrey (NZ)	77	73	72	71	293	1,209.00
	Geoff Parslow	72	78	68	75	293	1,209.00

NEW SOUTH WALES OPEN CHAMPIONSHIP
The Lakes Golf Club, Sydney   1–4 November 1979   Prize Money A$60,000

Pos	Player						A$
1	Jack Newton	69	70	70	72	281	12,000.00
2	Gary Vanier (USA)	69	72	77	72	290	4,956.67
	Wayne Grady	74	68	78	70	290	4,956.67
	Jeff Hall (GB)	72	72	71	75	290	4,956.67
5	Scott Simpson (USA)	74	76	70	71	291	2,400.00
6	Martin Foster (GB)	71	74	76	71	292	1,830.00
	Mike Ferguson	73	77	70	72	292	1,830.00
	Chris Tickner	72	75	72	73	292	1,830.00
	Maurice Bembridge (GB)	72	72	75	73	292	1,830.00
10	Tony Gresham*	75	71	75	72	293	–
	Greg Norman	73	70	76	74	293	1,277.75
	Barry Vivian (NZ)	75	75	72	71	293	1,277.75
	Richard Coombes (NZ)	74	71	72	76	293	1,277.75
	Chris Witcher	72	74	72	75	293	1,277.75

Amateur

THE MAYNE NICKLESS AUSTRALIAN PGA CHAMPIONSHIP
Royal Melbourne Golf Club, Victoria   8–11 November 1979   Prize Money A$125,000

Pos	Player						A$
1	Stewart Ginn	71	72	69	72	284	25,000.00
2	Bob Shearer	70	70	77	70	287	12,185.00
	Bob Charles (NZ)	75	71	71	70	287	12,185.00
4	Scott Simpson (USA)	71	73	76	69	289	5,690.00
	Simon Owen (NZ)	74	69	73	73	289	5,690.00
6	Hubert Green (USA)	68	79	77	69	293	3,812.00
	Bruce Devlin	73	72	77	71	293	3,812.00
	Bob Shaw	73	72	77	71	293	3,812.00
	Terry Kendall (NZ)	70	76	73	74	293	3,812.00
10	Greg Norman	73	75	70	76	294	2,750.00
	Peter Cowen (GB)	70	75	75	74	294	2,750.00
	Bruce Green	72	72	74	76	294	2,750.00
13	Mike Cahill	78	72	71	74	295	2,325.00
	Terry Gale	74	73	75	73	295	2,325.00
15	Jack Newton	74	77	71	74	296	2,000.00
	Gary Player (SA)	75	69	75	77	296	2,000.00
	Walter Godfrey (NZ)	73	73	74	76	296	2,000.00

THE DUNHILL AUSTRALIAN OPEN CHAMPIONSHIP
Metropolitan Golf Club, Melbourne, Victoria 15–18 November 1979 Prize Money A$150,000

Pos	Name					Total	A$
1	Jack Newton	74	72	70	72	288	30,000.00
2	Graham Marsh	76	68	73	72	289	14,635.00
	Greg Norman	73	69	73	74	289	14,625.00
4	Bob Shearer	73	76	69	72	290	7,650.00
5	Bill Britton (USA)	74	72	71	74	291	5,700.00
	Scott Tuttle (USA)	73	72	71	75	291	5,700.00
7	Gary Player (SA)	74	72	72	74	292	4,800.00
8	Severiano Ballesteros (S)	79	73	70	71	293	4,200.00
9	David Graham	74	74	73	73	294	3,750.00
	Bob Shaw	74	75	71	74	294	3,750.00
11	Hubert Green (USA)	76	75	70	74	295	3,300.00
12	Terry Kendall (NZ)	71	77	75	73	296	2,940.00
14	Rob McNaughton	78	72	74	72	296	2,940.00
	Bruce Devlin	76	71	78	72	297	2,400.00
	Mike Cahill	77	73	76	71	297	2,400.00
	Terry Gale	71	77	76	73	297	2,400.00
	Jim Nelford (C)	72	74	76	75	297	2,400.00
	John Lister (NZ)	74	73	73	77	297	2,400.00
19	Stuart Reese (NZ)	71	76	75	76	298	1,650.00
	Chris Tickner	78	73	70	77	298	1,650.00
	Trevor McDonald	75	74	73	76	298	1,650.00
	Trevor Johnson (GB)	70	81	68	79	298	1,650.00
	Deray Simon (USA)	70	74	75	79	298	1,650.00

THE WESTERN AUSTRALIAN ANNIVERSARY OPEN
Lake Karrinyup Golf Club, Perth 22–25 November 1979 Prize Money A$150,000

Pos	Name					Total	A$
1	Peter Jacobsen (USA)	71	70	68	70	279	30,000.00
2	David Graham	70	70	70	74	284	18,000.00
3	Bob Charles (NZ)	73	73	69	70	285	7,575.00
	Graham Marsh	72	71	72	70	285	7,575.00
	Severiano Ballesteros (S)	70	71	72	72	285	7,575.00
	Barry Jaeckel (USA)	74	69	70	72	285	7,575.00
7	Jerry Pate (USA)	69	73	70	74	286	4,500.00
	Bob Shearer	70	74	67	75	286	4,500.00
9	Peter Thomson	74	70	73	70	287	3,750.00
1	Greg Norman	77	71	66	73	287	3,750.00
11	Curtis Strange (USA)	73	73	72	70	288	3,300.00
12	John Cook (USA)	74	70	74	71	289	2,860.00
	Chris Tickner	71	70	76	72	289	2,860.00
	Terry Kendall (NZ)	72	72	70	75	289	2,860.00
15	Vaughan Somers	71	68	77	74	290	2,400.00
	John Lister (NZ)	70	69	74	77	290	2,400.00
	Mike Cahill	72	70	74	73	290	2,400.00

Since he first started playing at the age of 12 Jack Newton had set his sights on the Australian Open title.

THE AIR NEW ZEALAND-SHELL OPEN

Heretaunga Golf Club, Wellington   28 November–2 December 1979   Prize Money NZ$75,000

								NZ$
1	David Graham (AUS)	70	67	69	73	279		12,500.00
2	Rodger Davis (AUS)	69	70	72	76	287		8,500.00
3	Bob Charles	72	73	72	71	288		5,350.00
	Victor Regalado (MEX)	72	75	68	73	288		5,350.00
5	Simon Owen	71	71	72	76	290		3,333.00
	Barry Vivian	69	73	73	75	290		3,333.00
7	Tom Kite (USA)	67	72	76	76	291		2,250.00
								NZ$
8	Bob Gilder (USA)	70	72	72	78	292		1,875.00
9	Terry Kendall	78	73	71	71	293		1,650.00
10	Gene Littler (USA)	76	75	71	72	294		1,500.00
11	Rob Barker (NZ)	69	73	73	80	295		1,350.00
	John Schroeder (USA)	72	72	78	73	295		1,350.00
	John Godwin (USA)	72	67	84	72	295		1,350.00
	Brian Jones (AUS)	69	77	75	74	295		1,350.00

THE NEW ZEALAND OPEN CHAMPIONSHIP

St Clair Golf Club, Dunedin   6–9 December 1979   Prize Money NZ$50,000

								NZ$
1	Stewart Ginn (AUS)	70	68	71	69	278		7,500.00
2	Simon Owen	65	71	71	74	281		5,600.00
3	Rodger Davis (AUS)	67	73	73	70	283		4,250.00
4	Terry Gale (AUS)	71	74	72	67	284		3,250.00
5	Ted Ball (AUS)	63	78	72	72	285		2,475.00
								NZ$
6	Brian Jones (AUS)	72	72	78	64	286		1,660.00
	John Short (USA)	70	72	72	72	286		1,600.00
8	Barry Vivian	71	73	73	70	287		1,250.00
	Brian Barnes (GB)	69	71	71	76	287		1,250.00

THE SOUTH SEAS CLASSIC

Pacific Harbour Golf Club, Fiji   13–16 December 1979   Prize Money A$42,000

								A$
1	Rick Mallicoat (USA)	71	73	73	68	285		8,000.00
2	Wayne Grady (AUS)	66	75	70	75	286		3,900.00
	Mike Ferguson (AUS)	71	71	71	73	286		3,900.00
4	Maurice Bembridge (GB)	70	75	70	72	287		2,040.00
5	Greg Norman (AUS)	68	74	70	76	288		1,600.00
6	Bob Shearer (AUS)	74	71	73	72	290		1,360.00
	Terry Kendall (NZ)	70	76	72	72	290		1,360.00
								A$
8	Ted Ball (AUS)	66	74	76	75	291		1,120.00
9	Simon Owen (NZ)	71	74	74	73	292		1,040.00
10	Guy Wolstenholme (AUS)	76	76	70	71	293		880.00
	Vaughan Somers (AUS)	70	79	73	71	293		880.00
	Rodger Davis (AUS)	76	71	73	73	293		880.00
13	Richard Coombes (NZ)	74	73	73	74	294		768.00

WINNERS OF CONCLUDING TOURNAMENTS IN THE 1978–79 SEASON

26–29 January 1979, Traralgon A$15,000 Classic: Greg Norman 277
1–4 February 1979, Tasmanian A$20,000 Open: Martin Bohen (USA) 271
15–18 February 1979, Victorian A$60,000 Open: Rodger Davis 291
22–25 February 1979, Dunhill A$25,000 South Australian Open: Peter Senior 282

1–4 March 1979, Australian A$30,000 Masters: Barry Vivian (NZ) 289
15–18 March 1979, Western Australia PGA A$15,000: Richard Coombes (NZ) 285
22–25 March 1979, Royal Fremantle A$15,000 Open: Terry Gale 280
29 March–1 April 1979, WAY A$20,000 Celebration Open: Terry Kendall (NZ) 280

THE INTERNATIONAL SCENE 1979

THE SUN ALLIANCE RYDER CUP 1979
THE WALKER CUP 1979
THE PGA CUP 1979
THE WORLD CUP 1979
THE TRANSATLANTIC TROPHY
THE WOMEN'S PROFESSIONAL CIRCUIT 1979
THE PRO-AMATEUR YEAR

Larry Nelson won all of his five Ryder Cup matches to crown a great year in which he finished second to Tom Watson in the US Money-Winners List.

Stay one stroke ahead with Sun Alliance

In the course of life you're bound to come up against hazards of all kinds. So it's important you're as prepared as possible to meet them.

That's where Sun Alliance can help you.

We can provide you with all the insurance cover you need to protect your home, your business, your car, your savings, your retirement, your life itself.

That way you can stay one stroke ahead of many of life's hazards.

Talk to your broker or call in to see us.

There's a branch near you.

THE SUN ALLIANCE RYDER CUP 1979

USA MAKE IT 19–3

It was, so it is said, at the instigation of Jack Nicklaus that the shape of the Ryder Cup encounters was eventually adjusted from what was formerly a Great British and Irish team to a more widely representative European side, and so for the first time since the series began in 1927 Continental players made their appearance in the 1979 biennial international against the United States. That Europe, with the former World Cup winning pair Severiano Ballesteros and Antonio Garrido in their midst, still lost by 17 points to 11 at the luxurious Greenbrier Club in White Sulphur Springs, West Virginia, to an American team minus a non-qualifying Nicklaus himself and imminent father-to-be Tom Watson, was by no means the failure of an enterprise.

Europe fought them all the way, recovering from a shaky start in the opening fourballs, getting back to within a solitary point at the end of the second day, and in the end going down to four singles that ended successively on the 18th green.

Ironically the Spaniards, bravely though they competed, managed only one point between them, and with Mark James not 100 per cent fit, and his opening partner Ken Brown having non-communicative problems when re-paired with Des Smyth, the result reflected much credit on their fellow team members and their splendid captain John Jacobs.

Bernard Gallacher played his heart out, winning four points out of five. Inseparably paired on such occasions with Brian Barnes, they came from three down to beat Irwin and Mahaffey on the first day, and came back from two down to beat Zoeller and Hayes, and then disposed of Trevino and Zoeller on the second day.

Though Barnes was one of those who lost on the last green in the vital singles, Gallacher produced a magnificent 3 and 2 win over Wadkins whose Ryder Cup record to that point was seven points out of seven!

Like Barnes, Nick Faldo contributed three points, lifting himself from a bad patch that had been with him all summer. Resuming his reliable partnership with Peter Oosterhuis they got maximum points on the second day, after having been surprisingly dropped from the first afternoon's engagements, and Faldo got a singles point as well at the expense of Elder, the first coloured professional to win Ryder Cup honours.

When Oosterhuis went under on the 18th to Hubert Green it was his first singles defeat since he first played Ryder Cup golf in 1971.

Ballesteros and Garrido played better than their one point suggested. The Open Champion was an obvious target for the American side. Four times the draw brought him face-to-face with Larry Nelson, and four times the number two US money-winner put him to the sword.

Nelson had a 100 per cent five-out-of-five Ryder Cup baptism to crown his finest year. Teamed permanently with Wadkins they won both days' fourballs and foursomes, Nelson capping the achievement with a 3 and 2 victory over the Open Champion.

So the United States widened their lead in the series to 19 victories, three defeats, and one tied match. None the less Europe will line up against them 'at home' in 1981 with hopes higher than ever in recent years that they can come out of the wilderness that has engulfed them since 1957.

In 1979 it was agreed that the event should officially be called The Sun Alliance Ryder Cup.

Every right to be happy were Lee Elder, Fuzzy Zoeller, Andy Bean and their non-playing captain Billy Casper. But it was a closer Ryder Cup match than the final score indicated. (Golf Photography International)

THE SUN ALLIANCE RYDER CUP

The Greenbrier, White Sulphur Springs, West Virginia
14–16 September 1979

United States of America versus Europe

FIRST DAY
Fourballs (*USA names first*)

Lanny Wadkins and Larry Nelson beat Antonio Garrido and Severiano Ballesteros	2 and 1
Lee Trevino and Fuzzy Zoeller beat Ken Brown and Mark James	3 and 2
Andy Bean and Lee Elder beat Peter Oosterhuis and Nick Faldo	2 and 1
Hale Irwin and John Mahaffey lost to Brian Barnes and Bernard Gallacher	2 and 1

United States of America 3 Europe 1

Foursomes

Irwin and Tom Kite beat Brown and Des Smyth	7 and 6
Zoeller and Hubert Green lost to Ballesteros and Garrido	3 and 2
Trevino and Gil Morgan halved with Sandy Lyle and Tony Jacklin	
Wadkins and Nelson beat Barnes and Gallacher	4 and 3

United States of America 2½ Europe 1½
Match Position: USA 5½ Europe 2½

SECOND DAY
Foursomes

Elder and Mahaffey lost to Jacklin and Lyle	5 and 4
Bean and Kite lost to Oosterhuis and Faldo	6 and 5
Zoeller and Mark Hayes lost to Barnes and Gallacher	2 and 1
Wadkins and Nelson beat Ballesteros and Garrido	2 and 1

United States of America 1 Europe 3

Fourballs

Wadkins and Nelson beat Ballesteros and Garrido	5 and 4
Irwin and Kite beat Jacklin and Lyle	1 hole
Trevino and Zoeller lost to Barnes and Gallacher	3 and 2
Elder and Hayes lost to Oosterhuis and Faldo	1 hole

United States of America 2 Europe 2
Match Position: USA 8½ Europe 7½

THIRD DAY
Singles

Morgan halved with James*	
Nelson beat Ballesteros	3 and 2
Hayes beat Garrido	1 hole
Bean beat Mike King	4 and 3
Irwin beat Smyth	5 and 3
Trevino beat Lyle	2 and 1
Wadkins lost to Gallacher	3 and 2
Kite beat Jacklin	1 hole
Mahaffey beat Barnes	1 hole
Elder lost to Faldo	3 and 2
Green beat Oosterhuis	2 holes
Zoeller lost to Brown	1 hole

*James withdrew unfit – match counted as a half

United States of America 8½ Europe 3½

MATCH RESULT: United States of America 17   Europe 11

THE WALKER CUP 1979

Pat Ward-Thomas

ANTI-CLIMAX YET AGAIN

Anyone who has followed the Walker Cup matches over the years, with the unforgettable exception of 1971, will have long grown accustomed to anti-climax – from the British and Irish viewpoint. After the opening day in 1963 at Turnberry, the home side led by three points and the evening was alive with hope, but it swiftly eroded the next morning when all the foursomes were lost.

Two years later a British victory seemed certain in Baltimore. Only two points were needed from the last eight singles, but in the end Clive Clark had to hole a long putt to save his side from a humiliating defeat.

That was the supreme disappointment, but again in Milwaukee in 1969, and in Boston when the match was next in the United States, there was a lively possibility of victory until the last half-hour. Invariably there was a strong American reaction to adversity, but their recoveries were assisted by tremulous finishing from the opposition when the pressure grew severe.

Thus it was at Muirfield when the contest gave every promise of being agonisingly close until, after every match had passed the turn, parity suddenly vanished with appalling swiftness. Seven of the matches were lost and Allan Brodie alone saved his side from the humiliation of a 'whitewash'. Only once in 40 years had Britain and Ireland failed to get more than one point from the singles. Disappointment was the harder to bear because the preceding play had given no indication that such a collapse was imminent, and forever would look dreadful in the record books.

Neither was the failure due to withering blasts of birdies from the Americans, but was almost entirely due to British errors, mostly marginal but fatal nonetheless, over the last few holes which the Americans were able to win with pars. Every match finished on the 16th or 17th green – no-one was 'murdered'.

As always the Americans had emerged from a tougher competitive background than the British. When the dies were cast they missed fewer fairways and putted more soundly, but that hardly excused lapses by the home side in conditions that could not have been more sympathetic. The reason was the old fear of success, one of the greatest destructive influences in golf; or indeed in any sport. Having only won the Cup twice in 26 attempts the prospect of victory became a formidable burden.

Apart from the final outcome, the match made splendid watching. The opening series of foursomes finished even. Brian Marchbank and

Geoffrey Godwin, playing in their first Walker Cup matches, and Michael Kelley, won their singles. Had Peter McEvoy's short putting not been vulnerable he would have beaten Jay Sigel, who confirmed his stature as the most accomplished player on either side by winning the Amateur Championship the following week. As it was McEvoy halved and Britain ended the day a point behind.

Aided by some fortune the next morning the British again halved the foursomes. In the second match they seemed likely to go two down on the 14th, but McEvoy holed a long putt and one of their opponents, thinking his side had lost the hole, picked up their ball when in fact they had a short putt for a half. Reprieved, Marchbank and McEvoy raced ahead to victory.

A moment or so later Kelley, with his side one up, hit an imperial shank to the 17th and seemed certain to lose the 18th and the match, when he pulled wide of the green. Ian Hutcheon could only move the ball from deep rough into a bunker from where Kelley holed out with a beautiful little shot, and a half had been saved.

Now it was all to play for and a heavy responsibility rested on McEvoy in the leading single, but finely though he responded Scott Hoch proved just the stronger. His golf was the most impressive of the day and McEvoy lost with honour.

Meanwhile the scoreboards still revealed that in match after match there was nothing in it. At one stage the Americans, who needed four points to win, were ahead in only one. Then the sickly sequence of British blemishes began and within the hour the likelihood of a momentous climax had become a sorry tale.

At the outset few experienced observers anticipated a British victory. The team, admirably led by Rodney Foster, was not as strong as some

A familiar story! America's strength in the final singles saw them through to their 24th Walker Cup victory.

of its predecessors, but neither was the American. Dick Siderowf, the non-playing captain, alone had previous experience of British conditions. A misunderstanding over dates led to an unfortunate clash between the National Collegiate finals in the United States, and the Walker Cup match.

Eventually Bobby Clampett, the outstanding amateur golfer of the previous year, John Cook the US champion, and Gary Hallberg all of whom would have been in the team, played for their colleges instead of for their country. As it proved, their absence made little difference, but had they played defeat would have lost a little of its sting.

THE WALKER CUP

Muirfield, Gullane, East Lothian   30–31 May 1979

Great Britain and Ireland v United States of America

FIRST DAY
Foursomes (*GB & I names first*)

P. McEvoy and B. Marchbank lost to S. Hoch and J. Sigel	1 hole
G. Godwin and I. Hutcheon beat M. West and H. Sutton	2 holes
G. Brand and M. Kelley lost to D. Fischesser and J. Holtgrieve	1 hole
A. Brodie and I. Carslaw beat G. Moody and M. Gove	2 and 1

Great Britain and Ireland 2 United States of America 2

Singles

McEvoy halved with Sigel	
J. C. Davies lost to D. Clarke	8 and 7
J. Buckley lost to Hoch	9 and 7
Hutcheon lost to Holtgrieve	6 and 4
Marchbank beat M. Peck	1 hole
Godwin beat Moody	3 and 2
Kelley beat Fischesser	3 and 2
Brodie lost to Gove	3 and 2

Great Britain and Ireland 3½ United States of America 4½
Match position: *Great Britain and Ireland 5½ United States of America 6½*

SECOND DAY
Foursomes

Godwin and Brand lost to Hoch and Sigel	4 and 3
McEvoy and Marchbank beat Fischesser and Holtgrieve	2 and 1
Kelley and Hutcheon halved with West and Sutton	
Carslaw and Brodie halved with Clarke and Peck	

Great Britain and Ireland 2 United States of America 2

Singles

McEvoy lost to Hoch	3 and 1
Brand lost to Clarke	2 and 1
Godwin lost to Gove	3 and 2
Hutcheon lost to Peck	2 and 1
Brodie beat West	3 and 2
Kelley lost to Moody	3 and 2
Marchbank lost to Sutton	3 and 1
Carslaw lost to Sigel	2 and 1

Great Britain and Ireland 1 United States of America 7
MATCH RESULT: *Great Britain and Ireland 8½ United States of America 15½*

THE PGA CUP 1979

CLUB PROS TRIUMPH AGAIN

While the Ryder Cup and Walker Cup representative teams failed to break the American stranglehold on golf's major professional and amateur team trophies, the club professionals allowed no loosening of the grip on their opposite numbers from across the Atlantic. First glimmers of domination by the Great Britain and Ireland team had appeared at Mission Hills, in Palm Springs, California in 1977 when they achieved a memorable draw in the annual Club Professionals' international match for the PGA Cup. It culminated in victory in 1978 at the St Mellion Golf and Country Club, Plymouth, and that victory was underlined when the home team beat the United States by the wide margin of eight points over the Castletown golf links in the Isle of Man.

The PGA Cup Match was sponsored for the first time by Britannia Financial Services, and broke tradition in being staged for two successive years in the British Isles in order to form part of the Isle of Man's 1979 Millennium celebrations.

Though Peter Butler, Brian Waites, David Huish, David Jones, and John Morgan were all tournament hardened competitors, their club

An unfamiliar sight in international matches against America. The scoreboard displayed a second successive victory in the series by the Great Britain and Ireland team.

professional status was unchallengeable. With Paul Leonard, David Ridley, and Mike Steadman they occupied the top places in the Club Professionals' Championship, Jim Farmer replacing the ninth qualifier George Will who withdrew.

The home side took a 2½–1½ lead from the opening foursomes, Farmer and Morgan being the only ones to suffer when Gentile and Ferree birdied five of the first seven holes, and went on to win by eight and six. The outcome was really wrapped up on the second day when only a halved match between Jones and Morgan against Aycock and Collins prevented a clean sweep of the fourballs.

It left Great Britain and Ireland needing only 2½ points to retain the trophy, and they made no mistake by winning six and halving one of the final day's nine singles. Huish, Butler, and Waites were all three-out-of-three winners.

THE PGA CUP MATCH

Castletown Golf Club, Isle of Man   28–30 September 1979

CLUB PROFESSIONALS' INTERNATIONAL MATCH
Great Britain and Ireland v USA

FIRST DAY
Foursomes (*GB & I names first*)

David Huish and Peter Butler beat Tim Collins and Tommy Aycock	4 and 2
Brian Waites and David Ridley beat Bob Bruno and Jay Overton	2 and 1
John Morgan and Jim Farmer lost to John Gentile and Jim Feree	8 and 6
David Jones and Paul Leonard halved with Jack Sommers and George Shortridge	

Great Britain and Ireland 2½ United States of America 1½

SECOND DAY
Fourballs

Waites and Farmer beat Jim Wright and Overton	2 and 1
Butler and Mike Steadman beat Gentile and Ferree	4 and 3
Jones and Morgan halved with Collins and Aycock	
Huish and Ridley beat Sommers and Shortridge	1 hole

Great Britain and Ireland 3½ United States of America ½

THIRD DAY
Singles

Jones beat Overton	6 and 5
Waites beat Wright	1 hole
Farmer beat Gentile	5 and 4
Ridley halved with Shortridge	
Leonard lost to Ferree	2 holes
Steadman lost to Bruno	5 and 3
Morgan beat Aycock	5 and 4
Butler beat Collins	5 and 4
Huish beat Sommers	2 and 1

Great Britain and Ireland 6½ United States of America 2½

MATCH RESULT: *Great Britain and Ireland 12½ United States of America 4½*

THE WORLD CUP 1979

Glyfada Golf Club, Athens   8–11 November 1979

Leading Team Scores

1	**United States 575**					
	Hale Irwin	74	70	72	69	285
	John Mahaffey	67	71	80	72	290
2	**Scotland 580**					
	Sandy Lyle	72	73	73	69	287
	Ken Brown	73	72	77	71	293
3	**Spain 590**					
	Antonio Garrido	74	76	66	73	289
	Manuel Pinero	73	77	77	74	301
4	**Brazil 594**					
	Jaime Gonzalez	73	71	72	72	288
	Rafael Navarro	75	73	81	77	306
5	**Taiwan 595**					
	Lu Hsi-Chuen	71	73	72	77	293
	Chen Tze-Ming	73	76	74	79	302
6	**Canada 599**					
	Jim Nelford	73	74	73	74	294
	Dan Halldorson	77	74	82	72	305
7	**Japan 599**					
	Kazuo Yoshikawa	71	74	73	75	293
	Koichi Inoue	76	76	78	76	306
8	**France 600**					
	Jean Garaialde	74	74	76	75	299
	Bernard Pascassio	77	76	74	74	301
9	**England 601**					
	Mike King	72	73	72	79	296
	Mark James	81	72	75	77	305
10	**Malaysia 602**					
	Marimuthu Ramayah	75	75	74	74	298
	Nazamuddin Yusoff	74	79	75	76	304
11	**West Germany 602**					
	Bernard Langer	74	70	71	72	287
	Manfred Kessler	86	75	79	75	315
12	**Mexico 605**					
	Victor Regalado	76	76	73	75	300
	Enrique Serna	74	74	80	77	305

Leading Individual Scores

1	Hale Irwin (USA)	74	70	72	69	285
2	Bernard Langer (G)	74	70	71	72	287
	Sandy Lyle (SC)	72	73	73	69	287
4	Jaime Gonzalez (BZ)	73	71	72	72	288
5	Antonio Garrido (S)	74	76	66	73	289
6	John Mahaffey (USA)	67	71	80	72	290
7	Ramon Munoz (VEN)	72	78	70	72	292
8	Kazuo Yoshikawa (J)	71	74	73	75	293
	Ken Brown (SC)	73	72	77	71	293
	Lu Hsi-Chuen (TAI)	71	73	72	77	293
11	Jim Nelford (C)	73	74	73	74	294
12	Mike King (ENG)	72	73	72	79	296
13	Des Smyth (IRE)	74	79	74	71	298
	Marimuthu Ramayah (MAL)	75	75	74	74	298
15	Jean Garaialde (F)	74	74	76	75	299
	Juan Pinzon (COL)	70	74	79	76	299
	Eddie Polland (IRE)	76	74	74	75	299

For those people who still insist that British Caledonian fly only to Edinburgh.

British Caledonian
We never forget you have a choice.

THE TRANSATLANTIC TROPHY

LIONS AGAIN RAMPANT

Victory in the 1979 Transatlantic Golf Trophy in Texas rounded off a very successful season for British Caledonian's team of professional golfers, the Golfing Lions. For the second year in succession B.Cal's Lions defeated an eight-man team of Texan tour and club professionals in the return Trophy meeting at Waterwood National Country Club, near Huntsville.

The international, unlike 1978 when the Lions won all but one point, was more evenly matched. Led by non-playing President Dai Rees and the European number one Sandy Lyle, the squad shrugged off the Texan challenge, headed by Dave Marr, to clinch the trophy by five points to three.

The margin had looked like being much greater until Lyle dumped his approach into water at the 18th only to halve his match with top US club pro Tommy Aycock, when he had earlier seemed certain to win it. Sam Torrance recorded a superb one-hole victory over Don Massengale, the former Canadian Open Champion and captain of the Texan side.

Malcolm Gregson who captained the B.Cal side beat Bob Elliott three and two; Carl Mason held on to beat Ken Noll two and one; and John Morgan had a notable four and three win over Bert Baine. But Tommy Horton could only manage a half with Ras Allen; Ewen Murray lost to Texan Champion Clayton Cole three and two; and David Ingram, after leading most of the way, lost to Charlie Epps three and two.

For Lyle, the British Caledonian Transatlantic Trophy was just another stop-off on a 'world tour'. After finishing joint-second in the World Individual Championship at the World Cup in Greece he jetted off from Texas to Japan before returning home to collect his Harry Vardon Trophy at the PGA's Annual Dinner.

One notable absentee from the Transatlantic Trophy in Texas was Brian Barnes, who had already committed himself to a winter tour of New Zealand and Australia.

The Lions acquitted themselves with distinction in 1979. Barnes won the Zambian, Portuguese, and Italian Open Championships, tied for fourth place in the Carrolls and Colgate PGA Championship and won another European Ryder Cup team place. Sam Torrance played consistently all year finishing third in three major events; John Morgan continued his successful run, after winning the Nigerian and Lusaka Open Championships, by finishing sixth in the Spanish and runner-up in the Martini International.

Morgan was also in the Great Britain and Ireland side that defeated America in the PGA Cup match. Fourth place in the Nigerian Open Championship, eighth in the Swiss, and 10th place in the Zambian Open, helped Ewen Murray to his first appearance in the Transatlantic Trophy. He also finished third in the SOS/Talisman event, and Tommy Horton finished fourth in the European Open.

The other members of the Trophy squad, Carl Mason, David Ingram and Mike Miller all enjoyed a reasonable year on the tour.

The winning Transatlantic Trophy squad. Left to right: David Ingram, Ewen Murray, Malcolm Gregson, Sandy Lyle, Tommy Horton, Dai Ress (president), Sam Torrance, Carl Mason, John Morgan and Mike Miller.

THE WOMEN'S PROFESSIONAL CIRCUIT 1979

Bill Johnson

PROVING THE CRITICS WRONG

When, just before Christmas in 1978, the newly-formed Women's Professional Golf Association announced their tournament programme, there were some critics who gave them little chance of success. It was suggested that their programme was too ambitious. Others said that the women were not good enough, while some held the opinion that there was no interest in women's golf and that spectators would not take the trouble to watch their tournaments.

They were all wrong! The tour clearly was a success. Any doubts on the other counts were finally squashed by the large crowd who, on a beautiful autumn day, saw Jane Panter ring down the curtain on a rewarding season when she beat Muriel Thomson in a superb final to win the Lambert and Butler Match-play Championship at Moor Park in Hertfordshire. This, however, would never have been possible without the Carlsberg company, the well known lager brewers, who were the main sponsors of the tour. Without their support it is doubtful if even the energetic Barry Edwards, executive director of the WPGA, would have been able to get the new tour off the ground.

Carlsberg opened the season with their European Women's Championship Series of 12 successive tournaments, and with the first three months of the tournament programme thus settled, Edwards gained much-needed breathing space to accommodate other prospective sponsors. And it seemed the critics could be proved right when Mollie Anderson, a blonde Californian who had been playing on the American mini-tour, finished three strokes ahead of Jane Chapman to win the opening Tyrrells Wood event.

Home prospects could have looked even more gloomy had Karstin Ehrnlund from Sweden, winner of five European amateur titles in 1978, gone one stage better than her second-place finishes in the following two tournaments. Cathy Panton, daughter of the former Ryder Cup golfer, won the first of these at Willingdon. The other was won by Christine Langford at Long Ashton.

Two weeks later Christine Langford came within a whisker of breaking 70 when she won her second Carlsberg tournament at Whitecraigs. She then had another round of 70 at St Annes Old Links, where she won the first hole of a sudden death play-off against Jenny Lee Smith. Winner of three tournaments in only seven outings, Christine Langford emerged as the player to beat. And how well she carried the responsibility. Playing in America for two years had taught her the importance of

Get a grasp of Danish.

Probably the best lager in the world.

good public relations, and this experience helped her project the WPGA's image in the best possible manner.

Breaking 70 had become something of a thing with her. 'It is a barrier I have always wanted to break', she said at the time. The competition hotted up with the return from America of Mickey Walker, Jenny Lee Smith, and the brave Lynne Harrold who in 1978 so tragically lost an eye in a road accident.

Christine Langford's ambition was realised when the Carlsberg series reached the York club's attractive course at Strensall. She led the first round with a 69, but her record stood for only 24 hours, nor did she win the tournament. On the next day Cathy Panton and Mickey Walker both had 68s with Mickey Walker's effort producing the first win of her six-year-old professional career.

Another round of 69 came from Jenny Lee Smith. Cheered home by a big Geordie gallery, the former Newcastle hairdresser won the last of the Carlsberg tournaments at Arcot Hall, only five miles from her home. But it was Christine Langford who captured the Carlsberg European title as the well-deserved leader of the Order of Merit. Next stop on the tour was Southport and Ainsdale for the Women's British Open Championship. This was 'the big one'. Although war had not been openly declared, it soon became noticeable that the professionals and the amateurs were flexing their muscles in preparation for the showdown!

The professionals turned out in strength, but so too did the amateurs, with Maureen Madill, the British champion, along with Julia Greenhalgh, Gillian Stewart, Vicki Rawlings, and Mary McKenna, the respective champions of England, Scotland, Wales and Ireland, in the strong field. Alison Sheard left her Durban home in South Africa when she learned of the new tour in May. She was no stranger to Britain, having been a losing finalist to Cathy Panton in the 1976 British Amateur Championship at Silloth.

At Sand Moor three weeks earlier Alison Sheard, winner of 10 national titles when an amateur, had had four birdies in the first six holes of her final round to win her first tournament as a professional. In the difficult conditions which continued on the first day, Alison Sheard opened with a round of 83. As the weather improved she followed this with 74, 72, 72, to win by three strokes from Mickey Walker. Once again she produced the birdies at the crucial moment. They came on the last two holes when the pressure was at its greatest.

Alison Sheard also came from behind to win the Welsh Classic at Dinas Powis. She edged in front of Christine Trew, the former British international swimmer who, undaunted, won the Hitachi tournament which followed.

Cathy Panton beat Amanda Middleton in a play-off to win the State Express Tournament over gale-lashed Royal Portrush. It was Cathy Panton's second win of the year, and she duly headed the Order of Merit, thus emulating her father John who won the Harry Vardon Trophy for leading the men's table in 1951.

The WPGA made a first visit to the Continent, and at Valbonne in the South of France Susan Moon from Santa Barbara, who travelled the circuit by caravan with her British parents, became the second American to win a tournament.

So to Moor Park for the final act. When Jane Panter clinched the Match-play title she was left with a putt to complete the West Course in 68 – three-under-par. Jane possessed a very modest record as an amateur. Prior to Moor Park she had won a Carlsberg tournament at Coventry – proof of how dedication, hard work, and the chance to compete regularly, can improve a golfer's game.

Maybe the tour is without a Nancy Lopez. Such golfers are not born overnight. But there are a few around like Jane Panter who between them impressed the sponsors sufficiently for prize money to be increased from £80,000 to around £150,000 in 1980.

Carlsberg may, unfairly, have been accused of depriving the amateur game of its up-and-coming young golfers. But their faith in supporting an unknown venture has kept the new professionals on the course at a time when they may have turned their backs on golf because of mounting expenses. This, in turn, ought to encourage youngsters of the future to reach for the top in golf which, in the long run, should help to raise the standards of both amateur and professional golf.

CARLSBERG EUROPEAN CHAMPIONSHIP

Date	Venue	Winner	Score	Prize money
26–27 April	Tyrrells Wood	M. Anderson (USA)	145	£200
3–4 May	Willingdon	C. Panton (Cambs Hotel)	151	£200
10–11 May	Long Ashton	C. Langford (British Car Auctions)	73	£200
17–18 May	Baberton	J. Smurthwaite (Southampton City)	147	£200
24–25 May	Whitecraigs	C. Langford (British Car Auctions)	142	£200
31 May–1 June	Coventry	J. Panter (Clitheroe)	146	£200
7–8 June	South Staffs	V. Marvin (Easingwold)	143	£200
14–15 June	Ballater	B. Huke (Unattached)	146	£200
21–22 June	St Annes Old Links	C. Langford (British Car Auctions) (*after a play-off with J. Lee Smith*)	148	£200
28–29 June	York	M. Walker (Faversham)	140	£200
5–6 July	Sand Moor	A. Sheard (SA)	147	£200
12–13 July	Arcot Hall	J. Lee Smith (Barnham Broom)	140	£200

* *C. Langford, leader of the Order of Merit after Arcot Hall, won the Carlsberg European Championship*

Women's British Open Championship (Sponsored by Pretty Polly)

25–28 July	Southport and Ainsdale	A. Sheard (SA)	301	£3,000

McEwans Welsh Classic

29–31 August	Dinas Powis	A. Sheard (SA)	144	£400

Hitachi Tournament

12–14 September	Downshire	C. Trew (Bristol & Clifton)	145	£400

State Express Tournament

21–22 September	Royal Portrush	C. Panton (Cambs Hotel) (*after a play-off with A. Middleton*)	166	£775

WPGA European Championship

26–29 September	Valbonne	S. Moon (USA)	292	£1577

Lambert and Butler Match Play Championship

25–27 October	Moor Park	J. Panter (Clitheroe)		£2,000

THE PRO-AMATEUR YEAR

Alan Booth

As the European tournament circuit has attracted increasing sponsorship support, so too has the 'mini' world of pro-am events. Professional-amateur tournaments are now an integral part of the European tour. They are planned and organised with the same attention to detail and promotion accorded a major event.

In 1979 almost every tournament was preceded by such an event, and in 1980 even more emphasis will be placed on the importance of the pro-am as a desirable, indeed essential, feature of the tournament year. Sponsors today place great value on a successful pro-am as a social curtain-raiser to their own tournament. And, just as in America, where pre-tournament pro-ams feature the US Tour's top players, so too in Britain and on the Continent the leading players on the European Tour at the time regularly join with amateur partners in the season's programme.

Equally important are the officially approved individual pro-am events away from the tournament scene, which offer lucrative rewards for the professionals. Most of these developed as Sunday attractions, with the players travelling on from tournaments which had ended the previous day. But with tournaments now switching to Sunday finishes, these events have fitted smoothly, and with no lessening of popularity, into midweek dates.

Indeed, attendances increased at many of the big pro-am events in 1979, reflecting the ever-growing interest in golf as a spectacle to be watched and enjoyed. The attraction is not only the opportunity to see the most accomplished professionals in action – and in 1979, apart from the top European players on view, many from overseas countries, including America, competed – but also the chance to mingle with the 'personalities' who have become household names through their popularity on radio, television, films, or stage, or through their success in other branches of sport.

Nowhere else but on a golf course, one imagines, is it possible to find so many famous, talented and varied individuals together at one time. In pro-ams in Britain in 1979 it was possible to watch players like Gary Player, Hale Irwin, David Graham, Fuzzy Zoeller, Graham Marsh, Seve Ballesteros, Hubert Green, Isao Aoki, Tony Jacklin, Ray Floyd, Bob Charles, and Jerry Pate, playing alongside Jimmy Tarbuck, Henry Cooper, Bruce Forsyth, Alec Bedser, Colin Cowdrey, Bobby Charlton and Jimmy Hill. The reaction of the sponsors can be summed up by Derek Peaker, managing director of Associated Tyre Specialists, who annually stage one of the country's most successful pro-am tournaments.

ASSOCIATED TYRE SPECIALISTS BRITAIN'S No.1 TYRE SERVICE.

Head Office: 160 Brompton Road, London, SW3 1JL.

OVER 400 BRANCHES THROUGHOUT THE U.K.

Walker Cup star Geoff Godwin, pictured with ATS managing director Derek Peaker, won the Scratch prize at Woburn.

At their fifth such event, held for the second year in the spectacular surroundings of the new Woburn Golf and Country Club, Peaker commented: 'Every year, I receive shoals of letters from the players, our guests, and the public, all praising a wonderful occasion, notable for fine displays of golf, and providing the opportunity for everyone who attends to mix and talk with so many popular personalities.'

In common with the other companies who sponsor golf, Associated Tyre Specialists are naturally concerned with 'customer involvement'. Inviting clients to their pro-am and offering hospitality is one way of showing the company's appreciation for the support they have been given. Also, through the pro-ams, many charities benefit from generous donations. In the case of Associated Tyres, a sum in the region of £4,000 has been donated each year to SPARKS (Sportsmen Pledged to Aid Research into Crippling Diseases).

The 1978 ATS pro-am was the first big professional event to be staged at Woburn, and with its great success the company had no hesitation in going back there in 1979.

In 1978 the reigning Amateur Champion Peter McEvoy returned a record 68 for the 6,839yd, par 72, Duke's course, and there was another outstanding achievement in 1979 by the diminutive Spaniard, Manuel Pinero, who holed his tee shot at the 121yd third hole to win a new Austin Allegro car.

Pinero's ace helped him return a 69 and tie for first place with Eamonn Darcy, each winning £875 in this £8,000 event. The pro-am event was won by Simon Owen's team of comedian Jerry Stevens and John Morris with a better-ball score of 62. It was the third year in a row that the professional event had ended in a tie. In 1977, at Calcot Park, Martin Foster and Brian Huggett each returned 69 for joint first place, and in 1978 Bob Charles and Guy Hunt tied with rounds of 69.

Other successful official pro-ams during 1979 included the Allbright and Wilson event at Walton Heath, won by Peter Townsend with a record round of 65, and those for the Jewish National Fund at Dyrham Park, the Christy O'Connor tournament at the Hermitage, the Brent Walker International, the Coral Leisure Classic at Rowlands Castle, and the NSCR at the Cambridgeshire Hotel. Among personalities to finish in winning teams was the chairman of the England cricket selectors Alec Bedser, while one tournament professional, who on occasion during the year earned admonition for his conduct during pro-ams, put in a responsible performance to win the Dunlop Masters 'pipe-opener' at Woburn with its £900 first prize – a happy end-of-season finale for Ken Brown!

ASSOCIATED TYRE SPECIALISTS PRO-AM

Woburn Golf and Country Club, Bucks   22 May 1979
Prize Money £8,000

Leading Individual Professional Scores

			£
1	Manuel Pinero (S)	69	875.00
	Eamonn Darcy (IRE)	69	875.00
3	Nick Job	70	475.00
	Martin Foster	70	475.00
5	Bob Charles (NZ)	71	325.00
	Hugh Baiocchi (SA)	71	325.00
7	John Bland (SA)	72	225.00
	Ken Brown	72	225.00
	Brian Waites	72	225.00
10	Tienie Britz (SA)	73	152.00
	Bobby Verwey (SA)	73	152.00
	Angel Gallardo (S)	73	152.00
	John O'Leary (IRE)	73	152.00
	Noel Ratcliffe (AUS)	73	152.00
	Peter Butler	73	152.00
	Mike King	73	152.00

Leading Better-ball Net Team Scores

1	Simon Owen (£250), Jerry Stevens, John Morris	62
2	Brian Waites (£64), Mike Tredgett, John Sorg	64
	John Morgan (£64), Bobby Campbell, Peter Fox	64
	Hugh Baiocchi (£64), Jimmy Hill, Paul Head	64
	Martin Foster (£64), Alec Bedser, Gordon Fox	64
	Nick Job (£64), John Spencer, Gil Jones	64
	Ken Brown (£64), Roger Cooke, Jeremy Hine	64
	Garry Cullen (£64), Roger De Courcey, Alan Baker	64

Individual Amateur Scratch Prize

1 Geoff Godwin   76

THE AMATEUR YEAR

REPORT AND RESULTS

Jay Sigel (USA), Amateur Champion 1979.

THE AMATEUR YEAR

Pat Ward-Thomas

BRADSHAW'S CHALLENGE TO McEVOY

Although Peter McEvoy did not retain the Amateur title he had held for the previous two years, and his showing in some championships was unremarkable, he remained the most accomplished amateur golfer in Britain. His performance in the Open at Lytham, where in the early summer he had won the Trophy of that name, was the finest by any amateur since Guy Wolstenholme finished sixth in 1960. In a field of formidable overseas strength McEvoy, the only amateur to qualify for the final round, tied for 17th place. Mark James alone of the British professionals was ahead of him.

This achievement apart, McEvoy's overall record was challenged by Ian Bradshaw, long a solid golfer for Cheshire, who commanded a place in the England team for the first time at the comparatively late age of 30. Of short sturdy build, his golf was impressive in the firmness and pace of a sound swing; and he revealed an ability for keeping going in round after round, the mark of a first-class medal player. His consistency in the Lytham Trophy, while Geoffrey Birtwell and Charles Green notably were fading in the last round, enabled him to finish second. McEvoy had to get down in two from through the last green to win by a stroke.

Two weeks later, at Little Aston, Bradshaw tied second with Brian Marchbank, who turned professional at the end of the season, one stroke behind David Long of Belfast, the first Irishman to win the English Stroke-play Championship. Long avoided the anxiety of a play-off by holing from 15 feet on the last green, Bradshaw having missed from 20 feet. Long was one of a group of Irish golfers under the tutelage of Joe Carr, who competed in several early events. Raymond Kane, another of their company, won the West of England title at Saunton.

McEvoy caused considerable comment by withdrawing, an unusual action for an amateur, from the Championship at Little Aston after a poor second round. Aside from playing in the Masters at Augusta he had competed in numerous other events, probably too many, and told the English Golf Union officials that he needed a rest before the Walker Cup match 10 days later.

By a strange coincidence Bradshaw, who had hunted McEvoy so close at Lytham, dismissed him from the Amateur Championship which was played for the first time at Hillside. Bradshaw's steadiness prevailed in the third round and he won twice more before falling to Scott Hoch in the quarter-finals. By this stage Marchbank, alone of the five

British Walker Cup players who had entered, still survived. The next morning he faced a series of ruthless strokes from Tony Gresham whose beautiful style and rhythm had kept him in the forefront of Australian golfers for many years.

Meanwhile the American challenge was looking the more menacing as Hoch and Jay Sigel approached their meeting in the final. At the same time an Indian golfer, Lakshman Singh, had progressed much further in the Championship than any of his countrymen had ever done, and Douglas Roxburgh from Canada needed 19 holes to deny him a semi-final place. Never before in the 90-odd years of the Championship had there not been at least one British golfer in the last four.

The climax, involving the two best players, was entirely fitting with Sigel, an amateur of lasting status, beating the college golfer. His effortless swing, a model of unhurried patience, was a rare pleasure to watch, and his manner was always serene and impassive.

The European Team Championship at Esbjerg in Denmark was a triumph for the English. On a demanding course in continuous wind their qualifying score was 24 strokes lower than that of Sweden and Wales who, together with Ireland and Scotland were in the first flight.

For once Scotland failed, however. In the three matches England won all their foursomes and only two singles were lost. Bradshaw won all his five matches, as did Paul Downes. England were sorely pressed by Ireland. McEvoy and Downes won at the 21st against Long and Pat Mulcare; three other matches were won on the last green and two were halved.

Irish golf may be on the threshold of a revival and one not confined to the men. Inspired by having Maureen Madill, the British champion in their team, the Irish women gained their first victory in the European Championship. They crushed Germany in the final. France were third and England fourth.

Miss Madill, an unusually strong striker, won a notable victory in the British Championship at Nairn beating Jane Lock, one of the finest Australian golfers, in the final. She was the first Ulster woman to win since May Hezlet in 1907, and gained her place in the British team for the Vagliano Trophy match against the Continent of Europe, and for the Commonwealth tournament in Australia.

Two Welsh golfers in Tegwen Perkins and Vicki Rawlings also were chosen in the team of six for Australia, a singular distinction for Wales. Susan Hedges, runner-up in the English Championship, and third in the British Open at Southport, was the only English member of the side, an indication of the extent to which England have suffered from the formation of the professional circuit. After dominating the Home Internationals for some 20 years a largely inexperienced team finished last.

The Commonwealth team fared little better. Susan Hedges alone won a match against Canada, the eventual winners of the event, and Vicki Rawlings' halved single saved her side from complete rout by Australia. A narrow victory over New Zealand, in which Miss Madill and Miss Rawlings played a major part gave Britain place.

The ever-changing pattern at the head of amateur golf was reflected in the English Men's Championship at St George's, Sandwich. None of the seeded players reached the last eight, McEvoy having to withdraw because of stomach trouble on the third day. The continuing cause of youth was splendidly upheld by Roger Chapman, aged 20, from Kent who beat Andrew Carman, a Warwickshire county player, six and five in the final. The previous afternoon he disposed of David Williams, a spirited young golfer, who had won the Berkshire Trophy in impressive fashion.

The sad events in Northern Ireland led to the cancellation of the Home Internationals which were due to be played at Newcastle, Co. Down. This was particularly unfortunate for those who had been chosen to play for their countries for the first time. Happily there was consolation for all with the arrangement of friendly matches between Scotland and England at Royal Troon and Wales and Ireland at Royal Porthcawl.

Roger Chapman 'splendidly upheld the continuing cause of youth' in winning the English Amateur title at the age of 20.

THE PRESIDENT'S PUTTER
Rye Golf Club, Sussex   4–7 January 1979

(Event cancelled for the first time in its 59 years' history owing to inclement weather.)

AVIA INTERNATIONAL WOMEN'S FOURSOMES
The Berkshire Golf Club, Ascot   13–15 March 1979

1	Mrs A. Sander (Sunningdale) and Mrs L. Byman (Berkshire)	80	72	71	79	302
2	Mrs A. Uzielli (Berkshire) and Mrs S. Barber (Thorpe Hall)	71	78	79	80	308
3	Mrs J. Chapman (Breadsall Priory) and Miss C. Mackintosh (Royal Winchester)	76	81	80	79	316
4	Miss V. Marvin (Easingwold) and Miss C. Barker (Hartlepool)	78	78	85	78	319
5	Miss T. Perkins (Wenvoe Castle) and Miss M. McKenna (Donabate)	76	80	84	80	320
	Mrs S. Hedges (Wrotham Heath) and Mrs E. Boatman (Colchester)	77	77	80	86	320
	Miss V. Saunders (Tyrrells Wood) and Miss M. Everard (Hallamshire)	80	77	83	80	320

OXFORD UNIVERSITY v CAMBRIDGE UNIVERSITY
Royal St David's Golf Club, Harlech   23–24 March 1979

Result	Oxford U. 8½	Cambridge U. 6½
Foursomes	Oxford U. 4	Cambridge U. 1
Singles	Oxford U. 4½	Cambridge U. 5½

THE SUNNINGDALE FOURSOMES
Sunningdale Golf Club, Berkshire   21–24 March 1979

Final

G. Will (Sundridge Park) and R. Chapman (Langley Park) beat N.C. Coles (Dunlop Sports) and D. McClelland (Laleham)   3 and 2

Semi-finals

Will and Chapman beat M.S. Bavin (Downshire) and R.W. Seamer (West Kent)   3 and 2

Coles and McClelland beat I. Caldwell and Mrs C. Caldwell (Sunningdale)   3 and 2

Quarter-finals

Will and Chapman beat G.A. Caygill (Crimple Valley) and Miss J. Greenhalgh (Pleasington)   1 hole

Coles and McClelland beat J.C. Davies (Sunningdale) and G. Brand (Knowle)   4 and 2

Bavin and Seamer beat T. Healy (Rowlands Castle) and D. Hope (Bramshott Hill)   3 and 2

Caldwell and Mrs Caldwell beat N.R. Davies and G. Davies (Pontypool)   19th hole

THE HALFORD HEWITT CUP
Royal Cinque Ports Golf Club, Deal, Kent 5–8 April 1979

Final
Stowe beat Marlborough   3½–1½

Semi-finals
Stowe beat Rossall   3½–1½
Marlborough beat Loretto   5–0

Quarter-finals
Stowe beat Repton
Marlborough beat Whitgift   4–1
Rossall beat Eton   4–1
Loretto beat Rugby   3½–1½

THE LYTHAM TROPHY
Royal Lytham and St Annes Golf Club, Lancashire 5–6 May 1979

1	P. McEvoy (Copt Heath)	64	68	74	73	279
2	I. Bradshaw (Eastham Lodge)	66	67	75	72	280
3	C.W. Green (Dumbarton)	64	67	77	73	281
4	P.R. Thomas (Sudbury)	64	73	73	72	282
5	I.C. Hutcheon (Monifieth)	67	70	72	74	283
6	S.G. Birtwell (St Annes Old)	66	63	71	84	284
	I.A. Carslaw (Williamswood)	67	67	77	73	284
	J.R. Dickson (Royal Portrush)	65	66	76	77	284
9	D. McLean (Holyhead)	67	70	72	76	285
	G.F. Godwin (Thorndon Park)	67	69	73	76	285
11	J.C. Davies (Royal Mid-Surrey)	71	67	75	73	286
12	P. Carrigill (Moortown)	69	68	74	76	287
	G. MacGregor (Glencorse)	63	70	77	77	287

Tournament reduced to 68 holes because of inclement weather

GOLF ILLUSTRATED GOLD VASE
Walton Heath Golf Club, Surrey 12 May 1979

1	K.J. Miller (Fulford)	71	69	140
2	P.R. Thomas (Sudbury)	71	71	142
3	R. Chapman (Langley Park)	71	74	145
4	S.D. Keppler (Walton Heath)	72	74	146
5	J.G. Bennett (Croham Hurst)	76	71	147
	M.F. Bonallack (Thorpe Hall)	72	75	147
7	G.F. Godwin (Thorndon Park)	76	72	148
	M.L. Weir (Sudbury)	73	75	148
	J.E. Ambridge (West Herts)	79	69	148
	N. Mitchell (Ifield)	73	75	148

WELSH WOMEN'S AMATEUR CHAMPIONSHIP
Caernarvonshire Golf Club, Conwy 16–18 May 1979

Final
Miss V. Rawlings (Bargoed) beat Mrs A. Briggs (Royal   2 holes

Semi-Final
Miss Rawlings beat Miss J. Rhys (Glamorgan)   2 and 1
Mrs Briggs beat Mrs C.E. Thomas (Holyhead)   2 and 1

Quarter-finals
Miss Rawlings beat Mrs B. Chambers (Monmouthshire)   6 and 4
Mrs Briggs beat Miss S. Rowlands (Prestatyn)   4 and 3
Miss Rhys beat Mrs A. Johnson (Ludlow)   3 and 1
Mrs Thomas beat Mrs K. Bradley (Bargoed)   1 hole

IRISH WOMEN'S AMATEUR CHAMPIONSHIP

Donegal Golf Club 17–19 May 1979

Final

Miss M. McKenna (Donabate) beat Miss C. Nesbitt 5 and 4

Semi-finals

Miss McKenna beat Miss M. Madill (Portstewart) 6 and 5
Miss Nesbitt beat Miss M. Gorry (Baltinglass) 5 and 4

Quarter-finals

Miss McKenna beat Miss P. Moran (Donabate) 5 and 4
Miss Nesbitt beat Miss S. O'Brien-Kenney (Grange) 4 and 3
Miss Madill beat Miss C. Hourihane (Woodbrook) 5 and 4
Miss Gorry beat Miss P. Wickham (Laytown & Bettystown) 3 and 2

SCOTTISH WOMEN'S AMATEUR CHAMPIONSHIP

Gullane Golf Club, East Lothian 22–26 May 1979

Final

Miss G. Stewart (Inverness) beat Miss L. Hope (Gullane) 2 and 1

Semi-finals

Miss Stewart beat Miss F.C. Anderson (Craigie Hill) 4 and 3
Miss Hope beat Mrs J. Marshall (Baberton) 3 and 2

Quarter-finals

Miss Stewart beat Miss M. Stavert (Craigmillar Park) 2 and 1
Miss Hope beat Miss D. Reid (Ladybank) 6 and 5
Miss Anderson beat Miss J. Connachan (Royal Musselburgh) 3 and 2
Mrs Marshall beat Miss C.J. Lugton (Gullane) 1 hole

AER LINGUS SCHOOLS' CHAMPIONSHIP
(in association with The Golf Foundation)

Co. Louth Golf Club, Baltray 20 May 1979

Boys

1	St Fachtna's High School, Skibbereen (Ireland)	484
2	Buckie High School, Banff (Scotland)	494
3	Bishop Gore School, Swansea (Wales)	494
4	Birkenhead School (England)	495
5	Per Brahe Skolan, Jonkoping (Sweden)	497

Individual title:
Brendan McDaid (St Fachtna's) 152

Girls

1	Prudhoe High School, Northumberland (England)	173
2	St Larsskolan, Linkoping (Sweden)	184
3	Aboyne Academy, Aberdeenshire (Scotland)	185
4	Syr Thomas Jones School, Amlwch (Wales)	191
	Vocational School, Tipperary (Ireland)	191

Individual title:
Janet Soulsby (Prudhoe) 82

ENGLISH WOMEN'S AMATEUR CHAMPIONSHIP

Royal Liverpool Golf Club, Hoylake 22–25 May 1979

Final
Miss J. Greenhalgh (Pleasington) beat Mrs S. Hedges (Wrotham Heath) 2 and 1

Semi-Final
Miss Greenhalgh beat Miss C. Barker (Hartlepool) 1 hole
Mrs Hedges beat Mrs P. Deman (Colchester) 7 and 6

Quarter-finals
Miss Greenhalgh beat Miss B. New (Lansdown) 4 and 3
Mrs Hedges beat Mrs R. Slark (Long Ashton) 2 and 1
Miss Barker beat Miss J. Walter (St Ives) 3 and 2
Mrs Deman beat Mrs A. Howard (Whitefield) 4 and 3

ENGLISH OPEN AMATEUR STROKE-PLAY CHAMPIONSHIP (Brabazon Trophy)

Little Aston Golf Club, West Midlands 18–20 May 1979

1	D. Long (Shandon Park)	71	70	78	72	291
2	B. Marchbank (Auchterarder)	72	72	74	74	292
	I. Bradshaw (Eastham Lodge)	74	69	74	75	292
4	C.R. Smethurst (Crewe)	69	71	73	73	294
5	H.B. Green (Doncaster)	77	71	74	73	295
6	P. Curry (Braintree)	75	73	76	72	296
	P.F. Garner (Wentworth)	74	73	73	76	296
8	S. Bennett (Grimsby)	76	77	73	72	298
9	T.R. Shingler (Blackwell)	69	76	79	75	299
	J.L. Plaxton (Scarborough South Cliff)	72	74	77	76	299
11	G. Godwin (Thorndon Park)	77	76	74	73	300
	R. Chapman (Langley Park)	81	72	72	75	300
	T. Allen (Maxstoke Park)	71	73	80	76	300
14	R. Kane (Island)	78	75	73	75	301
15	S. East (York)	74	76	79	73	302
	S. Fernyhough (Whittington Barracks)	71	74	79	78	302

THE AMATEUR CHAMPIONSHIP

Hillside Golf Club, Southport, Merseyside 4–9 June 1979

Final
J. Sigel (USA) beat S. Hoch (USA) 3 and 2

Semi-finals
Sigel beat D. Roxburgh (C) 6 and 5
Hoch beat A. Gresham (AUS) 3 and 2

Quarter-finals
Sigel beat S.F. Robson (Walton Heath) 5 and 3
Hoch beat I. Bradshaw (Eastham Lodge) 2 and 1
Roxburgh beat L. Singh (IN) 19th hole
Gresham beat B. Marchbank (Auchterarder) 3 and 2

Fifth round

Sigel beat G. Moody (USA)	3 and 2
Hoch beat A.D. Ferguson (Drumpellier)	4 and 3
Roxburgh beat D. Whelan (Seaton Carew)	20th hole
Gresham beat M.P.D. Walls (Hillside)	5 and 4
Robson beat D.H. Fischesser (USA)	1 hole
Bradshaw beat K.W. Macintosh (Cardross)	5 and 3
Singh beat S. Cipa (Upminster)	6 and 5
Marchbank beat S. Andrews (Effingham)	1 hole

Fourth round

Sigel beat M.F. Bonallack (Thorpe Hall)	2 holes
Hoch beat R. Van Nieker (SA)	20th hole
Roxburgh beat T.W. Williams (Maesdu)	5 and 3
Gresham beat J. Holtgrieve (USA)	7 and 5
Robson beat F.J. Speight (Northwood)	2 and 1
Bradshaw beat J.B. Dickinson (Hindley Hall)	2 and 1
Singh beat D. Blakeman (Trentham)	2 holes
Marchbank beat P. Buckles (Hillside)	4 and 3
Moody beat W. Player (SA)	20th hole
Ferguson beat T.P. Gifford (Middlesbrough)	3 and 1
Whelan beat M. Peck (USA)	3 and 1
Walls beat N.R.W. Lucas (Southport & Ainsdale)	4 and 3
Fischesser beat P.G.J. Hoad (Prince's)	1 hole
Macintosh beat A.J. Dobson (Royal Mid-Surrey)	2 and 1
Cipa beat C.R. Dalgleish (Helensburgh)	4 and 2
Andrews beat P. Curry (Braintree)	1 hole

BRITISH WOMEN'S OPEN AMATEUR CHAMPIONSHIP

Nairn Golf Club, Scotland 5–9 June 1979

Final

Miss M. Madill (Portstewart) beat Miss J. Lock (AUS)	2 and 1

Semi-finals

Miss Madill beat Miss M. McKenna (Donabate)	1 hole
Miss Lock beat Miss E. Kennedy (AUS)	20th hole

Quarter-finals

Miss Madill beat Mrs S. Hedges (Wrotham Heath)	3 and 2
Miss Lock beat Miss M. de Lorenzi (F)	4 and 3
Miss McKenna beat Mrs C. Mourgue d'Algue (F)	3 and 2
Miss Kennedy beat Mrs C. Artasona (S)	2 and 1

Second round

Miss Madill beat Miss J. Greenhalgh (Pleasington)	3 and 2
Miss Lock beat Miss D. Dowling (Royal Mid-Surrey)	5 and 4
Miss McKenna beat Miss D. Reid (Ladybank)	5 and 4
Miss Kennedy beat Miss T. Perkins (Wenvoe Castle)	3 and 2
Mrs Hedges beat Mrs C. Bailey (Tandridge)	4 and 3
Miss de Lorenzi beat Mrs A. Sander (Sunningdale)	5 and 4
Mrs Mourgue d'Algue beat Miss G. Stewart (Inverness)	1 hole
Mrs Artasona beat Miss J. Smith (Carnoustie)	1 hole

THE BERKSHIRE TROPHY

The Berkshire Golf Club, Ascot 16–17 June 1979

1	D. Williams (Ashridge)	68 68	68 70		274
2	P. Curry (Braintree)	72 68	67 69		276
3	H.B. Green (Doncaster)	72 68	68 72		280
4	S.D. Keppler (Walton Heath)	70 70	71 70		281
	P.F. Garner (Wentworth)	65 72	74 70		281
6	J.C. Davies (Royal Mid-Surrey)	68 71	69 75		283
7	P. Downes (Coventry)	69 76	70 69		284
	M.P.D. Walls (Hillside)	71 75	67 71		284
9	P.G.J. Hoad (Prince's)	75 69	71 70		285
10	R. Mugglestone (Worksop)	73 70	73 70		286
	R.W. Guy (Gog Magog)	72 71	69 74		286

SCOTTISH OPEN AMATEUR STROKE-PLAY CHAMPIONSHIP

Blairgowrie Golf Club, Perthshire   16–17 June 1979

1	I.C. Hutcheon (Monifieth)	75	70	73	78	296
2	G.C. MacGregor (Glencorse)	73	77	76	71	297
	D.B. Howard (Cochrane Castle)	74	76	76	71	297
4	A. Brodie (Balmore)	78	74	73	75	300
5	P. Smith (Pumpherston)	73	80	75	75	303
	C. Christy (Pitlochry)	72	78	79	74	303
7	C.W. Green (Dumbarton)	74	76	80	77	307
	E.R. Lindsay (Blairgowrie)	76	76	73	82	307
	J. Cuddihy (West Lothian)	76	79	75	77	307
10	J. Huggan (Winterfield)	75	76	82	75	308
	J.A. McIntyre (Dunnikier Park)	77	76	78	77	308
	J.H. Anderson (East Renfrewshire)	75	78	79	76	308
	W.L. Gray (Dunbar)	77	77	75	79	308
	R. Blackwood (Cochrane Castle)	78	77	77	76	308
	C.R. Dalgliesh (Helensburgh)	73	82	78	75	308

THE EUROPEAN MEN'S AMATEUR TEAM CHAMPIONSHIP

Esbjerg Golf Club, Denmark   27 June–1 July 1979

Stroke-play Qualifying
England 755; Sweden 779; Wales 779; Ireland 783;
Scotland 787; France 788; Denmark 802; Germany 804;
Switzerland 817; Netherlands 822; Italy 823; Norway 823;
Austria 827; Belgium 828; Spain 834; Iceland 839;
Finland 850; Luxemburg 860; Czechoslovakia 868

Match-Play – First Flight
England 5½ Germany 1½; Denmark 4 Sweden 3; Wales 4½
France 2½; Ireland 4 Scotland 3; England 5 Ireland 2;
Wales 5½ Denmark 1½; Scotland 5 France 2;
Ireland 5½ Denmark 1½.

Final
England 6 Wales 1

Foursomes

| P. Downes and P. McEvoy beat D. McLean and H.J. Evans | 5 and 4 |
| P. Deeble and I. Bradshaw beat J.R. Jones and T. Melia | 5 and 4 |

Singles

Downes beat Jones	1 hole
McEvoy beat McLean	5 and 4
M.J. Kelley halved with Evans	
Bradshaw beat M. Mouland	7 and 6
G. Godwin halved with Melia	

Final Classification
1 England; 2 Wales; 3 Ireland; 4 Denmark; 5 Scotland; 6 France; 7 Sweden; 8 Germany.
(Italy headed the Second Flight.)

THE EUROPEAN WOMEN'S AMATEUR TEAM CHAMPIONSHIP
Hermitage Golf Club, Lucan, Dublin   4–8 July 1979

Stroke-play Qualifying
France 756; Spain 759; Germany 764; Ireland 769;
Sweden 771; Switzerland 774; England 781;
Scotland 782; Netherlands 785; Wales 789; Italy 792;
Belgium 801; Norway 848; Austria 849.

Match-Play – First Flight
England 5 Spain 2; France 5 Scotland 2; Ireland 4½
Sweden 2½; Germany 4 England 3; Ireland 5½
France 1½; Scotland 4 Sweden 3; France 5½ England 1½;
Spain 5½ Scotland 1½

Final
Ireland 6 Germany 1

Foursomes
M. McKenna and C. Nesbit beat N. Thannhaeuser and
S. Blecher   3 and 2
M. Madill and M. Gorry lost to N. Eicke and I. Umsen   22nd hole

Singles
McKenna beat Thannhaeuser   6 and 5
Madill beat B. Boehn   3 and 2
S. Gorman beat Blecher   3 and 1
Nesbit beat Umsen   1 hole
Gorry beat C. Felixmueller   4 and 3

Final Classification
1 Ireland; **2** Germany; **3** France; **4** England; **5**
Spain; **6** Scotland; **7** Sweden; **8** Switzerland.
(Wales, in the Second Flight, finished 10th.)

ENGLISH WOMEN'S COUNTY CHAMPIONSHIP
Gog Magog Golf Club, Cambridgeshire   17–19 July 1979

Finals
Essex 4 Lancashire 5
Essex 6 Staffordshire 3
Essex 5 Glamorgan 4
Staffordshire 5 Glamorgan 4
Glamorgan 5 Lancashire 4

Lancashire 5 Staffordshire 4

Final classification
1 Essex 15pts; **2** Lancashire 14 pts; **3** Glamorgan 13pts;
4 Staffordshire 12 pts.

WELSH AMATEUR CHAMPIONSHIP
Ashburnham Golf Club, Dyfed   23–28 July 1979

Final
T.J. Melia (Cardiff) beat M. Roper (Llanwern)   5 and 4

Semi-finals
Melia beat M.W. Calvert (Royal St David's)   19th hole
Roper beat D. McLean (Holyhead)   4 and 2

Quarter-finals
Melia beat A.L. Strange (Oswestry)   19th hole
Roper beat C. Stedman (Pontypool)   1 hole
Calvert beat M. Skinner (Pontypool)   2 and 1

McLean beat N.R. Davies (Pontypool)   2 and 1

Fourth round
Melia beat E.N. Davis (Prestatyn)   3 and 2
Roper beat J.A. Evans (Frilford Heath)   21st hole
Calvert beat D.L. Stevens (Llantrisant and Pontyclun)   1 hole
McLean beat I. Duffy (Tenby)   5 and 4
Stedman beat J.R. Jones (Langland Bay)   2 and 1
Skinner beat N.B. Morgan (Holyhead)   8 and 6
Strange beat B. Rolfe (Ashburnham)   20th hole
Davis beat J.K.D. Povall (Whitchurch)   4 and 2

SCOTTISH AMATEUR CHAMPIONSHIP

Prestwick Golf Club, Ayrshire 23–28 July 1979

Final
K. Macintosh (Cardross) beat P.J. McKellar (East Renfrewshire) 5 and 4

Semi-finals
Macintosh beat G. Hay (Hilton Park) 2 and 1
McKellar beat G. MacGregor (Glencorse) 6 and 5

Quarter-finals
Macintosh beat G. Brand (Knowle) 5 and 4
McKellar beat S. Taylor (East Kilbride) 21st hole
MacGregor beat A. Coles (King James VI) 5 and 4

	19th hole
Hay beat F. Coutts (Deeside)	5 and 4

Fifth round
Macintosh beat I. Doig (Monifieth) 1 hole
McKellar beat I. Gillan (Bishopbriggs) 5 and 4
MacGregor beat I. Brotherston (Dumfries and County) 2 and 1
Hay beat A. Brodie (Balmore) 3 and 2
Brand beat I. Ford (Kelso) 4 and 3
Taylor beat I. Harris (Royal Troon) 2 and 1
Coles beat D.B. Howard (Cochrane Castle) 1 hole
Coutts beat B. Aitken (West Kilbride) 1 hole

BRITISH WOMEN'S OPEN STROKE-PLAY CHAMPIONSHIP

Southport and Ainsdale Golf Club, Merseyside 25–28 July 1979

1	Miss A. Sheard (SA)*	83	74	72	72	301
2	Miss M. Walker (Faversham)*	83	72	75	74	304
3	Mrs. S. Hedges (Wrotham Heath)	82	80	78	69	309
4	Miss Beverley Huke (Unattached)*	79	76	75	81	311
5	Miss J. Lee-Smith (Barnham Broom)*	76	88	77	71	312
	Miss M. McKenna (Donabate)	78	79	77	78	312
7	Miss J. Panter (Clitheroe)*	83	80	75	75	313
	Miss C. Chamberlain (USA)*	79	80	77	77	313
	Miss M. Mills (USA)*	83	76	77	77	313
10	Miss M. Thomson (GB)*	75	78	82	79	314
	Miss M. Madill (Portstewart)	81	79	75	79	314
	Miss J. Greenhalgh (Pleasington)	82	75	77	80	314
13	Miss V. Saunders (Tyrells Wood)*	81	84	74	76	315
	Miss D. Dowling (Royal Mid-Surrey)	82	78	78	77	315
	Miss V. Rawlings (Bargoed)	78	82	76	79	315
16	Miss C. Nesbitt (Knock)	80	78	77	82	317
17	Miss A. Gemmill (Kilmarnock)	80	83	78	77	318
	Miss T. Fernando (USA)	78	84	77	79	318
	Miss C. Hourihane (Woodbrook)	78	82	77	81	318

(Pretty Polly provided £10,000 in prize money – Miss Sheard winning £3,000 and Miss Walker £1,500.)
* *Professional*

THE CARRIS BOYS' TROPHY

Moor Park Golf Club, Rickmansworth, Herts 25–26 July 1979

1	P. Hammond (Bognor Regis)	72	69	73	74	288
2	C.W. Gray (Chilwell Manor)	74	68	74	76	292
	R. Roper (Catterick)	73	67	76	76	292
	D. Rosier (Newbury)	73	75	69	75	292
5	M.P. McLean (Knole Park)	74	69	74	76	293
6	P.G. Way (Nevill)	73	70	78	73	294
7	S.A. Scott (Calcot Park)	77	71	76	71	295
8	M. Reynard (Moseley)	74	73	72	78	297

ENGLISH AMATEUR CHAMPIONSHIP
Royal St George's Golf Club, Sandwich, Kent   30 July–4 August 1979

Final

R. Chapman (Langley Park) beat A. Carman (Coventry)   6 and 5

Semi-finals

Chapman beat D. Williams (Ashridge)   6 and 4
Carman beat A.J. Wells (Hayling)   4 and 3

Quarter-finals

Chapman beat I.T. Simpson (Notts)   19th hole
Carman beat C.W. Gray (Chilwell Manor)   3 and 1
Williams beat R.L. Glading (Addington Palace)   22nd hole

Wells beat C. Catford (Canterbury)   2 and 1

Fifth round

Chapman beat P. Deeble (Alnmouth)   3 and 2
Carman beat S. Smith (Newbiggin-by-sea)   19th hole
Williams beat P. Hammond (Bognor Regis)   4 and 3
Wells beat E.I. Bradshaw (Eastham Lodge)   20th hole
Simpson beat I.W. Boyd (Berkshire)   6 and 5
Gray beat H.B. Green (Doncaster)   22nd hole
Glading beat S.R. Leake (Middlesbrough)   2 and 1
Catford beat A.R. Kerr (Worplesdon)   3 and 2

BRITISH SENIORS AMATEUR CHAMPIONSHIP
Royal St David's Golf Club, Harlech   8–10 August 1979

1	R.J. White (Royal Birkdale)	76	74	76	226
2	H.D. Moseley (Robin Hood)	72	78	76	226
3	L.L. Shelley (Tamworth)	77	74	75	226

White won play-off for first three places at first extra hole

4	J.L. Whitworth (Handsworth)	77	79	73	229
5	L. Lippitt (Handsworth)	70	81	79	230
6	J.W. Munro (Cathkin Braes)	75	81	75	231

	R.C. Oliver (Hull)	78	77	76	231
	T.A. Spooner (Leamington & County)	77	76	78	231
	J.N. Wardle (Wheatley)	75	80	76	231
	J.R. Wroe (Southport & Ainsdale)	75	77	79	231
11	T.E.D. Harker (Sunningdale)	84	75	74	233
	J. Lawrence (Stoke Pogs)	77	79	77	233

IRISH AMATEUR CHAMPIONSHIP
Ballybunion Golf Club, Co Kerry   11–15 August 1979

Final

J. Harrington (Adare Manor) beat M. Gannon (Co Louth)   2 and 1

Semi-finals

Harrington beat V. Nevin (Limerick)   3 and 2
Gannon beat B. McDaid (Skibbereen)   6 and 5

Quarter-finals

Harrington beat T. Cleary (Fermoy)   2 and 1
Gannon beat T. Corridan (Ballybunion)   19th hole
Nevin beat E. Dunne (Athlone)   3 and 2
McDaid beat R. Moran (Woodenbridge)   1 hole

Third Round

Harrington beat B.P. Malone (Elm Park)   conceded
Gannon beat G. Carr (Sutton)   2 and 1
Nevin beat M. Wolseley (Belvoir Park)   6 and 5
McDaid beat G. McGimpsey (Bangor)   2 and 1
Cleary beat B.A. McBride (Narin and Portnoo)   21st hole
Corridan beat M.F. Morris (Portmarnock)   1 hole
Dunne beat H.B. Smyth (Royal Co Down)   2 and 1
Moran beat M. McGinley (Naas)   4 and 3

BRITISH BOYS' CHAMPIONSHIP
Kilmarnock (Barassie) Golf Club, Ayrshire 13–17 August 1979

Final
R. Rafferty (Warrenpoint) beat D. Ray (Long Ashton)   6 and 5

Semi-finals
Rafferty beat P. Walton (Malahide)   2 and 1
Ray beat A. Canessa (Italy)   1 hole

Quarter-finals
Rafferty beat D. Boughey (Trentham Park)   3 and 1

Ray beat M. Russell (Manchester)   2 holes
Walton beat B. Hobson (Malone)   4 and 2
Canessa beat G.D. Dalgleish (Helensburgh)   1 hole

International Matches
Great Britain and Ireland 9½ Europe 2½
England 11 Scotland 4
Ireland 9½ Wales 2½

BRITISH GIRLS' CHAMPIONSHIP
Edgbaston Golf Club, West Midlands 15–18 August 1979

Final
Miss S. Lapaire (F) beat Miss P. Smillie (Pannal)   19th hole

Semi-finals
Miss Lapaire beat Miss B. Gleeson (Killarney)   3 and 2
Miss Smillie beat Miss J. Rhodes (West Bowling)   1 hole

Quarter-finals
Miss Lapaire beat Miss D. Christison (Whittington Barracks)   1 hole
Miss Smillie beat Miss M. Rawlings (Bargoed)   1 hole

Miss Gleeson beat Miss S. Binks (Ponteland)   5 and 4
Miss Rhodes beat Miss M. Gallagher (Cowdray Park)   6 and 5

International Matches
England 7 Ireland 0; England 5½ Scotland 1½;
England 3½ Wales 3½; Wales 4½ Ireland 2½;
Wales 4½ Scotland 2½; Ireland 4 Scotland 3.

Final placings
1 England and Wales; 3 Ireland; 4 Scotland. (England retained the title.)

The Championship and International Matches were sponsored by Gor-Ray

BRITISH WOMEN'S OPEN AMATEUR STROKE-PLAY CHAMPIONSHIP
Moseley Golf Club, West Midlands 22–24 August 1979

1	Miss M. McKenna (Donabate)	83	73	75	74	305
2	Miss V. Rawlings (Bargoed)	74	83	78	72	307
3	Miss T. Fernando (USA)	77	78	81	75	311
	Miss S. Cohen (Roehampton)	76	79	75	81	311
5	Miss T. Perkins (Wenvoe Castle)	77	78	80	77	312
6	Miss W. Aitken (Old Ranfurly)	77	77	82	77	313
7	Mrs C. Caldwell (Canterbury)	78	76	79	81	314
8	Miss L. Moore (Truro)	81	74	80	82	317
	Miss J. Connachan (Royal					
	Mrs A. Booth (Little Aston)	77	76	84	80	317
11	Miss L. Isherwood (Swansea Bay)	75	77	83	83	318
	Mrs A. Sheldon (Copt Heath)	79	88	73	78	318
	Miss C. Barker (Hartlepool)	80	79	79	80	318
14	Miss P. Smillie (Pannal)	78	84	76	81	319
15	Miss G. Stewart (Inverness)	78	81	79	83	321
	Miss S. Hedges (Wrotham Heath)	80	79	79	83	321
	Mrs A. Johnson (Ludlow)	79	79	82	81	321

BRITISH YOUTHS CHAMPIONSHIP

Woodhall Spa Golf Club, Lincolnshire   23–25 August 1979

1	G. Brand (Knowle)	70	75	74	72	291
2	P.W. Gallagher (Peebles)	76	69	74	73	292
	C. Dalgleish (Helensburgh)	77	72	73	70	292
4	D. Evans (Leek)	77	70	73	73	293
5	B. Marchbank (Auchterarder)	74	68	78	75	295
6	A.R. Gelsthorpe (Renishaw Park)	74	75	76	72	297
	J.S. Taylor (East Kilbride)	74	75	74	74	297
	J.G. Bennett (Croham Hurst)	76	72	77	72	297
9	R. Chapman (Langley Park)	76	74	74	74	298
	R.J. Mugglestone (Worksop)	72	71	78	77	298
11	N. Lucas (Ellesborough)	72	72	76	79	299
12	C. Cox (Royal Epping Forest)	76	73	74	77	300
	M.E. Lewis (Henbury)	76	76	76	72	300
14	S.D. Keppler (Woodcote Park)	71	75	78	77	301
	P. Curry (Braintree)	77	77	76	71	301
16	A.G. Dobson (Royal Mid-Surrey)	76	72	80	74	302
	M. Johnson (Wentworth)	75	77	77	73	302

International Matches

England 7½ Scotland 7½

Great Britain and Ireland 12 Continent of Europe 3

THE VAGLIANO TROPHY

Great Britain and Ireland v Continent of Europe

Royal Porthcawl Golf Club, Mid Glamorgan   7–8 September 1979

FIRST SERIES

Foursomes (*GB & I names first*)

Miss M. Madill and Miss V.R. Rawlings beat Mrs C. Morgue d'Algue and Miss D.M. de Lorenzi (F) — 1 hole

Miss M. McKenna and Miss C. Nesbitt beat Mrs M. Thannhauser and Miss B. Bohm (G) — 5 and 4

Mrs S. Hedges and Miss C. Cohen lost to Mrs M. Ragher (I) and Miss M. Figueras-Dotti (S) — 2 holes

Miss T. Perkins and Miss G. Stewart lost to Miss A. Janmaat (Nld) and Miss E. Berthet (F) — 5 and 3

Great Britain and Ireland 2 Continent of Europe 2

Singles

Perkins beat Ragher — 4 and 3

Cohen lost to Morgue d'Algue — 4 and 2

Stewart beat Janmaat — 5 and 4

Miss J. Melville beat Berthet — 6 and 4

Madill beat Figueras-Dotti — 3 and 2

McKenna beat Thannhauser — 2 and 1

Rawlings lost to de Lorenzi — 4 and 3

Nesbitt lost to Miss H. Hagstrom (SW) — 2 and 1

Great Britain and Ireland 5 Continent of Europe 3

SECOND SERIES

Foursomes

McKenna and Nesbitt halved with Morgue d'Algue and de Lorenzi

Madill and Rawlings lost to Ragher and Figueras-Dotti — 4 and 3

Perkins and Stewart beat Thannhauser and Hagstrom — 3 and 1

Cohen and Melville lost to Berthet and Janmaat — 5 and 3

Great Britain and Ireland 1½ Continent of Europe 2½

Singles

McKenna beat de Lorenzi — 5 and 4

Madill lost to Ragher — 4 and 2

Perkins halved with Morgue d'Algue

Stewart lost to Figueras-Dotti — 2 and 1

Rawlings beat Thannhauser — 1 hole

Nesbitt beat Janmaat — 1 hole

Hedges lost to Berthet — 3 and 2

Melville lost to Hagstrom — 3 and 2

Great Britain and Ireland 3½ Continent of Europe 4½

MATCH RESULT

Great Britain and Ireland 12 Continent of Europe 12

WOMEN'S AMATEUR HOME INTERNATIONALS

Royal St David's Golf Club, Harlech, Gwynedd   12–14 September 1979

Scotland 5 Wales 4
England 4 Ireland 5
England 6 Wales 3
Scotland 3½ Ireland 5½
Scotland 7 England 2
Ireland 3½ Wales 5½

Final placings	P	W	H	L	Pts
Scotland	3	2	0	1	4
Ireland	3	2	0	1	4
Wales	3	1	0	2	2
England	3	1	0	2	2

Scotland won the Championship on aggregate of games won

ENGLISH COUNTY CHAMPIONS' TOURNAMENT

Olton Golf Club, West Midlands   23 September 1979

1	N. Burch (Essex)	70	70	140
2	D. Evans (Staffordshire)	72	71	143
3	D.F. Williams (Hertfordshire)	74	70	144
	R. Broad (Gloucestershire)	71	73	144
	M. Walls (Lancashire)	71	73	144
6	P. Bailey (Cheshire)	72	75	147
7	J. Naisby (Durham)	80	68	148
	A. Payne (Cumbria)	73	75	148
	J. Parkhill (Norfolk)	75	73	148
	G. Wilson (Isle of Man)	77	71	148

WOMEN'S COMMONWEALTH TEAM CHAMPIONSHIP

Lake Karrinyup Golf Club, Perth, Australia   27–29 September 1979

Australia 5 New Zealand 1
Canada 4½ Great Britain 1½
Canada 4 New Zealand 2
Australia 5½ Great Britain ½
Canada 4 Australia 2
Great Britain 3½ New Zealand 2½

Final placings

1 Canada; **2** Australia; **3** Great Britain
(Mrs S. Hedges, Miss M. Madill, Miss T. Perkins,
Miss V. Rawlings, Miss G. Stewart);
4 New Zealand.

ENGLISH MEN'S COUNTY CHAMPIONSHIP

Formby Golf Club, Merseyside   29–30 September 1979

Final

Gloucestershire 6½ Berks, Bucks and Oxon 2½

Semi-finals

Gloucestershire 5 Yorkshire 4
Berks, Bucks and Oxon 5 Leicester & Rutland 4

Play-off for Third Place

MEN'S AMATEUR INTERNATIONALS

(Official Home International matches, scheduled for Royal Co.
Down, Northern Ireland, were cancelled)

Unofficial matches

Wales 17 Ireland 15 (at Royal Porthcawl, 10–11 October)
Scotland 17 England 13 (at Royal Troon, 16–17 October)

THE YEAR IN SCOTLAND, WALES AND IRELAND

REPORT AND RESULTS

David Jones had a great year, retaining his Club Professionals' and Irish Dunlop titles, winning the Carrolls Irish Match-Play, and being undefeated in the PGA Cup matches against America.

THE YEAR IN SCOTLAND, WALES AND IRELAND

Jock MacVicar, John Moody, and John Redmond

TELEVISION TO THE RESCUE

There were times during the PGA Scottish region's season of plenty when it seemed as though officials had laboured in vain to procure the centrepiece of their annual show. In a year of more than two dozen tournaments and record prize money of some £108,000, there was no sponsor for the long-established Scottish Professional Championship. The irony of the situation cast a deep gloom over secretary David Begg and his committee at a time when they should have been rejoicing. Then at the 11th hour, Scottish Television arrived like the US Cavalry and rescued the Championship to the tune of £13,000. Glasgow Gailes was the venue in late August, and the new sponsors were rewarded for their enterprise with the most memorable finish in years.

The holder Sam Torrance, tied at 10 under par on 274 with Sandy Lyle, and it was the 21-year-old son of the Hawkstone Park professional, Alex Lyle, who finally triumphed at the third extra hole after Torrance had driven out of bounds! Two months later Lyle had become the European Open champion, played in the Ryder Cup in the United States, and beaten Severiano Ballesteros for the coveted Harry Vardon Trophy by topping the European Order of Merit. Rarely, if ever, can Scotland have had a more illustrious professional champion. Yet there was a final irony. The rescuers were unable to cover the Championship because of industrial trouble within Independent Television.

Many months earlier the 'Tartan Tour' began at Nairn with the Clydesdale Bank Northern Open. Brian Barnes defended the title he won at Elgin. But this time the winner of the £1,400 first prize was the former professional footballer, Jim Farmer. It was the start of a great year for Farmer, both as a tournament player and as a club professional. He was fourth in the Scottish Championship behind Ronnie Shade, lost first place in the new Peterhead Tournament to Alastair Thomson in October only after a sudden-death play-off, and finished leading the Scottish Order of Merit with 580 points and nearly £7,000 in prize money. He achieved all that in spite of the upheaval of moving from Drumpellier to take over the late John Shade's post at Duddingston.

Second to Farmer in the Merit Table with 478.96 points was one of Bob Jamieson's famous Turnberry Hotel squad, Ross Drummond. In a way it was a frustrating year for Drummond, who was joint runner-up in the Northern Open, second to David Huish in the Coca-Cola at North Berwick, and shared first place with Sam Torrance and John Hay in the

£7,500 Royal Bank Tournament at Mortonhall. He left many with the feeling that only one outright victory stands between young Ross and a successful career in tournaments.

Sam Torrance once again completed the season among the top 20 money-winners in Europe, and in early July forced Brian Barnes into second place in the Skol Tournament at Cowglen with a blistering aggregate of 265. But he suffered two major disappointments – the loss of his Scottish title after such a sterling defence, and his failure to win his first Ryder Cup cap.

There were disappointments, too, on the amateur scene, among them Scotland's poor showing, as holders, in the European Team Championship at Esbjerg. But nearer home there were many notable deeds. Keith Macintosh, after nearly a decade on the fringe of international selection, finally broke through by beating Paul McKellar five and four in the final of the Scottish Amateur Championship at Prestwick.

It was sad that Keith was prevented from leading Scotland in the Home International at Newcastle, County Down, because of the troubles in Ireland. But the arranging of a friendly international against England at Royal Troon in late October at least assured first caps for Macintosh and three other newcomers to the full squad, Garry Hay, Barclay Howard, and Stuart Taylor. And there was consolation for all when Scotland defeated England 17–13.

The year was a good one for youth. Gillian Stewart, the 20-year-old from Inverness, captured the Scottish Women's Championship at Gullane by beating Lesley Hope two and one in the final; 15-years-old Jane Connachan was the star of the Women's Home Internationals in Wales; and four Scots, Gordon Brand, Colin Dalgleish, Paul Gallagher and Brian Marchbank, took up four of the first five places in the British Youths' Championship at Woodhall Spa in August.

Marchbank, son of Gleneagles Hotel professional Ian Marchbank, promptly turned professional, and made an immediate impact. He won close to £1,000 in the final month of the 'Tartan Tour' and finished equal 15th in his very first European tournament, the SOS Talisman TPD Championship, at Moor Park, Hertfordshire.

Two more internationals, Alastair Webster and John Cuddihy, subsequently switched to the professional game, Webster winning fourth place in the Douglas Gillespie Plant Tournament at Drumpellier behind Gordon Gray, Bill Murray, and Bernard Gallacher.

DISAPPOINTMENTS IN WALES

A much-heralded new £30,000 tournament which should have been the centre-piece of the golfing scene in Wales but flopped, and a scheduled £12,000 Welsh Professional Championship which fell through for lack of sponsorship clouded the Welsh Professional season.

The multi-sponsored Welsh Classic at the Wenvoe Castle club, near Cardiff, seemed to have everything in its favour, notably a top-class field chasing Ryder Cup points. But poor weather and pathetically small crowds put a damper on the tournament, won by Mark James after a play-off with Mike Miller and Eddie Polland. New hope for the event came at the end of the year, with the announcement that in 1980 Coral, the bookmakers, were to take over the sponsorship of the Welsh Classic.

The failure to secure the necessary funds by the promoters for the Professional Championship, which was to have been played at St Pierre, Chepstow, in September, brought the first break in the tournament, apart from the war years, since its inception in 1904.

On the amateur front, David McLean, undoubtedly the most consistent amateur in the country, won the Stroke-play Championship over his home course at Holyhead for a second time with an aggregate of 289, and so had the distinction of holding both Stroke and Match-play titles, having won the latter at Conwy in 1978.

Leading the field by three strokes with 18 holes to play, the 32-year-old Post Office engineer could afford the luxury of a 76, his worst round of the tournament, and still win by two shots from 18-year-old Jonathan Morrow who had dominated junior golf in the Principality over the previous three years.

The selectors had no hesitation in naming Morrow for the side which later travelled to Esbjerg, Denmark for the European Team Championship and he fully justified his inclusion, helping the side to its best-ever performance in reaching the final where they were beaten by England.

Terry Melia, another stalwart in the side's fine run, returned from Denmark with added confidence to win the Welsh title at Ashburnham where only three of the eight 'seeds' survived to the last 16 – Melia, John Roger Jones, twice Stroke-play Champion, and the holder McLean.

Jones was then eliminated by Chris Stedman, a competent Gwent county player who had helped Pontypool to retain the Welsh team title earlier in the meeting, but McLean and Melia duly reached the last four – the latter with the aid of a two at the 19th to win a close battle with 20-year-old Alan Strange – and seemed destined to meet in the final.

But McLean's form deserted him, and Mike Roper, the Gwent county captain, played his usual steady game to win at the 16th to emerge as a surprise finalist. Melia, on the other hand, had to go to the 19th for the second time during the day, this time to defeat Mike Calvert, an 18-year-old junior international whose mature play impressed everyone. Roper, who later led Gwent to their first Channel League success, proved no match for Melia in the 36-hole final over the scorched Ashburnham links, and was beaten at the 32nd.

Vicki Rawlings, for several years one of the best players in Wales, but who because of her physical education studies had been unable to compete in many major events, proved a popular first-time winner of the Women's title at Conwy, where the first-round defeat of Tegwen Perkins provided an early shock.

She was beaten at the 19th by Pamela Whitley, who thus avenged her defeat in the 1977 final but was herself defeated in the second round by Christine Thomas, captain-elect of the Welsh team. That proved to be the only surprise of the week. Vicki Rawlings went on to beat four-times champion Audrey Briggs on the last green in the final.

Earlier in the week Vicki Rawlings, Glamorgan title-holder and later runner-up in the British Open Amateur Stroke-Play Championship, along with her younger sisters Kerri and Mandy and mother Joyce, had made history by supplying four members of the five-strong Bargoed side which won the National Team Championship, while 15-year-old Mandy brought further honours to the family by winning the Welsh Girls' title later in the season.

On the international scene Welsh players gained more recognition than ever before. Jimmy Buckley became only the second Welsh player to win Walker Cup recognition; Terry Melia was included in the European side which met South America in Caracas, Venezuela; and Tegwen Perkins and Vicki Rawlings were members of both the Vagliano Cup side and the British team which competed in the Commonwealth tournament in Australia.

At the end of the season, in a match arranged as a replacement for the 11th hour cancellation of the Home Internationals, Wales gained an encouraging win over Ireland – only their second success in contests between the two countries in the space of 21 years – by 17 matches to 15 over two days at Royal Porthcawl.

But the Welsh Women's Open Amateur Stroke-play title went to an English player for the third successive year. Sue Crowcroft, a 25-year-old Worcestershire County player, emerged as a surprise winner at Aberdovey finishing three strokes ahead of a strong field with a 54-hole total of 228. Somerset's title-holder Beverley New, who set up a new course record of 69, was the runner-up a stroke in front of Janet Melville, the 1978 British Womens' Stroke-play Champion.

HEADY DAYS FOR IRELAND

David Jones and Des Smyth could not have been more timely in their emergence to the forefront of the international professional golf scene in 1979. They came good at a stage when, for once, it seemed as if Ireland's professionals were going to be completely overshadowed by the amateurs – men and women! For until the time when the 'unlikely lads' Jones and Smyth produced the goods on behalf of the paid ranks, the headlines had been entirely, and quite deservedly, monopolised by the amateurs. While the normal mainstays – Darcy, Polland, O'Connor Jnr, O'Leary – even in Ireland now it is accepted that Christy O'Connor Snr is in semi-retirement – failed to make any impact on the European tour, the amateurs blazed a trail right across Europe.

Raymond Kane won the West of England title; David Long followed up by becoming the first Irishman to win the prestigious Brabazon Trophy as the English Stroke-play Champion; the boy prodigy Ronan Rafferty won the British Youths' title; Maureen Madill captured the British Women's Match-play Championship; and Mary McKenna was crowned British Stroke-play queen.

It was a tremendous accomplishment by the amateurs, and added to it was the first-time victory for Ireland in the European Women's Team Championship, and a second success in three years for Ireland's under-22 brigade in the European Youths' Team Championship in Czechoslovakia, the first time that a major golf event had been staged behind the Iron Curtain.

With such an unprecedented haul by the amateurs, the pros were certainly put to shame. But thanks to the 32-year-old Jones, and to Smyth, six years younger, their standing was honourably restored by the end of the year. Indeed, the manner in which this pair salvaged the dented pride of the professionals was all the more exciting considering that not so much could have been expected from them at the outset.

A good late 1978 season effort by Smyth suggested he had more to offer, albeit he was still among the pre-qualifying 'rabbits' for 1979. And Jones was a club professional at Bangor who occasionally went out to rub shoulders with his country cousins on the glamour European tour.

Yet what an impact they made! Smyth's haul of £15,553 from the tigerishly-contested kitty of the European circuit bore testament to an achievement highlighted by being crowned Sun Alliance European Match-Play Champion, and being rewarded in becoming Ireland's 13th player of Ryder Cup status – the only Irish member of the new European side. Appropriately, as well as his exploits abroad, he endorsed his class by winning the Rank Xerox National Championship.

Jones's feats were perhaps not quite so grandiose. But in retaining both the Irish Dunlop tournament and also the PGA Club Professionals' title, he added further to his rising stock by being the key member of the winning British and Irish PGA club professionals' team in the Isle of Man against the Americans. And he emulated Smyth's match-play achievement when winning the Carrolls Irish confined title at Killarney beating Eamonn Darcy – Smyth having gone out in the semi-finals to Paul Leonard.

For the amateurs, it was a dazzling case of one record being established after another as Ireland's gifted men and women plundered two European titles and five in Britain. It was all due to a professional approach to the job that had not been witnessed previously in Irish golf.

The huge financial outlay undertaken by the Golfing Union of Ireland to ensure that newly-installed 'Supremo' Joe Carr could do things his way – and that included squad training and sponsored trips to play in the major events in Britain – worked wonders.

A third-place finish in the men's European Cup in Denmark had all the indications of a nation on the way back to the top, and this cherished hope could not be in more capable hands for the immediate future than in those of the wonder boys Ronan Rafferty, aged 15, and Philip Walton, 17, who produced a string of performances that eventually won them senior international team recognition. Speculation about their potential abounds, but judgement must be reserved as they have yet to shine in senior competition, the 1979 titles going to David Long (West of Ireland), Arthur Pierse (East), Padraig O'Rourke (South), and Jackie Harrington in the Irish Championship at Ballybunion.

The Irish women's scene was equally healthy. Mary McKenna's fifth National title win, along with her contribution to the winning European Cup team and her victory in the British Women's Stroke-play, made her Ireland's Queen of the Fairways for another year. It was a close-run thing, however, for Maureen Madill's effort to pull off the British Match-play crown bridged a 22-year gap since the legendary Philomena Garvey went back to Ireland with the title.

Overall, 1979 was such a good one for Irish golfers that many were recalling the heady deeds of Garvey, Carr, Bruen, Ewing, etc., and thanks to the emerging Smyth and Jones they had good reasons, too, to be making comparisons with Daly, Bradshaw, and O'Connor!

THE SCOTTISH TELEVISION/SCOTTISH PROFESSIONAL CHAMPIONSHIP

Glasgow Gailes Golf Club, Ayrshire
31 August–2September 1979   Prize Money £13,000

							£
1	S. Lyle (Hawkstone Park)	66	71	70	67	274	2,500.00
2	S. Torrance (Caledonian Hotel, Ayr)	65	66	73	70	274	1,750.00
	Lyle won play-off at third extra hole						
3	R. D. Shade (Unatt)	70	70	74	68	282	1,000.00
4	J. Farmer (Duddingston)	67	72	74	72	285	720.00
5	D. Huish (North Berwick)	71	70	73	72	286	560.00
	G. McKay (Ham Manor)	71	67	74	74	286	560.00
7	A. Thomson (Glencorse)	73	66	77	71	287	445.00
	J. Chillas (Stirling)	69	68	80	70	287	445.00
9	F. Rennie (Prestwick)	73	72	75	69	289	375.00
10	G. Cunningham (Troon Mun.)	72	67	76	75	290	330.00

RANK XEROX IRISH PROFESSIONAL CHAMPIONSHIP

Royal Dublin Golf Club   24–26 September 1979   Prize Money £10,000

						£
1	D. Smyth (Laytown and Bettystown)	77	69	69	215	1,600.00
2	D. Jones (Bangor)	70	75	71	216	1,200.00
3	C. O'Connor, Snr (Royal Dublin)	72	75	70	217	1,000.00
4	E. Darcy (Ballybunion)	73	76	70	219	800.00
5	P. Posnett (Shandon Park)	70	78	73	221	700.00
6	J. Purcell (Mullingar)	74	79	69	222	506.00
	J. Kinsella (Skerries)	70	80	72	222	506.00
	P. Skerritt (St Annes)	71	78	73	222	506.00
9	L. Owens (Royal Dublin)	71	79	73	223	300.00
	T. Halpin (Bodenstown)	74	75	74	223	300.00
	C. O'Connor, Jnr (Shannon)	73	77	73	223	300.00

Probably the best 10 minutes in the world.

THE TOP SIXTY

George Simms

INTRODUCTION

The 60 biographies which follow are not intended to be a one to 60 rating of the world's top golfers. They are those who made the news in 1979, mostly on their own tournament circuits but in many cases internationally as well, and in so doing are featured in the results, reports, and statistics that comprise the *World of Golf 1980* yearbook.

It is a fair assumption that most of them will be making the news again in 1980, in press, television, and radio, in the nerve-stretching quest for prize money and titles.

ISAO AOKI (J)

As far as 1979 was concerned, Japan's number one will forever be remembered as the man who won a £55,000 furnished apartment in Gleneagles, Scotland, for a hole-in-one than for the four further victories he added to his illustrious career which confirmed him as Japan's greatest golfer of all time. All four victories were successful title defences – the Chunichi Crowns, the Japanese PGA Match-Play, the Kanto PGA and the Japan Series – while he was in a losing four-way play-off for the Japanese Open, won by Taiwan's Kuo Chie-Hsiung. It was in 1978 that he became a golfing household name when always in the forefront of the 1978 Open Championship, and he was back in 1979 to repeat his joint-seventh place. He finished joint-second in the Dunlop Masters, and put up a valiant defence of his World Match-play title, going under only on the 36th green to America's Bill Rogers. Aoki is 36 and from Yokohama.

1979 summary

1st:	Chunichi Crowns; Japanese PGA Match-play Championship; Kanto PGA Championship; Japan Series of Golf	3rd equal: 4th equal:	ANA Sapporo Tournament Pepsi-Wilson Tournament; Suntory Open
2nd:	Fuji-Sankei Classic; Suntory World Match-play Championship (GB)	5th equal: 6th:	Dunlop International (J) Mitsubishi Galant Tournament
2nd equal:	Japanese Open Championship; Dunlop Masters (GB)	6th equal: 7th equal:	Kanto Open The Open Championship

HUGH BAIOCCHI (SA)

Since his first trip to the European circuit in 1972 Hugh has earned a reputation as something of a Continental specialist. His record includes victories in the Swiss, Dutch, and Scandinavian Opens, and true to such form he won again in Switzerland in 1979, his five-shot victory being one of the biggest of the season. The 33-year-old South African thus kept up his record of having won either in his native land or abroad since 1973. He won the South African Open title in 1978, but his best year was 1977 when he won the Sun Alliance PGA Match-play title, finished a frustrating second in four of the Continental Championships, and was second in the final Order. In 1979 he was 12th, and there was deep disappointment for him and Dale Hayes when politics excluded them from the World Cup in Greece.

1979 summary

1st:	Swiss Open Championship	7th equal:	British Airways/Avis Tournament;
3rd equal:	French Open Championship		South African Open Championship
6th equal:	Madrid Open Championship; Lada	10th equal:	South African PGA Championship
	English Classic; German Open		
	Championship; South African		
	Masters		

SEVERIANO BALLESTEROS (S)
(See 'Golfers of the Year')

Ballesteros has now been named among the five Golfers of the Year by this yearbook continuously since 1976 – and justifiably so. His has had a phenomenal rise. Seve, 23 in April and the youngest of four golfing brothers, first tried his luck on the European tournament circuit in 1974 and finished 118th in the Order of Merit. Twelve months later he had shot up to 26th, and by July 1976 was world-famous as a result of his great battle with Johnny Miller for the Open title at Royal Birkdale. He topped the Order that year, and again in 1977 and 1978, but last year he had to hand over the crown to Sandy Lyle and failed to match the four straight Harry Vardon Trophy successes of Peter Oosterhuis. Seve has scored a total of 17 international victories in Europe, the United States, Africa, Japan, and New Zealand, and helped Spain to successive World Cup victories in 1976 and 1977.

1979 summary

1st:	The Open Championship; Lada English Classic	5th equal:	Italian Open Championship
		6th equal:	European Open Championship
2nd:	Scandinavian Open Championship	7th equal:	Martini International; Japanese Open Championship
3rd equal:	French Open Championship; Western Australian Open	8th:	Australian Open Championship
4th:	Suntory World Match-play Championship	9th equal:	Madrid Open Championship
		10th equal:	Colgate PGA Championship

BRIAN BARNES (GB)

Two tournament wins in 1978 were followed by two more in 1979, but still the really big title eludes the Scot. Brian won the Portuguese and Italian Opens, having earlier won in Zambia, for a career tally of over a dozen tournament victories, and was runner-up in defence of his Spanish Open title. He ended the season in sixth place in the Order of Merit winning £28,203 – the ninth successive year in which he has finished in the top eight. He has, however, yet to finish higher than fourth. Brian's win in Portugal was one better than in 1978 when he lost by a shot, while his victory at Monticello after a play-off with Dale Hayes was reward for two previous runners-up spots in the Italian Open.

Barnes, now 34, won Ryder Cup honours for the sixth successive time – and also endured a £500 fine for outspoken comments on The Belfry course, scene of the new English Classic.

1979 summary

1st:	Portuguese Open Championship; Italian Open Championship; Zambian Open Championship	7th:	Sun Alliance European Match-play Championship
2nd :	Spanish Open Championship	8th equal:	New Zealand Open Championship
4th equal:	Colgate PGA Championship; Carrolls Irish Open	9th equal:	Greater Manchester Open
		10th equal:	Martini International

ANDY BEAN (USA)

Since he moved from a notable amateur career into the professional ranks in 1975 Andy has been one of the success stories of American golf. In his first full year in 1976 he finished an indifferent 139th in the Order of Merit, rocketed into 12th place in 1977, after winning his first tournament at Doral, and then in 1978 was one of the stars of the season with victories in the Kemper Open, Memphis Classic, and Western Open, winnings of $267,241, and third place behind Watson and Morgan. Andy cleared the magic $200,000 mark again in 1979 for a seventh-place finish and a fifth tournament victory which he gained at Atlanta. Additionally he lost a three-way play-off with Mark Hayes and Lon Hinkle for the Crosby title. The 6ft 4in Georgian, who is 27, shot a course and tournament record 61 (32–29) en route to victory at Atlanta.

1979 summary

1st:	Atlanta Golf Classic	5th equal:	Tohkai Classic (Japan)
2nd equal:	Bing Crosby National Pro-Am	8th:	Tournament Players' Championship
3rd equal:	Glen Campbell-Los Angeles Open; Bay Hill Citrus Classic; Kemper Open	8th equal:	Danny Thomas-Memphis Classic
		10th equal:	Tournament of Champions; World Series
4th equal:	Phoenix Open		

KEN BROWN (GB)

Brown will surely wish to forget 1979 and make new resolutions for 1980. It was a year in which he suffered a £1,000 fine, and was suspended for a year from international golf in the disciplinary aftermath of an unhappy second Ryder Cup appearance. Charges of indifference in pro-am events, and slow play, surrounded him as well. Yet he had a highly-successful playing season despite not adding to his one career victory – the Carrolls in 1978. He finished second behind Maurice Bembridge in the Benson and Hedges, had nine finishes in the top-10 placings, and ended up seventh in the Order of Merit with £25,406, just three places lower than in 1978. At the end of the season he paired with Sandy Lyle to take Scotland into second place behind the United States in the World Cup meeting in Greece.

1979 summary

2nd:	Benson and Hedges International	7th equal:	Welsh Classic
4th equal:	Martini International; Scandinavian Open Championship	8th equal:	Dunlop Masters Tournament
		9th equal:	Belgian Open Championship
5th equal:	Swiss Open Championship	10th equal:	Portuguese Open Championship; South African Masters
6th:	Greater Manchester Open		

NEIL COLES (GB)

When Neil Coles stepped up to receive his fourth-place cheque for £4,227 at the end of the European Open at Turnberry, he entered the record books as the first man to pass the £200,000 mark in career earnings on the European tournament circuit. He won his first prize money back in 1955 and since finishing fifth in the Order of Merit in 1961 has only once been out of the top 10 in the Final Order – and that was in 1977 when he was 11th! Despite being not 100 per cent fit in 1979 'Mr Consistency' was second twice, including a one-shot defeat in the Dunlop Masters, and was 10th in the Order of Merit. When he missed the cut in the Benson and Hedges it was the first time he had failed to make the last day since the PGA Championship in 1973 – a run of 68 tournaments. Neil, 46 in September, is Chairman of the European Tournament Players' Division Committee.

1979 summary

2nd equal:	*Dunlop Masters; Lada English Classic*	*6th equal:*	*Tournament Players' Championship*
4th equal:	*European Open Championship; Greater Manchester Open*	*7th equal:*	*Welsh Classic*
		10th equal:	*Colgate PGA Championship*

BEN CRENSHAW (USA)

Ben will remember 1979 as another frustrating year to put with 1978, even though he began the season by winning the rain-hit Phoenix and ended it winning the Walt Disney Team in partnership with George Burns. Between times the 28-year-old Texan, who so much yearns for a 'major' title, lost a play-off for the US PGA Championship with David Graham, and took six at the 71st when he looked to have the Open Championship in his grasp. Crenshaw had another losing play-off, with Larry Nelson in the Western Open, which was part of a six-tournament stretch in which he was five times the runner-up! He ended the season with $236,770 for fifth place in the Money Winners' List, a performance second only to 1976 when he won over $250,000 in finishing second to Jack Nicklaus. He should pass the gross million-dollars mark in 1980.

1979 summary

1st:	*Phoenix Open; Walt Disney World Team Championship (with George Burns)*	*2nd equal:*	*The Open Championship*
		5th equal:	*San Antonio-Texas Open; Italian Open Championship*
2nd:	*US PGA Championship; Canadian Open Championship; Western Open; American Optical Classic*	*8th equal:*	*Tournament of Champions; IVB-Philadelphia Classic*

LEE ELDER (USA)

Perhaps it was reaction to his two victories in 1978 – a peak year in which he also cemented his place in the Ryder Cup side for 1979 – but whatever it was Lee skidded down the slopes last year and managed only three top-10 finishes, the highest being a tie for fourth at Inverrary. A disappointing season ended with Lee banking only $65,247 and a 64th place that was in stark contrast to his 13th of 1978. He also lost three of his four Ryder Cup matches. Lee has been touring since 1968 and is 45. He beat Peter Oosterhuis in a play-off to win the Monsanto Open in 1974, and took the Houston Open two years later. One play-off he lost was in 1968 when Nicklaus beat him at the fifth extra hole in the American Golf Classic. In 1975 Lee was the first black professional to be invited into the US Masters.

1979 summary

4th equal:	Jackie Gleason-Inverrary Classic
6th equal:	Greater Greensboro Open
8th equal:	Tournament of Champions

NICK FALDO (GB)

In an end-of-the-year trip out to South Africa Nick Faldo found compensation for a disappointing season. With a final round of 65 he won the ICL International in Johannesburg by three shots, his first win since the Laurent Perrier Invitational in Belgium the previous season. Modest performances in Europe had seen the 22-year-old slip from his third place and £37,900 of 1978 down to 21st and £14,910. His best performance had come in the Belgian Open where he finished in a tie for second behind South Africa's Gavin Levenson. Nick joined the professional tour in 1976. The following year he finished eighth in the Order of Merit, with a victory in the Skol Individual event. Then in 1978 came a triumph in the PGA Championship, a fourth in the European Open, and a tie for seventh in the Open itself.

1979 summary

1st:	ICL International (SA)	9th:	South African Masters
2nd equal:	Belgian Open Championship	9th equal:	Cacharel World Under-25 Championship
4th equal:	Lada English Classic	10th:	Welsh Golf Classic
5th equal:	French Open Championship	10th equal:	Colgate PGA Championship

RAY FLOYD (USA)

It was a fair prophecy that Ray would not spend too long in his 1978 doldrums, and he came back a winner in 1979. Ray put in a closing five-under-par 67 at Forest Oaks to come from six shots back to win the Greater Greensboro Open by a solitary stroke. It was his first victory since his triumphs in the Byron Nelson Classic and the Pleasant Valley Classic in 1977 which were followed by a winless slump to 30th place the following year. Ray, who is 37 and from Fort Bragg, North Carolina, has been campaigning since 1963. He has won 11 times in America, the high spot being his eight-shot victory in the 1976 US Masters, and his US PGA Championship win in 1969. He won $122,872 in 1979 for 26th place in the Final Money List, and had six US top-10 finishes in all.

1979 summary

1st:	Greater Greensboro Open		
2nd equal:	Chilean Open	6th:	Jackie Gleason-Inverrary Classic
4th:	Lancôme Trophy Tournament	6th equal:	Colgate PGA Championship (GB)
5th:	Kemper Open	8th equal:	IVB-Philadelphia Classic
5th equal:	Sea Pines Heritage Classic	10th equal:	Sammy Davis-Greater Hartford Open

BERNARD GALLACHER (GB)

Bernard shot to the front of professional golf in Europe at the tender age of 20 back in 1969 when he won the PGA Championship, the Wills Open, a couple of tournaments in Zambia, gained his first Ryder Cup badge, and topped the Order of Merit. He has been a credit to the game ever since. Bernard combines one of golf's top jobs as club professional at fashionable Wentworth, in Surrey, with competition in selected events on the tournament circuit, and he did so to good effect once again in 1979. He followed a successful sojourn in Spain with victory in the French Open where he finished a shot ahead of fellow-Scot Willie Milne. Bernard had sharpened his early-season form with a trip out to Kenya where he lost the Kenya Open first prize in a play-off with Maurice Bembridge. He was the star performer for Europe in the Ryder Cup, notching four points out of five.

1979 Summary

1st:	French Open Championship	5th:	SOS Talisman Tournament Players'
2nd:	Kenya Open Championship		Championship; Madrid Open Cham-
3rd equal:	Spanish Open Championship; British		pionship
	Airways/Avis Tournament		

ANTONIO GARRIDO (S)

After a setback in 1978 when he slipped down to 23rd place, Antonio came bounding back in 1979 to finish eighth in the European Order of Merit with highest ever winnings of £24,664. He also went into the history books, together with Ballesteros, as the first Continentals to play in the re-styled European Ryder Cup team. While not possessing the charisma of Ballesteros he has nevertheless long been a prominent figure in professional golf, and has scored victories in the Spanish Open, the Madrid Open, and the Benson and Hedges International. He had none of the luck that was going in 1979, trying for second place on four occasions, two of which – the Martini and Dutch Open – he lost by a shot. At the end of the season Garrido, who is 40, paired with Manuel Pinero to finish third for Spain behind USA and Scotland in the World Cup, which he and Ballesteros had won in 1977.

1979 summary

2nd equal:	Martini International; Dutch Open	5th equal:	Italian Open Championship
	Championship; German Open Cham-	6th:	Portuguese Open Championship
	pionship; Swiss Open Championship	7th equal:	Greater Manchester Open
3rd:	Sun Alliance European Match-play	9th equal:	Spanish Open Championship;
	Championship		Madrid Open Championship
5th:	World Cup Individual		

AL GEIBERGER (USA)

Back in 1975 Al Geiberger won the Tournament Players' Championship over the course of the Colonial Country Club in Fort Worth, Texas, and Al went back there again in 1979 to win Colonial National Invitational – his 12th victory on the US circuit. Al won a 'battle of the veterans', pipping Don January and Gene Littler by a shot. It was, strangely, the only top-10 finish Al had in the US in what is now for him a restricted schedule after the surgical operation which laid him low in 1978. The 42-year-old Californian, whose record includes the 1966 PGA Championship, will forever be remembered for his second round in the Danny Thomas-Memphis Classic in 1977 when he went out in 30 and back in 29 for a 13-under-par 59 – the lowest score in the history of the US Tour. It contained 11 birdies, one eagle, six pars – and 23 putts!

1979 summary

1st:	*Colonial National Invitational*
9th equal:	*Swiss Open Championship*

BOB GILDER (USA)

Bob is not unknown in Europe where he campaigned for a while in 1975 after winning the 1974 New Zealand Open Championship in a play-off with Bob Charles and Jack Newton. Bob performed creditably for 21st place in the European Order of Merit, obtained his US Players' Card in the autumn of 1975, and made an immediate impact by winning the early-season 1976 Phoenix Open. He went on to reach six figures in prize money, and only Jerry Pate, who won the US Open, kept the 'Rookie of the Year' award from him. Bob finished 24th that year, slipped to 72nd, and was back to 36th in 1978. In 1979 he made further progress, winning a highest-ever $134,428 for 22nd finishing spot, amassed from eight top-10 placements. His best result was third in Jack Nicklaus's Memorial Tournament behind Tom Watson.

1979 summary

3rd:	*Memorial Tournament*	*8th equal:*	*Jackie Gleason-Inverrary Classic*
3rd equal:	*Houston Open*	*9th:*	*World Series*
4th:	*Canadian Open Championship*	*9th equal:*	*Anheuser-Busch Classic; San*
6th equal:	*First NBC New Orleans Open*		*Antonio-Texas Open*

DAVID GRAHAM (AUS)

David's record as an international winner got another boost in 1979 when he captured the US PGA Championship, went home to win the West Lakes Classic, then crossed to Wellington to take the Air New Zealand-Shell Open. His victory at Oakland Hills did not come without some tense moments, for he had the title in his grasp, only to double-bogey the final hole and let himself in for a play-off with Ben Crenshaw. Justice was done when the Australian, now 34, won at the third extra hole. It was a good title to put on top of others he had won in Britain, France, Japan, South America, Asia, South Africa, and his own Australian Open which he won in 1977. A Florida-based 'regular' on the US Tour, his peak year was in 1976 when he won the Westchester and American Golf Classics for eighth place in the Final Order. In 1979 he won a best-ever $177,684 for 16th.

1979 summary:

1st:	*US PGA Championship; West Lakes Classic; Air New Zealand-Shell Open*	*2nd:*	*Western Australia Open*
		2nd equal:	*Manufacturers Hanover-Westchester Classic*

3rd equal:	Atlanta Golf Classic		7th equal:	Greater Milwaukee Open
5th equal:	Canadian Open Championship		8th equal:	Buick-Goodwrench Open
6th equal:	IVB-Philadelphia Classic		9th:	Australian Open Championship
7th:	US Open Championship		9th equal:	Doral-Eastern Open

LOU GRAHAM (USA)

Lou achieved a distinction he could probably have done without in 1979, going into the record books as the man to reach the $1,000,000 mark in tournament earnings with the fewest number of victories. He joined the US Tournament circuit in 1964, and when he won the US Open title in 1975 had registered only three wins in that time. No more winner's cheques materialised until the end of July 1979, to which point he had not finished in the top-10 placings. Then he shot a closing 64 in the Philadelphia Classic to catch Bobby Wadkins and beat him in a play-off. It started a seven-tournament streak in which he won the American Optical Classic and the San Antonio-Texas Open – three wins in 11 weeks. Lou, who is 42 and from Nashville, Tennessee, won his first tournament in 1967, and only once since has he been out of the top 60. In 1979 he finished 12th with $190,827.

1979 summary

1st:	IVB-Philadelphia Classic; American Optical Classic; San Antonio-Texas Open		5th equal:	Sammy Davis-Greater Hartford Open
			10th equal:	US PGA Championship

HUBERT GREEN (USA)

It was back in 1971 that Hubert won his first tournament, the Houston Open, the year after gaining his Player's Card. He missed out in 1972, but has been an annual winner ever since. Last year was no exception, his victories in the Hawaiian Open and at New Orleans taking his career total to 16 during which time he has banked over $1,300,000. Hubert's win in Hawaii was his second there in succession and included a third round of 63, nine-under-par. In 1976 Green, who is 33 and comes from Birmingham, Alabama, had the distinction of winning three successive tournaments, and he reached a landmark the following year when he led all the way to win the US Open title at Southern Hills, Tulsa, and played the final holes knowing that his life had been threatened by a telephone caller. He was placed 13th in 1979.

1979 summary

1st:	Hawaiian Open; First NBC New Orleans Open		8th equal:	Sammy Davis-Greater Hartford Open
4th equal:	Suntory Open (Japan)		10th:	Australian Open Championship
6th equal:	Australian PGA Championship		10th equal:	Tournament of Champions;
7th equal:	Atlanta Golf Classic			US Masters

DALE HAYES (SA)

Nothing has held back Dale Hayes since he forsook the United States circuit in 1977 and returned to the European scene which he had dominated pre-Ballesteros. Second in the Order of Merit in 1978, with nearly

£44,000 in prize money, the 27-year-old South African placed fourth with £32,540 in 1979, putting in some splendid finishes in a restricted European programme. He finished 67–66 to come from eight behind to win the Spanish Open title for the second time, and lost in a play-off with Brian Barnes for the Italian Open. He tied for second in both the European Open and Swiss Open Championships. Big disappointment for Dale came at the end of the season when political pressures forced him and Hugh Baiocchi to withdraw from the World Cup in Greece. He and Bobby Cole had won it for South Africa in 1974. However at the end of the year he got compensation by winning in Bogota.

1979 summary

1st:	Spanish Open Championship; Bogota Open	3rd:	Portuguese Open Championship
2nd:	Italian Open Championship	4th equal:	Scandinavian Open Championship
2nd equal:	European Open Championship; Swiss Open Championship	6th equal:	South African PGA Championship
		9th equal:	French Open Championship

MARK HAYES (USA)

When Mark Hayes won the Tournament Players' Championship in 1977 he earned a 10-year exemption as well, and although he has not won again since then he is never far from the reckoning. In the last four years the 30-year-old Oklahoman has finished 11, 19, 15, 23 in the Money Winners' lists, and the $130,878 he garnered in 1979 took his six-year total to around $650,000. He had a third place in the opening Bob Hope event, two shots behind winner John Mahaffey, and three weeks later lost a three-way play-off with Lon Hinkle and Andy Bean for the Bing Crosby first prize – Hinkle winning with a birdie at the third hole. In an eight-week stretch later in the year Mark had 3, 4, 5, 6 finishes, third place coming in the Philadelphia, where only one stroke kept him out of the Lou Graham-Bobby Wadkins play-off.

1979 summary

2nd equal:	Bing Crosby National Pro-am	5th equal:	Sammy Davis-Greater Hartford Open
3rd:	Bob Hope Desert Classic	6th:	Kemper Open
3rd equal:	IVB-Philadelphia Classic	6th equal:	Western Open
4th equal:	Danny Thomas-Memphis Classic	9th equal:	Sun City Classic (SA)

LON HINKLE (USA)

In 1979 Lon Hinkle won himself instant fame with two victories, a tree, and a pond. They were all in the season's saga of $247,693 in money-winnings and a consequent best-ever finishing place of third behind Watson and Nelson. Lon won the Crosby after a play-off with Andy Bean and Mark Hayes, and later captured the rich World Series with its first prize of $100,000 finishing a stroke ahead of Trevino, Nelson, and Rogers. He made news at Inverness in the US Open where the USGA planted a tree overnight to try to prevent him from playing the eighth via the 17th, while at Firestone in the World Series he deliberately skimmed a shot across the surface of the pond at the 16th on his way to victory! The tall Hinkle – he is 6ft 2in and 15½st – spent five years trying to get into the top 100. Then came 60th in 1977, and 16th in 1978 when he won his previous lone victory at New Orleans.

1979 summary

1st:	Bing Crosby National Pro-Am; World Series	6th equal:	Anheuser-Busch Classic
		8th equal:	Dunlop Phoenix (Japan)
2nd:	Glen Campbell-Los Angeles Open	9th equal:	Taiheiyo (Pacific) Masters
4th equal:	Phoenix Open	10th equal:	Tournament of Champions;
5th equal:	Japanese Open Championship; Buick-Goodwrench Open		Manufacturers Hanover Westchester Classic

SIMON HOBDAY (ZIM)

With South Africa's Dale Hayes and Hugh Baiocchi finishing in the top dozen in the European Order of Merit, Simon Hobday contributed his bit from Zimbabwe-Rhodesia by occupying 11th place – his second-best showing in 10 years of campaigning. Simon won the South African Open in 1971, and the German Open in 1976, and added to these with the Madrid Open and his own Zimbabwe-Rhodesian Open when he returned home. He led from first to last in Madrid, and had two shots to spare despite taking a final 74. To capture his own national title he had to go to extra holes in a play-off with Denis Watson. Simon's season, which netted him £21,218, also included a tie for second place behind Severiano Ballesteros in the Lada English Classic. He will be 40 in June.

1979 summary

1st:	Madrid Open Championship; Zimbabwe-Rhodesia Open	4th:	German Open Championship
		4th equal:	Carrolls Irish Open
2nd equal:	Lada English Classic	10th equal:	Portuguese Open Championship
3rd equal:	South African Open Championship		

HSIEH MIN-NAN (TAI)

Like his compatriot Kuo, Hsieh Min-Nan found he had to go to Japan for most of his successes in 1979. On the Asian Circuit he could manage only three high finishes without a victory, but he crossed to Japan to win the Japanese PGA Championship, and was beaten finalist in the Japanese PGA Match-play Championship, as well as registering two other runners-up spots. Hsieh shot four sub-par rounds, including a six-under 66 to win the PGA title, and lost on the last green to Aoki in the Match-play having beaten Nakamura and Yamamoto en route. Nakamura beat him in a play-off for the Tohoku Classic title. Min-Nan, who is 39, has been among the best in the Far East for a decade. He was number one in 1971, 1975, and 1977 and in 1979 won $102,051 to finish 6th in the Japanese Order of Merit.

1979 summary

1st:	Japanese PGA Championship	5th equal:	Nihon Kokudo Keikaku Summers Tournament (J)
2nd:	Japanese PGA Match-play Championship; Tohuku Classic	7th equal:	Malaysia Open; Fuji-Sankei Classic (J)
2nd equal:	Tohkai Classic (J)	8th equal:	Kanto PGA Championship (J)
3rd equal:	Singapore Open	9th equal:	Japan Series of Golf
4th:	Taiwan Open	10th:	Jun Classic (J)

HALE IRWIN (USA)
(See 'Golfers of the Year')

Paradoxically Hale Irwin in 1979, on paper at least, had his worst year since 1970 in so far as a final finishing position was concerned! His 19th place was his lowest since his 49th in 1970, while his $154,168 in prize money was his lowest for four years. But nothing could detract from his achievement in winning the United States Open for the second time, plus the World Individual title whilst helping John Mahaffey win the World Cup in Greece. His victory at Inverness broke a long spell – for Hale at least – without a winner's cheque. He went throughout 1978 making every cut and finishing 13 times in the top-10 in 23 tournaments without once winning! He has been on the US Circuit now for 11 years, has amassed almost $1,600,000, and won 11 US victories. Hale will be 35 in June.

1979 summary

1st:	United States Open Championship; World Cup Team (with John Mahaffey); World Cup Individual	5th equal:	World Series
		6th:	The Open Championship
3rd:	Jackie Gleason-Inverarry Classic	9th equal:	Hawaiian Open
3rd equal:	Bay Hill Citrus Classic; Houston Open		

TONY JACKLIN (GB)

The clouds finally rolled away for Tony Jacklin in 1979. Although he had won the English Professional title in 1977, the former Open and US Open Champion had not chalked up a really big win since he ran away with the Scandinavian Open in 1974. But last year saw his return to form, which was rightly rewarded with a two-shot victory in the German Open in which he fought off Lanny Wadkins (66) and Antonio Garrido (67) in the closing round. Late in the year he won the Venezuela Open. It was a year in which Tony finished nine times in the top 10 placings in Europe which saw him end the season in ninth place in the Final Order of Merit – his highest finish since 1974. His European winnings of £22,178 were also his best since 1973. Despite his five years without a really big win, Tony, now 35, remains Britain's most successful golfer in terms of victories gained around the world.

1979 summary

1st:	German Open Championship; Venezuela Open	6th equal:	Canadian PGA Championship
		7th equal:	Portuguese Open Championship; Carrolls Irish Open
3rd equal:	British Airways/Avis Tournament		
4th:	Dunlop Masters Tournament	9th equal:	French Open Championship; Belgian Open Championship
5th:	Benson and Hedges International		
5th equal:	Italian Open Championship		

MARK JAMES (GB)

Like his friend Ken Brown, James will surely remember 1979 as a good and bad one. Breaches of team etiquette in what was his second Ryder Cup appearance earned him a fine of £1,500 – the heaviest ever imposed by the European Tournament Players' Division. Yet on the course he had a great year – his best since leaving the amateur ranks after Walker Cup honours in 1975. He added the Welsh Classic and the Carrolls Irish Open titles to the Sun Alliance Match-play crown he had won in 1978, putting in a record-equalling final 65 in Dublin to win by a shot over Ed Sneed. With seven top-10 finishes in Europe, James climbed to third place in the Final Order of Merit, winning £38,534. What must have given him most pleasure was the huge putt he holed on the 72nd at Royal Lytham to secure fourth place in the Open Championship.

1979 summary

1st:	*Carrolls Irish Open; Welsh Classic*	*6th equal:*	*European Open Championship*
4th:	*The Open Championship*	*7th equal:*	*Martini International; Belgian*
4th equal:	*Portuguese Open Championship*		*Open Championship*

MICHAEL KING (GB)

Michael 'got his head down' in 1979 and in his fifth year on the professional circuit finally burst through to the top. Early in the season it was a case of so near and yet so far as promising early challenges came to nought, but he finished consistently high and was handsomely rewarded for that consistency towards the end of the season. He won a Ryder Cup place, and although he played in only one single at Greenbrier, he came straight back to win the Tournament Players' Championship at Moor Park. The fifth place in the Dunlop Masters that followed meant a season of 11 top-10 finishes and a highest-ever fifth place in the Final Order of Merit with £29,724. Previous best – 35th in 1978. King, 30, was on two Walker Cup sides in his amateur days which he left in 1975.

1979 summary

1st:	*SOS Talisman Tournament Players' Championship*	*9th:*	*Martini International*
		9th equal:	*Italian Open Championship;*
2nd equal:	*Belgian Open Championship*		*Carrolls Irish Open*
3rd equal:	*British Airways/Avis Tournament*	*10th equal:*	*South African Masters*
5th:	*Dunlop Masters Tournament*		
6th equal:	*Madrid Open Championship; Scandinavian Open Championship; Dutch Open Championship; Benson and Hedges International*		

TOM KITE (USA)

Few players matched Tom Kite for consistency on the US Tour in 1979, but the 30-year-old bespectacled Texan nevertheless failed to add to the two solitary victories that have gone his way since he turned professional in 1972 following a notable amateur career. These victories were at Whitemarsh, Pennsylvania, in the 1976 Bicentennial Classic, and in 1978 at the BC Open. Tom had 11 top 10 finishes in 1979 and three times finishes third. He shot a tremendous eight-under-par 63 at Phoenix to finish three shots behind Ben Crenshaw in an event reduced by rain to 54 holes, and failed by two shots to join Gil Morgan and Larry Nelson in a play-off in Memphis. Tom also had a creditable fifth in the

US Masters. He is a former Walker Cup and Eisenhower Trophy international, and was runner-up in 1970 to Lanny Wadkins for the US Amateur title.

1979 summary

3rd:	Phoenix Open; Danny Thomas-Memphis Classic	7th:	World Series; Tournament of Champions; Air New Zealand – Shell Open
3rd equal:	Sea Pines Heritage Classic	9th equal:	Doral-Eastern Open; Tournament
4th equal:	Memorial Tournament; BC Open		Players' Championship
5th:	US Masters		
6th:	Manufacturers Hanover Westchester Classic		

BILL KRATZERT (USA)

Those who two and three years ago were predicting that Bill Kratzert was destined to become one of the game's superstars must be crossing their fingers as he moves into 1980. After his initial 'rookie' year of 1976 when he and Woody Blackburn combined to win the Walt Disney World Team title, Bill picked up the Greater Hartford Open in 1977 and wound up in 10th place at the end of the year. Best of 1978 however, were second places in the Hawaiian Open, Memorial, and Hartford events, but even so Bill moved up to eighth position with over $180,000. Came the slide in 1979, down to 35th place, again with a couple of runners-up spots, but nothing to add to his previous two victories. Nearest he came to it was at Pensacola where, after an opening record-equalling 64, he lost by a shot to Curtis Strange.

1979 summary

2nd:	Pensacola Open	6th equal:	IVB-Philadelphia Classic
2nd equal:	Andy Williams-San Diego Open	8th:	Doral-Eastern Open
5th equal:	Tournament Players' Championship; Buick-Goodwrench Open		

KUO CHIE-HSIUNG (TAI)

Kuo has for long been a leading force in golf in the Far East, but the 39-year-old Taiwanese from Tamsui had to go to Japan for his 1979 successes. He travelled well, returning home with the Japanese Open Championship, the Jun Classic, and the Golf Digest tournament, all won in the space of five tremendous weeks. He showed, too, that his tournament-hardened nerves were still sound, winning the rain-hit Jun event in a five-hole play-off with Funatogawa, and the prestige Japanese Open in a four-way play-off with Yamamoto, Aoki, and Uehara in which he got home at the fourth extra hole. He was three shots clear when rain cut the Golf Digest to 54 holes. Top money-winner in Asia in 1978, he won $125,073 in Japan in 1979 for fifth place in their Order of Merit.

1979 summary

1st:	Japanese Open Championship; Jun Classic; Golf Digest Tournament	5th equal:	Yomiuri Open (J); Malaysia Open
		6th:	Taiwan Open
2nd:	KBC August Tournament (J)	6th equal:	Bridgestone Tournament (J); Japan Series of Golf
3rd equal:	Korea Open	7th equal:	Singapore Open
4th equal:	Philippine Open	10th equal:	Pepsi-Wilson Tournament (J)

WAYNE LEVI (USA)

It was at the end of the 1978 season that young Wayne Levi (he pronounces it as in 'heavy') really got his game going. He finished third behind the play-off pair Mac McLendon and Mike Reid at Pensacola, then paired with Bob Mann to win the Walt Disney World team title. This gave Wayne exemption from the grind of qualifying in 1979 and he made splendid use of it by winning the Houston Open, tying for second in San Diego, and amassing $141,612 for an impressive 20th finishing spot in the Final standings. Wayne showed his class in winning the Houston when, after opening rounds of 69 and 65, he shot an eight-under-par course record of 63 which virtually clinched the title. Wayne is 27 and from Little Falls, New York, although at 19 he moved to Florida for the sunshine that allowed him to play the year round.

1979 summary

1st:	Houston Open	8th equal:	Phoenix Open; Colonial
2nd equal:	Andy Williams-San Diego Open		National Invitational
5th equal:	Tournament Players' Championship	10th equal:	Tallahassee Open
7th equal:	Walt Disney World Team Championship (with Bob Mann)		

BRUCE LIETZKE (USA)

Apart from his opening year on the US Tour in 1975, Bruce has been a consistent top 60 money-winner, and in the past three years has finished fifth, 18th, and eighth in the Final standings. In that stretch he has won four tournaments, two of them in 1977 when he took the Tucson and Hawaiian Opens in the space of three weeks, and later lost a three-hole play-off with Jack Nicklaus in the Tournament of Champions. That year he just topped the magic $200,000 mark. In 1979 he was less than $2,000 under it in writing up his fourth victory – again at Tucson, where he opened with a seven-under-par 63. He led all the way. He also led the first round of the US Masters with 67 but faded thereafter. Bruce, 28, is a former Texas Amateur Champion.

1979 summary

1st:	Joe Garagiola-Tucson Open	6th:	US Masters
2nd equal:	Tournament of Champions; First NBC New Orleans Open	7th equal:	Taiheiyo (Pacific) Masters
		8th equal:	Colonial National Invitational
4th equal:	Danny Thomas-Memphis Classic	9th equal:	Anheuser-Busch Classic
5th:	Western Open	10th equal:	World Series
5th equal:	Canadian Open Championship		

GENE LITTLER (USA)

It may be a couple of years since Gene last won a tournament in the United States, but that takes nothing away from an illustrious career which reaches a milestone in 1980 with his 50th birthday on 21 July. Gene turned pro soon after winning the 1953 US Amateur title. He won his first tournament in 1954, and since then has won 29 on the US circuit. The incredible fact is that since turning professional Littler has

Brian Barnes

Neil Coles

Ben Crenshaw

Al Geiberger

Tony Jacklin

Mark James

Bill Kratzert

Bruce Lietzke

Gene Littler

John Mahaffey

Graham Marsh

Johnny Miller

only once been out of the top 60 – and that was in 1972 when he underwent an operation for cancer of the lymph glands. He came back, and 16 months afterwards won yet again. It was no fluke, for in 1975 he won the Crosby, the Memphis Classic, and the Westchester Classic, netted $182,883 in prize money and finished fifth in the Money List. In 1979 he won over $70,000 for 59th place to maintain his top-60 traditions.

1979 summary

2nd equal:	Colonial National Invitational	10th:	Air New Zealand-Shell Open
9th equal:	Byron Nelson Classic	10th equal:	US Masters

LU HSI-CHUEN (TAI)

The Lu family has had a prominent name in golf for many a year now, entirely through the efforts of 'Mr Lu' Liang-Huan. But a new arm of the family added to its accomplishments in 1979 when nephew 'Master Lu' Hsi-Chuen decided to play for money instead of fun. As an amateur, the 26-year-old Hsi-Chuen had won 13 events, and turned professional in October 1978. Six months later he had won three Open Championships, and had had seven top-10 finishes in the 10 events that make up the Asian Circuit. He headed the Order of Merit 'by a street'. He won US $43,670, some $16,000 more than anyone else. Crossing over for the Japanese Circuit he added five more top-10 places to his 'rookie' professional year. Ironically he had to give best to Uncle Liang-Huan in their native Taiwan Open!

1979 summary

1st:	Singapore Open; Malaysia Open; Indonesia Open	5th equal:	Yomiuri Open (J)
		7th:	Mitsubishi Galant Tournament (J)
2nd equal:	Hong Kong Open	7th equal:	Taiwan Open
3rd:	Korea Open	9th equal:	India Open
4th:	Chunichi Crowns (J)	10th equal:	Fuji-Sankei Classic (J)
4th equal:	Golf Digest Tournament (J)		

SANDY LYLE (GB)
(See 'Golfers of the Year')

When Alexander Walter Barr Lyle turned professional at the end of 1977 it is doubtful whether he had his sights set on reaching any sort of pinnacle in two years. But that is precisely what happened to the former England international who had twice won the English Stroke-play title, the British Youths' Championship, and a Walker Cup badge. In an amateur career rich in promise he had represented England at all three levels – boy, youth, and senior – while still only 17. Soon after forsaking the amateur ranks he won the Nigerian Open, achieved a comfortable 49th place in the 1978 Order of Merit, and then swept into the European spotlight in 1979 to bring to an end the three-year domination of Severiano Ballesteros. In doing so, 21-year-old Sandy won £49,232.

1979 summary

1st:	European Open Championship; Scandinavian Open Championship; British Airways/Avis Tournament; STV Scottish Professional Championship	2nd:	Zambian Open Championship
		2nd equal:	World Cup Individual; Lancôme Trophy Tournament
		3rd equal:	Lusaka Open Championship

4th equal:	Welsh Classic; Lada English Class-	7th equal:	Portuguese Open Championship;
	ic; Dunlop Phoenix (Japan)		Greater Manchester Open; Kenya
6th equal:	Spanish Open Championship		Open Championship
7th:	Nigerian Open Championship		

JOHN MAHAFFEY (USA)

Though again hit by injuries, which have assailed him in recent years, John nevertheless kept to the forefront of the game and for the second successive year won the World Cup for America. In 1978 it was in partnership with Andy North when he won the Individual Title as well; in 1979 he teamed with Hale Irwin to win in Greece. John started the season where he had left off in his comeback year of 1978, in which he had won the US PGA Championship and the American Optical Classic. He promptly took the 90-hole Bob Hope by a single shot from Lee Trevino, and had seven successive birdies along the way, but three weeks later an injured wrist kept him idle and took almost the year to recover. John is 32 and from Texas. In winning the US PGA title in 1978 he made up seven shots on Watson with a closing 66 and won in a play-off with Watson and Pate.

1979 summary

1st:	Bob Hope Desert Classic; World	6th:	World Cup Individual
	Cup Team (with Hale Irwin)	6th equal:	South African Masters.
3rd equal:	Pensacola Open		

GRAHAM MARSH (AUS)

Graham's reputation as an international winner was further enhanced in 1979 when he won in the Netherlands, in the United Kingdom, and in Japan. His victories since turning professional in 1968 are now well in excess of 30, and include wins in Asia and the United States. Probably the victory that gave him most pleasure last year came in the prestige Dunlop Masters where his three-wood second to the par-five 72nd finished 10ft from the hole when he needed a birdie to win. His victory in the Dutch Open ended a 1978 drought following 1977 in which he had won the World Match-Play at Wentworth, the Sea Pines in the US, two events in Japan, and the Lancôme in Paris. He was named 'Rookie of the Year' in the States, finishing 22nd and topped $100,000. Graham is 36 and from Kalgoorie in Western Australia.

1979 summary

1st:	Dunlop Masters (UK); Dutch	4th equal:	Danny Thomas-Memphis Classic
	Open Championship; ANA	7th equal:	The Open Championship; Hong
	Sapporo Open (J)		Kong Open; Chunichi Crowns (J)
2nd equal:	Australian Open Championship	10th equal:	Western Open (USA); KBC
3rd equal:	Western Australian Open		Augusta Tournament (J)

JERRY McGEE (USA)

Legal problems involving his sponsor seemed to inspire JerryMcGee in 1979, for he won two tournaments on occasions before he was due to appear in court! At the Kemper Open he shot an opening 11-under-par

61 to set a new course record for the Quail Hollow course, but drifted to 74 and in the end got home only by a shot over Jerry Pate; while at Wethersfield his closing 65 for a 17-under total of 267 gave him a similar slender victory, this time over Jack Renner. These successes and two other top-10 finishes helped towards an aggregate of $166,735 in season's earnings – 18th in the standings. Jerry joined the US Tour in 1967. He won the Pensacola in 1975 and the IVB-Philadelphia Classic in 1977 which earned him a Ryder Cup place at Royal Lytham & St Annes. He is 36 and from New Lexington, Ohio.

1979 summary

| 1st: | Kemper Open; Sammy Davis-Greater Hartford Open | 5th equal: | Byron Nelson Classic |
| | | 6th equal: | Andy Williams-San Diego Open |

JOHNNY MILLER (USA)

Johnny came marching home again in 1979 to the delight of the thousands who had watched him struggle so painfully to regain the form that disappeared after 1976. While he did not exactly set the world alight, he nevertheless beat a strong field to win the invitational Lancôme tournament in Paris, and more importantly lost a play-off with Tom Watson for the winner's cheque in the Colgate Hall of Fame tournament. His 63 in the second round of that event over tough Pinehurst No. 2 was reminiscent of the 63 in his heyday which won him the 1973 US Open. Johnny, a million-dollars winner, has 17 US victories to his credit and won a record $353,021 in topping the Money Winners List in 1974. He was second to Jack Nicklaus in 1975, 14th in 1976, but then came the wilderness and a drop to 48th and 111th. In 1979 he moved up to 79th.

1979 summary

| 1st: | Lancôme Trophy Tournament | 9th equal: | Canadian Open Championship |
| 2nd: | Colgate Hall of Fame Classic | | |

GIL MORGAN (USA)

After finishing second in the 1978 Final Order behind Tom Watson, Gil Morgan suffered a reaction and fell back to 29th place. His $115,857 compared none too well with the $267,459 of the previous year, and although Gil did win another tournament to add to the three in his record, he had only one other top 10 placement. Gil's victory came in the Danny Thomas-Memphis event where he shot a six-under-par 66 in the last round to earn a play-off with Larry Nelson and beat him at the second extra hole. His cheque for $54,000 and the $10,000 he got for 10th place at Westchester made up a great part of his season's total. Gil won two events in 1978, his peak year – the Los Angeles and the World Series. The previous year he won the BC Open. He is 33, comes from Oklahoma, and is a qualified doctor of optometry.

1979 summary

| 1st: | Danny Thomas-Memphis Classic | 10th equal: | Manufacturers Hanover Westchester Classic |
| 9th equal: | Taiheiyo (Pacific) Masters | | |

TOHRU NAKAMURA (J)

When Tohru Nakamura turned professional at the age of 18 he was the youngest in the 'paid ranks' at that time. That was in 1968, and he had to wait five years before chalking up two victories and a World Cup place with Aoki in Spain. He has been prominent ever since, winning twice in 1974 and 1975, once in each of the following two years, and twice again in 1978. Then 1979 brought him his finest year. In a hot June streak he won the Mitsubishi Galant and Tohoku Classic in succession, and the following month took the Kansai PGA title for a career total of 13 victories. He went close as well, finishing tied for second, one shot behind Aoki in the Chunichi Crowns, and the Japan Series, and losing again by a stroke to Miyamoto in the Kansai Open. Tohru who is 30, stands only 5ft 5in and weighs barely 10st.

1979 summary

1st:	Mitsubishi Galant Tournament; Tohoku Classic; Kansai PGA Championship	3rd:	Fuji-Sankei Classic
		5th equal:	Japanese PGA Championship
		8th equal:	Dunlop Phoenix
2nd:	Kansai Open	10th:	Nihon Kokudo Keikaku Summers Tournament
2nd equal:	Chunichi Crowns; Japan Series of Golf	10th equal:	Pepsi-Wilson Tournament

LARRY NELSON (USA)

When he set out on the 1979 tournament trail Larry had still not got a US victory to his credit despite six years of trying. But when the last putt went down the 32-year-old, 11st, Georgian had chalked up wins in the Jackie Gleason and the Western Open, lost a play-off in the Memphis Classic with Gil Morgan, won all five of his Ryder Cup encounters, and wound up second only to Tom Watson in the Money Winners' List with over $280,0000. Six times he finished in the top three, including a tie for second in the World Series. He also had a fourth in the US Open. And he had only been playing golf for 10 years. It began with 1969 when he went to try his luck on a driving range, and that was the end of his earlier involvement with baseball and basketball. Two years later he turned professional.

1979 summary

1st:	Jackie Gleason Inverarry Classic; Western Open	4th equal:	US Open Championship
		5th equal:	Tournament of Champions
2nd:	Danny Thomas-Memphis Classic	10th equal:	Andy Williams-San Diego Open
2nd equal:	World Series		
3rd:	Hawaiian Open; Byron Nelson Classic		

JACK NICKLAUS (USA)

Jack stuck to his declared intention of playing only a limited season, failed to win a tournament, and ended up 'down among the dead men' in 71st place in the US Money Winners' List. Jack could afford the lapse. Since playing professionally from 1962 he has won 66 tournaments alone in the United States, and 18 other championships around the world. One of the greatest golfers the game has known, Nicklaus has won the US Masters five times, the US PGA title four times, and the Open and US Open titles three times, all of which combined with his two US Amateur Championships give him 17 'Majors'. In his 17 years on the professional circuit he has won over $3,400,000, topped the US Order of Merit eight times, and was never out of the top four until 1979. Despite missing out in victories in 1979 he finished second in the defence of his Open title, and was in the top 10 in two of the other major championships.

1979 summary

2nd equal:	The Open Championship	4th:	US Masters
3rd equal:	IVB-Philadelphia Classic	9th equal:	US Open Championship

GREG NORMAN (AUS)

With three victories to add to his fast-developing career, Greg was considering rationing his appearances in Europe at the season's end, and concentrating on the Far East. He won in Australia, Asia, and Europe, and hit the hole from a yard at the 72nd in the Australian Open to be robbed of a play-off with Jack Newton for the title. His victory in Europe came in the Martini International at Wentworth, an event he had won two years earlier in Blairgowrie. After finishing 17th in Europe, including a creditable joint-10th at Royal Lytham, the 25-year-old Queenslander went home to figure prominently in almost every event on the Australasian circuit. Greg shot to the front just four tournaments after turning pro in 1976, when he won the West Lakes Classic.

1979 summary

1st:	Traralgon Classic (1978/79); Hong Kong Open; Martini International	6th equal:	Lada English Classic
		9th equal:	Western Australian Open
2nd equal:	Australian Open Championship	10th equal:	Australian PGA Championship;
4th equal:	Garden State PGA Championship;		New South Wales Open; The Open
	West Lakes Classic		Championship; Colgate PGA
5th:	South Seas Classic		Championship

ANDY NORTH (USA)

Maybe it was reaction from the heady heights of 1978, but the fact was that Andy North completely failed to carry the flag into 1979 with the same flourish. It is in the record books that Andy North won the United States Open Championship in 1978 at Cherry Hills, where he had a four strokes lead with five to play, frittered it slowly away, and finally won with a bogey on the last hole! Andy's only previous win in America had been the 1977 Westchester Classic, and he did not add to it in 1979 where he in fact managed only three top 10 finishes, the best being a fifth in the Colgate Hall of Fame. It meant only $73,873 in prize money and a dramatic drop from 14th to 54th place, the worst since his 'rookie' year of 1973. He crossed to St Andrews for the Colgate-PGA Championship where he finished tied for sixth.

1979 summary

5th:	Colgate Hall of Fame Classic		PGA Championship (GB)
6th equal:	Anheuser-Busch Classic; Colgate	7th:	Jackie Gleason-Inverarry Classic

MASASHI OZAKI (J)

It is a rare event in Japanese golf for 'Jumbo' to go through a season without a victory, but that is what happened to Ozaki in 1979. Nevertheless, despite the fact that Isao Aoki has taken over the mantle of Japan's number one, Ozaki remains a big attraction wherever he plays and is one of the finest professionals his country has ever produced. Seven times he finished in the top five placements and he was twice a runner-up, losing a play-off with Sugihara in the Yomiuri Open at the second extra hole, and being beaten on the post by Masaru Amano's closing 65 after Jumbo had held a clear third round lead. He again came to Britain with Aoki for the Open Championship, improving on his joint-14th in 1978 with a share of 10th place.

1979 summary

2nd:	Yomiuri Open	5th:	Ana Sapporo Tournament
2nd equal:	Kanto Open	5th equal:	Fuji-Sankei Classic
3rd equal:	Mitsubishi Galant Tournament	6th equal:	Japan Series of Golf
4th equal:	Shizuoka Open; Kanto PGA Championship	8th equal:	Dunlop Phoenix
		10th equal:	The Open Championship

JERRY PATE (USA)

The year 1979 was one in which Jerry had the mortification of winning more than in any previous season – $193,707 from 11 top-10 placings – but failing to add to the five US tournament wins to his credit since turning pro in 1975. He had three near misses, losing by a shot to Jerry McGee in the Kemper, finishing second with Gary Player behind Hale Irwin in the US Open, and sharing second spot in the Tournament of Champions. He also tied for fifth in the US PGA Championship, and his final finishing place of 11th was only one spot down on his 1976 and 1978 performances. It was his victories in the US Open, the Canadian Open, and the Pacific Masters in Japan that won him this yearbook's vote of Golfer of the Year in 1976. The 26-year-old Georgian won the US Amateur title in 1974, and was a member of the US Walker Cup and Eisenhower Trophy teams.

1979 summary

2nd:	Kemper Open	6th equal:	Andy Williams-San Diego Open;
2nd equal:	US Open Championship; Tournament		Bay Hill Citrus Classic
	of Champions	7th equal:	Western Australia Open
4th:	Byron Nelson Classic	8th equal:	IVB-Philadelphia Classic
4th equal:	Phoenix Open	9th equal:	BC Open; Southern Open
5th equal:	US PGA Championship		

CALVIN PEETE (USA)

Prior to the start of 1979 it could be said that Calvin Peete was in something of a groove. Calvin, 36 years old and one of 19 children, had finished 105th in 1977 with $20,525 prize money, and 108th in 1978 with $20,459. How well he came out of the rut! He shot a seven-under 65 in the last round to win the Greater Milwaukee Open, with Trevino, Miller, and Green among those behind him, and the following week fired a closing seven-under 63 at Oakwood which only just failed to catch D.A.Weibring in the Quad Cities. His win in Milwaukee made him only the second black player to gain a place in the US Masters. Lee Elder was the first. Calvin had seven top 10 finishes in all, and won $122,481 in filling 27th place. He is said to be the first golfer to win on the US Tour with diamonds in his front teeth!

1979 summary

1st:	Greater Milwaukee Open	5th equal:	Byron Nelson Classic
2nd:	Ed McMahon–Quad Cities Open	6th equal:	First NBC New Orleans Open
3rd equal:	Southern Open	7th equal:	Houston Open
4th:	South African Masters	10th equal:	Western Open

GARY PLAYER (SA)

Gary's phenomenal career was further enhanced at the age of 44 in 1979 with the domination of his own South African circuit. In four tremendous weeks he won the South African PGA, the South African Masters, the South African Open Championship, and the Sun City Classic to take his tally of wins around the world to 118. His victory in the South African Open was his 12th since he first won it in 1956. Outside his own country he has won the Open Championship three times, the US Open once, the US Masters three times, and the US PGA title twice. He has been seven times Australian Open champion, and has five victories in the World Match-play Championship at Wentworth, Surrey. His run of victories on the South African 'Sunshine Circuit' was reminiscent of the previous year in America when he won the US Masters, the Tournament of Champions, and the Houston Open – also in successive weeks.

1979 summary:

1st:	South African Open Championship; South African Masters; South African PGA Championship; Sun City Classic	4th:	Tournament Players' Championship (GB); Tournament of Champions (USA)
2nd equal:	US Open Championship; Greater Greensboro Open; Colgate PGA Championship (GB)	7th:	Australian Open Championship
		9th equal:	French Open Championship

JACK RENNER (USA)

The Renners are a golfing family. Jack's parents moved from Illinois to California for the sunshine soon after the birth of Jane, now in her fourth year on the LPGA Tour; Jack began knocking a ball about soon after he could walk; and younger brother Jim has followed them in by turning professional. Jack, a Ben Hogan devotee down to Hogan clubs and a Hogan flat white hat, won the World Junior title in 1972 and the US Juniors' crown the following year. He went through the US Qualifying School in the spring of 1977 and won a creditable $12,000. Next year he won over $73,000 for 33rd placing, and last year he got his first tournament, the Westchester Classic with its first prize of $72,000. The previous week he was beaten by one shot at Hartford by Jerry McGee. At 23, Jack banked $182,808 in prize money and rocketed into 14th place in the Final Standings.

1979 summary

1st:	Manufacturers Hanover Westchester Classic	7th equal:	Atlanta Golf Classic
		8th equal:	Colonial National Invitational
2nd:	Sammy Davis-Greater Hartford Open	9th equal:	Greater Greensboro Open
3rd:	Tournament Players' Championship		

BILL ROGERS (USA)

When Bill Rogers journeyed to Wentworth, Surrey, for the Suntory World Match-Play, there were many who said 'Bill who?' and made him the outsider. That was to ignore his blossoming career which began on the US Tour in 1975, saw him place 29th in 1977, and 17th in 1978 when he won the Bob Hope Desert Classic. The 6ft, 10½st Texan confounded everyone and the bookmakers by beating Isao Aoki in the final of the Suntory to go home with the first-prize cheque of £30,000. Along the way he beat US Open Champion Hale Irwin and US Masters winner Fuzzy Zoeller. Back home Bill had a tremendous 12 top 10 finishes, being second four times including a play-off with Tom Watson for the Byron Nelson Classic. His best-ever season saw him finish sixth with $230,500 in US tournament winnings, a record for a player without a win during the season.

1979 summary

1st:	Suntory World Match-Play Championship	4th equal:	US Open Championship
		5th:	Anheuser-Busch Classic
2nd:	Doral-Eastern Open; Byron Nelson Classic	5th equal:	Sea Pines Heritage Classic
		6th:	Colgate Hall of Fame Classic
2nd equal:	World Series; San Antonio-Texas Open; Taiheiyo (Pacific) Masters	7th equal:	Houston Open; Memorial Tournament; Kemper Open
3rd equal:	Bay Hill Citrus Classic		

ED SNEED (USA)

The fact that Ed Sneed won a best-ever $123,606, and finished an equally best-ever 25th at the end of the season could not compensate for what happened to him at Augusta. It was there in April that Ed became known as The Man who Blew the Masters. The 35-year-old Virginian led by three shots with three holes to play, bogeyed all three, and lost the play-off with Fuzzy Zoeller and Tom Watson at the second extra hole. Ed has had no victories since 1977, the year he gained a place on the US Ryder Cup side at Royal Lytham & St Annes. He joined the US Tour in 1969, and since 1973 has never been out of the top 60. He has three victories to his credit – the Kaiser International in 1973, Milwaukee in 1974, and Tallahassee in 1977. During 1979 he crossed to Dublin and lost in the Carrolls Irish Open by a single shot after a brave final 65.

1979 summary

2nd:	Sea Pines Heritage Classic; Carrolls Irish Open	5th equal:	Glen Campbell-Los Angeles Open
		6th:	Memorial Tournament
2nd equal:	US Masters	8th equal:	Colonial National Invitational

CURTIS STRANGE (USA)

Curtis was one of the success stories of the US Tour in 1979. The former Wake Forest University product who won World Amateur Team and

Walker Cup honours, turned professional in 1977, and in his first full year in 1978 finished 88th in the standings. He shot to the front last year with a victory in the Pensacola and a tally of nine top 10 placings in all. He amassed a total of $138,368 in prize money and ended the year in a commendable 21st place. His victory at Pensacola sprang from a third round of 62, 10-under-par, which shattered the course record. He won by a shot from Bill Kratzert. It was a remarkable surge forward from the previous year when Curtis had managed only three top 10 finishes in 29 tournaments.

1979 summary

1st:	Pensacola Open	8th equal:	Ed McMahon-Quad Cities Open;
3rd equal:	Sammy Davis-Greater Hartford		Bing Crosby National Pro-Am
	Open	9th equal:	Greater Greensboro Open
5th equal:	Joe Garagiola-Tucson Open	10th equal:	Atlanta Golf Classic
6th equal:	First-NBC New Orleans Open		
7th equal:	BC Open		

LEE TREVINO (USA)

In terms of money won, Lee's $238,732 was the most he had won in a single season in America, whilst a third victory in the Canadian Open took his total of tournament titles on the US tour to 22. He could also look on his fourth finishing spot as his best effort since 1974, but at the same time could be forgiven for wondering just when his luck was really going to change. The previous year, the wisecracking Mexican from Dallas, Texas, had five second-place finishes, while in 1979 he was four times in the runner-up spot. On three of these occasions – the Bob Hope, New Orleans, and World Series – he was beaten only by a solitary shot. Trevino, twice winner of the Open and US Open titles, went back over the border to win the Canadian PGA title, and has now passed the $2,000,000 mark in career earnings, second only to Jack Nicklaus. He is now 40.

1979 summary

1st:	Canadian Open Championship;	3rd:	Colombian Open
	Canadian PGA Championship	5th equal:	Tournament Players' Championship;
2nd:	Bob Hope Desert Classic		Tournament of Champions; San
2nd equal:	1st NBC New Orleans Open; Greater		Antonio-Texas Open
	Milwaukee Open; World Series; Lan-	6th equal:	Andy Williams-San Diego Open
	côme Trophy Tournament	9th equal:	Joe Garagiola-Tucson Open

HOWARD TWITTY (USA)

Twice after turning professional in 1973 the 6ft 5in, 15½st Howard Twitty from Phoenix, Arizona, failed to get the necessary credentials at the US Tour Qualifying School. So he went out to Asia, won the Thailand Open, and returned in the spring of 1975 to try again. That time he made it, and after an indifferent opening year he has never looked back since 1976. That year he was 51st, in 1977 he was 49th, and in 1978 he finished 25th without quite making the six-figure mark. In 1979 came his first tournament victory – the BC Open, built on a third round 64 – and with eight top-10 finishes he amassed $179,619 in prize cheques, ending the season in a commendable 15th position. High spot of his career was his closing 62 at Silverado in the Anheuser-Busch in 1977 which gave him vital top 60 exemption.

1979 summary

1st:	*BC Open*	*7th equal:*	*Memorial Tournament; US*
2nd equal:	*Manufacturers Hanover Westchester*		*PGA Championship*
	Classic	*8th:*	*World Series*
5th equal:	*Joe Garagiola-Tucson Open; Cana-*	*10th equal:*	*Andy Williams-San Diego Open*
	dian Open Championship		

BOBBY WADKINS (USA)

The Wadkins brothers have played golf together since they were juniors, but when it came to the paid ranks it has been Lanny who has had the greater achievement and consequent limelight. But now Bobby is coming to the front. At 28, some 20 months the younger in age and professionalism, Bobby won exemption for the first time in 1979 as a result of his 41st place in 1978 – the year incidentally when he won the inaugural European Open in Britain. Bobby thoroughly justified his new status. Among seven top 10 placings was a losing play-off with Lou Graham in Philadelphia in which Lou had to shoot 64 to catch him, and a tie for second in the Anheuser-Busch, just a shot off in-form John Fought. Satisfied with $121,373 for 28th place, Bobby went out to Japan to win the prestige Dunlop Phoenix from a strong field.

1979 summary

1st:	*Dunlop Phoenix Tournament (Japan)*	*4th:*	*Greater Greensboro Open*
2nd:	*IVB-Philadelphia Classic*	*7th equal:*	*Bob Hope Desert Classic*
2nd equal:	*Anheuser-Busch Classic*	*9th equal:*	*Doral-Eastern Open*
3rd:	*Tallahassee Open*	*10th equal:*	*Western Open*

LANNY WADKINS (USA)

Lanny threatens to be the 'comeback' man on the US Tournament circuit. Soon after turning professional in 1971 he had a brilliant 1972–73 spell, winning the Sahara Invitational, the Byron Nelson Classic, and the USI Classic and ending 1973 with $200,455 and fifth spot in the Money-Winners' List. In 1974 he slumped to 54th, underwent a gall-bladder operation and returned too soon to golf, which meant an 88th place in 1975 and 64th in 1976. Then the former US Amateur Champion hit the recovery road, winning the PGA Championship in 1977 after a play-off with Gene Littler, and the World Series, and finishing third with just under $250,000. Again he fell back in 1978 to 61st, but in 1979 he rebounded with victories in the Tournament Players' Championship by three shots from Tom Watson in winds of 45mph. He won in Los Angeles, as well as in Japan, and ended up with over $195,000, finishing in 10th place.

1979 summary

1st:	*Tournament Players' Championship;*	*4th equal:*	*Memorial Tournament*
	Glen Campbell–Los Angeles Open;	*5th equal:*	*Bob Hope Desert Classic*
	Bridgestone Tournament (Japan)	*7th equal:*	*US Masters*
2nd:	*Canadian PGA Championship*	*9th equal:*	*Sea Pines Heritage Classic*
2nd equal:	*German Open Championship*		

TOM WATSON (USA)
(See 'Golfers of the Year')

Watson's tremendous achievement in topping the US Order of Merit for three successive years are fully documented in the yearbook. He was without doubt the world's number one in 1979, and the game's star attraction now that Jack Nicklaus – whom he is gradually succeeding – is playing a very restricted tournament schedule. Tom is from Kansas City, Missouri. He began playing golf at the age of six, and in 1971 graduated with a degree in psychology at Stanford University. That same year he turned professional and joined the US Tour in 1972. His US tournament winnings since then are now in excess of $1,600,000, and his five victories in 1979 took his total to 16 including the 1977 US Masters. In addition he has won two Open Championships (1975 and 1977) and the World Series (1975). It wasn't just the golf course that made 1979 great for Tom. His wife Linda presented him with a daughter, Margaret Elizabeth, on the eve of the Ryder Cup match.

1979 summary

1st:	Sea Pines Heritage Classic; Tournament of Champions; Byron Nelson Classic; Memorial Tournament; Colgate Hall of Fame Classic	3rd:	Canadian Open Championship; Canadian PGA Championship
		4th equal:	Colonial National Invitational
2nd:	Tournament Players' Championship	5th equal:	World Series
2nd equal:	US Masters; Andy Williams–San Diego Open; Joe Garagiola–Tucson Open; Taiheiyo (Pacific) Masters	6th equal:	Western Open; Bay Hill Citrus Classic; Dunlop Phoenix (Japan)
		10th equal:	Manufacturers Hanover–Westchester Classic

TOM WEISKOPF (USA)

Like his friend Jack Nicklaus, Tom Weiskopf will find 1979 easily forgettable despite a late-season win in Argentina. For the first time since 1970 he failed to reach the six-figure mark in tournament winnings, and also was unable to add to the 13 victories he had achieved on the US circuit since he joined it in 1965. He did, however, get within an ace of winning, for he came from one behind to catch Ed Fiori in the late-season Southern Open only to lose to Fiori's birdie at the second extra hole. He was in second place going into the last round of the US Open but finished fourth with an indifferent 76. Tom, who finished the season 48th with $76,999, had his finest year in 1973. He won the Open Championship at Troon, four US Tour events, the World Series, and the South African PGA title.

1979 summary

1st:	Argentine Open Championship	4th equal:	US Open Championship
2nd:	Southern Open	8th equal:	Buick-Goodwrench Open

FUZZY ZOELLER (USA)

Frank Urban Zoeller was largely unknown outside America at the start of 1979, but by the end of it he was in the record books as the reigning US Masters champion, and the winner of the San Diego Open besides. Fuzzy's previous claim to fame had been a permanent place in the top

60 money winners since 1976 in which year he equalled a Tour record by birdying eight successive holes during the Quad Cities Open at Oakwood Country Club. Big-hitting Zoeller had to be grateful to Ed Sneed for his Masters' title, for Ed threw it away by bogeying the last three holes. Nevertheless Fuzzy's nerves were equal to the play-off test which he won at the second extra hole. Middle rounds of 67 gave the wisecracking Fuzzy his victory in a howling gale at San Diego where he won by five shots – his first Tour victory. He finished ninth in the final money list.

1979 summary

1st:	*US Masters; Andy Williams–San Diego Open*	*5th:*	*Atlanta Golf Classic*
2nd:	*Hawaiian Open*	*5th equal:*	*Glen Campbell–Los Angeles Open*
3rd:	*Suntory World Match-Play Championship*	*6th equal:*	*Colonial National Invitational*
		8th equal:	*Dunlop Masters (GB)*

Jack Renner *Howard Twitty*

CHAMPIONSHIP ROLLS

THE OPEN CHAMPIONSHIP

Year	Winner		Venue	Score
1860	W. Park	Musselburgh	Prestwick	174
1861	T. Morris Sr	Prestwick	Prestwick	163
1862	T. Morris Sr	Prestwick	Prestwick	163
1863	W. Park	Musselburgh	Prestwick	168
1864	T. Morris Sr	Prestwick	Prestwick	167
1865	A. Strath	St Andrews	Prestwick	162
1866	W. Park	Musselburgh	Prestwick	169
1867	T. Morris Sr	St Andrews	Prestwick	170
1868	T. Morris Jr	St Andrews	Prestwick	157
1869	T. Morris Jr	St Andrews	Prestwick	154
1870	T. Morris Jr	St Andrews	Prestwick	149
1872	T. Morris Jr	St Andrews	Prestwick	166
1873	T. Kidd	St Andrews	St Andrews	179
1874	M. Park	Musselburgh	Musselburgh	159
1875	W. Park	Musselburgh	Prestwick	166
1876	B. Martin	St Andrews	St Andrews	176
1877	J. Anderson	St Andrews	Musselburgh	160
1878	J. Anderson	St Andrews	Prestwick	157
1879	J. Anderson	St Andrews	St Andrews	170
1880	B. Ferguson	Musselburgh	Musselburgh	162
1881	B. Ferguson	Musselburgh	Prestwick	170
1882	B. Ferguson	Musselburgh	St Andrews	171
1883	W. Fernie	Dumfries	Musselburgh	159
1884	J. Simpson	Carnoustie	Prestwick	160
1885	B. Martin	St Andrews	St Andrews	171
1886	D. Brown	Musselburgh	Musselburgh	157
1887	W. Park Jr	Musselburgh	Prestwick	161
1888	J. Burns	Warwick	St Andrews	171
1889	W. Park Jr	Musselburgh	Musselburgh	155
1890	Mr J. Ball	Royal Liverpool	Prestwick	164
1891	H. Kirkaldy	St Andrews	St Andrews	166
After 1891 the competition was extended to seventy-two holes and for the first time entry money was imposed.				
1892	Mr H.H. Hilton	Royal Liverpool	Muirfield	305
1893	W. Auchterlonie	St Andrews	Prestwick	322
1894	J.H. Taylor	Winchester	Sandwich	326
1895	J.H. Taylor	Winchester	St Andrews	322
1896	H. Vardon	Ganton	Muirfield	316
1897	Mr H.H. Hilton	Royal Liverpool	Hoylake	314
1898	H. Vardon	Ganton	Pretwick	307
1899	H. Vardon	Ganton	Sandwich	310
1900	J.H. Taylor	Mid-Surrey	St Andrews	309
1901	J. Braid	Romford	Muirfield	309
1902	A. Herd	Huddersfield	Hoylake	307
1903	H. Vardon	Totteridge	Prestwick	300
1904	J. White	Sunningdale	Sandwich	296
1905	J. Braid	Walton Heath	St Andrews	318
1906	J. Braid	Walton Heath	Muirfield	300
1907	A. Massy	La Boulie	Hoylake	312
1908	J. Braid	Walton Heath	Prestwick	291
1909	J.H. Taylor	Mid-Surrey	Deal	295
1910	J. Braid	Walton Heath	St Andrews	299
1911	H. Vardon	Totteridge	Sandwich	303
1912	E. Ray	Oxhey	Muirfield	295
1913	J.H. Taylor	Mid-Surrey	Hoylake	304
1914	H. Vardon	Totteridge	Prestwick	306
1915–19	*No Championship*			

Year	Winner		Venue	Score
1920	G. Duncan	Hanger Hill	Deal	303
1921	J. Hutchinson	USA	St Andrews	296
1922	W. Hagen	USA	Sandwich	300
1923	A.G. Havers	Coombe Hill	Troon	295
1924	W. Hagen	USA	Hoylake	301
1925	J. Barnes	USA	Prestwick	300
1926	Mr R.T. Jones	USA	Royal Lytham & St Annes	391
1927	Mr R.T. Jones	USA	St Andrews	285
1928	W. Hagen	USA	Sandwich	292
1929	W. Hagen	USA	Muirfield	292
1930	Mr R.T. Jones	USA	Hoylake	291
1931	T.D. Armour	USA	Carnoustie	296
1932	G. Sarazen	USA	Prince's, Sandwich	283
1933	D. Shute	USA	St Andrews	292
1934	T.H. Cotton	Waterloo, Belgium	Sandwich	283
1935	A. Perry	Leatherhead	Muirfield	283
1936	A.H. Padgham	Sundridge Park	Hoylake	287
1937	T.H. Cotton	Ashridge	Carnoustie	290
1938	R.A. Whitcombe	Parkstone	Sandwich	295
1939	R. Burton	Sale	St Andrews	290
1940–45	*No Championship*			
1946	S. Snead	USA	St Andrews	290
1947	F. Daly	Balmoral	Hoylake	293
1948	T.H. Cotton	Royal Mid-Surrey	Muirfield	284
1949	A.D. Locke	SA	Sandwich	283
1950	A.D. Locke	SA	Troon	279
1951	M. Faulkner	Unattached	Royal Portrush	285
1952	A.D. Locke	SA	Royal Lytham	287
1953	B. Hogan	USA	Carnoustie	282
1954	P.W. Thomson	AUS	Royal Birkdale	283
1955	P.W. Thomson	AUS	St Andrews	281
1956	P.W. Thomson	AUS	Hoylake	286
1957	A.D. Locke	SA	St Andrews	279
1958	P.W. Thomson	AUS	Royal Lytham & St Annes	278
1959	G.J. Player	SA	Muirfield	284
1960	K.D.G. Nagle	AUS	St Andrews	278
1961	A.D. Palmer	USA	Royal Birkdale	284
1962	A.D. Palmer	USA	Troon	276
1963	R.J. Charles	NZ	Royal Lytham & St Annes	277
1964	A. Lema	USA	St Andrews	279
1965	P.W. Thomson	AUS	Royal Birkdale	285
1966	J.W. Nicklaus	USA	Muirfield	282
1967	R. de Vicenzo	ARG	Hoylake	278
1968	G.J. Player	SA	Carnoustie	289
1969	A. Jacklin	Potters Bar	Royal Lytham & St Annes	280
1970	J.W. Nicklaus	USA	St Andrews	283
1971	L. Trevino	USA	Royal Birkdale	278
1972	L. Trevino	USA	Muirfield	278
1973	T. Weiskopf	USA	Troon	276
1974	G.J. Player	SA	Royal Lytham & St Annes	282
1975	T. Watson	USA	Carnoustie	279
1976	J. Miller	USA	Royal Birkdale	279
1977	T. Watson	USA	Turnberry	268
1978	J.W. Nicklaus	USA	St Andrews	281
1979	S. Ballesteros	S	Royal Lytham & St Annes	283

AMERICAN OPEN CHAMPIONSHIP

Year	Winner	Venue	Score
1894	Willie Dunn, GB	New York, defeated Willie Campbell	2 holes
1895	H.J. Rawlins	Newport	173
1896	J. Foulis	Southampton	152

Year	Winner	Venue	Score
1897	J. Lloyd	Wheaton, Illinois	162
1898	F. Herd	Shinnecock Hills	328
1899	W. Smith	Baltimore	315
1900	H. Vardon, GB	Wheaton, Illinois	313
1901	W. Anderson	Myopia, Massachusetts	315
1902	I. Auchterlonie, GB	Garden City	305
1903	W. Anderson	Baltusrol	307
1904	W. Anderson	Glenview	304
1905	W. Anderson	Myopia, Massachusetts	335
1906	A. Smith	Onwentsia	291
1907	A. Ross	Chestnut Hill, Pennsylvania	302
1908	F. M'Leod	Myopia, Massachusetts	322
1909	G. Sargent	Englewood, New Jersey	290
1910	A. Smith	Philadelphia	289
1911	J.J. M'Dermott	Wheaton, Illinois	307
1912	J.J. M'Dermott	Buffalo, New York	294
1913	Mr F. Ouimet	Brookline, Massachusetts	304
1914	W. Hagen	Midlothian	297
1915	Mr J.D. Travers	Baltusrol	290
1916	Mr Charles Evans	Minneapolis	286
1919	W. Hagen	Braeburn	301
1920	E. Ray, GB	Inverness	295
1921	J. Barnes	Washington	289
1922	G. Sarazen	Glencoe	288
1923	Mr R.T. Jones	Inwood, Long Island	296
1924	C. Walker	Oakland Hills	297
1925	W. MacFarlane	Worcester	291
1926	Mr R.T. Jones	Scioto	293
1927	T.D. Armour	Oakmont	301
1928	J. Farrell	Olympia Fields	294
1929	Mr R.T. Jones	Winged Foot, New York	294
1930	Mr R.T. Jones	Interlachen	287
1931	B. Burke	Inverness	292
1932	G. Sarazen	Fresh Meadow	286
1933	Mr J. Goodman	North Shore	287
1934	O. Dutra	Merion	293
1935	S. Parks	Oakmont	299
1936	T. Manero	Springfield	282
1937	R. Guldahl	Oakland Hills	281
1938	R. Guldahl	Cherry Hills	284
1939	B. Nelson	Philadelphia	284
1940	W. Lawson Little	Canterbury, Ohio	287
1941	C. Wood	Fort Worth, Texas	284
1942–45	*No Championship*		
1946	L. Mangrum	Canterbury	284
1947	I. Worsham	St Louis	282
1948	B. Hogan	Los Angeles	276
1949	Dr C. Middlecoff	Medinah, Illinois	286
1950	B. Hogan	Merion, Pa.	287
1951	B. Hogan	Oakland Hills, Michigan	287
1952	J. Boros	Dallas, Texas	281
1953	B. Hogan	Oakmont	283
1954	E. Furgol	Baltusrol	284
1955	J. Fleck	San Francisco	287
1956	Dr C. Middlecoff	Rochester	281
1957	R. Mayer	Inverness	282
1958	T. Bolt	Tulsa, Oklahoma	283
1959	W. Casper	Mamaroneck	282
1960	A.D. Palmer	Cherry Hills	280
1961	G. Littler	Birmingham, Michigan	281
1962	J.W. Nicklaus	Oakmont	283
1963	J. Boros	Brookline, Massachusetts	293
1964	K. Venturi	Washington	278
1965	G.J. Player, SA	St Louis, Massachusetts	282

Year	Winner	Venue	Score
1966	W. Casper	San Francisco	278
1967	J.W. Nicklaus	Baltusrol	275
1968	L. Trevino	Rochester	275
1969	O. Moody	Houston, Texas	281
1970	A. Jacklin, GB	Chaska, Minnesota	281
1971	L. Trevino	Merion, Pennsylvania	280
1972	J.W. Nicklaus	Pebble Beach	290
1973	J. Miller	Oakmont	279
1974	H. Irwin	Winged Foot, New York	287
1975	L. Graham	Medina, Illinois	287
1976	J. Pate	Atlanta, Georgia	277
1977	H. Green	Tulsa, Oklahoma	278
1978	A. North	Cherry Hills	285
1979	H. Irwin	Inverness	284

AMERICAN MASTERS TOURNAMENT
Augusta National Golf Course, Augusta, Georgia

Year	Winner	Score	Year	Winner	Score
1934	H. Smith	284	1958	A.D. Palmer	284
1935	G. Sarazen	282	1959	A. Wall	284
1936	H. Smith	285	1960	A.D. Palmer	282
1937	B. Nelson	283	1961	G.J. Player. SA	280
1938	H. Picard	285	1962	A.D. Palmer	280
1939	R. Guldahl	279	1963	J.W. Nicklaus	286
1940	J. Demaret	280	1964	A.D. Palmer	276
1941	C. Wood	280	1965	J.W. Nicklaus	271
1942	B. Nelson	280	1966	J.W. Nicklaus	288
1943–45	*No Championship*		1967	G. Brewer	280
1946	H. Keiser	282	1968	R. Goalby	277
1947	J. Demaret	281	1969	G. Archer	281
1948	C. Harmon	279	1970	W. Casper	279
1949	S. Snead	283	1971	C. Coody	279
1950	J. Demaret	282	1972	J.W. Nicklaus	286
1951	B. Hogan	280	1973	T. Aaron	283
1952	S. Snead	286	1974	G.J. Player. SA	278
1953	B. Hogan	274	1975	J.W. Nicklaus	276
1954	S. Snead	289	1976	R. Floyd	271
1955	C. Middlecoff	279	1977	T. Watson	276
1956	J. Burke	289	1978	G.J. Player, SA	277
1957	D. Ford	283	1979	F. Zoeller	280

AMERICAN PGA CHAMPIONSHIP

Year	Winner	Runner-up	Venue	Result
1916	J. Barnes	J. Hutchinson	Siwanoy	1 hole
1919	J. Barnes	F. M'Leod	Engineer's Club	6 and 5
1920	J. Hutchinson	D. Edgar	Flossmoor	1 hole
1921	W. Hagen	J. Barnes	Inwood Club	3 and 2
1922	G. Sarazen	E. French	Oakmont	4 and 3
1923	G. Sarazen	W. Hagen	Pelham	38th hole
1924	W. Hagen	J. Barnes	French Lick	2 holes
1925	W. Hagen	W.E. Mehlhorn	Olympia Fields	6 and 4
1926	W. Hagen	L. Diegel	Salisbury	4 and 3
1927	W. Hagen	J. Turnesa	Dallas, Texas	1 hole
1928	L. Diegel	A. Espinosa	Five Farms	6 and 5
1929	L. Diegel	J. Farrell	Hill Crest	6 and 4
1930	T.D. Armour	G. Sarazen	Fresh Meadow	1 hole

Year	Winner	Runner-up	Venue	Result
1931	T. Creavy	D. Shute	Wannamoisett	2 and 1
1932	O. Dutra	F. Walsh	St Paul, Minnesota	4 and 3
1933	G. Sarazen	W. Goggin	Milwaukee	5 and 4
1934	P. Runyan	C. Wood	Buffalo	38th hole
1935	J. Revolta	T.D. Armour	Oklahoma	5 and 4
1936	D. Shute	J. Thomson	Pinehurst	3 and 2
1937	D. Shute	H. McSpaden	Pittsburgh	38th hole
1938	P. Runyan	S. Snead	Shawnee	8 and 7
1939	H. Picard	B. Nelson	Pomonok	37th hole
1940	B. Nelson	S. Snead	Hershey, Pennsylvania	1 hole
1941	V. Ghezzie	B. Nelson	Denver, Colorado	38th hole
1942	S. Snead	J. Turnesa	Atlantic City	2 and 1
1943	*No Championship*			
1944	R. Hamilton	B. Nelson	Spokane, Washington	1 hole
1945	B. Nelson	S. Byrd	Dayton, Ohio	4 and 3
1946	B. Hogan	E. Oliver	Portland	6 and 4
1947	J. Ferrier	C. Harbert	Detroit	2 and 1
1948	B. Hogan	M. Turnesa	Norwood Hills	7 and 6
1949	S. Snead	J. Palmer	Richmond, Virginia	3 and 2
1950	C. Harper	H. Williams	Scioto, Ohio	4 and 3
1951	S. Snead	W. Burkemo	Oakmont, Pennsylvania	7 and 6
1952	J. Turnesa	C. Harbert	Big Spring, Louisville	1 hole
1953	W. Burkemo	F. Lorza	Birmingham, Michigan	2 and 1
1954	C. Harbert	W. Burkemo	St Paul, Minnesota	4 and 3
1955	D. Ford	C. Middlecoff	Detroit	4 and 3
1956	J. Burke	T. Kroll	Boston	3 and 2
1957	L. Hebert	D. Finsterwald	Miami Valley, Dayton	3 and 1
1958*	D. Finsterwald	W. Casper	Havertown, Pennsylvania	276
1959	B. Rosburg	J. Barber	Minneapolis	277
1960	J. Herbert	J. Ferrier	Akron, Ohio	281
1961	J. Barber	D. January	Olympia Fields	277
1962	G.J. Player, SA	R. Goalby	Newtown Square	278
1963	J.W. Nicklaus	D. Ragan	Dallas, Texas	279
1964	R. Nichols	A.D. Palmer and J.W. Nicklaus	Columbus, Ohio	271
1965	D. Marr	W. Casper and J.W. Nicklaus	Ligonier, Pennsylvania	280
1966	A. Geiberger	D. Wysong	Akron, Ohio	280
1967	D. January	D. Massengale	Denver, Colorado	281
1968	J. Boros	A.D. Palmer and R.J. Charles	San Antonio	281
1969	R. Floyd	G.J. Player	Dayton, Ohio	276
1970	D. Stockton	A.D. Palmer and B. Murphy	Tulsa, Oklahoma	279
1971	J. Nicklaus	W. Casper	Palm Beach, Florida	281
1972	G.J. Player, SA	T. Aaron and J. Jamieson	Birmingham, Michigan	281
1973	J.W. Nicklaus	B. Crampton	Canterbury, Cleveland	277
1974	L. Trevino	J. Nicklaus	Tanglewood, Winston Salem	276
1975	J.W. Nicklaus	B. Crampton	Akron, Ohio	276
1976	D. Stockton	R. Floyd and D. January	Congressional, Bethesda, Maryland	281
1977	L. Wadkins	G. Littler	Pebble Beach, California	282
1978	J. Mahaffey	J. Pate and T. Watson	Oakmont, Pennsylvania	276
1979	D. Graham, AUS	B. Crenshaw	Oakland Hills	272

* From 1958, decided by stroke play.

CANADIAN OPEN CHAMPIONSHIP
Instituted 1904   Winners since 1945

Year	Winner	Club	Venue	Score
1945	B. Nelson	Toledo	Toronto	280
1946	G. Fazio	Los Angeles, Ca.	Montreal	278
1947	A.D. Locke	SA	Toronto	268
1948	C. Congdon	Tacoma, Washington	Vancouver, British Columbia	280
1949	E.J. Harrison	Little Rock, Arkansas	Toronto	271
1950	J. Ferrier	San Francisco	Montreal	271
1951	J. Ferrier	San Francisco	Toronto	273
1952	J. Palmer	Badin, NC	Saint Charles	263
1953	D. Douglas	Newark (Delaware)	Toronto	273
1954	P. Fletcher	Saskatoon	Vancouver	280
1955	A.D. Palmer	Latrobe, Pa.	Toronto	265
1956	Mr D. Sanders	Cedartown, Ga.	Quebec	273
1957	G. Bayer	California	Kitchener	271
1958	W. Ellis, Jr	Ridgewood, NJ	Edmonton	267
1959	D. Ford	Paradise, Fla.	Montreal	276
1960	A. Wall	USA	Toronto	269
1961	J. Cupit	Texas, USA	Winnipeg	270
1962	E. Kroll	USA	Montreal	278
1963	D. Ford	USA	Toronto	280
1964	K.D.G. Nagle	AUS	Montreal	277
1965	G. Littler	USA	Toronto	273
1966	D. Massengale	USA	Vancouver	280
1967	W. Casper	USA	Montreal	279
1968	R.J. Charles	NZ	Toronto	274
1969	T. Aaron	USA	Montreal	275
1970	K. Zarley	USA	London, Ontario	279
1971	L. Trevino	USA	Montreal	275
1972	G. Brewer	USA	Ridgeway, Ontario	275
1973	T. Weiskopf	USA	Montreal	278
1974	R. Nichols	USA	Mississaugua, Ontario	270
1975	T. Weiskopf	USA	Montreal	274
1976	J. Pate	USA	Windsor, Ontario	267
1977	L. Trevino	USA	Oakville, Ontario	280
1978	B. Lietzke	USA	Oakville, Ontario	283
1979	L. Trevino	USA	Oakville, Ontario	281

AUSTRALIAN OPEN CHAMPIONSHIP
Instituted 1904   Winners since 1946

Year	Winner	Club	Venue	Score
1946	H.O. Pickworth	Manly	Royal Sydney	289
1947	H.O. Pickworth	Victoria	Brisbane	285
1948	H.O. Pickworth	Royal Melbourne	Melbourne	289
1949	E. Cremin	Unattached	Australian	287
1950	N.G. Von Nida	Sydney	Kooyonga	286
1951	P.W. Thomson	Riversdale	Metropolitan	283
1952	N.G. Von Nida	Royal Sydney	Lake Karrinyup	278
1953	N.G. Von Nida	New South Wales	Melbourne	278
1954	H.O. Pickworth	Royal Melbourne	Kooyonga	280
1955	A.D. Locke	SA	Gailes	290
1956	B. Crampton	Sydney	Royal Sydney	289
1957	F. Phillips	Sydney	Melbourne	287
1958	G.J. Player	SA	Adelaide	271
1959	K.D.G. Nagle	Unattached	Australian	284
1960	B.J. Devlin	The Lakes	Lake Karrinyup	282

Year	Winner		Venue	Score
1961	F. Phillips	Pymble	Royal Melbourne	275
1962	G.J. Player	SA	Adelaide	281
1963	G.J. Player	SA	Melbourne	278
1964	J.W. Nicklaus	USA	Royal Sydney	287
1965	G.J. Player	SA	Adelaide	264
1966	A.D. Palmer	USA	Royal Queensland	276
1967	P.W. Thomson	AUS	Commonwealth	281
1968	J.W. Nicklaus	USA	Lake Karrinyup	270
1969	G.J. Player	SA	Royal Sydney	288
1970	G.J. Player	SA	Melbourne	280
1971	J.W. Nicklaus	USA	Royal Hobart	269
1972	P.W. Thomson	AUS	Kooyonga	281
1973	J.C. Snead	USA	Royal Queensland	280
1974	G.J. Player	SA	Lake Karrinyup	277
1975	J.W. Nicklaus	USA	Australian	282
1976	J.W. Nicklaus	USA	Australian	286
1977	D. Graham	AUS	Australian	284
1978	J.W. Nicklaus	USA	Australian	284
1979	J. Newton	AUS	Metropolitan, Melbourne	288

SOUTH AFRICAN OPEN CHAMPIONSHIP
Instituted 1930   Winners since 1946

Year	Winner	Club	Venue	Score
1946	A.D. Locke	Unattached	Royal Johannesburg	285
1947	Mr R.W. Glennie	Rondebosch	Mowbray, Cape Town	293
1948	Mr M. Janks	Houghton	East London	298
1949	S.F. Brews	Houghton	Maccauvlei	291
1950	A.D. Locke	Ohenimuri	Durban	287
1951	A.D. Locke	Ohenimuri	Houghton	275
1952	S.F. Brews	Houghton	Humewood	300
1953	J.R. Boyd	East Rand	Royal Cape	302
1954	R.C. Taylor	Kensington	East London	289
1955	A.D. Locke	Unattached	Zwartkop	283
1956	G.J. Player	Killarney	Durban	286
1957	H. Henning	Johannesburg	Humewood	289
1958	Mr A.A. Stewart	Randfontein Estates	Blomfontein	281
1959	Mr D. Hutchinson	E. Rand Prop. Mines	Johannesbrg	282
1960	G.J. Player	Killarney	Mowbray	288
1961	R. Waltman	Springs CC	East London	289
1962	H.R. Henning	SA	Johannesburg	285
1963	R. Waltman	Springs CC	Durban	281
1964	A. Henning	SA	Bloemfontein	278
1965	G.J. Player	SA	Cape Town	273
1966	G.J. Player	SA	Johannesburg	274
1967	G.J. Player	SA	East London	279
1968	G.J. Player	SA	Houghton	278
1969	G.J. Player	SA	Durban	273
1970	T. Horton	GB	Royal Durban	285
1971	S. Hobday	RH	Mowbray, Cape Town	276
1972	G.J. Player	SA	Royal Johannesburg	274
1973	R.J. Charles	NZ	Durban	282
1974	R. Cole	SA	Royal Johannesburg	272
1975	G.J. Player	SA	Mowbray, Cape Town	278
1976*	D. Hayes	SA	Houghton	287
1976*	G.J. Player	SA	Durban	280
1977	G.J. Player	SA	Royal Johannesburg	273
1978	H. Baiocchi	SA	Mowbray, Cape Town	285
1979	G. J. Player	SA	Houghton, Johannesburg	279

The South African Open Championship was played twice in 1976 – in January and December – due to a change in the domestic circuit calendar.

THE AMATEUR CHAMPIONSHIP

Year	Winner	Runner-up	Venue	Result
1885	A.F. MacFie	H.G. Hutchinson	Hoylake	7 and 6
1886	H.G. Hutchinson	H. Lamb	St Andrews	7 and 6
1887	H.G. Hutchinson	J. Ball	Hoylake	1 hole
1888	J. Ball	J.E. Laidlay	Prestwick	5 and 4
1889	J.E. Laidlay	L.M.B. Melville	St Andrews	2 and 1
1890	J. Ball	J.E. Laidlay	Hoylake	4 and 3
1891	J.E. Laidlay	H.H. Hilton	St Andrews	20th hole
1892	J. Ball	H.H. Hilton	Sandwich	3 and 1
1893	P. Anderson	J.E. Laidlay	Prestwick	1 hole
1894	John Ball	S.M. Fergusson	Hoylake	1 hole
1895	L.M.B. Melville	John Ball	St Andrews	19th hole
1896*	F.G. Tait	H.H. Hilton	Sandwich	8 and 7
1897	A.J.T. Allan	James Robb	Muirfield	4 and 2
1898	F.G. Tait	S.M. Fergusson	Hoylake	7 and 5
1899	J. Ball	F.G. Tait	Prestwick	37th hole
1900	H.H. Hilton	J. Robb	Sandwich	8 and 7
1901	H.H. Hilton	J.L. Low	St Andrews	1 hole
1902	C. Hutchings	S.H. Fry	Hoylake	1 hole
1903	R. Maxwell	H.G. Hutchinson	Muirfield	7 and 5
1904	W.J. Travis, USA	E. Blackwell	Sandwich	4 and 3
1905	A.G. Barry	Hon. O. Scott	Prestwick	3 and 2
1906	J. Robb	C.C. Lingen	Hoylake	4 and 3
1907	J. Ball	C.A. Palmer	St Andrews	6 and 4
1908	E.A. Lassen	H.E. Taylor	Sandwich	7 and 6
1909	R. Maxwell	Capt. C.K. Hutchison	Muirfield	1 hole
1910	J. Ball	C. Aylmer	Hoylake	10 and 9
1911	H.H. Hilton	E.A. Lassen	Prestwick	4 and 3
1912	J. Ball	A. Mitchell	Westward Ho!	38th hole
1913	H.H. Hilton	R. Harris	St Andrews	6 and 5
1914	J.L.C. Jenkins	C.O. Hezlet	Sandwich	3 and 2
1915–19	*No Championship*			
1920	C.J.H. Tolley	R.A. Gardner, USA	Muirfield	37th hole
1921	W.I. Hunter	A.J. Graham	Hoylake	12 and 11
1922	E.W.E. Holderness	J. Caven	Prestwick	1 hole
1923	R.H. Wethered	R. Harris	Deal	7 and 6
1924	E.W.E. Holderness	E.F. Storey	St Andrews	3 and 2
1925	R. Harris	K.F. Fradgley	Westward Ho!	13 and 12
1926	J. Sweetser, USA	A.F. Simpson	Muirfield	6 and 5
1927	Dr W. Tweddell	D.E. Landale	Hoylake	7 and 6
1928	T.P. Perkins	R.H. Wethered	Prestwick	6 and 4
1929	C.J.H. Tolley	J.N. Smith	Sandwich	4 and 3
1930	R.T. Jones, USA	R.H. Wethered	St Andrews	7 and 6
1931	E. Martin Smith	J. De Forest	Westward Ho!	1 hole
1932	J. De Forest	E.W. Fiddian	Muirfield	3 and 1
1933	Hon. M. Scott	T.A. Bourn	Hoylake	4 and 3
1934	W. Lawson Little, USA	J. Wallace	Prestwick	14 and 13
1935	W. Lawson Little, USA	Dr W. Tweddell	Royal Lytham & St Annes	1 hole
1936	H. Thomson	J. Ferrier, AUS	St Andrews	2 holes
1937	R. Sweeny Jr, USA	L.O. Munn	Sandwich	3 and 2
1938	C.R. Yates, USA	R.C. Ewing	Troon	3 and 2
1939	A.T. Kyle	A.A. Duncan	Hoylake	2 and 1
1940–45	*No Championship*			
1946	J. Bruen	R. Sweeney, USA	Birkdale	4 and 3
1947	W.P. Turnesa, USA	R.D. Chapman, USA	Carnoustie	3 and 2
1948	F.R. Stranahan, USA	C. Stowe	Sandwich	5 and 4
1949	S.M. McCready	W.P. Turnesa, USA	Portmarnock	2 and 1
1950	F.R. Stranahan, USA	R.D. Chapman, USA	St Andrews	8 and 6
1951	R.D. Chapman, USA	C.R. Coe, USA	Porthcawl	5 and 4
1952	E. Harvie Ward, USA	F.R. Stranahan, USA	Prestwick	6 and 5
1953	J.B. Carr	E. Harvie Ward, USA	Hoylake	2 holes
1954	D.W. Bachli, AUS	W.C. Campbell, USA	Muirfield	2 and 1

Year	Winner	Runner-up	Venue	Result
1955	J.W. Conrad, USA	A. Slater	Royal Lytham & St Annes	3 and 2
1956†	J.C. Beharrell	L.G. Taylor	Troon	5 and 4
1957†	R. Reid Jack	H.B. Ridgley, USA	Formby	2 and 1
1958‡	J.B. Carr	A. Thirlwell	St Andrews	3 and 2
1959	D.R. Beman, USA	W. Hyndman, USA	Sandwich	3 and 2
1960	J.B. Carr	R. Cochran, USA	Portrush	8 and 7
1961	M.F. Bonallack	J. Walker	Turnberry	6 and 4
1962	R.D. Davies, USA	J. Povall	Hoylake	1 hole
1963	M.S.R. Lunt	J.G. Blackwell	St Andrews	2 and 1
1964	G.J. Clark	M.S.R. Lunt	Ganton	39th hole
1965	M.F. Bonallack	C.A. Clark	Porthcawl	2 and 1
1966	R.E. Cole, SA	R.D.B.M. Shade	Carnoustie (18 holes)	3 and 2
1967	R.B. Dickson, USA	R.J. Cerrudo, USA	Formby	2 and 1
1968	M.F. Bonallack	J.B. Carr	Troon	7 and 6
1969	M.F. Bonallack	W. Hyndman, USA	Hoylake	3 and 2
1970	M.F. Bonallack	W. Hyndman, USA	Newcastle Co. Down	8 and 7
1971	S. Melnyk, USA	J. Simons, USA	Carnoustie	3 and 2
1972	T.W.B. Homer	A. Thirlwell	Royal St George's	4 and 3
1973	R. Siderowf, USA	P.H. Moody	Royal Porthcawl	5 and 3
1974	T.W.B. Homer	J. Gabrielson	Muirfield	2 holes
1975	M. Giles, USA	M. James	Hoylake	8 and 7
1976	D. Siderowf, USA	J.C. Davies	St Andrews	37th hole
1977	P. McEvoy	H.M. Campbell	Ganton	5 and 4
1978	P. McEvoy	P.J. McKellar	Royal Troon	4 and 3
1979	J. Sigel, USA	S. Hoch, USA	Hillside	3 and 2

* *Thirty-six holes played on and after this date.*
† *In 1956 and 1957 the Quarter-Finals, Semi-Finals and Final were played over 36 holes.*
‡ *In 1958 Semi-Finals and Final only were played over 36 holes.*

ENGLISH AMATEUR CHAMPIONSHIP

Year	Winner	Runner-up	Venue	Result
1925	T.F. Ellison	S. Robinson	Hoylake	1 hole
1926	T.F. Ellison	Sq. Ldr. C.H. Hayward	Walton Heath	6 and 4
1927	T.P. Perkins	J.B. Beddard	Little Aston	2 and 1
1928	J.A. Stout	T.P. Perkins	Royal Lytham & St Annes	3 and 2
1929	W. Sutton	E.B. Tipping	Northumberland	3 and 2
1930	T.A. Bourn	C.E. Hardman	Burnham	3 and 2
1931	L.G. Crawley	W. Sutton	Hunstanton	1 hole
1932	E.W. Fiddian	A.S. Bradshaw	Royal St George's	1 hole
1933	J. Woollam	T.A. Bourn	Ganton	4 and 3
1934	S. Lunt	L.G. Crawley	Formby	27th hole
1935	J. Woollam	E.W. Fiddian	Hollinwell	2 and 1
1936	H.G. Bentley	J.D.A. Langley	Deal	5 and 4
1937	J.J. Pennink	L.G. Crawley	Saunton	6 and 5
1938	J.J. Pennink	S.E. Banks	Moortown	2 and 1
1939	A.L. Bentley	W. Sutton	Royal Birkdale	5 and 4
1940–45	*No Championship*			
1946	I.R. Patey	K. Thom	Royal Mid-Surrey	5 and 4
1947	G.H. Micklem	C. Stowe	Ganton	1 hole
1948	A.G.B. Helm	H.J. Roberts	Little Aston	2 and 1
1949	R.J. White	C. Stowe	Formby	5 and 4
1950	J.D.A. Langley	I.R. Patey	Deal	1 hole
1951	G.P. Roberts	H. Bennett	Hunstanton	39th hole
1952	E. Millward	T.J. Shorrock	Burnham and Berrow	2 holes
1953	G.H. Micklem	R.J. White	Royal Birkdale	2 and 1
1954	A. Thirlwell	H.G. Bentley	Royal St George's	2 and 1
1955	A. Thirlwell	M. Burgess	Ganton	7 and 6
1956	G.B. Wolstenholme	H. Bennett	Royal Lytham & St Annes	1 hole
1957	A. Walker	G. Whitehad	Royal Liverpool	4 and 3
1958	D.N. Sewell	D.A. Procter	Walton Heath	8 and 7

Year	Winner	Runner-up	Venue	Result
1959	G.B. Wolstenholme	M.F. Bonallack	Formby	1 hole
1960	D.N. Sewell	M.J. Christmas	Hunstanton	41st hole
1961	I. Caldwell	G. Clark	Wentworth	37th hole
1962	M.F. Bonallack	M.S.R. Lunt	Moortown	2 and 1
1963	M.F. Bonallack	A. Thirlwell	Burnham and Berrow	4 and 3
1964	Dr D. Marsh	R. Foster	Hollinwell	1 hole
1965	M.F. Bonallack	C. Clark	Berkshire	3 and 2
1966	M.S.R. Lunt	D.J. Millensted	Royal Lytham & St Annes	3 and 2
1967	M.F. Bonallack	G.E. Hyde	Woodhall Spa	4 and 2
1968	M.F. Bonallack	P.D. Kelly	Ganton	12 and 11
1969	J.H. Cook	P. Dawson	Royal St George's	6 and 4
1970	Dr D. Marsh	S.G. Birtwell	Royal Birkdale	6 and 4
1971	W. Humphreys	J. Davies	Burnham and Berrow	9 and 8
1972	H. Ashby	R. Revell	High Gosforth Park	5 and 4
1973	H. Ashby	J.C. Mason	Formby	5 and 4
1974	M. James	J.A. Watts	Woodhall Spa	6 and 5
1975	N. Faldo	D.J. Eccleston	Royal Lytham & St Annes	6 and 4
1976	P. Deeble	J.C. Davies	Ganton	3 and 1
1977	T.R. Shingler	J.M. Mayell	Walton Heath	4 and 3
1978	P. Downes	P.G. Hoad	Royal Birkdale	1 hole
1979	R. Chapman	A. Carman	Royal St. George's	6 and 5

SCOTTISH AMATEUR CHAMPIONSHIP

Year	Winner	Runner-up	Venue	Result
1922	J. Wilson	E. Blackwell	St Andrews	19th hole
1923	T.M. Burrell	Dr A.R. M'Callum	Troon	1 hole
1924	W.W. Mackenzie	W. Tulloch	Royal Aberdeen	3 and 2
1925	J.T. Dobson	W.W. Makenzie	Muirfield	3 and 2
1926	W.J. Guild	S.O. Shepherd	Leven	2 and 1
1927	A. Jamieson Jr	Rev D.S. Rutherford	Gailes	22nd hole
1928	W.W. Mackenzie	W.E. Dodds	Muirfield	5 and 3
1929	J.T. Bookless	J.E. Dawson	Royal Aberdeen	5 and 4
1930	K. Greig	T. Wallace	Carnoustie	9 and 8
1931	J. Wilson	A. Jamieson Jr	Prestwick	2 and 1
1932	J. McLean	K. Greig	Dunbar	5 and 4
1933	J. McLean	K.C. Forbes	Aberdeen	6 and 4
1934	J. McLean	W. Campbell	Western Gailes	3 and 1
1935	H. Thomson	J. McLean	St Andrews	2 and 1
1936	E.D. Hamilton	R. Neill	Carnoustie	1 hole
1937	H. McInally	K.G. Patrick	Barassie	6 and 5
1938	E.D. Hamilton	E. Rutherford	Muirfield	4 and 2
1939	H. McInally	H. Thomson	Prestwick	6 and 5
1940–45	*No Championship*			
1946	E.C. Brown	R. Rutherford	Carnoustie	3 and 2
1947	H. McInally	J. Pressley	Glasgow Gailes	10 and 8
1948	A.S. Flockhart	G.N. Taylor	Royal Aberdeen	7 and 6
1949	R. Wight	H. McInally	Muirfield	1 hole
1950	W.C. Gibson	D.A. Blair	Prestwick	2 and 1
1951	J.M. Dykes	J.C. Wilson	St Andrews	4 and 2
1952	F.G. Dewar	J.C. Wilson	Carnoustie	4 and 3
1953	D.A. Blair	J.W. McKay	Western Gailes	3 and 1
1954	J.W. Draper	W.G.H. Gray	Nairn	4 and 3
1955	R.R. Jack	A.C. Miller	Muirfield	2 and 1
1956	Dr F.W.G. Deighton	A. MacGregor	Old Troon	8 and 7
1957	J.S. Montgomerie	J. Burnside	Royal Aberdeen	2 and 1
1958	W.D. Smith	J.R. Harris	Prestwick	6 and 5
1959	Dr F.W.G. Deighton	R.M.K. Murray	St Andrews	6 and 5
1960	J.R. Young	S. Saddler	Carnoustie	5 and 3
1961	J. Walker	S.W.T. Murray	Western Gailes	4 and 3

Year	Winner	Runner-up	Venue	Result
1962	S.W.T. Murray	R.D.B.M. Shade	Muirfield	2 and 1
1963	R.D.B.M. Shade	N. Henderson	Troon	4 and 3
1964	R.D.B.M. Shade	J. McBeath	Nairn	8 and 7
1965	R.D.B.M. Shade	G.B. Cosh	St Andrews	4 and 2
1966	R.D.B.M. Shade	C. Strachan	Western Gailes	9 and 8
1967	R.D.B.M. Shade	A. Murphy	Carnoustie	5 and 4
1968	G.B. Cosh	R.L. Renfrew	Muirfield	4 and 3
1969	J.M. Cannon	A.H. Hall	Troon	6 and 4
1970	C.W. Green	H.B. Stuart	Royal Aberdeen	1 hole
1971	S. Stephen	C.W. Green	St Andrews	3 and 2
1972	H.B. Stuart	A.K. Pirie	Prestwick	3 and 1
1973	I. Hutcheon	A. Brodie	Carnoustie	3 and 2
1974	G.H. Murray	A.K. Pirie	Western Gailes	2 and 1
1975	D.G. Greig	G.H. Murray	Montrose	7 and 6
1976	G.H. Murray	H.B. Stuart	St Andrews	6 and 5
1977	A. Brodie	P.J. McKellar	Troon	1 hole
1978	I. Carslaw	J. Cuddihy	Downfield	7 and 6
1979	K. Macintosh	P.J. McKellar	Prestwick	5 and 4

WELSH AMATEUR CHAMPIONSHIP

Instituted 1895   Finalists since 1930

Year	Winner	Runner-up	Venue	Result
1930	H.R. Howell	D.R. Lewis	Tenby	2 and 1
1931	H.R. Howell	W.G. Morgan	Aberdovey	7 and 6
1932	H.R. Howell	H.E. Davies	Ashburnham	7 and 6
1933	J.L. Black	A.A. Duncan	Porthcawl	2 and 1
1934	S.B. Roberts	G.S. Noon	Prestatyn	4 and 3
1935	R. Chapman	G.S. Noon	Tenby	1 hole
1936	R.M. de Lloyd	G. Wallis	Aberdovey	1 hole
1937	D.H. Lewis	R. Glossop	Porthcawl	2 holes
1938	A.A. Duncan	S.B. Roberts	Rhyl	2 and 1
1939–45	*No Championship*			
1946	J.V. Moody	A. Marshman	Porthcawl	9 and 8
1947	S.B. Roberts	G. Breen Turner	Harlech	8 and 7
1948	A.A. Duncan	S.B. Roberts	Porthcawl	2 and 1
1949	A.D. Evans	Mervyn A. Jones	Aberdovey	2 and 1
1950	J.L. Morgan	D.J. Bonnell	Southerndown	9 and 7
1951	J.L. Morgan	W.I. Tucker	Harlech	3 and 2
1952	A.A. Duncan	J.L. Morgan	Ashburnham	4 and 3
1953	S.B. Roberts	D. Pearson	Prestatyn	5 and 3
1954	A.A. Duncan	K. Thomas	Tenby	6 and 5
1955	T.J. Davies	P. Dunn	Harlech	38th hole
1956	A. Lochley	W.I. Tucker	Southerndown	2 and 1
1957	E.S. Mills	H. Griffiths	Harlech	2 and 1
1958	H.C. Squirrell	A.D. Lake	Conway	4 and 3
1959	H.C. Squirrell	N. Rees	Porthcawl	8 and 7
1960	H.C. Squirrell	P. Richards	Aberdovey	2 and 1
1961	A.D. Evans	J. Toye	Ashburnham	3 and 2
1962	J. Povall	H.C. Squirrell	Royal St David's	3 and 2
1963	W.I. Tucker	J. Povall	Southerndown	4 and 3
1964	H.C. Squirrell	W.I. Tucker	Royal St David's	1 hole
1965	H.C. Squirrell	G. Clay	Royal Porthcawl	6 and 4
1966	W.I. Tucker	E.N. Davies	Aberdovey	6 and 5
1967	J.K. Povall	W.I. Tucker	Ashburnham	3 and 2
1968	J. Buckley	J. Povall	Conway	8 and 7
1969	J.I. Toye	E.N. Davies	Royal Porthcawl	1 hole
1970	E.N. Davies	J. Povall	Royal St David's	1 hole
1971	C.T. Brown	H.C. Squirrell	Southerndown	6 and 5
1972	E.N. Davies	J.L. Toye	Prestatyn	40th hole

Year	Winner	Runner-up	Venue	Result
1973	D. McLean	T. Holder	Ashburnham	6 and 4
1974	S. Cox	E.N. Davies	Caernarvonshire	3 and 2
1975	J.L. Toye	W.I. Tucker	Royal Porthcawl	5 and 4
1976	M.P.D. Adams	W.I. Tucker	Royal St David's	6 and 5
1977	D. Stevens	J. Povall	Southerndown	3 and 2
1978	D. McLean	A. Ingram	Caernarvonshire	11 and 10
1979	T.J. Melia	M. Roper	Ashburnham	5 and 4

IRISH AMATEUR CHAMPIONSHIP

Instituted 1893   Finalists since 1930

Year	Winner	Runner-up	Venue	Result
1930	J. Burke	F.P. McConnell	Lahinch	6 and 5
1931	J. Burke	F.P. McConnell	Rosses Point	6 and 4
1932	J. Burke	M. Crowley	Royal Portrush	6 and 5
1933	J. Burke	G.T. M'Mullan	Cork	3 and 2
1934	J.C. Brown	R. McConnell	Rosslare	6 and 5
1935	R. McConnell	J. Burke	Galway	2 and 1
1936	J. Burke	R. McConnell	Castlerock	7 and 6
1937	J. Bruen, Jr	J. Burke	Ballybunion	3 and 2
1938	J. Bruen, Jr	R. Simcox	Rathfarnham Castle	3 and 2
1939	G.H. Owens	R.M. McConnell	Rosses Point	6 and 5
1940	J. Burke	W.M. O'Sulliyan	Dollymount	4 and 3
1941–45	*No Championship*			
1946	J. Burke	R.C. Ewing	Dollymount	2 and 1
1947	J. Burke	J. Fitzsimmons	Lahinch	2 holes
1948	R.C. Ewing	B.J. Scannell	Royal Portrush	3 and 2
1949	J. Carroll	Pat Murphy	Galway	4 and 3
1950	B. Herlihy	B.C. McManus	Baltray	4 and 3
1951	M. Power	J.B. Carr	Cork	3 and 2
1952	T.W. Egan	J.C. Brown	Royal Belfast	41st hole
1953	J. Malone	M. Power	Rosses Point	2 and 1
1954	J.B. Carr	I. Forsythe	Carlow	4 and 3
1955	Dr James Mahon	G. Crosbie	Lahinch	3 and 2
1956	G. Love	G. Crosbie	Malone	37th hole
1957	J.B. Carr	G. Crosbie	Galway	2 holes
1958	R.C. Ewing	G.A. Young	Ballybunion	5 and 3
1959	T. Craddock	J.B. Carr	Portmarnock	38th hole
1960	M. Edwards	N. Fogarty	Portstewart	6 and 5
1961	D. Sheahan	J. Brown	Rosses Point	5 and 4
1962	M, Edwards	J. Harrington	Baltray	42nd hole
1963	J.B. Carr	E.C. O'Brien	Killarney	2 and 1
1964	J.B. Carr	A. McDade	Royal Co. Down	6 and 5
1965	J.B. Carr	T. Craddock	Rosses Point	3 and 2
1966	D. Sheahan	J. Faith	Dollymount	3 and 2
1967	J.B. Carr	P.D. Flaherty	Lahinch	1 hole
1968	M. O'Brien	F. McCarroll	Royal Portrush	2 and 1
1969	V. Nevin	J. O'Leary	Co. Sligo	1 hole
1970	D.B. Sheahan	M. Bloom	Grange	2 holes
1971	R. Kane	M. O'Brien	Ballybunion	3 and 2
1972	K. Stevenson	B. Hoey	Royal Co. Down	2 and 1
1973	R.K.M. Pollin	R.M. Staunton	Rosses Point	1 hole
1974	R.M. Kane	M. Gannon	Portmarnock	5 and 4
1975	M.D. O'Brien	J.A. Bryan	Cork	5 and 4
1976	D. Branigan	D. O'Sullivan	Royal Portrush	2 holes
1977	M. Gannon	A. Hayes	Westport	19th hole
1978	M. Morris	T. Cleary	Carlow	1 hole
1979	J. Harrington	M. Gannon	Ballybunion	2 and 1

BRITISH WOMEN'S CHAMPIONSHIP

Year	Winner	Runner-up	Venue	Result
1893	Lady M. Scott	Miss I. Pearson	St Annes	7 and 5
1894	Lady M. Scott	Miss I. Pearson	Littlestone	3 and 2
1895	Lady M. Scott	Miss E. Lythgoe	Royal Portrush	5 and 4
1896	Miss Pascoe	Miss L. Thomson	Hoylake	3 and 2
1897	Miss E.C. Orr	Miss Orr	Gullane	4 and 2
1898	Miss L. Thomson	Miss E.C. Neville	Yarmouth	7 and 5
1899	Miss M. Hezlet	Miss Magill	Newcastle, Co. Down	2 and 1
1900	Miss Adair	Miss Neville	Westward Ho!	6 and 5
1901	Miss Graham	Miss Adair	Aberdovey	3 and 1
1902	Miss M. Hezlet	Miss E. Neville	Deal	19th hole
1903	Miss Adair	Miss F. Walker-Leigh	Royal Portrush	4 and 3
1904	Miss L. Dod	Miss M. Hezlet	Troon	1 hole
1905	Miss B. Thompson	Miss M.E. Stuart	Cromer	3 and 2
1906	Mrs Kennion	Miss B. Thompson	Burnham	4 and 3
1907	Miss M. Hezlet	Miss F. Hezlet	Newcastle, Co. Down	2 and 1
1908	Miss M. Titterton	Miss D. Campbell	St Andrews	19th hole
1909	Miss D. Campbell	Miss F. Hezlet	Royal Birkdale	4 and 3
1910	Miss Grant Suttie	Miss L. Moore	Westward Ho!	6 and 4
1911	Miss D. Campbell	Miss V. Hezlet	Royal Portrush	3 and 2
1912	Miss G. Ravenscroft	Miss S. Temple	Turnberry	3 and 2

Final played over 36 holes after 1912

1913	Miss M. Dodd	Miss Chubb	St Annes	8 and 6
1914	Miss C. Leitch	Miss G. Ravenscroft	Hunstanton	2 and 1
1915–19	*No Championship*			
1920	Miss C. Leitch	Miss M. Griffiths	Newcastle, Co. Down	7 and 6
1921	Miss C. Leitch	Miss J. Wethered	Turnberry	4 and 3
1922	Miss J. Wethered	Miss C. Leitch	Princes, Sandwich	9 and 7
1923	Miss D. Chambers	Mrs A. Macbeth	Burnham, Somerset	2 holes
1924	Miss J. Wethered	Mrs Cautley	Royal Portrush	7 and 6
1925	Miss J. Wethered	Miss C. Leitch	Troon	37th hole
1926	Miss C. Leitch	Mrs Garon	Harlech	8 and 7
1927	Mlle T. de la Chaume, F	Miss Pearson	Newcastle, Co. Down	5 and 4
1928	Mlle N. Le Blan, F	Miss S. Marshall	Hunstanton	3 and 2
1929	Miss J. Wethered	Miss G. Collett	St Andrews	3 and 1
1930	Miss D. Fishwick	Miss G. Collett	Formby	4 and 3
1931	Miss E. Wilson	Miss W. Morgan	Portmarnock	7 and 6
1932	Miss E. Wilson	Miss C.P.R. Montgomery	Saunton	7 and 6
1933	Miss E. Wilson	Miss D. Plumpton	Gleneagles	5 and 4
1934	Mrs A.M. Holm	Miss P. Barton	Royal Porthcawl	6 and 5
1935	Miss W. Morgan	Miss P. Barton	Newcastle. Co. Down	3 and 2
1936	Miss P. Barton	Miss B. Newell	Southport & Ainsdale	5 and 3
1937	Miss J. Anderson	Miss E. Park	Turnberry	6 and 4
1938	Mrs A.M. Holm	Miss E. Corlett	Burnham	4 and 3
1939	Miss P. Barton	Mrs T. Marks	Royal Portrush	2 and 1
1940–45	*No Championship*			
1946	Mrs G.W. Hetherington	Miss P. Garvey	Hunstanton	1 hole
1947	Mrs G. Zaharias, USA	Miss J. Gordon	Gullane	5 and 4
1948	Miss L. Suggs, USA	Miss J. Donald	Royal Lytham	1 hole
1949	Miss F. Stephens	Mrs V. Reddan	Harlech	5 and 4
1950	Vicomtesse de Saint Sauveur, F	Mrs G. Valentine	Newcastle, Co. Down	3 and 2
1951	Mrs P.G. MacCann	Miss F. Stephens	Broadstone	4 and 3
1952	Miss M. Paterson	Miss F. Stephens	Troon	38th hole
1953	Miss M. Stewart, C	Miss P. Garvey	Royal Porthcawl	7 and 6
1954	Miss F. Stephens	Miss E. Price	Ganton	4 and 3
1955	Mrs G. Valentine	Miss B. Romack	Royal Portrush	7 and 6
1956	Miss M. Smith, USA	Miss M.P. Jansen	Sunningdale	8 and 7
1957	Miss P. Garvey	Mrs G. Valentine	Gleneagles	4 and 3
1958	Mrs G. Valentine	Miss E. Price	Hunstanton	1 hole
1959	Miss E. Price	Miss B. McCorkindale	Berkshire	37th hole
1960	Miss B. McIntire, USA	Miss P. Garvey	Harlech	4 and 2

Year	Winner	Runner-up	Venue	Result
1961	Mrs A.D. Spearman	Miss D.J. Robb	Carnoustie	7 and 6
1962	Mrs A.D. Spearman	Mrs M.F. Bonallack	Royal Birkdale	1 hole
1963	Mlle B. Varangot, F	Miss P. Garvey	Newcastle, Co. Down	3 and 1
1964	Miss C. Sorenson, USA	Miss B.A.B. Jackson	Prince's, Sandwich	37th hole
1965	Mlle B. Varangot, F	Mrs I. Robertson	St Andrews	4 and 3
1966	Miss E. Chadwick	Miss V. Saunders	Ganton	3 and 2
1967	Miss E. Chadwick	Miss M. Everard	Harlech	1 hole
1968	Mlle B. Varangot, F	Mrs C. Rubin, F	Walton Heath	20th hole
1969	Mlle C. Lacoste, F	Miss A. Irvin	Royal Portrush	1 hole
1970	Miss D. Oxley	Mrs I.C. Robertson	Gullane	1 hole
1971	Miss M. Walker	Miss B. Huke	Alwoodley	3 and 1
1972	Miss M. Walker	Mrs C. Rubin, F	Hunstanton	2 holes
1973	Miss A. Irvin	Miss M. Walker	Carnoustie	3 and 2
1974	Miss C. Semple	Mrs A. Bonallack	Royal Porthcawl	2 and 1
1975	Mrs N. Syms, USA	Miss S. Cadden	St Andrews	3 and 2
1976	Miss C. Panton	Miss A. Sheard, SA	Silloth	1 hole
1977	Mrs A. Uzielli	Miss V. Marvin	Hillside	6 and 5
1978	Miss E. Kennedy, AUS	Miss J. Greenhalgh	Hollinwell	1 hole
1979	Miss M. Madill	Miss J. Lock, AUS	Nairn	2 and 1

ENGLISH WOMEN'S CHAMPIONSHIP
Instituted 1912   Finalists since 1947

Year	Winner	Runner-up	Venue	Result
1947	Miss M. Wallis	Miss E. Price	Ganton	3 and 1
1948	Miss Frances Stephens	Mrs Zara Bolton	Hayling	1 hole
1949	Mrs A.C. Critchley	The Lady Katherine Cairns	Burnham	3 and 2
1950	Hon Mrs A. Gee	Miss Pamela Davies	Sheringham	8 and 6
1951	Miss J. Bisgood	Mrs A. Keiller	St Annes Old Links	2 and 1
1952	Miss Pamela Davies	Miss Jacqueline Gordon	Westward Ho!	6 and 5
1953	Miss J. Bisgood	Miss J. McIntyre	Prince's, Sandwich	6 and 5
1954	Miss Frances Stephens	Miss Elizabeth Price	Woodhall Spa	37th hole
1955	Mrs R. Smith Stephens	Miss E. Price	Moor Town	4 and 3
1956	Miss Bridget Jackson	Mrs Ruth Ferguson	Hunstanton	2 and 1
1957	Miss J. Bisgood	Miss M. Nichol	Bournemouth	10 and 8
1958	Mrs M.F. Bonallack	Miss Bridget Jackson	Formby	3 and 2
1959	Miss R. Porter	Mrs F. Smith	Aldeburgh	5 and 4
1960	Miss M. Nichol	Mrs M.F. Bonallack	Burnham	3 and 1
1961	Miss R. Porter	Mrs P. Reece	Littlestone	2 holes
1962	Miss J. Roberts	Mrs M.F. Bonallack	Woodhall Spa	3 and 1
1963	Mrs M.F. Bonallack	Miss E. Chadwick	Liphook	7 and 6
1964	Mrs A.D. Spearman	Miss M. Everard	Royal Lytham & St Annes	6 and 5
1965	Miss R. Porter	Miss G. Cheetham	Whittington Barracks	6 and 5
1966	Miss J. Greenhalgh	Mrs J.C. Holmes	Hayling Island	3 and 1
1967	Miss A. Irvin	Mrs A. Pickard	Alwoodley	3 and 2
1968	Mrs S. Barber	Miss D. Oxley	Hunstanton	5 and 4
1969	Miss B. Dixon	Miss M. Wenyon	Burnham and Berrow	6 and 4
1970	Miss D. Oxley	Mrs S. Barber	Rye	3 and 2
1971	Miss D. Oxley	Mrs S. Barber	Royal Liverpool	5 and 4
1972	Miss M. Everard	Mrs M.F. Bonallack	Woodhall Spa	2 and 1
1973	Miss M. Walker	Miss C. Le Feuvre	Broadstone	6 and 5
1974	Miss A. Irvin	Mrs J. Thornhill	Sunningdale	1 hole
1975	Miss B. Huke	Miss L. Harrold	Royal Birkdale	2 and 1
1976	Miss L. Harrold	Mrs A. Uzielli	Hollinwell	3 and 2
1977	Miss V. Marvin	Miss M. Everard	Burnham and Berrow	1 hole
1978	Miss V. Marvin	Miss R. Porter	West Sussex	2 and 1
1979	Miss J. Greenhalgh	Mrs S. Hedges	Royal Liverpool	2 and 1

ENGLISH AMATEUR OPEN STROKE-PLAY CHAMPIONSHIP

Year	Winner	Venue	Score
1957	D. Sewell	Moortown	287
1958	A.H. Perowne	Royal Birkdale	289
1959	D. Sewell	Hollinwell	300
1960	G.B. Wolstenholme	Ganton	286
1961	R.D.B.M. Shade	Hoylake	284
1962	A. Salter	Woodhall Spa	209
1963	R.D.B.M. Shade	Royal Birkdale	306
1964	M.F. Bonallack	Royal Cinque Ports	290
1965	C.A. Clark, D.J. Millensted and M.J. Burgess tied	Formby	289
1966	P.M. Townsend	Hunstanton	282
1967	R.D.B.M. Shade	Saunton	299
1968	M.F. Bonallack	Walton Heath	210
1969	R. Foster and M.F. Bonallack tied	Moortown	290
1970	R. Foster	Little Aston	287
1971	M.F. Bonallack	Hillside	294
1972	P.H. Moody	Royal Liverpool	296
1973	R. Revell	Hunstanton	294
1974	N. Sundelson	Moortown	291
1975	A.W.B. Lyle	Hollinwell	298
1976	P. Hedges	Saunton	294
1977	A.W.B. Lyle	Royal Liverpool	293
1978	G. Brand	Woodhall Spa	289
1979	D. Long	Little Aston	291

SCOTTISH AMATEUR OPEN STROKE-PLAY CHAMPIONSHIP

Year	Winner	Venue	Score
1967	B.J. Gallacher	Muirfield	291
1968	R.D.B.M. Shade	Prestwick	282
1969	J.S. Macdonald	Carnoustie	288
1970	D. Hayes	Glasgow Gailes	275
1971	I.C. Hutcheon	Leven	277
1972	B.N. Nicholson	Dalmahoy	290
1973	D.M. Robertson and G.J. Clark tied	Dunbar	284
1974	I.C. Hutcheon	Blairgowrie	283
1975	C.W. Green	Nairn	295
1976	S. Martin	Monifieth	283
1977	P.J. McKellar	Muirfield	299
1978	A.R. Taylor	Cawder	281
1979	I.C. Hutcheon	Blairgowrie	296

WELSH AMATEUR OPEN STROKE-PLAY CHAMPIONSHIP

Year	Winner	Venue	Score
1967	E.N. Davies	Royal St David's	295
1968	J.A. Buckley	Royal St David's	294
1969	D.L. Stevens	Tenby	288
1970	J.K. Povall	Newport	292
1971	E.N. Davies and J.L. Toye tied	Royal St David's	296
1972	J.R. Jones	Pyle and Kenfig	299
1973	J.R. Jones	Llandudno	300
1974	J.L. Toye	Tenby	307
1975	D. McLean	Wrexham	288

Year	Winner	Venue	Score
1976	W.I. Tucker	Newport	282
1977	J.A. Buckley	Prestatyn	302
1978	H.J. Evans	Pyle and Kenfig	300
1979	D. McLean	Holyhead	289

WALKER CUP

Year	Venue	Result			
1922	National Links, Long Island	USA	8	Britain	4
1923	St Andrews, Fife	Britain	5½	USA	6½
1924	Garden City, New York	USA	9	Britain	3
1926	St Andrews, Fife	Britain	5½	USA	6½
1928	Chicago Golf Club, Wheaton	USA	11	Britain	1
1930	Royal St George's, Sandwich	Britain	2	USA	10
1932	Brookline, Massachusetts	USA	9½	Britain	2½
1934	St Andrews, Fife	Britain	2½	USA	9½
1936	Pine Valley, New Jersey	USA	10½	Britain	1½
1938	St Andrews, Fife	Britain	7½	USA	4½
1947	St Andrews, Fife	Britain	4	USA	8
1949	Winged Foot, New York	USA	10	Britain	2
1951	Royal Birkdale, Lancashire	Britain	4½	USA	7½
1953	Kittansett, Marion	USA	9	Britain	3
1955	St Andrews, Fife	Britain	2	USA	10
1957	Minikahda, Minnesota	USA	8½	Britain	3½
1959	Muirfield, East Lothian	Britain	3	USA	9
1961	Seattle, Washington	USA	11	Britain	1
1963	Turnberry, Ayrshire	Britain	10	USA	14
1965	Baltimore, Maryland	USA	12	Britain	12
1967	Royal St George's, Sandwich	Britain	9	USA	15
1969	Milwaukee, Wisconsin	USA	13	Britain	11
1971	St Andrews, Fife	Britain	13	USA	11
1973	Brookline, Massachusetts	USA	14	Britain	10
1975	St Andrews, Fife	Britain	8½	USA	15½
1977	Shinnecock Hills, Long Island	USA	16	Britain	8
1979	Muirfield, East Lothian	Britain	8½	USA	15½

To date, USA 24 wins, Britain 2 wins, with 1 tie.

CURTIS CUP

Year	Venue	Result			
1932	Wentworth, Surrey	Britain	3½	USA	5½
1934	Chevy Chase, Maryland	USA	6½	Britain	2½
1936	Gleneagles, Perthshire	Britain	4½	USA	4½
1938	Essex Country Club, Massachusetts	USA	5½	Britain	3½
1948	Royal Birkdale, Lancashire	Britain	2½	USA	6½
1950	Buffalo, New York	USA	7½	Britain	1½
1952	Muirfield, East Lothian	Britain	5	USA	4
1954	Merion, Pennsylvania	USA	6	Britain	3
1956	Prince's, Sandwich, Kent	Britain	5	USA	4
1958	Brae Burn, Massachusetts	USA	4½	Britain	4½
1960	Lindrick, Yorkshire	Britain	2½	USA	6½
1962	Broadmoor, Colorado	USA	8	Britain	1
1964	Royal Porthcawl, Glamorganshire	Britain	7½	USA	10½
1966	Hot Springs, Virginia	USA	13	Britain	5
1968	Newcastle, Co. Down	Britain	7½	USA	10½
1970	Brae Burn, Massachusetts	USA	11½	Britain	6½
1972	Western Gailes, Ayrshire	Britain	8	USA	10
1974	San Francisco, California	USA	13	Britain	5

Year	Venue	Result			
1976	Royal Lytham & St Annes	Britain	6½	USA	11½
1978	Apawamis, New York	USA	12	Britain	6

To date, USA 16 wins, Britain 2 wins, with 2 ties.

THE SUN ALLIANCE RYDER CUP

Year	Venue	Result			
1927	Worcester Country Club, Worcester, Mass.	USA	9½	Britain	2½
1929	Moortown Golf Club, Leeds	Britain	7	USA	5
1931	Scioto Country Club, Columbus, Ohio	USA	9	Britain	3
1933	Southport & Ainsdale Golf Club, Southport	Britain	6½	USA	5½
1935	Ridgewood Country Club, Ridgewood, NJ	USA	9	Britain	3
1937	Southport & Ainsdale Golf Club, Southport	Britain	4	USA	8
1947	Portland Golf Club, Portland, Oregon	USA	11	Britain	1
1949	Ganton Golf Club, Scarborough	Britain	5	USA	7
1951	Pinehurst Country Club, Pinehurst, NC	USA	9½	Britain	2½
1953	Wentworth Golf Club, Surrey	Britain	5½	USA	6½
1955	Thunderbird Country Club, Palm Springs	USA	8	Britain	4
1957	Linkrick Golf Club, Yorkshire	Britain	7½	USA	4½
1959	Eldorado Country Club, Palm Desert, Calif.	USA	8½	Britain	3½
1961	Royal Lytham & St Annes Golf Club, Lancs.	Britain	9½	USA	14½
1963	East Lake Country Club, Atlanta, Georgia	USA	23	Britain	9
1965	Royal Birkdale Golf Club, Southport	Britain	12½	USA	19½
1967	Champions Golf Club, Houston, Texas	USA	23½	Britain	8½
1969	Royal Birkdale Golf Club, Southport	Britain	16	USA	16
1971	Old Warson Country Club, St Louis	USA	18½	Britain	13½
1973	Muirfield, East Lothian	Britain	13	USA	19
1975	Laurel Valley Golf Club, Ligonier, Penn.	USA	21	Britain	11
1977	Royal Lytham & St Annes Golf Club, Lancs.	Britain	7½	USA	12½
1979	The Greenbrier Club, West Virginia	USA	17	Europe	11

To date, USA 19 wins, Britain 3 wins, with 1 tie.
In 1973 and 1977 sponsored by the Sun Alliance Insurance Group.
In 1979 the format was altered to include Europe.

WORLD CUP

Year	Winners		Venue	Score
1953	Argentine	A. Cerda and R. de Vicenzo	Montreal	287
		Individual: A. Cerda, Argentina, 140		
1954	Australia	P.W. Thomson and K. Nagle	Laval-sur-Lac	556
		Individual: S. Leonard, Canada, 275		
1955	United States	C. Harbert and E. Furgol	Washington	560
		Individual: E. Furgol, USA, 279		
1956	United States	B. Hogan and S. Snead	Wentworth	567
		Individual: B. Hogan, USA, 277		
1957	Japan	T. Nakamura and K. Ono	Tokyo	557
		Individual: T. Nakamura, Japan, 274		
1958	Ireland	H. Bradshaw and C. O'Connor	Mexico City	579
		Individual: A. Miguel, Spain, 286		
1959	Australia	P.W. Thomson and K.D.G. Nagle	Melbourne	563
		Individual: S. Leonard, Canada, 275		
1960	United States	S. Snead and A.D. Palmer	Portmarnock	565
		Individual: F. van Donck, Belgium, 279		
1961	United States	S. Snead and J. Demaret	Puerto Rico	560
		Individual: S. Snead, USA, 272		
1962	United States	S. Snead and A.D. Palmer	Buenos Aires	557
		Individual: R. de Vicenzo, Argentina, 276		

Year	Winners		Venue	Score
1963	United States	A.D. Palmer and J.W. Nicklaus Individual: J.W. Nicklaus, USA, 237 (63 holes)	St Nom-La- Bretèche	482
1964	United States	A.D. Palmer and J.W. Nicklaus Individual: J.W. Nicklaus, USA, 276	Maui, Hawaii	554
1965	South Africa	G.J. Player and H.R. Henning Individual: G. Player, SA, 281	Madrid	571
1966	United States	J.W. Nicklaus and A.D. Palmer Individual: G. Knudson, Canada and H. Sugimoto, Japan each 272. Knudson won play-off	Tokyo	548
1967	United States	J.W. Nicklaus and A.D. Palmer Individual: A. Palmer, USA, 276	Mexico City	557
1968	Canada	A. Balding and G. Knudson Individual: A. Balding, Canada, 274	Olgiata, Rome	569
1969	United States	O. Moody and L. Trevino Individual: L. Trevino, USA, 275	Singapore	552
1970	Australia	B.J. Devlin and D. Graham Individual: R. de Vicenzo, Argentina, 269	Buenos Aires	545
1971	United States	J.W. Nicklaus and L. Trevino Individual: J.W. Nicklaus, USA, 271	Palm Beach, Florida	555
1972	Taiwan	Lu Liang Huan and Hsieh Min Nan Individual: Hsieh Min Nan, Taiwan, 217 (54 holes)	Royal Melbourne	438
1973	United States	J.W. Nicklaus and J. Miller Individual: J. Miller, USA, 277	Nueva Andalucia, Spain	558
1974	South Africa	R. Cole and D. Hayes Individual: R. Cole, SA, 271	Caracas	554
1975	United States	J. Miller and L. Graham Individual: J. Miller, USA, 275	Bangkok	554
1976	Spain	S. Ballesteros and M. Pinero Individual: E. Acosta, MEX, 282	Palm Springs, California	574
1977	Spain	S. Ballesteros and A. Garrido Individual: G. Player, SA, 289	Manila	591
1978	United States	J. Mahaffey and A. North Individual: J. Mahaffey, USA, 281	Hawaii	564
1979	United States	J. Mahaffey and H. Irwin Individual: H. Irwin, USA, 285	Athens	575

EISENHOWER TROPHY

Year	Winners		Venue	Score
1958	Australia	B.J. Devlin, P. Toogood. R.F. Stevens D. Bachli After a tie, Australia won the play-off by two strokes, Australia 222, United States 224	St Andrews	918
1960	United States	D.R. Beman, R.W. Gardner, W. Hyndman, J.W. Nicklaus Best individual score: J. Nicklaus, USA 269	Ardmore, USA	834
1962	United States	D.R. Beman, W.J. Patton, R. Sikes, L. Harries Best individual score, G. Cowan, Canada, 280	Kawana, Japan	854
1964	Great Britain and Ireland	R.D.B.M. Shade, R. Foster, M.S.R. Lunt, M.F. Bonallack Best individual score, Hsieh Min Nan, Taiwan, 294	Olgiata, Rome	895
1966	Australia	K.W. Hartley, P.K. Billings, W. Berwick, K.K. Donohoe Best individual score, R.D.B.M. Shade, Great Britain, 283	Mexico City	877

Year	Winners		Venue	Score
1968	United States	M. Giles, B. Fleisher, J. Lewis Jr, R. Siderowf Best individual score, M.F. Bonallack, Great Britain and M. Giles, USA. 286	Melbourne	868
1970	United States	M. Giles, T. Kite, A. Miller, L. Wadkins Best individual score, V. Regalado, Mexico, 280	Madrid	857
1972	United States	M. Giles, B. Crenshaw, M. Hayes, M. West Best individual score, A. Gresham, Australia, 285	Buenos Aires	865
1974	United States	G. Burns, G. Koch, J. Pate, C. Strange Best individual score, J. Pate and J. Gonzales, Brazil, 294	Dominican Republic	888
1976	Great Britain and Ireland	I. Hutcheon, J. Davies, M. Kelley, S. Martin Best individual score, I. Hutcheon and Tze-Ming Chen, Taiwan, 293	Penina, Portugal	892
1978	United States	R. Clampett, J. Cook, S. Hoch, J. Sigel, Best individual score, R. Clampett, USA, 287	Fiji	873

WORLD WOMEN'S AMATEUR TEAM CHAMPIONSHIP ESPIRITO SANTO TROPHY

Year	Winners		Runners-up	Venue	Score
1964	France	Mlle C. Lacoste, Mlle B. Varangot, Mlle C. Cros	United States	St Germain, France	588
1966	United States	Miss S. Hamlin, Miss B. Boddle, Mrs A. Welts	Canada	Mexico	580
1968	United States	Mrs Welts, Miss J. Bastanchury, Miss S. Hamlin	Australia	Melbourne	616
1970	United States	Miss C. Hill Miss J. Bastanchury, Miss M. Wilkinson	France,	Madrid	598
1972	United States	Miss L. Baugh, Mrs J. Booth, Miss M. Budke	France	Buenos Aires	593
1974	United States	Miss C. Hill, Miss D. Massey, Miss C. Semple	British Isles & South Africa	Dominican Republic	620
1976	United States	Miss N. Lopez, Miss D. Massey, Miss D. Horton	France	Vilamoura, Portugal	605
1978	Australia	Miss L. Goggin, Miss E. Kennedy, Miss J. Lock Best individual score, Miss C. Sherk, Canada, 294	Canada	Fiji	596

THE BOYS' CHAMPIONSHIP

Year	Winner	Runner-up	Venue	Score
1921	A.D.D. Mathieson	G.H. Lintott	Royal Ascot	37th hole
1922	H.S. Mitchell	W. Greenfield	Royal Ascot	4 and 2
1923	A.D.D. Mathieson	H.S. Mitchell	Dunbar	3 and 2
1924	R.W. Peattie	P. Manuevrier	Coombe Hill	2 holes
1925	R.W. Peattie	A. M'Nair	Royal Burgess	4 and 3
1926	E.A. M'Ruvie	C.W. Timmis	Coombe Hill	1 hole
1927	E.W. Fiddian	K. Forbes	Royal Burgess	4 and 2
1928	S. Scheftel	A. Dobbie	Formby	6 and 5
1929	J. Lindsay	J. Scot-Riddell	Royal Burgess	6 and 4
1930	J.Lindsay	J. Todd	Fulwell	9 and 8

Year	Winner	Runner-up	Venue	Score
1931	H. Thomson	F. McGloin	Killermont	5 and 4
1932	I.S. MacDonald	L.A. Hardie	Royal Lytham & St Annes	2 and 1
1933	P.B. Lucas	W. M'Lachlan	Carnoustie	3 and 2
1934	R.S. Burles	F.B. Allpass	Moorstown	12 and 10
1935	J.D.A. Langley	R. Norris	Royal Aberdeen	6 and 5
1936	J. Bruen	W. Innes	Birkdale	11 and 9
1937	I.M. Roberts	J. Stewart	Bruntsfield	8 and 7
1938	W. Smeaton	T. Snowball	Moor Park	3 and 2
1939	S.B. Williamson	K.G. Thom	Carnoustie	4 and 2
1940-45	*No Championship*			
1946	A.F.D. MacGregor	D.F. Dunstan	Bruntsfield	7 and 5
1947	J. Armour	I. Caldwell	Royal Liverpool, Hoylake	5 and 4
1948	J.D. Pritchett	D. H. Reid	Barassie	37th hole
1949	H. MacAnespie	N.V. Drew	St Andrews	3 and 2
1950	J. Glover	I. Young	Royal Lytham & St Annes	2 and 1
1951	N. Dunn	M.S.R. Lunt	Prestwick	6 and 5
1952	M. Bonallack	A.E. Shepperson	Formby	37th hole
1953	A.E. Shepperson	A.T. Booth	Dunbar	6 and 4
1954	A.F. Bussell	K. Warren	Hoylake	38th hole
1955	S.C. Wilson	B.J.K. Aitken	Troon	39th hole
1956	J.F. Ferguson	C.W. Cole	Sunningdale	2 and 1
1957	D. Ball	J. Wilson	Carnoustie	2 and 1
1958	R. Braddon	I.M. Stungo	Moortown	4 and 3
1959	A.R. Murphy	E.M. Shamash	Pollok	3 and 1
1960	P. Cros	P.O. Green	Olton	5 and 3
1961	F.S. Morris	C. Clark	Dalmahoy	3 and 2
1962	P.M. Townsend	D.C. Penman	Royal Mid-Surrey	1 hole
1963	A.H.C. Soutar	D.I. Rigby	Prestwick	2 and 1
1964	P.M. Townsend	R.D. Gray	Formby	9 and 8
1965	G.R. Milne	D.K. Midgley	Gullane	4 and 2
1966	A. Phillips	A. Muller	Moortown	12 and 11
1967	L.P. Tupling	S.C. Evans	Western Gailes	4 and 2
1968	S.C. Evans	K. Dabson	St Annes Old Links	3 and 2
1969	M. Foster	M. Gray	Dunbar	37th hole
1970	I.D. Gradwell	J.F. Murray	Hillside	1 hole
1971	H. Clark	G. Harvey	Barassie	6 and 5
1972	G. Harvey	R. Newsome	Moortown	7 and 5
1973	D.M. Robertson	S. Betti	Blairgowrie	5 and 3
1974	T.R. Shannon	A.W.B. Lyle	Hoylake	10 and 9
1975	B. Marchbank	A.W.B. Lyle	Bruntsfield	1 hole
1976	M. Mouland	G. Hargreaves	Sunningdale	6 and 5
1977	I. Ford	C.R. Dalgleish	Downfield	1 hole
1978	S. Keppler	M. Stokes	Seaton Carew	3 and 2
1979	R. Rafferty	D. Ray	Barassie	6 and 5

THE GIRLS' CHAMPIONSHIP

Year	Winner	Runner-up	Venue	Score
1919	Miss A. Croft	Miss C. Clarke		1 hole
1920	Miss C. Clarke	Miss A. Croft		21st hole
1921	Miss W. Sarson	Miss M. Parkinson		5 and 3
1922	Miss M. Wickenden	Miss B. Griffiths		4 and 3
1923	Miss M. Mackay	Miss Strohmenger		3 and 2
1924	Mlle T. de la Chaume	Miss D. Pearson	Stoke Poges	4 and 2
1925	Miss E. Wilson	Miss K.M. Nicholls		5 and 3
1926	Miss D. Esmond	Miss M. Ramsden		6 and 5
1927	Miss D. Fishwick	Miss I. Taylor		7 and 6
1928	Miss D. Fishwick	Miss M. Jolly		3 and 2
1929	Miss N. Baird	Miss S. Bailey		4 and 3

Year	Winner	Runner-up	Venue	Score
1930	Miss P. Doran	Miss D. Wilkins		19th hole
1931	Miss P. Doran	Miss D. Wilkins		2 and 1
1932	Miss P. Doran	Mlle A. de Gunzbourg		19th hole
1933	Miss J. Anderson	Miss F.M. Pears		5 and 3
1934	Miss N. Jupp	Miss J. Mountford	Stoke Poges	3 and 1
1935	Miss P. Falkner	Miss J. Pemberton		1 hole
1936	Miss P. Edwards	Miss J. Gordon		3 and 2
1937	Mlle I. Vagliano	Miss P. Edwards		5 and 4
1938	Miss S. Stroyan	Miss J. Pemberton		4 and 3
1949	Miss P. Davies	Mlle A. Jacquet	Beaconsfield	1 hole
1950	Miss I. Robertson	Miss A. Phillips	Formby	5 and 4
1951	Miss J. Redgate	Miss I. Robertson	Gullane	19th hole
1952	Miss A. Phillips	Miss S. Marbrook	Stoke Poges	7 and 6
1953	Miss S. Hill	Miss A. Ward	Woodhall Spa	3 and 2
1954	Miss B. Jackson	Miss D. Winsor	West Kilbride	20th hole
1955	Miss A. Ward	Miss A. Gardner	Beaconsfield	5 and 4
1956	Miss R. Porter	Miss A. Nicholson	Seaton Carew	5 and 4
1957	Mlle B. Varangot	Miss R. Porter	North Berwick	3 and 2
1958	Miss T. Ross-Steen	Mlle Varangot	Cotswold Hills	2 and 1
1959	Miss S.M. Vaughan	Miss J.A. Greenhalgh	Nottingham	1 hole
1960	Miss S. Clarke	Miss A.L. Irvin	Barassie	2 and 1
1961	Miss D. Robb	Miss J. Roberts	Beaconsfield	3 and 2
1962	Miss S. McLaren-Smith	Miss A. Murphy	Foxton Hall	2 and 1
1963	Miss D. Oxley	Miss B. Whitehead	Gullane	2 and 1
1964	Miss P. Tredinnick	Miss K. Cumming	Camberley Heath	2 and 1
1965	Miss A. Willard	Miss S. Ward	Formby	3 and 2
1966	Miss J. Hutton	Miss D. Oxley	Troon Portland	20th hole
1967	Miss P. Burrows	Miss J. Hutton	Liphook	2 and 1
1968	Miss C. Wallace	Miss C. Reybroeck	Leven	4 and 3
1969	Miss J. de Witt Puyt	Miss C. Reybroeck	Ilkley	2 and 1
1970	Miss C. Le Feuvre	Miss Michelle Walker	North Wales	2 and 1
1971	Miss J. Mark	Miss Maureen Walker	North Berwick	4 and 3
1972	Miss Maureen Walker	Miss S. Cadden	Royal Norwich	2 and 1
1973	Miss A.M. Palli	Miss N. Jeanson	Northamptonshire	2 and 1
1974	Miss R. Barry	Miss T. Perkins	Dunbar	1 hole
1975	Miss S. Cadden	Miss L. Isherwood	Henbury	4 and 3
1976	Miss G. Stewart	Miss S. Rowlands	Pyle and Kenfig	5 and 4
1977	Miss W. Aitken	Miss S. Bamford	Formby	2 and 1
1978	Miss M. de Lorenzi	Miss D. Glenn	Largs	2 and 1
1979	Mlle S. Lapaire	Miss P. Smillie	Edgbaston	19th hole

THE BRITISH YOUTHS' CHAMPIONSHIP

Year	Winner	Venue	Score
1954	J.S. More	Erskine	287
1955	B. Stockdale	Pannal	297
1956	A.F. Bussell	Royal Burgess	287
1957	G. Will	Pannal	290
1958	R.H. Kemp	Dumfries and County	281
1959	R.A. Jowle	Pannal	286
1960	C.A. Caygill	Pannal	279
1961	J.S. Martin	Bruntsfield	284
1962	C.A. Caygill	Pannal	287
1963	A.J. Low	Pollok	283
1964	B.W. Barnes	Pannal	290
1965	P.M. Townsend	Gosforth Park	281
1966	P.A. Oosterhuis	Dalmahoy (54 holes)	219
1967	P.J. Benka	Copt Heath	278
1968	P.J. Benka	Ayr Belleisle	281

Year	Winner	Venue	Score
1969	J.H. Cook	Lindrick	289
1970	B. Dassu	Barrton	276
1971	P. Elson	Northamptonshire	277
1972	A.H. Chandler	Glasgow Gailes	281
1973	S.C. Mason	Southport and Ainsdale	284
1974	D.M. Robertson	Downfield	284
1975	N.A. Faldo	Pannal	278
1976	M.E. Lewis	Gullane	277
1977	A.W.B. Lyle	Moor Park	285
1978	B. Marchbank	East Renfrewshire	278
1979	G. Brand	Woodhall Spa	291

EUROPEAN MEN'S AMATEUR TEAM CHAMPIONSHIP

Year	Winner	Runner-up	Venue
1959	Sweden		
1961	Sweden	England	Brussels, Belgium
1963	England	Sweden	Falsterbo, Sweden
1965	Ireland	Scotland	Royal St George's, England
1967	Ireland	France	Turin, Italy
1969	England	West Germany	Hamburg, West Germany
1971	England	Scotland	Lausanne, Switzerland
1973	England	Scotland	Penina, Portugal
1975	Scotland	Italy	Killarney, Ireland
1977	Scotland	Sweden	The Hague, The Netherlands
1979	England	Wales	Esjberg, Denmark

EUROPEAN WOMEN'S TEAM CHAMPIONSHIP

Year	Winner	Runner-up	Venue
1967	England	France	Penina, Portugal
1969	France	England	Tylosand, Sweden
1971	England	France	Ganton, England
1973	England	France	Brussels, Belgium
1975	France	Spain	Paris, France
1977	England	Spain	Sotogrande, Spain
1979	Ireland	Germany	Hermitage, Dublin

VAGLIANO CUP – BRITISH ISLES v EUROPE

Year	Venue	Result			
1959	Wentworth, Surrey	Britain	12	Europe	3
1961	Ville d'Este, Italy	Europe	7	Britain	8
1963	Muirfield, East Lothian	Britain	20	Europe	10
1965	Cologne, West Germany	Europe	17	Britain	13
1967	Royal Lytham & St Annes, Lancashire	Britain	4½	Europe	15½
1969	Chantilly, France	Europe	16	Britain	14
1971	Worplesdon, Surrey	Britain	17½	Europe	12½
1973	Eindhoven, The Netherlands	Europe	10	Britain	20
1975	Muirfield, East Lothian	Britain	13½	Europe	10½
1977	Malmo, Sweden	Europe	8½	Britain	15½
1979	Royal Porthcawl, Mid Glamorgan	Britain	12	Europe	12

To date, Britain 7 wins, Europe 3 wins, one match halved.

THE PGA MATCH-PLAY CHAMPIONSHIP

Year	Winner	Runner-up	Venue
1903	J. Braid	E. Ray	Sunningdale
1904	J.H. Taylor	A. Toogood	Mid-Surrey
1905	J. Braid	T. Vardon	Walton Heath
1906	A. Herd	C. Mayo	Hollinwell
1907	J. Braid	J.H. Taylor	Sunningdale
1908	J.H. Taylor	F. Robson	Mid-Surrey
1909	T. Ball	A. Herd	Walton Heath
1910	J.G. Sherlock	G. Duncan	Sunningdale
1911	J. Braid	E. Ray	Walton Heath
1912	H. Vardon	E. Ray	Sunningdale
1913	G. Duncan	J. Braid	Walton Heath
1914–1918	*No Championship*		
1919	A. Mitchell	G. Duncan	Walton Heath
1920	A. Mitchell	Josh. Taylor	Mid-Surrey
1921	B. Seymour	J. Gaudin	Oxhey
1922	G. Gadd	F. Leach	Sunningdale
1923	R.G. Wilson	T. Renouf	Walton Heath
1924	E.R. Whitcombe	G. Gadd	St George's Hill
1925	A. Compston	G. Gadd	Moor Park
1926	A. Herd	J. Bloxham	Mid-Surrey
1927	A. Compston	J. Braid	Walton Heath
1928	C.A. Whitcombe	T.H. Cotton	Stoke Poges
1929	A. Mitchell	P. Rodgers	Wentworth
1930	C.A. Whitcombe	T.H. Cotton	Oxhey
1931	A.H. Padgham	M. Seymour	Royal Mid-Surrey
1932	T.H. Cotton	A. Perry	Moor Park
1933	P. Alliss	M. Seymour	Purley Downs
1934	J.J. Busson	C.A. Whitcombe	Walton Heath
1935	A.H. Padgham	P. Alliss	Royal Mid-Surrey
1936	D.J. Rees	E.R. Whitcombe	Oxhey
1937	P. Alliss	J. Adams	Stoke Poges
1938	D.J. Rees	E.E. Whitcombe	Walton Heath
1940	T.H. Cotton	A.H. Padgham	Royal Mid-Surrey
1941–1944	*No Championship*		
1945	R.W. Horne	P. Alliss	Walton Heath
1946	T.H. Cotton	J. Adams	Hoylake
1947	F. Daly	F. van Donck	St Annes
1948	F. Daly	L. Ayton	Royal Birkdale
1949	D.J. Rees	T.H. Cotton	Walton Heath
1950	D.J. Rees	F. Jowle	Carnoustie
1951	H. Weetman	J. Adams	Hoylake
1952	F. Daly	F. van Donck	Walton Heath
1953	M. Faulkner	D.J. Rees	Ganton
1954	P. Thomson	J. Fallon	St Andrews
1955	K. Bousfield	E.C. Brown	Walton Heath
1956	J. Panton	H. Weetman	Hoylake
1957	C. O'Connor	T.B. Haliburton	Turnberry
1958	H. Weetman	B.J. Hunt	Walton Heath
1959	D. Snell	H. Weetman	Royal Birkdale
1960	E.C. Brown	H. Weetman	Turnberry
1961	P.W. Thomson	R.L. Moffitt	Walton Heath
1962	E.C. Brown	E. Whitehead	Walton Heath
1963	D.C. Thomas	J. MacDonald	Turnberry
1964	N.C. Coles	P.J. Butler	Walton Heath
1965	N.C. Coles	L. Platts	Walton Heath
1966	P.W. Thomson	N.C. Coles	Walton Heath
1967	P.W. Thomson	D.J. Rees	Walton Heath
1968	B.G.C. Huggett	J. Panton	Walton Heath
1969	M. Bembridge	D.J. Rees	Walton Heath
1970	T.A. Horton	R.D. Shade	Moor Park

Year	Winner	Runner-up	Venue
1971	*No Championship*		
1972	J.R. Garner	N.C. Coles	Moor Park
1973	N.C. Coles	D.W. McClelland	Hillside
1974	J. Newton	C. Sanudo	Downfield
1975	E. Polland	P.J. Butler	Lindrick
1976	B.W. Barnes	C. DeFoy	Kings Norton
1977	H. Baiocchi	B.G.C. Huggett	Stoke Poges

From 1975 sponsored by the Sun Alliance Insurance Group

THE SUN ALLIANCE EUROPEAN MATCH-PLAY CHAMPIONSHIP

Year	Winner	Runner-up	Venue
1978	M. James	N. Coles	Dalmahoy
1979	D. Smyth	N. Price	Fulford, York

DUNLOP MASTERS TOURNAMENT

Year	Winner	Venue	Score
1946	A.D. Locke and J. Adams tied	Stoneham	286
1947	A. Lees	Little Aston	286
1948	N. Von Nida	Sunningdale	272
1949	C.H. Ward	St Andrews	290
1950	D.J. Rees	Hoylake	281
1951	M. Faulkner	Wentworth	281
1952	H. Weetman	Mere	281
1953	H. Bradshaw	Sunningdale	272
1954	A.D. Locke	Prince's, Sandwich	291
1955	H. Bradshaw	Little Aston	277
1956	C. O'Connor	Prestwick	277
1957	E.C. Brown	Hollinwell	275
1958	H. Weetman	Little Aston	276
1959	C. O'Connor	Portmarnock	276
1960	J. Hitchcock	Sunningdale	275
1961	P.W. Thomson	Royal Porthcawl	284
1962	D.J. Rees	Wentworth	278
1963	B.J. Hunt	Little Aston	282
1964	C. LeGrange	Royal Birkdale	288
1965	B.J. Hunt	Portmarnock	283
1966	N.C. Coles	Lindrick	278
1967	A. Jacklin	Royal St George's	274
1968	P.W. Thomson	Sunningdale	274
1969	C. LeGrange	Little Aston	281
1970	B.G.C. Huggett	Royal Lytham & St Annes	293
1971	M. Bembridge	St Pierre	273
1972	R.J. Charles	Northumberland GC, Newcastle	277
1973	A. Jacklin	St Pierre	272
1974	B. Gallacher	St Pierre	282
1975	B. Gallacher	Ganton	289
1976	B. Dassu	St Pierre	271
1977	G.L. Hunt	Lindrick	291
1978	T.A. Horton	St Pierre	279
1979	G. Marsh	Woburn	283

THE PGA CHAMPIONSHIP

Year	Winner	Venue	Score
1972	A. Jacklin	Wentworth	279
1973	P. Oosterhuis	Wentworth	280
1974	M. Bembridge	Wentworth	278
1975	A. Palmer	Royal St George's	285
1976	N.C. Coles	Royal St George's	280
1977	M. Pinero	Royal St George's	283
1978	N. Faldo	Royal Birkdale	278
1979	V. Fernandez	St Andrews	288

From 1972 to 1974 sponsored by Carrington Viyella Ltd.
From 1975 sponsored by the Penfold Golf Company/Craigton Golf Company.
Re-named The Colgate PGA Championship in 1978.

THE WORLD MATCH-PLAY CHAMPIONSHIP

Year	Winner	Runner-up	Venue	Result
1964	A.D. Palmer	N.C. Coles	Wentworth	2 and 1
1965	G.J. Player	P.W. Thomson	Wentworth	3 and 2
1966	G.J. Player	J.W. Nicklaus	Wentworth	6 and 4
1967	A.D. Palmer	P.W. Thomson	Wentworth	2 holes
1968	G.J. Player	R.J. Charles	Wentworth	1 hole
1969	R.J. Charles	G. Littler	Wentworth	at 37th
1970	J.W. Nicklaus	L. Trevino	Wentworth	2 and 1
1971	G.J. Player	J.W. Nicklaus	Wentworth	5 and 4
1972	T. Weiskopf	L. Trevino	Wentworth	4 and 3
1973	G.J. Player	G. Marsh	Wentworth	at 40th
1974	H. Irvin	G.J. Player	Wentworth	2 and 1
1975	H. Irwin	A. Geiberger	Wentworth	4 and 2
1976	D. Graham	H. Irwin	Wentworth	at 38th
1977	G. Marsh	R. Floyd	Wentworth	5 and 3
1978	I. Aoki	S. Owen	Wentworth	3 and 2
1979	W. Rogers	I. Aoki	Wentworth	1 hole

From 1964–76 sponsored by Piccadilly.
From 1977–78 sponsored by Colgate
In 1979 sponsored by Suntory, Japan.